RAINWATER CATCHMENT SYSTEMS
FOR DOMESTIC SUPPLY

0

Rainwater Catchment Systems for Domestic Supply

Design, construction and implementation

JOHN GOULD
and
ERIK NISSEN-PETERSEN

PUBLISHING

Published by ITDG Publishing
The Schumacher Centre for Technology and Development,
Bourton Hall, Bourton-on-Dunsmore, Rugby, CV23 9Q2, UK.
www.itdgpublishing.org.uk

First published in 1999
Reprinted in 2002, 2005

ISBN 1 85339 456 4

A catalogue record for this book is available from the British Library.

ITDG Publishing is the publishing arm of the Intermediate Technology Development Group.
Our mission is to build the skills and capacity of people in developing countries through the
dissemination of information in all forms, enabling them to improve the quality of their lives
and that of future generations.

Typeset by Dorwyn Ltd, Rowlands Castle, Hants
Printed in Great Britain by Antony Rowe Ltd., Chippenham, Wiltshire

Contents

Acknowledgements

This book has been a truly international effort, with the authors and publishers based in three different continents and reviews and other assistance being provided from people all over the world. While this has had its difficulties, it has, we hope, helped to give the book a broad global flavour. It is impossible to mention all of the hundreds of people who have assisted us over the last few years in developing ideas and material for this book; at the risk of forgetting someone we would nevertheless specifically like to acknowledge the following individuals and organizations for their assistance. Special thanks are due to Stephen Burgess, Eriko Kamikubo and Ralph Rogge for reading and commenting on the whole manuscript and for providing constructive criticism throughout the project. Also to Mark Winstanley for assisting with the production of diagrams and June Laird for facilitating information searches and inter-library loans.

For reviewing chapters of the book we are especially grateful to Alan Fewkes, Roger Fujioka, Hans Hartung, Kevin Hewison, Julie Jarman, Peter Morgan, Dai Rees, Rick Scott, Brian Skinner, Greg Simmons and Terry Thomas. For comments and material relating to case-studies we thank John Pigram (Australia), Eagilwe Segosebe (Botswana), Zhu Qiang and Mou Haisheng (China), Klaus König (Germany), Makoto Murase (Japan), Sacha Sethaputra (Thailand) and Richard Heggen (USA) and, on other sections of the text, Jane Heyworth, Brian Latham, Nigel Horan, Robert Schemenauer and Donald Waller.

Others who have assisted significantly but indirectly in the development of this book include: Gurmeet Bambrah, Adrian Cullis, Yu-Si Fok, Jamal Ghoddousi, Ambro Gieske, Johann Gnadlinger, Krib Gurusamy, Liang Haitang, Li Lijuan, Andrew Lo, Changming Liu, Johann Gnadlinger, the late Isao Minami, John Mbugua, Chayatit Vadhanavikkit, Vyas Vikram, Prakob and Wanpen Wirojanagud. Appreciation is also due to Crile Doscher, Kieran O'Boyle, Andrew Dakers, Alan Cox, Shelley Evans in New Zealand and to Brian Kirke, Marilla Barnes and John Day in Australia for providing useful information and encouragement.

Several organizations have also contributed to the contents of this book by providing background materials and other forms of support, including ASAL Consultants Ltd, the Botswana Technology Centre, the University of Botswana, the Health Department of Western Australia, the Intermediate Technology Development Group, the International Rainwater Catchment Systems Association, the Kenya Rainwater Association, the Rainwater Harvesting Information Service, the South Australia Water Corporation,

WaterAid and WISY (Winkler Systems). Others who provided useful information, comments and suggestions include Renate Steinkrauss (WISY), Ingvar Andersson and Lennart Nilsson (SIDA), Robert Spencer (IT) and Klaus Sandstrom (GWP).

A number of figures have been taken or adapted from other sources and these are acknowledged individually. Thanks are due to Bob Schemenaue for the loan of plate 2.2; to WISY AG for plates 9.9, 9.10, and 9.11 and to Makoto Murase for plates 9.12 and 9.13.

Finally, we acknowledge the support of the Swedish International Development Agency (SIDA) for providing financial assistance for the project, and especially to Rolf Winberg in Nairobi for co-ordinating the project. Thanks are also due to IT Publications in London and especially to Neal Burton for encouragement and support throughout the project.

Preface

As THE 20TH CENTURY draws to a close the world faces two diametrically opposed water problems: the use of too much of the earth's limited high-quality water resources by the rich, and the supply of too little high-quality water to the poor. Rainwater catchment systems for domestic supply can, to some extent, help to address both these problems through improving water provision where required, and by encouraging water conservation, thereby reducing demand on existing water sources.

Despite the phenomenal rate of technological development in recent decades, solutions to many technically simple problems continue to elude the world community. The provision of clean water within easy reach of every household is one of them. Intensive efforts to address this issue during and since the International Drinking Water Supply and Sanitation (IDWSS) Decade 1981–1990 by a variety of agencies (donors, NGOs, national governments, community groups) have had an impact in increasing water provision but, as the 20th century draws to a close, around a billion people still lack convenient access (within 400m) to clean water.

This book focuses on one technical option for improving domestic water supply provision, namely the collection and storage of rainwater runoff, a technology which has not generally been given the attention it deserves. This is unfortunate in the light of the huge numbers of people in the South still lacking access to improved supplies. Every day, millions of women have the thankless chore of carrying water from distant sources. The water is often contaminated and the task wastes valuable time and energy which could be put to more productive uses. In most cases, a simple roof catchment system, costing as little as US$100 or less, could relieve most of this daily burden and provide cleaner water at the same time. Even where alternative supplies exist, rainwater can provide a useful supplementary supply and important backup during periods when the main supply breaks down or dries up during droughts. The reasons for the failure of the world community to meet even the most basic needs of its citizens, such as clean reliable water supplies, are complex and lie mainly in the realm of politics and economics, at both global and national levels. While this book does not touch on this aspect of the problem, it is vital to realize that development at a grassroots level takes place within a broader global framework. Without a favourable political climate – particularly at the local level – solutions, where they are available, may be hard to implement and even harder to sustain.

In the past, rainwater catchment systems have often been looked upon as a technology of last resort to be used only when no other alternative could be found, such as on coral islands lacking fresh surface or groundwater. While it is true that rainwater catchment systems cannot generally compete in economic terms with shallow wells, gravity-fed spring supplies or even with conventional reticulated groundwater-based systems in areas with abundant good-quality water sources, in many other circumstances rainwater can provide a viable option. Rainwater catchment systems also have a number of advantages, which may make them preferable to other alternatives. Since rainfall occurs virtually everywhere that people live, rainwater use is almost always an option either as a total, partial or backup water supply. Even in places where the precipitation is predominantly in the form of snow, dew or fog, these too can be harnessed and provide valuable water supplies. Since most people live in dwellings with either roofs, yards (compounds) or both, they already have catchment surfaces from which rainwater runoff can be collected. Fortuitously, even in the rural parts of the developing world, currently the most poorly served by improved water supplies, traditional mud and thatched roofs are increasingly being replaced by impervious tiles or corrugated iron. An opportunity is thus being created to provide household roof catchment water supplies at an increasing number of homes worldwide. The individual ownership and control of these systems also helps to ensure their proper operation and maintenance.

Worldwide pressure on water resources continues to mount as population growth, increasing consumption, pollution and climatic change take their toll. The over-exploitation and mineralization of groundwater in some areas, and contamination and drying up of surface waters in others, are making author-ities seriously consider alternatives to help relieve the growing strain. As a result, interest in rainwater catchment systems is now increasing in many industrialized countries, where growing attention is also being focused on several indirect benefits that can be derived from widespread collection of rainwater in urban contexts. Among these benefits are better flood control due to the temporary storage of stormwater runoff in rainwater cisterns, reduced pressure on ground and surface water sources, and economic benefits due to the down-scaling and deferring of the construction or enlargement of major storm-drainage and sewer networks. It is particularly in a number of mega-cities in Asia which are already suffering from problems of flooding, subsidence and periodic water shortages such as Tokyo, Bangkok and Shang-hai that this interest is greatest. These aspects of the technology have not been widely addressed in previous publications and, while not the primary focus of this book, some examples are cited in the last two chapters.

This is not the first book dealing with rainwater catchment systems for domestic supply, and hopefully it will not be the last. It is now 12 years since *Rainwater Harvesting* by Pacey and Cullis (1986) was published, and 20 years since *Ferrocement Water Tanks and their Construction* by Watt (1978) was written. *Rain Catchment and Rural Water Supplies* by Nissen-Petersen (1982) and *Rainwater Reservoirs above Ground Structure for Roof Catchment* by Hasse (1989) are also becoming dated. Considerable progress and develop-ment have occurred regarding both system design and implementation strategies over the last ten years which deserve highlighting. Several other aspects of rainwater catchment systems not covered in detail in earlier texts, such as water-quality issues, system sizing and project implementation, are also included here. During the time of writing some very useful new books on rainwater catchment systems aimed at specific countries have been published: e.g. Australia (Cuncliffe 1998) and Germany (König 1996). Perhaps the most significant recent contribution to the literature on the topic is *Dying Wisdom: the Rise, Fall and Potential of India's Traditional Water Harvesting Systems* (Agarwal and Narain 1997). This groundbreaking re-evaluation of traditional water harvesting systems makes a strong case for returning to a technology that has served people's water needs in India for millennia.

The objective of this book is thus to provide an up-to-date review of recent developments and lessons learnt with respect to rainwater catchment systems for domestic supply, and to consider possible future opportunities relating to the technology. In Chapter 1, rainwater use is examined in the context of other water sources. A review is then given of the historical development, current state of the art and recent developments of rainwater catchment systems for domestic supply. Some important lessons learned relating to the technology are also discussed. Chapter 2 examines the different types of rainwater catchment systems and their main features: catchments, delivery devices and storage systems. Dew, fog and snow collection are also considered here as well as rainwater harvesting for domestic agriculture. Chapter 3 deals with rainwater-quantity aspects, such as calculating domestic demand and potential supply, and tank-sizing techniques. In Chapter 4 system components and design considerations are examined, and in Chapter 5 construction techniques and materials are detailed. Chapter 6 covers aspects relating to rainwater quality. Social, cultural, political, environmental and economic aspects are considered in Chapter 7. Various aspects of project implementation are considered in Chapter 8. Specific case-studies from Australia and New Zealand, Botswana, China, Germany, Kenya, Japan, Thailand and the USA are presented in Chapter 9. Finally, in Chapter 10, the future of rainwater utilization around the world is discussed.

Much of the material quoted comes from a wide range of articles, booklets and manuals which are not always easily accessible to fieldworkers and practitioners. These sources are listed in the bibliography, and the addresses of some of the organizations that can supply some of the materials listed and further information on the technology are included in Appendices 2 and 3. This book attempts to provide a broad overview of various different designs as well as outlining construction procedures and different project-implementation strategies; it does not provide the detailed step-by-step information ideally required for actually constructing the systems. Any reader wishing to build any of the rainwater catchment systems discussed is advised to acquire the relevant design drawings and manual, if possible.

John Gould
Erik Nissen-Petersen
October 1998

Disclaimer

The tank designs and construction procedures described in this book are based on the authors' experiences and observations around the world. The tanks described, when properly built and maintained, have performed well. Local climatic, geological, seismic and soil conditions vary widely, as does the quality of materials and workmanship. While the authors are keen to encourage the replication of rainwater catchment systems for domestic supply around the world, they cannot accept liability for the failure of any system based on the designs described in this book.

Acronyms

ACK	Anglican Church of Kenya
ALDEP	Arable Lands Development Programme (Botswana)
ALDEV	African Land Development (Kenya)
ASAL	Arid and Semi-arid land
BRC	British Reinforcement
BTC	Botswana Technology Centre
CIDA	Canadian International Development Agency
DANIDA	Danish International Development Agency
EPA	Environmental Protection Agency (US)
FAO	Food and Agriculture Organization (United Nations)
GI	Galvanized Iron
HESAWA	Health, Sanitation and Water (Project)
IDRC	International Development and Research Centre (Canada)
IDWSSD	International Drinking Water Supply and Sanitation Decade (1981–1990)
IRC	International Reference Centre for Community Water Supply and Sanitation (Netherlands)
IRCSA	International Rainwater Catchment Systems Association
ITDG	Intermediate Technology Development Group
KRA	Kenya Rainwater Association
KWAHO	Kenya Water and Sanitation for Health Organization
NGO	Non-Governmental Organization
PC	Personal Computer
PVC	Polyvinyl Chloride
RIIC	Rural Industries Innovation Centre
SIDA	Swedish International Development Agency
TIRUC	Tokyo International Rainwater Utilization Conference
UNCHS	United Nations Centre for Human Settlements (Habitat)
UNEP	United Nations Environment Programme
UNICEF	United Nations Children's Fund
USAID	United States Agency for International Development
WASH	Water and Sanitation for Health
WEDC	Water, Engineering and Development Centre (UK)
WHO	World Health Organization

1

Introduction

AT THE DAWN of the new millennium, the future relevance and potential of rainwater catchment systems for domestic water supply is increasingly being recognized around the world. In the last 20 years, the ancient practice of rainwater collection has undergone a major renaissance in many countries. Africa and South-east Asia, in particular, have been at the heart of this revival during which tens of millions of roof catchment systems have been constructed (Figure 1.1). Some countries, such as Kenya and Thailand, have been focal points for technological innovation, while others have followed their lead. In other places, systems and technologies have gradually evolved specifically to meet local conditions and needs. This is the case in Iran, for example, where many modern systems are based on ancient traditional designs (Aminipori and Ghoddousi, 1997). Perhaps most significant of all has been the recent growing interest in the technology in China and India, which together comprise more than a third of the global population. Both these rapidly developing countries are facing growing pressures on their finite water resources and both are now recognizing the important role that traditional rainwater harvesting technologies can play in integrated water resources management (Agarwal and Narain, 1997; Zhu and Liu, 1998). Since most modern rainwater systems are upgraded or modified forms of traditional technologies, based on the same design principles, they too offer the promise of providing sustainable water supplies with low environmental impact.

There are several reasons for the rediscovery of this simple yet highly appropriate method of water supply. Perhaps the most significant is the growing number of potential catchment surfaces available worldwide due to the use of modern impervious roofing materials and paved surfaces. Another less direct but still important reason is the failure of conventional improved water supply systems to meet the challenges of providing 'clean water for all'. One of the goals of the International Drinking Water Supply and Sanitation Decade (1981–1990) was to provide clean, convenient supplies for all by 1990. Despite the achievements of the Decade, including the provision of improved water supplies to an estimated 1 billion people (Mather 1996), at the end of the decade around 1.2 billion still remained unserved (Bastermeyer and Lee 1992). Lack of investment, growing water demand, over-exploitation of existing sources, pollution and maintenance problems, leading to frequent breakdowns meant that the Decade's ambitious goals 'of clean water supply provision for all' were met in only a few developing countries. While rainwater catchment systems do not by themselves provide a cornucopia of water

Figure 1.1 Common types of rainwater catchment tank

(a)

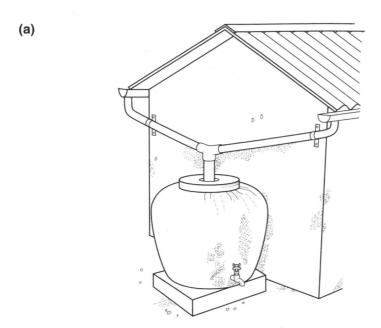

(a) 2m³ 'Thai Jar' wire reinforced cement roof catchment tank, popular in Thailand and other parts of South-east Asia.
(Source: Waterlines)

(b) A rural household with roof and ground catchments and surface and sub-surface tanks in southern Africa. This system designed for a rural household in East Botswana (mean rainfall 400-500mm/year) can meet essential household water needs in most years.
(Adapted from a drawing by A. Gieske, 1995)

(b)

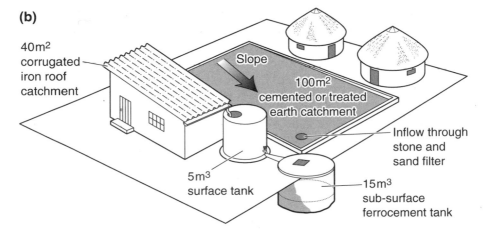

40m² corrugated iron roof catchment

Slope

100m² cemented or treated earth catchment

Inflow through stone and sand filter

5m³ surface tank

15m³ sub-surface ferrocement tank

provision, they are an important additional source of supply and one which can often complement other sources. Rainwater collection is almost always one available option, but until recently it has all too often been ignored.

The purpose and function of rainwater utilization varies enormously in different settings around the world. While, for a household in rural Kenya, rainwater may provide the only source of domestic water supply, in Tokyo, its prime purpose may be for flood control with domestic consumption limited to the watering of plants or flushing of toilets. In Denmark and Germany it has recently become popular to harvest rainwater from roofs because of the increased cost of water which now often has to be treated due to groundwater contamination in many areas. Whatever particular niche rainwater catchment systems occupy in any society, in one form or another they can always play a useful role.

The growing pressures on the earth's finite resources, and especially the worsening water crisis in many regions, has been extensively discussed (Postel 1992, Falkenmark 1989). Considering the acute problems of water scarcity that many are likely to face in the near future, it would seem prudent not to ignore the direct exploitation of nature's simplest and most fundamental source of renewable freshwater – rain. To overlook rainwater utilization would be incompatible with the growing desire worldwide for more sustainable modes of development. Rain falls in at least moderate quantities almost everywhere that people live and, except in hostile arid desert and polar environments, rainwater collection is usually viable to some degree (Figure 1.2a).

In this chapter, rainwater is first considered in the context of other water sources. A review is then given of the historical development, current state of the art and recent developments in rainwater catchment systems for domestic supply. These are examined in both rural and urban areas of developing and industrialized countries and consideration is also given to key lessons learnt.

Sources of water

All rainwater originates from the oceans from where it is distilled through the process of evaporation and about 20 per cent is carried over the land as clouds by atmospheric winds. Once it falls on the land as precipitation (rain, snow, hail or dew) it starts its journey via glaciers, rivers or groundwater back to the sea. This familiar cycle is known as the hydrological cycle (Figure 1.2b). Fresh water for human use is accessible at several points in the cycle and even seawater can be used if desalinated. The most common sources, however, are groundwater, surface water and rainwater. Although these sources are briefly discussed below, the literature on these topics is vast. This book and its references, for example, cover only smaller-scale rainwater sources. Those interested in large-scale floodwater and runoff farming water schemes should refer to UNEP (1983), NAS (1974), Hudson (1987) and Reij et al. (1988). For a more detailed discussion of the technicalities and issues surrounding surface water and groundwater exploitation, the following references might provide a

(a)

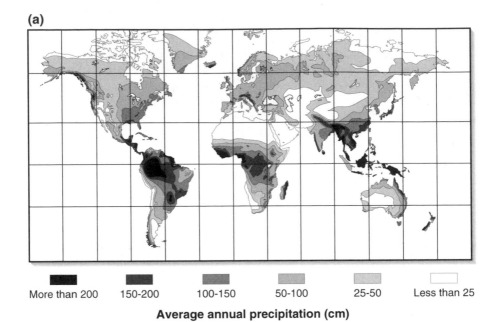

More than 200   150-200   100-150   50-100   25-50   Less than 25

Average annual precipitation (cm)

Figure 1.2a Global rainfall pattern
(Adapted from H.L. Penman, 1970)

Figure 1.2b The hydrological cycle and rainwater catchment systems
(Adapted from Technical Brief No.7, *Waterlines*, Vol. 4, No. 3, 1986)

(b)

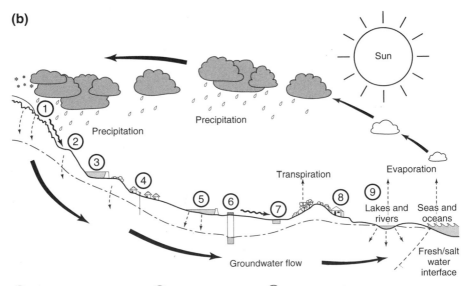

① Surface runoff   ④ Hand pump   ⑦ Ground catchment system
② Rock catchment   ⑤ Earth pump   ⑧ Roof catchment system
③ Rock catchment dam   ⑥ Hand-dug well   ⑨ Potential for dam or sub-surface dam

useful starting point (Agnew and Anderson, 1992; Postel, 1992; WRI, 1996; Morgan, 1990).

Groundwater is normally accessed through wells, protected springs and boreholes. Where groundwater is abundant, fresh, uncontaminated and close to the surface, it provides an excellent source of water supply. Consequently, it is widely used around the world, especially in rural areas. Unfortunately, in some areas where good groundwater was once available, over-exploitation and contamination from agricultural, industrial or domestic sources have degraded both the quality and quantity of the available water. In other places, natural causes such as aridity, droughts or climatic change have led to groundwater sources being unreliable or drying up altogether. Sometimes falls in groundwater levels or deterioration in water quality may be temporary problems, whereas in other cases they may be permanent. Once groundwater becomes contaminated it can take many decades or centuries for its quality to be restored naturally. Treatment of polluted water is expensive – as is desalination when groundwater becomes too saline to use.

Surface-water sources are also widely used around the world, with rivers, lakes and man-made reservoirs providing the major water source for most larger towns and cities. Surface sources are often more accessible than groundwater, since they do not need to be pumped from underground, and water can often be piped from reservoirs to settlements at lower elevation using only gravity. Surface water is, however, more susceptible to contamination from both natural and man-made sources and normally requires treatment. Because of the high cost of constructing dams, treatment facilities and reticulation systems, many surface-water projects are subject to economies of scale. Consequently, while they may provide a cost-effective option for large towns and cities, they are less attractive options for smaller settlements and scattered populations, especially in areas such as the semi-arid tropics which are subject to seasonal and erratic rainfall and high evaporation rates. If a very long-term view is taken, most large-scale dam and reservoir developments are also inherently unsustainable since they will eventually fill with sediment.

Rainwater sources can be sub-divided into small, medium and large-scale systems, as illustrated in Figure 1.3. Large-scale systems include floodwater harvesting where bunds, diversion structures and small dams are used to divert flood waters for spate irrigation, groundwater recharge and flood control. Runoff farming using external catchment areas and larger water harvesting systems using within-field catchments are also categorized here as large-scale systems. Some micro-catchments and smaller water harvesting structures designed for runoff gardening, household subsistence production and water for domestic vegetable plots and individual trees are categorized as medium-scale systems. Since some of these smaller systems use rainwater for domestic cultivation centred around the household, they also fit neatly within the scope of this book. Rainwater catchment systems are all categorized here as small-scale systems, even though some rock and ground catchments can be quite large. Rainwater catchment includes the direct collection of rainwater

5

Figure 1.3 Sources of water and the context of rainwater catchment: the tinted box shows the scope of this book

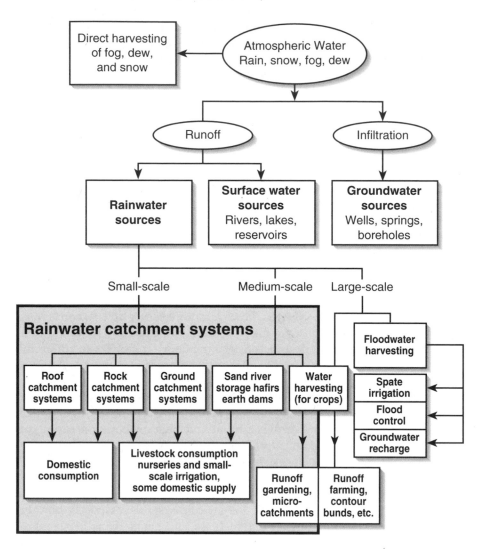

from roofs and other purpose-built catchments, the collection of sheet runoff (overland flow) from small man-made ground or natural surface catchments, and rock catchments (Figure 1.2b). In the case of natural ground catchment systems, this runoff should not normally flow for more than 100 metres or so before being channelled or directed into a storage reservoir. This is because surface runoff flowing for greater distances over bare and gently sloping earth surfaces will normally be concentrated into rills and gullies (Pacey and Cullis, 1986). This process occurs in conjunction with a change to turbulent flow and the initiation of soil erosion. In such circumstances the collection of rainwater runoff in small reservoirs becomes impractical. In the case of rock catchments, erosion is not a problem and runoff over slopes of several hundred metres or more is possible. As with rock catchments, earth dams, and hafirs, sand river storage systems vary considerably in scale and are described here as medium-scale systems (Figure 1.3). These are discussed briefly in Chapters 2 and 4 since, as well as providing water for livestock, they sometimes act as domestic water supplies.

Rainwater runoff occurs at many different scales and is used in a variety of ways, e.g. for domestic purposes, livestock and irrigation. Figure 1.3 shows these and illustrates the relationship between them and how rainwater catchment for domestic supply fits into the overall scheme of water sources. Groundwater, surface water and rainwater sources, although sometimes in competition with each other, also frequently complement each other. Where water scarcity is a problem, often one source will provide a supplementary or backup supply to the other. In other cases, two sources may be used for different things; for example, rainwater for drinking and sightly saline groundwater for other purposes. Apart from the main water sources discussed above, there are many minor sources including the direct utilization of fog, dew and snow. These sources are discussed in detail in the next chapter.

Historical development

Rainwater catchment systems have a long history and their origin, while not known precisely, seems to stem from the early civilizations of the Middle East and Asia several thousand years ago. In Baluchistan in India, evidence of simple stone-rubble structures for impounding rainwater dates back to the third millennium BC (Agarwal and Narain, 1997). In the Negev desert in Israel, cisterns for storing runoff from hillsides, for both domestic and agricultural purposes, have allowed habitation and cultivation in areas with as little as 100mm of rain per year since 2000 BC or earlier (Evenari et al., 1961). In the Mediterranean, archaeologists have uncovered some very early rainwater systems, such as the sophisticated collection and storage system used at the Palace of Knossos perhaps as early as 1700 BC (Hasse, 1989). On Sardinia, the Phoenicians and Carthaginians also practised the widespread collection and storage of roof runoff as the main water source for many settlements from the sixth century BC onwards (Crasta et al., 1982). Eventually, the Romans took control of the region and the technology was further developed. Roman villas and even whole cities were designed to take advantage of rainwater as the principal water source for drinking and domestic purposes (Kovacs, 1979).

In North Africa and around the Mediterranean, thousands of large cisterns for rainwater storage have been in existence for many centuries, with the oldest having been constructed at least 2000 years ago. These sub-surface cisterns with volumes ranging from 200 to 2000m^3 are found mainly around the Western Mediterranean coastal desert in northern Egypt and some are still in use today (Shata, 1982). The world's largest rainwater cistern is

7

probably the Yerebatan Sarayi in Istanbul, Turkey. This was constructed under the rule of Caesar Justinian (AD 527–565); it measures 140m by 70m and has a capacity of 80 000m³ (Hasse, 1989; Ozis, 1982). In his review of ancient cisterns in Anatolia, Ozis (1982), observes that the region is the home of many of the largest and oldest cisterns and dams in the world, some dating back almost 3500 years.

In East and South-east Asia, rainwater collection for domestic purposes also has a long tradition, with evidence of the practice having been traced back almost 2000 years in Thailand (Prempridi and Chatuthasry, 1982). In Japan, rainwater catchment systems have allowed habitation for centuries on numerous, small off-shore volcanic islands such as Miyake-jima and Mikura-jima in the Pacific, as well as many islands in the Japan Inland Sea which lack alternative sources of supply. In parts of China, the history of rainwater utilization may extend back even further. Clay pots being produced in Gansu Province, central China over 6000 years ago, may well have been filled with rainwater runoff from the roofs of ancient shelters and other structures in times of need. Much larger systems specifically developed for rainwater collection were the bottle-shaped water cellars cut into the loess soils of Gansu and Shanxi Province to store surface runoff. These underground tanks, known locally as *shuijiao*, are often up to 30m³ in volume and have provided hundreds of thousands of households with their domestic water requirements for many centuries (Figure 1.4b).

The Indian sub-continent, too, has a long tradition of rainwater collection for both domestic supply and agriculture (Pakianathan, 1989; Kolarkar et al., 1980; Ray, 1983). Examples of traditional water harvesting systems dating back more than 4000 years have been documented from all over India, from the trans-Himalayan mountains to the eastern coastal plains. In the drier regions of northern India in Rajasthan, Uttar Pradesh and Bihar, runoff farming by inundation has been widely practised for centuries. The technique involves the construction of large bunds known locally as *khadin* (in Rajasthan) and *ahar* (in Bihar). These bunds, which are up to 3m high and vary in length from 100m to 10km or more, trap surface runoff and create temporary storage reservoirs from which water may be extracted directly. Overflow via spillways or sluice gates may be used to fill further reservoirs downstream. The water stored behind the bunds eventually infiltrates into the ground where it recharges groundwater, thereby sustaining well-water supplies downslope. Similar types of systems are used in other semi-arid regions of Asia. In Pakistan these are known as *sailabas* or *kuskabas*. People in the arid regions around the Thar desert have long used sub-surface cisterns to store rainwater runoff to supplement limited groundwater supplies (Pacey and Cullis, 1986). Traditional systems based on lining excavated pits with fired lime mortar have been used for over 500 years. These traditional family *tankas*, as they are known locally, are especially common in Jodhpur, Rajasthan. Another traditional system common in the Churu district of Rajasthan is the *kundi* – these huge, concrete saucer-shaped structures gather rainwater, which is stored in a central sub-surface cistern covered with a domed roof shaped like a Buddhist

Figure 1.4 Some examples of traditional rainwater catchment systems

(a) *Abanbar*
Traditional sub-surface
communal cistern, Iran.
(Source: Hassanizadeh, 1984)

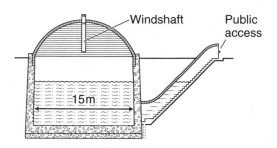

(b) *Shuijiao*
Excavated clay-lined
water cellar, loess
plateau, Central China
(Source: UNEP, 1979)

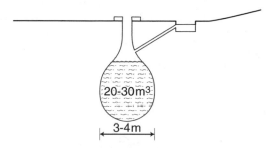

(c) *Chultun*
Mayan stucco
cement/lime-plastered
underground tank
and ground catchment
system in limestone
region, Yucatan
Peninsula, Mexico.
(Source: Gordillo, 1982)

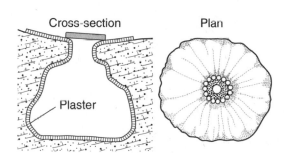

(d) *Adobe Granary Bins*
Lined with
ferrocement to
convert to water
tank, Mali.
(Source: Watt, 1978)

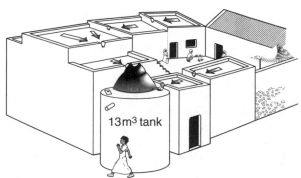

stupa (Agarwal and Narain, 1997). Rainwater utilization also has a long history in other South Asian states, notably Sri Lanka, Nepal and Bangladesh where use of rainwater systems is still common today (Ariyabandu, 1991; Dixit and Upadyaya, 1991; Hoque, 1991).

The Islamic world, from Algeria to Indonesia, and especially throughout the arid Middle East, is also rich in ancient examples of rainwater harvesting used both for agriculture and domestic supply, e.g. Iran, Iraq, Yemen (Pacey and Cullis, 1986). Conical dome shaped structures used to house sub-surface rainwater cisterns for communal use, known locally as *abanbars*, have been used in Iran for many centuries and are still being used and constructed today (Hassanizadeh, 1984; Ghoddousi, 1995; Ghoddousi and Aminipori, 1997; Eslam and Nejad, 1997). These *abanbars* typically have volumes of between 100 and 300m^3 but are sometimes larger – up to 1000m^3 or more (Figure 1.4a).

In sub-Saharan Africa, the small-scale collection of rainwater from the eaves of roofs, or via simple gutters into traditional jars and pots, has been practised for millennia. The Kalahari bushmen (the San peoples) traditionally collected and stored rainwater in ostrich eggs which they sometimes buried in remote locations for months or even years, recovering them when needed during the next dry period or drought. Such practices by hunter/gatherer communities suggest that in one form or another, rainwater collection, like the use of fire, has its origins far back in human history. Astonishingly, in some remote rural areas, some of these early methods of rainwater utilization are still used today, the collection of rainwater runoff from trees being another example (Opiro, 1993). Along the east coast of Africa, traditional roof catchment and ground catchment systems (known as *djabirs*) were introduced by arab traders and settlers and have been in use for several centuries. On Wasini island near the Kenya/Tanzania border, one rich arab businessman donated a large ground catchment system, with a catchment apron of several hundred square metres to the community in the 1950s at a time of extreme water shortages. During droughts, fresh water had previously had to be imported from the mainland by dugout canoe. In other parts of Africa, more formalized roof catchment systems were introduced in the late nineteenth century as missionaries and other settlers built more structures with impervious tiled or corrugated-iron roofs. One cistern, built at a German mission in south-east Ghana at the turn of the century, was still operational when observed in the early 1970s by Parker (1973).

In Western Europe, historical records show that, in Venice, rooftop collection and storage of rainwater was the principal source of water for 1300 years up until the sixteenth century (Hare, 1900). In France, a plan presented to the French Academy of Science in 1703 included the provision of a rainwater cistern with a sand filter in every house (La Hire, 1742). Roof tanks have also been required by public ordinance on Gibraltar since 1869. Until recently, a 6ha rock catchment and 14ha artificial corrugated-iron catchment together provided around 10 per cent of the peninsula's water requirements (Doody, 1980).

In the Americas, although early historic evidence is scant, archaeological remains in Mexico indicate that ground catchment systems known as *chultuns* were being used in the Yucatan Peninsula from as early as 300 AD

(Figure 1.4c; Gordillo et al., 1982). Records in the Caribbean show that on the Island of Bermuda evidence of roof catchment systems dates back to 1628 (McCallan, 1948), and today regulations require tanks by law. Roof catchment systems are in fact widespread in much of the West Indies and have been used there for a long time. In north-east Brazil, hand-dug cisterns made from lime mortar and bricks were introduced by the Portuguese and were commonly used until about 40 years ago according to Gnadlinger (1995). In the USA and Canada, rainwater cisterns have been common features of isolated homesteads and farms since the times of earliest settlement (Bailey, 1959; Moysey and Mueller, 1962) and in many areas continue to be commonplace.

In Australia, Kenyon (1929) made reference to a 2400m² ironclad catchment, able to provide sufficient water for 6 people, 10 horses, 2 cows and 150 sheep in a region with a mean annual rainfall of just 300mm. Roof catchment systems have a long history of use in the Australian outback. Many settlers frequently relied exclusively on rainwater for their freshwater, and many still do. This is particularly the case in areas, such as South Australia, lacking good groundwater supplies. In New Zealand, roof catchment systems have been widely used since major European colonization began around 1850 and the practice remains common in many rural areas today. Elsewhere in the Pacific, many communities have always been dependent on rainwater collection as their main source of water. The use of the technology in one form or another dates back to the time of the first colonization of the islands by early Polynesian travellers. Due to the problems of water supply frequently faced on small islands, especially those of volcanic origin or low-lying atolls, rainwater collection is still an important primary water source throughout most of the South Pacific (Marjoram, 1987).

The current state of the art

Although there was a decline in rainwater utilization in many parts of the world during the middle part of the twentieth century, a period when there was great interest in and enthusiasm for dam building, groundwater development and piped water schemes, during the last two decades interest in rainwater collection has steadily increased. While rainwater collection has always been used in locations where other water sources are scarce, such as on coral and volcanic islands and in arid areas, its use in semi-arid and semi-humid regions has recently expanded rapidly, particularly in Africa and Asia.

Rainwater collection in rural areas
In many rural areas in the developing world the renewed interest in rainwater catchment technologies has spread rapidly both in regions where they have been used traditionally and those where the technology was previously unknown. The number of rainwater tanks with volumes in excess of 1m³ is now of the order of many tens of millions worldwide. Most of these have

been built since 1980, mainly in the rural parts of developing countries. In Thailand alone, somewhere in excess of 10 million 'jars' – 1 to 2m³ ferrocement rainwater tanks – have been constructed since 1983 (Figure 1.1a, Figure 9.6).

The rapid expansion in the use of rainwater catchment systems technology worldwide has coincided with a period of growing interest in community-based, grassroots, self-help development. Indeed, the success of privately owned roof catchment systems, more than any other technology in the water-supply field, has demonstrated that individual ownership and small-scale communal effort can bring impressive results. The rapid replication of the technology in several countries supports this proposition. These recent developments have been documented in Kenya, Indonesia, Thailand and the Philippines by Lee and Visscher (1990), Latham (1984), Wirojanagud and Vanvarothorn (1990) and Appan et al. (1989).

The enthusiastic adoption of rainwater catchment systems in the rural areas of the developing world is perhaps not surprising, given that only 60 per cent of rural dwellers have access to any improved water services, and in sub-Saharan Africa the figure is just 28 per cent (World Bank, 1992). In Asia, many tens of millions of people are dependent on rainwater supplies, most notably in north-east Thailand and central China (see case studies in Chapter 9). In Africa, too, formal and informal roof and ground catchment systems are found throughout the continent (Plates 1.1 and 1.2). These are especially common in parts of Kenya (Chapter 9) and in Mpumalanga and KwaZulu Natal in South Africa, where many hundreds of thousands of informal systems are to be found. Although hardly recognized in most official assessments of water provision, informal roof catchment systems using grass or palm thatch, iron sheets, clay tiles and mud roofs connected to a variety of storage containers are playing a vital role in rural South Africa, (Figure 1.5). These systems, which due to their limited storage capacities are most effective in wetter climates with year-round rainfall, often provide poorer households with their only convenient water source.

Although rainwater catchment systems were an established and widely accepted technology in many parts of the world at the beginning of the century, interest then declined. This was partly due to the development of pumping technologies allowing more groundwater exploitation and the construction of numerous large dams. During the last 20 years, however, the technology has started to spread rapidly from isolated pockets to many areas worldwide. It is particularly in the rural parts of the developing world, especially in East Africa and South-East Asia, where this renaissance has been most marked. Before 1970, rainwater catchment systems were mainly limited to areas lacking any alternative forms of supply, e.g. coral islands such as the US Virgin Islands (Krishna, 1989) and remote, arid locations lacking suitable surface or groundwater sources, such as much of the Australian outback (Perrens, 1975). From the 1970s onwards, a number of preconditions led to the introduction of rainwater catchment systems into the

Plate 1.1 *A simple but effective roof catchment system with a wire-reinforced cement jar at a household in Laikipia, Kenya.* (Photo: John Gould, 1991)

Plate 1.2 *A ground catchment system for community supply constructed on the side of a salt pan at the remote settlement of Zutshwa, Kgalagadi District, Botswana.* (Photo: John Gould, 1994)

13

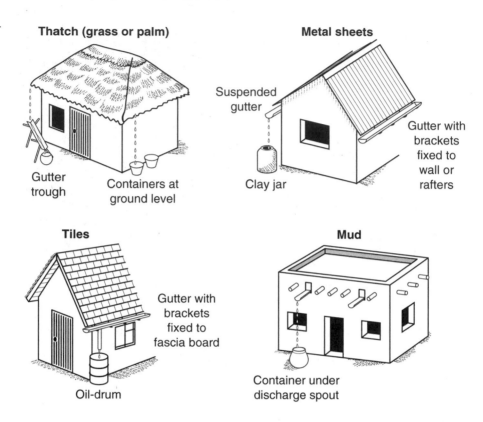

Figure 1.5 Typical roofing materials and some of the many varieties of informal rainwater collection methods
(Adapted from Skinner, 1990)

rural areas of many developing regions suffering water shortages. These included:

- the rapid spread of impervious roofing materials, such as tiles and corrugated iron, replacing the traditional grass and palm thatch in many regions
- the development of effective, low-cost tank designs, e.g. ferrocement water jars
- problems with ground- and surface-water supplies such as salinity, contamination and unreliability caused by increased demand, more intensive agricultural practices and deforestation
- increasing pressure on rural water supplies due to population growth and the trend towards settlement by nomadic people and their livestock
- an increased emphasis on rural development, in an attempt to stem rapidly growing populations flooding into the new urban slums
- failure of traditional piped systems in many developing countries due to problems with operation and maintenance

Although interest in rainwater collection is still predominantly focused on the rural parts of the developing world, there are notable examples of widespread

14

use of the technology in rural areas of industrialized countries. In Australia, hundreds of thousands of people in rural areas are served by some sort of domestic rainwater tank system, either as a primary or secondary supply (Perrens, 1982; Hoey and West, 1982) and in the USA it has been estimated that there are probably over 200 000 rainwater cisterns supplying small communities and individual households (Lye, 1992a). Further details of the use of the technology in Australia and the US are given in the case studies in Chapter 9.

Rainwater collection in urban areas
During the 1990s, there has also been a growing interest in the use of rainwater catchment systems in urban contexts. This may seem surprising, given the constraints of using rainwater systems in urban areas, especially for domestic water supply. The main problem relates to the much higher levels of atmospheric pollution in and around large cities, particularly those with heavy industry and coal-fired power stations. Such pollution often makes rainwater unsuitable for higher-quality uses such as drinking or cooking (Thomas and Greene, 1993). Another factor which may limit the appropriateness of rainwater catchment systems, particularly in large crowded cities, is the shortage of space and high cost of land which may make the installation of large surface storage reservoirs expensive and impractical. A further consideration is that whereas rainwater catchment systems may be cost effective vis-à-vis other water sources in some rural locations, urban water supplies are subject to major economies of scale, enabling the unit price of water to be kept very low and allowing for the piping of water from distant sources. For these various reasons, rainwater catchment systems can seldom compete directly with conventional municipal supplies in terms of cost, reliability or quality, except in situations where water resources are scarce or contaminated. There are, nevertheless, several other important functions that rainwater catchment systems can provide in an urban context.

It should not be forgotten that in many of the towns and cities of the developing world, large segments of the population remain unserved by improved water supplies. Millions of urban dwellers around the world still carry water from unimproved sources or standposts some distance from their homes, and often have to queue for long periods. In developing countries as a whole, around 13 per cent of urban dwellers still lacked access to improved water supplies in 1994; the figure rising to 25 per cent in the least developed countries (World Bank, 1996). As a result, there are many instances where rainwater collection provides a valuable supplementary source of domestic water, for example, in the peri-urban peripheries of many of the rapidly expanding towns and cities of Africa, Latin America and Asia. The *favelas* on the sleep slopes of Rio de Janeiro provide a good example of this phenomenon, as do many of the *barrios* of the Honduran capital, Tegucigalpa. Many of these shanty towns are very new and have poor infrastructure. Even where piped water supplies do exist, the steep slopes create difficulties and supplies are at best intermittent and often absent altogether. A major incentive encouraging people to collect rainwater is the fact that they often use up a substantial portion of their income buying water from water sellers.

In a survey of two low-income shanties in Tegucigalpa by Brand and Bradford (1991), it was found that more than half the households used rainwater as their principal water source, while 90 per cent of the inhabitants collected at least some rainwater from roof catchments. The mean area of the iron-sheet roofs varied from 23 to 45m². In most cases, only half of the roof or less was fitted with makeshift gutters, often made from recycled materials. Most households stored rainwater in old 200-litre oil drums, although about a quarter had somewhat larger cement tanks known as *pila*. The findings of the survey revealed that the introduction of more effective rainwater catchment systems was both feasible and desirable. The provision of loans for fully equipping roofs with guttering and for building *pila* up to 2000 litres in capacity could be repaid over a relatively short time, using money saved from not having to purchase water from vendors.

In India, leakage problems encountered with some of the traditional *tanka* designs have led to a major initiative to upgrade and replace these systems with new designs. In the city of Jodhpur alone, over 11 500 new systems with capacities ranging from 10 to 60m³ were constructed, according to Khan and Faroda (1997).

Apart from the growing interest in the potential role of rainwater catchment systems for supplementing water supplies in the towns and cities of the developing world, the advantages of rainwater collection in urban areas in 'developed' countries are also being recognized. There are several important beneficial secondary functions that rainwater utilization can provide. Explored by Fok (1994), König (1998), Murase (1994), and others (TIRUC, 1994), these include improved flood control, reduced river pollution, countering over-exploitation of groundwater and associated subsidence problems, and substantial cost savings on drainage infrastructure. The economic benefits of deferring and scaling down major infrastructural development of storm-drain and sewer networks provide powerful incentives for the promotion of rainwater utilization in large cities. Many of these secondary functions of rainwater utilization were examined in detail at the Tokyo International Rainwater Utilization Conference (TIRUC) in 1994. This was the first major meeting devoted exclusively to examining rainwater utilization in the context of modern urban development. Other interesting ideas presented at the conference included the growing need to try to restore the urban hydrological cycle, the role of rainwater utilization in countering the problems of the urban heat island effect, and the importance of rainwater tanks for fire-fighting purposes. The role of rainwater cisterns in fire protection and emergency water supply is of particular significance to the Japanese and residents of other earthquake-prone countries. Firestorms, like those following the Great Kanto Earthquake of 1923 which killed more than 100 000 people in Tokyo, are one of the greatest hazards associated with earthquakes. The provision of individual reservoirs in every building aid fire-fighting when mains supplies are ruptured, and can therefore also be of vital importance for providing emergency, safe water supplies in the wake of disasters.

Other benefits of stored rainwater in the urban context include providing backup supplies during dry spells, droughts or periods of mains-supply breakdown. These problems are especially acute in many of the rapidly expanding megacities of the South. Although the cost of installing rainwater catchment tanks is high, the catchment and delivery systems (gutters, downpipes, etc.) are normally already present in the urban context. Furthermore, the economic benefits of installing such systems may be substantial and include deferring major new water developments and reducing capacity of drainage infrastructure, e.g. stormwater drains. Other possible benefits of rainwater catchment systems within cities include the use of rainwater for snow melting on roofs and pavements, and use of rainwater for urban aquaculture and vegetable-production projects.

Currently, Japan is leading the way in Asia with regard to the utilization of rainwater in a modern urban context, and subsidies are increasingly being used to encourage the adoption of household rainwater collection for non-potable uses. In Europe, Germany has been at the forefront in encouraging household rainwater collection in urban areas through the provision of generous subsidies by local government authorities. Due to pollution problems and high drinking-water-quality standards, rainwater is mainly used for non-potable purposes such as washing clothes, watering gardens and flushing toilets. The rise of environmental consciousness and the 'Greens' as a political force, particularly at local government level, may have contributed to this development. Problems resulting from the over-exploitation of surface and groundwater sources have also been an important factor encouraging the promotion of rainwater utilization. Further specific examples of developments in these countries are given in Chapter 9.

Recent developments

Since the early 1980s, there has been an important trend of growing international collaboration with regard to the development and promotion of rainwater catchment systems worldwide. Important initiatives, such as growing donor interest and project support over the period, illustrate this. There has also been an increasing willingness by some national and many local government authorities to invest in the promotion and implementation of the technology, e.g. China, Thailand, Burma, Japan, Botswana and Kenya. Details of some of these individual initiatives are discussed in Chapter 9. Among the main donor initiatives is support by several bilateral government aid agencies, in particular those of Scandinavia for projects in Africa, and those of Canada and Australia for projects in Asia. Multilateral donor support has also been forthcoming from a number of UN agencies, such as UNICEF, UNCHS and WHO. There have also been numerous cases of small-scale project support from NGOs, charities, and church and community groups.

Another sign of growing collaboration internationally has been the initiation of a series of international conferences on rainwater catchment systems which began in Hawaii in 1982, initiated by Professor Yu-Si Fok. These continued with subsequent meetings in the US Virgin Islands (1984), Thailand (1987), the Philippines (1989), Taiwan (1991), Kenya (1993), China (1995), Iran (1997) and Brazil (1999). The conference proceedings provide a wealth of information on developments relating to the design, construction and implementation methods being employed and developed around the world. More recently, the conferences have been co-ordinated and supported by the International Rainwater Catchment Systems Association (IRCSA) formed in 1991. The IRCSA has also spawned a number of associated national bodies and national and regional meetings. A newsletter *Raindrop*, originally produced by the USAID-funded WASH project, was subsequently taken over by the IRCSA in 1993. For contact details see Appendix 2. Other important recent meetings include the Tokyo International Rainwater Utilization Conference (TIRUC, 1994); the first conference focusing exclusively on rainwater utilization in urban areas, and the Traditional Water Harvesting Systems Conference in New Delhi, India (1998), where findings from a decade-long investigation into the development and future potential role of these systems in India were presented. For further information and proceedings from these and other recent conferences see the contact addresses in Appendix 2.

Lessons learned

Although it is the successful rainwater-tank implementation projects and innovative designs which tend to receive the most attention in the literature, there have also been some notable failures. It is important that these should also be highlighted and examined as important lessons can be learned and future mistakes avoided. Some of these issues are technical in nature while others are social, such as the importance of community participation discussed in Chapter 7.

The high initial cost of the large storage tanks required, particularly in areas with low or erratic rainfall, is a major disadvantage of rainwater catchment systems. An important lesson learnt in recent years is that any attempt to overcome this problem by trying to reduce the cost of the tank must be approached cautiously to ensure that the quality of the finished product is not seriously jeopardized. If cost-cutting measures result in durability being seriously compromised, or an increased risk of tanks cracking or failing, the exercise will have been self-defeating. The high cost of the tank means that, in most circumstances, efficient systems design is essential, in order to maximize the supply from the tank while avoiding over-design.

Crucial role of sound software and community involvement
A key lesson learned from rainwater catchment system implementation projects is that the single most important factor in ensuring long-term success relates to the degree to which both individual system recipients and the community as a whole are involved. It is absolutely vital that the stakeholders in any project, whether it is conducted at household or community level, are fully engaged from the outset. In community projects, everyone involved should

participate in the planning process, the selection of the technology to be used, and the construction, operation and maintenance of the system(s). Failure to engage individuals and communities in the planning, managing and maintenance of their own water supply projects will almost certainly ensure that the project does not succeed. Such a situation occurred at a project at Kilifi in Kenya in the mid-1980s where, despite excellent quality hardware and substantial financial resources, the project failed because the rainwater-tank recipients were never engaged in the project, which was planned, managed and implemented entirely by an external agency (see Chapter 7 for further details).

The importance of field-testing new designs
The adoption and widespread replication of new designs, however promising they may seem at the development and demonstration phase, is extremely risky if they are not first subjected to thorough field-testing through carefully monitored pilot projects. The failure of various low-cost cement tank designs using organic reinforcement (bamboo, sisal and basketwork) in both East Africa and South-east Asia during the early 1980s provides an important lesson in this respect. The development and hasty promotion of low-cost bamboo and basketwork-reinforced tank designs, in Thailand and Kenya respectively, and their widespread adoption, resulted in one of the most serious failures of rainwater-tank technology to date (Latham and Gould, 1986). In the case of the bamboo-reinforced tank, insufficient field-testing and premature promotion of the design resulted in extensive replication in Indonesia and Thailand (where more than 50 000 were constructed). Unfortunately, after a couple of years, many instances of tank failure were reported due to damage of the bamboo reinforcement, resulting from termite, bacterial or fungal attack. Apart from the problem of cracking and leakage of the 5–12m³ tanks, the risk and related danger of a tank bursting and causing injury, or even death, had to be taken seriously.

A similar problem occurred with the basketwork-reinforced Ghala basket tanks which were widely promoted in East Africa and particularly Kenya in the early 1980s. Several thousand of these were constructed, but within a couple of years most tanks suffered failure due to rotting or termite attack of the organic 'reinforcement'. The lessons in both these instances are clear. It is vital that new designs are thoroughly field-tested before widespread promotion and replication of the technology. This is not always easy to ensure in practice due to the urgent need to find solutions to pressing water problems, especially when an apparently appropriate solution is found.

The importance of training, quality control and good management
While many projects fail as a result of the use of inappropriate technologies and designs, frequently the technology may be sound but failure is due to a lack of training, quality control or poor management. Specific problems stemming from this include poor workmanship, inadequate maintenance and lack of the necessary skills, training and supervision to ensure high-quality construction. Use of inappropriate materials, such as saline water or poorly

graded sand may also act as obstacles to long-term project success. In one major project in Kenya, for example, widespread tank cracking and failure resulted after a few years due to the 'disappearance' of cement during construction, resulting in inadequate quantities being used in the building of large ferrocement tanks. It is probably fair to say that the chequered history of ferrocement tanks in Africa, and particularly problems with the construction of larger rainwater tanks in Botswana and Namibia (Gould, 1995b), stem mainly from insufficient attention having been given to thorough training, careful quality control and project management.

The importance of proper operation and maintenance
Manuals and literature relating to rainwater catchment system operation and maintenance generally recommend that regular system maintenance should be carried out. In reality it seems that, based on field observations, regular cleaning of systems tends to be the exception rather than the rule. Maintenance is also frequently neglected, often to the detriment of the system's lifespan. Leaking taps, blocked or broken gutters and downpipes are very simple to maintain and repair but, if left unattended, these frequently result in total system failure. Even such obvious measures, like closing a dripping tap properly so water loss is avoided, are sometimes not done, especially in the case of communal tanks. Unless specific training is provided and responsibilities allocated, it is probably safest to assume that very little effort will be made regarding operation and maintenance, particularly with communal systems, at least until they fail or break down completely. The situation regarding privately owned systems is somewhat better, but even here it sometimes helps to raise awareness among system owners about the necessity and benefits to be derived from regular system cleaning and maintenance.

Summary of key points

- Rainwater catchment systems have a long history, stretching back thousands of years in several parts of the world.
- Rainwater collection for domestic water supply has increased greatly in rural areas around the world in recent decades, especially in Africa and Asia.
- Interest in rainwater use has also been growing in urban areas, where its benefits include helping in flood control and reducing pressures on existing water resources.
- Several important lessons have been learned from experiences in recent decades; these include the:
  - importance of fully engaging local communities in rainwater projects
  - need to field-test new designs fully
  - crucial role of good training, quality control and management
  - need for proper operation and maintenance of systems.

2

Types and features of rainwater catchment systems

RAINWATER CATCHMENT SYSTEMS can be categorized according to a number of criteria. The most common approach, and the one used here, is to subdivide systems according to the type of catchment surface used, e.g. roof, ground or rock (Figure 2.1). Other approaches to categorizing rainwater systems may be based on the type of storage tank used, whether surface or sub-surface, and on the material used for reservoir construction, e.g. ferrocement, concrete, wood staves, plastic, fibreglass, bricks and so forth. Systems can also be categorized in terms of the purpose for which the water is being collected, e.g. domestic use, livestock, plant production or flood control. In this book the focus is on rainwater catchment for domestic supply. For a broader discussion, *Rainwater Harvesting* by Pacey and Cullis (1986) provides a good overview. Several useful texts focus specifically on water harvesting for plant production, including NAS (1974), Hudson (1987), Reij et al. (1988) and Critchley and Siegert (1991). A brief discussion of the applications of rainwater catchment systems for flood control, climate control, reducing pressure on existing sources and restoring the natural hydrological cycle in urban contexts was touched on in Chapter 1 and is discussed again with respect to Japan in Chapter 9.

Every rainwater catchment system consists of a number of components:

- a catchment surface where the rainwater runoff is collected
- a storage reservoir where the rainwater is stored until required
- a delivery system for transporting the water from the catchment to the storage reservoir, e.g. gutters or drains.

In addition, systems always need some form of extraction device to take the water from the reservoir, e.g. a tap, rope and bucket, or pump. In this chapter a wide variety of rainwater catchment systems are discussed in terms of their different catchment and reservoir types. The various components of typical systems are also examined.

Catchment types

A wide variety of catchment surfaces can be used to collect and concentrate rainwater runoff. These range from natural sloping soil or rock surfaces to artificially treated, constructed or compacted catchments. Purpose-built catchments can be constructed from various materials including cement, tiles or metal sheets. The only key requirements for a catchment surface is that it has to be impermeable and does not seriously contaminate the water. Many

Figure 2.1 Examples of roof, ground and rock catchment systems

(a) Roof catchment

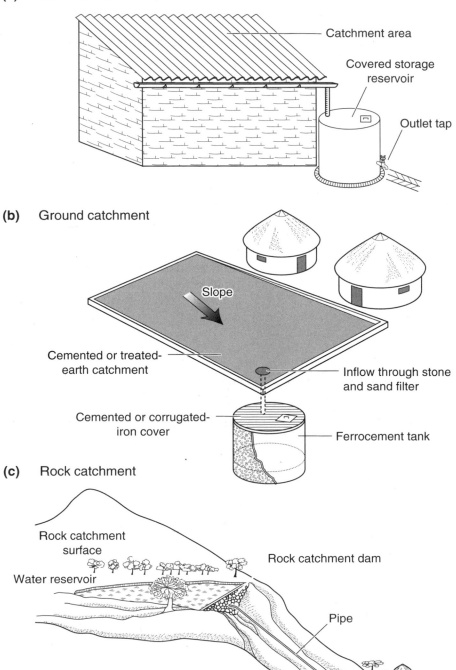

Catchment area

Covered storage
reservoir

Outlet tap

(b) Ground catchment

Slope

Cemented or treated-
earth catchment

Inflow through stone
and sand filter

Cemented or corrugated-
iron cover

Ferrocement tank

(c) Rock catchment

Rock catchment
surface

Rock catchment dam

Water reservoir

Pipe

man-made structures such as roofs, roads, car-parks, airport runways, children's playgrounds and threshing floors are specifically designed to shed water, and these provide excellent artificial catchments with high runoff coefficients. An added advantage of most artificial catchments is that they have generally been constructed for reasons other than rainwater collection, e.g. as a roof on a building, so their cost has already been covered. This is important because, where catchment surfaces have to be purpose-built, they often represent a substantial portion of the total system-cost. Usually the storage reservoir structure comprises the single most costly element of most rainwater catchment systems.

Roof catchments

Roofs are the most common type of catchment used for harvesting rainfall (Figure 2.1a). Galvanized, corrugated-iron sheets, corrugated plastic and tiles all make good roof catchment surfaces. Flat cement or felt-covered roofs can also be used provided they are clean. Corrugated iron is now widely used as a roofing material in much of the developing world. In Africa it is rapidly replacing traditional roofing materials such as grass thatch in rural areas. Since a well-constructed, corrugated, galvanized iron roof provides an ideal catchment surface, the potential for utilizing rainwater supplies is increasing steadily in much of the developing world. In many of the poorest areas, however, especially in Asia including much of rural China and the Indian subcontinent, corrugated iron is too expensive for most households. Here, locally produced clay tiles often provide a cheaper, effective alternative. Elsewhere, traditional roofing materials are still widespread.

Thatched roofs can make good catchments when certain palms are tightly thatched, e.g. coconut and anahaw palms (Plate 2.1). Most palms and almost all grasses, however, do not produce thatch suitable for high-quality rainwater collection, since they discolour the water and make it less palatable and attractive for domestic purposes. Grass-thatched catchments should be used only when no other alternatives are available, and ideally not for the collection of potable water. Mud roofs are generally not suitable as catchment surfaces, although they are used in some places, e.g. Mali, (Kone, 1991; Figure 1.1d). Although painted roofs can be used for rainwater collection, it is important the paint is non-toxic. Acrylic paints can be used provided the first few runoffs after application are not collected (Cuncliffe, 1998). Roofs painted with lead-based paints should *not* be used to collect rainwater for drinking. It is important that painted roofs are in good condition as flakes of paint may otherwise wash into the tank. Unpainted and uncoated roof surfaces are best.

Lead flashing should ideally not be used on roofs used for collecting rainwater; if small quantities are used they must be coated or painted over. There is no evidence that the use of asbestos fibro-cement roofs for rainwater collection poses any health risk; nevertheless, any work involving cutting or drilling into the roof material must be done with great caution as airborne asbestos fibres are dangerous to health if inhaled. It is also important that any pesticide-treated wood used in the construction of the tank or catchment does not come into contact with any rainwater collected for domestic purposes.

Plate 2.1 *Palm-thatch roof supplying a 2m³ ferrocement tank in Cuartero, Capiz, Philippines. (Photo: John Gould, 1989).*

Plate 2.2 *Poorly designed roof and tank system at Masunga, Botswana. One of 70 identical systems utilizing only a small fraction of the catchment and storage potential (see Box 2.1).* (Photo: John Gould, 1991)

For smaller dwellings, a single sloped roof will save on the costs of guttering, since less material will be used (Figure 2.1a). It is essential that gutters are fitted properly with a constant gentle slope to lead water to the tank and prevent blockages. Metal and PVC gutters are the most durable, but wood and bamboo may provide cheaper alternatives. In practice, the efficiency of many systems is often greatly reduced because gutters have been poorly installed or are in need of repair. In other instances, only part of the total available roof area is utilized (see Box 2.1 and Plate 2.2). These are all problems that are very simple to rectify, yet they can make the difference between a system functioning effectively or failing totally.

Roof catchments have a number of advantages over other forms of catchment. If buildings with impervious roofs are already in place, the catchment area is effectively available free of charge. Since roofs are designed to shed water they have a high runoff coefficient. For a well-designed roof, a runoff coefficient of around 0.7–0.9 can normally be expected in most localities, depending on the roofing material. Unlike most other water supplies, which either have to be collected from some distance and transported or piped to households, roof catchment systems provide a supply at the point of consumption.

Sometimes roof catchments are purpose-built specifically for rainwater collection. This is the case with the Arable Lands Development Programme's (ALDEP) water-tank project in Botswana, due to the absence of impermeable roofs in remote rural locations (Figure 2.2c; Plate 9.3). This project is discussed in detail in Chapter 9. Another method which has been tried in Kenya to overcome the limitations imposed by thatched roofs is to cover them with a polythene sheet. While this provides an effective method of increasing roof runoff in the short term, after some time the plastic degrades due to exposure to sunshine. In parts of Bangladesh and Kenya, a similar problem has been addressed by making small catchments from hessian sacks sewn together and hung between four wooden poles (Figure 2.2d).

Ground catchments
'Ground catchment system' is a general term describing all systems which use the ground surface as a catchment area. These include natural, treated and covered surfaces. Cement or tarmac-covered surfaces such as roads, runways, pavements, car parks and courtyards are designed to shed water and thus all provide potentially useful catchment areas. Ground catchment systems are cheaper than roof catchments and are normally employed where suitable roof surfaces are not available. The main advantage with using the ground as a catchment surface is that water can be collected from a larger area. This is particularly advantageous in areas of low rainfall. The main disadvantage in using the ground as a collecting surface is that the water supply can easily become contaminated, and since it can only be stored below the surface it is generally less convenient to withdraw it for use. Although ground catchment systems are sometimes used to collect rainwater for drinking purposes, it is strongly recommended, where possible, that this water should be boiled,

Box 2.1
Common problems with roof catchment design

Many roof catchment systems are poorly designed. Common mistakes include:

- gutters that are horizontal or sloping away from the tanks
- overflow pipes placed well below the top of the tank
- outlet taps high above the base of the tank
- down pipes leading to waste
- only part of the roof area being used

The following diagram compares a good and bad roof catchment system. The poorly designed system is probably only about 10 per cent efficient. Less than a quarter of the roof area is being effectively utilized, and only half of the storage capacity. Unfortunately, this is based on a real example observed in Masunga, Botswana (Plate 2.2). About 70 systems of this type had been built, each costing about US$2000. Since about 90 per cent of the rainwater runoff was not being collected, the money wasted in this project equals $0.90 \times 70 \times \$2000$ (90% of $\$140\,000$) or more than $\$125\,000$.

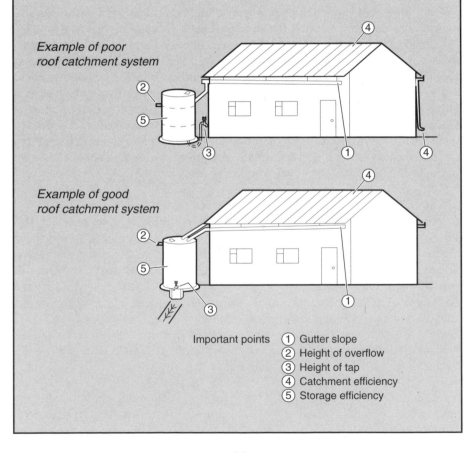

Example of poor
roof catchment system

Example of good
roof catchment system

Important points
1. Gutter slope
2. Height of overflow
3. Height of tap
4. Catchment efficiency
5. Storage efficiency

Figure 2.2 **(a)** Bermuda roof glides and **(b)** Chinese courtyard system.
(Source: Pacey and Cullis, 1986, p.101)

(a)

(b)

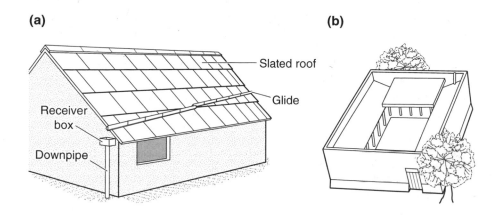

(c) Purpose-built 40m² corrugated-iron 'roof' catchment from Botswana.
(Source: Pacey and Cullis, 1986, p.101)

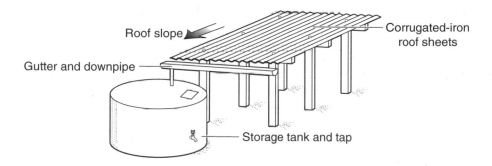

(d) Stretched-woven hessian sacks used for a 6m² 'Sarisa' purpose-built catchment in Kenya.

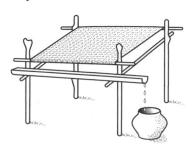

chlorinated, or at least passed through a slow sand filter before being consumed (see Chapter 6). For other domestic purposes, however, the water is generally suitable. It is also essential that where ground catchment systems use sub-surface tanks, these have a robust cover to prevent children and animals falling into them. Any open reservoir should be fenced. A number of cases of drowning of both livestock and children have been reported to the authors in eastern and southern Africa.

Most of the land surface is covered by soils which are pervious with high infiltration capacities and hence low runoff coefficients, e.g. loamy and sandy soils. Soils normally support vegetation which intercepts rainfall, increasing infiltration and reducing direct runoff. If vegetation is removed and the soil surface compacted, the runoff coefficient increases. Compounds around rural households are often subject to much human trampling, and frequently provide useful catchment surfaces. Threshing floors, where cereal and other grain crops are threshed after harvest are also usually compacted or plastered with mud, dung or cement. These can provide useful catchment aprons for rural households, especially those lacking impervious roofs or requiring some additional catchment area (Figure 2.1b). The catchment area will normally be enclosed by a low wall or raised surround to prevent debris blowing on to the catchment surface. It should be kept clean and, ideally, fenced to keep children and animals away. The catchment itself may be purpose-built and have a single purpose, or it may serve dual or multiple purposes, e.g. threshing floor, playground or road. The catchment area will normally slope towards the tank and ideally be plastered with cement or other non-toxic, impervious material. Natural, treated soil or compacted surfaces may form suitable catchment surfaces, although excess sediment may need to be removed from the captured water. Natural ground surfaces are not normally as efficient for collecting rainwater as roof catchment systems. A possible exception to this rule are steeply sloping, unjointed, bare rock surfaces, and where these exist they can provide excellent catchment surfaces. Since these rock catchments differ markedly from other ground catchment systems, they are discussed separately below.

In some cases, rainwater runoff can be collected directly from natural bare ground surfaces. Often, however, due to the low runoff coefficients of many natural soil surfaces, especially where the slope is small, various techniques have been developed to increase the amount of rainwater runoff. These basically involve three approaches – covering, treating or compacting of the surface.

(i) Coverings for ground catchments include butyl rubber, plastic sheeting, cement, tiles, metal sheets and various other impervious materials. While this is an effective way to ensure a high runoff coefficient and reduce surface contamination of the water, it is expensive. This approach is, therefore, most often appropriate only for small catchments. In Botswana, for example, traditional mud and dung or cement-plastered threshing floors have been used since the late 1970s for household supplies in remote areas (Gould, 1991). Only in a few exceptional circumstances is the use of larger purpose-built catchments viable because, with increasing size, costs soon become prohibitive. The 14ha corrugated iron sheet covered catchment on the east side of the Rock of Gibraltar is one such exception. This purpose-built catchment operating in conjunction with a 6ha rock catchment on the west side of the peninsula provides 10 per cent of Gibraltar's water needs (Gonzalez, 1972; Doody, 1980). The use of such approaches for addressing critical water needs are not new. The system on Gibraltar has been used since 1869, and a similar approach on level ground was adopted in Australia in the 1920s (Kenyon, 1929). Trials with gravel-covered plastic sheeting have also been undertaken in Jamaica, and with butyl rubber in Hawaii (Maddocks, 1973; Pacey and Cullis, 1986).

(ii) The treatment of catchment surfaces is a cheaper alternative for increasing the runoff from natural surfaces. Various methods are discussed by Maddocks (1975). Among the materials added to soil surfaces to try to seal them and reduce infiltration are cement, lime, paraffin wax, oil, bitumen and asphalt. Sodium salts may also be used to encourage crusting in soils containing clay. The application of water-repellant silicone or the addition of clays are another approach that can be used. Although less expensive than covering surfaces, the cost of these treatments can still be substantial, especially as meticulous supervision and maintenance is required and their durability is often limited due to erosion, weed growth or damage by insects and large animals.

(iii) The compaction and shaping of natural soil surfaces using machinery to form catchments made of a series of cambered roadways known as 'roaded catchments' have been used in Australia since the 1950s. These catchments feed parallel drains, normally leading into a single surface reservoir. They are typically between 2 and 4ha in size although some of 40ha and more have been constructed. The systems are used mainly to provide water for livestock. They have been widely adopted in Western Australia where they have met with considerable success, especially in areas with clay or clay-loam soils (Pacey and Cullis, 1986). Although not generally used to provide community supplies, due to the poor quality of the water, there is no reason in principle why, with appropriate treatment, the water could not be used for domestic purposes. The potential for developing roaded catchments exists wherever road construction and earth-moving machinery are available.

Another type of ground catchment system, which has been developed in the Kalahari Desert in western Botswana is one that uses the edge of a salt pan as its catchment apron (Figure 2.3; Petersen, 1993). Due to the very flat nature of the terrain in the Kalahari, the only slopes available are the sides of wind-blown pans. During occasional heavy downpours, these yield runoff which can be collected and stored in sub-surface lined tanks excavated into the surface of calcrete pans. A pilot project at Zutshwa in southwest Botswana which began in 1992 has demonstrated that sufficient runoff can be generated to fill storage tanks with a capacity of over 200m^3 in most years. Although the quantity of runoff seems promising, quality problems in the form of turbidity from fine clay still need to be addressed (Gould, 1997).

Figure 2.3 Sedimentation chamber and 68m³ sub-surface brick tanks cut
into calcrete pan at Zutshwa, Botswana.

(Source: Adapted from Petersen, 1993, pp.170 and 171)

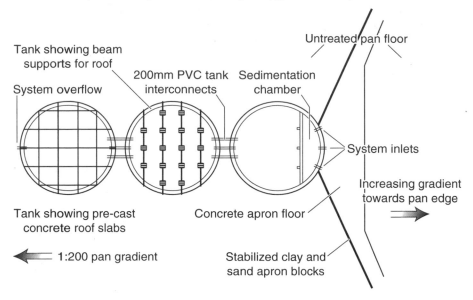

Rock catchments

Technically, rock catchments are a type of ground catchment system. They
are, however, included here as a separate category because they are so different from other ground catchment systems, having several distinctive features such as gravity flow supplies (Figure 2.1c). Rock catchments are also
generally constructed for communal supplies in areas with suitable rock outcrops. The runoff is channelled along stone and cement gutters constructed on
the rock surface into reservoirs contained by concrete or stone masonary
dams (Plate 2.3). Massive, unjointed rock surfaces provide excellent freely
available catchment surfaces, often with very substantial surface areas –
typically several hectares or more. These can yield large quantities of water.
100mm of rain is equivalent to 1000m³ (1000 tonnes) of water per hectare, so
such systems are often capable of providing sufficient water for whole communities if suitable dam sites can be located.

Where the dams lie above settlements, water can be supplied to standposts
through a gravity-fed pipe network. The main drawback with rock catchment
systems is the fact that water-quality problems can result from contamination
of the catchment surface, particularly if defecation by humans or animals
takes place in the vicinity. Ideally, any soil or vegetation on the rock catchment surface should be removed and animals excluded from the area. Since
rock catchment reservoirs are often large, it is normally not practical to cover
them, and as a result they are subject to significant evaporative losses. For a
brief history of rock catchment systems in Kitui, Kenya, an area with probably

30

Plate 2.3 *Rock catchment system at Kaseva, Mutomo in Kitui District, Kenya. Note the stone gutters connected to the sides of the dam wall.* (Photo: Erik Nissen-Petersen)

Plate 2.4 *Fog-water collectors at El Tofo, Chile (altitude 780m).* (Photo: R. Schemenauer, 1997)

more systems than anywhere else on earth (see Box 2.2). A detailed discussion of site assessment, design features, costing, construction, maintenance and management of rock catchment systems is provided in Chapter 4 and by Lee and Visscher (1992) and Nissen-Petersen (1985; 1990a; 1998b).

Runoff delivery systems

In order to convey rainwater runoff from the catchment surface to the storage reservoir, some sort of delivery system is normally required.

Roof catchment delivery systems
The delivery systems used for roof catchment systems usually consist of gutters suspended from the eaves sloping towards a downpipe and tank. In some instances, however, surface drains are used as an alternative. This is the case in many parts of China, where the 'courtyard' system is employed (Figure 2.2b) (Mou and Wang, 1995). Such systems are found in Gansu Province where in rural areas people simply cannot afford metal gutters. Since no cheap alternatives exist, they construct cement channels on the surface of their courtyards to divert the roof runoff into sub-surface tanks (Zhu and Wu, 1995a and 1995b). These are swept regularly to keep them clean.

Another alternative to gutters are stone or cement glides which are used on roofs in Bermuda (Figure 2.2a). These slanting ridges are constructed on the roof itself to direct rainwater runoff towards the tank inlet or a receiver box. In many parts of rural Africa, troughs made of wood, or metal supported by simple frames and slanting towards drums, or other storage containers on the ground, are common sights, (Figure 1.5).

Ground catchment delivery systems
Delivery systems for ground catchments vary depending on the size and nature of the catchment. In the case of the small (about 100m²) threshing-floor ground catchments in Botswana, the floor normally slopes to a single tank inlet and coarse stone-and-mesh filter. Here at one corner of the catchment the water enters the sub-surface tank through a short length of pipe (Figure 1.1b). For larger systems, such as roaded catchments or other large ground catchments, a network of drains and channels is required to direct runoff quickly and efficiently via an inlet filter for removing coarse debris to the reservoir. Ground catchment systems normally include a coarse stone filter to prevent sticks, leaves and other debris from entering the storage tank. Wire-mesh screens placed over the inlet pipe may also help to exclude finer debris. Dust, fine silt and other dirt can also be removed by using a sedimentation chamber constructed in front of the inlet pipe or coarse stone filter. To be effective, it must be cleaned regularly to remove any sediment accumulations. Another approach to sediment removal is to put a line of reservoirs in series and use part of the first as a sedimentation chamber. This approach is illustrated in Figure 2.3 for the system constructed on the edge of Zutshwa Pan in Botswana (Petersen, 1993).

Rock catchment delivery systems

In the case of rock catchments, standard drains are not appropriate. Instead, large flat stones can be placed upright and cemented in lines to form 'stone gutters' approximately 20cm high (Plate 2.3). These should be carefully aligned so they rise gently with a gradient of 3cm per 100cm (3 in 100) relative to the contour. The junction between the stone gutter and the rock surface creates a channel sloping downwards at about 2 degrees towards the reservoir. These stone gutters can extend for several hundred metres and even run around to the opposite side of a rock outcrop or inselberg (see Figure 2.4), provided the stone gutter can divert the water down to the reservoir.

Figure 2.4 Runoff for rock catchment dam collected from the reverse side
of an inselberg.
(Source: Adapted from Nissen-Petersen, 1990a, p.6)

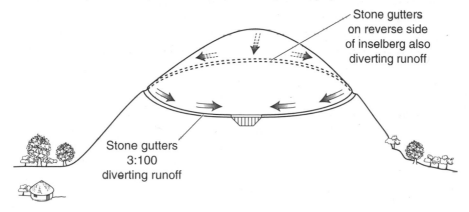

Storage reservoirs

Rainwater storage reservoirs can be subdivided into three distinct categories: (i) surface or above-ground tanks, which are common in the case of roof catchment systems, where the catchment surface is elevated; (ii) sub-surface or underground tanks which are normally associated with purpose-built ground catchment systems; (iii) dammed reservoirs for larger catchment systems using natural catchments, e.g. rock catchment dams, earthdams and sub-surface or sand dams in sand rivers.

Since the tank is generally the most expensive part of the system, careful design and construction are essential. A detailed discussion of the design (including reservoir-sizing methods) and construction methods for rainwater tanks and other rainwater storage reservoirs can be found in Chapters 3, 4 and 5. Sources of other useful information are listed in Appendices 2, 3 and 4, and for those interested in constructing systems themselves, detailed step-by-step construction procedures, design drawings and bills of quantity details for seven tanks ranging from 3m³ to 90m³ are given in Appendix 5.

Surface tanks

These can be constructed from a wide range of materials: metal, wood, plastic, fibreglass, brick, interlocking blocks, compressed-soil or rubble-stone blocks, ferrocement and concrete. The key features of any tank are that it should be watertight, durable, affordable and not contaminate the water in any way. The most appropriate choice of tank in any situation will depend on local conditions. Various environmental factors may preclude certain types of tank. Metal tanks are not suitable in areas of saline soils and coastal areas; wood may be inappropriate if termites are present; and plastic (even UV-stabilized) may be less durable in the presence of strong sunlight. The comparative costs of locally available alternatives will also be a key factor in choosing the most appropriate tank.

Surface tanks may vary in size from $1m^3$ to more than $40m^3$ for households, and up to $100m^3$ or more for schools, hospitals, etc. The tank size is dependent on the rainfall regime (the pattern of rainfall throughout the year) and the demand. Areas with seasonal rainfall will require larger tanks. In locations with long dry seasons lasting several months, a large tank ($25m^3$–$35m^3$) and a roof probably exceeding $100m^2$ would be required if total household demand was to be satisfied throughout the dry period. Rationing schedules or the use of alternative supplies during drought periods can, however, help to reduce tank-size requirements significantly. In general, the roof area of catchment systems increases as total rainfall decreases, or where rainfall patterns become erratic. This is due to the larger roof area and tank size needed for a permanent supply. Consequently, in some more arid areas, cost may dictate that rainwater catchment is most effectively used only as a supplementary water-supply source. In many semi-arid areas, however, roof catchment supplies are much cheaper than water either trucked or piped over long distances from deep boreholes.

Smaller surface tanks have the advantage that they do not necessarily have to be made on site. If centrally made and transported to site it may be easier to ensure quality control in their construction. This is especially important for tanks which require a high level of workmanship, such as ferrocement. In New Zealand, ferrocement tanks as large as $25m^3$ have been constructed centrally and transported to site. This does, however, require considerable care and reasonable roads. Plastic tanks up to $10m^3$ or $20m^3$ in volume can more easily be transported almost anywhere as they are light and flexible.

Another benefit of surface tanks (compared to sub-surface tanks) is that water can be extracted simply and easily through a tap just above the base of the tank. If the tank is elevated by placing it on a stand or base, water can be piped by gravity to where it is required. The main disadvantage of surface tanks is that they are relatively expensive when compared with sub-surface storage. Where roof catchment systems are incorporated in the initial plans and designs for houses it is, however, often possible to make substantial cost savings by incorporating the rainwater storage reservoirs into the house structure itself. This is the case in the US Virgin Islands where most homes have a tank constructed as standard within the basement of the house (Krishna, 1989).

Box 2.2

History of rock catchments
Rock catchment dams in Kitui, Kenya

Elephants created the first rock catchment dams or rock pools by scooping soil out of natural depressions in rocks long before the Wakamba people arrived in Kitui in eastern Kenya. The oldest known rock catchment dam in Kitui is a 150 000-litre depression on a rock outcrop at a village named Mutomo. Unfortunately for the elephants, rock catchment dams have rather steep sides making it difficult for them to climb out after having consumed water. The Wakamba found it easy to kill elephants caught in these dams and named one rock YaMutomo which means 'easy place to kill elephants'. The last elephant going for water at YaMutomo was killed at the rock by the Game Department in 1983.

In pre-colonial days, rock catchment dams situated along the slave routes, such as YaMutomo, were used and improved by slave-dealers on transit to and from the coast. The colonial government of Kenya implemented a programme called ALDEV (African Land Development) in the 1950s during which some 20 large rock catchment dams were built. Dynamite was used to increase rock depressions and the fractured rocks were used for building the dam walls. Forced labour – men and women separated in thorn-fenced camps – carried out the manual labour while a British agricultural officer designed and supervised the work. Although these first rock catchment dams were built by forced labour, the dams proved to be the most reliable and popular water source for the Wakamba people over the next 40 years.

Around 1970, the Kenyan Government built some 80 rock catchment dams in Kitui, but due to lack of experience most of these dams were not very successful in design and construction. The Diocese of Kitui has been assisting the Wakamba in building many good rock catchment dams since the mid-1970s. The water users have to pay for every tenth bag of cement and provide free labour, and the programme continues to be implemented without problems. USAID started the construction of some 40 rock catchment dams between 1984 and 88. Unfortunately, most of these dams were never completed because the water users were paid for their labour and completion would result in losing a stable income.

From 1983 to 1989, DANIDA's Mutomo Soil and Water Conservation Project assisted hundreds of self-help groups in repairing and completing 20 existing rock catchment dams. Ninety new rock catchment dams of various designs were also built, the biggest having a reservoir capacity of 6000m^3. Today, some 200 000 Wakamba people fetch nearly all their domestic water from about 350 rock catchment dams in Kitui District. Building new rock catchment dams, as well as extending existing ones is on-going because rock catchment dams are the most popular water source for rural communities in Kitui.

Sub-surface tanks

Several of the techniques used for building surface tanks can also be used for sub-surface tanks. For these, the tanks are constructed in excavations with the soil being backfilled around the outside of the tank on completion. Where the soil is firm, some of the forces of the water against the side of the tank are absorbed by the soil and the walls do not have to be as strong as for an equivalent surface tank. For ferrocement tanks, it is possible to line a carefully excavated hole with chicken wire and barbed wire reinforcement and plaster directly on to it. This dispenses with the need for formwork for the walls of the main tank and helps to reduce costs significantly.

Soil water and soil pressure will also exert external pressure on the tank walls. While this is counterbalanced by the internal water pressure when the tank is full, when the tank is empty this may produce substantial pressures and the walls must be strong enough to resist these. In order to overcome this, the tanks must be cylindrical or hemispherical in shape. Seasonal rises in ground-water levels may also create a situation where an empty tank can float like a boat. Care, therefore, has to be taken when siting the tanks! Raising the sides of the tanks above ground level and ensuring the tanks are never completely empty can also help to counter this problem. Surface water should also be diverted away from the tanks by raising the ground around them.

Where impervious soils exist, such as clay or loess, it is often possible to construct unlined sub-surface reservoirs. Invariably these suffer from problems of seepage, evaporation, and poor water quality. Lining these reservoirs and treating the water collected from them can, however, help to improve its quality to a degree. The main advantage with sub-surface tanks is that they are generally cheaper per unit volume than surface tanks. Where space is in short supply they may also be more appropriate. The main disadvantage is that to access the water, some form of pump or other extraction method is required. An alternative to this is to construct steps to a tap stand from where the water can be extracted under gravity (Figure 1.1b). Where sub-surface tanks use surface catchments, they are also more likely to risk contamination and may suffer from problems of excessive sediment inflow.

Rock catchment dams, earth dams and hafirs
Where suitable sites exist, rock catchment dams are one of the cheapest and most effective types of rainwater storage system (Figures 2.1c and 4.9). Where impermeable, exposed, unjointed bedrock exists, potential dam sites can normally be found in natural valleys or hollows, which can easily be converted into storage reservoirs by constructing rubble-stone-masonry dams. Granitic inselbergs in Africa are ideal locations for rock catchments, which normally vary from 500 to 10 000m³ in volume. Water can normally be piped by gravity to tap stands or storage tanks at the base of the outcrops or to nearby villages to improve accessibility.

Earth dams and ponds consist of raised banks of compacted earth and can be constructed to retain water, where it regularly flows into small valleys, depressions or at hill-sides. The dam wall is normally 2–5m high and has a clay core and stone aprons and spillways to discharge excess runoff (Figure 4.11). Volumes range from hundreds to tens of thousands of cubic metres. Reservoirs with volumes of less than 5000m³ are usually called ponds.

Hafirs are excavated reservoirs normally 500–10 000m³ in volume (Figure 4.12). Originating in the Sudan, these sources still provide important, traditional water supplies in many parts of semi-arid Africa for both people and livestock. Hafirs are located in natural depressions and the excavated soil is used to form banks around the reservoir to increase its capacity. Bunds and improvements to the catchment apron may help to increase runoff into the reservoir, but seepage and evaporation often result in them drying out late in the dry season. In common with earth dams, high water turbidity and sedimentation problems are a major drawback with hafirs, which require periodic cleaning to remove silt. Sediment traps and delivery wells may help to improve water quality but, as with water from earth dams, it is not usually suitable for drinking without some form of treatment. Despite this, untreated water from these sources is still widely used for human consumption due to the lack of any better alternatives. The populations affected, and especially the very young, are exposed to substantial health risks.

Sand river storage
In many semi-arid regions, rivers are ephemeral and surface water flow may be visible for only a few weeks a year. Once the water subsides, the sandy river bed is exposed but, while the river may appear dry, water is normally found flowing very slowly under the sand. These sand rivers provide important traditional water sources, especially in Africa. During the dry season, pits dug into the sand can provide important water sources for both people and livestock. The water level in the river bed tends to fall throughout the dry season and sometimes dries up altogether. To increase the upstream storage capacity in the river bed a sub-surface dam can be built across the river channel so its top is level with the sandy river bed. Sub-surface dams are constructed of either earth or stone-masonry where the sand is shallow (Figure 4.10b).

Sand dams are similar to sub-surface dams except that the top of the dam wall exceeds the level of the sandy river bed (Figure 4.10a). These dams are built in stages, with the dam wall height being increased by 0.3m after floods have deposited sand to the level of the spillway. This allows sand to be trapped upstream of the dam wall, increasing the overall storage capacity of the river bed. Natural underground dykes of clay or murram can be exploited to facilitate the construction of sub-surface and sand dams. Coarse river sand provides the best and greatest storage potential, which often amounts to several thousand cubic metres for a single dam.

The advantage with sand river storage is that it normally represents an upgrading of a traditional and hence socially acceptable water source. Because the water is stored under the sand it is protected from significant evaporation losses and is also less liable to be contaminated. The construction of river intakes and hand-dug wells with handpumps on the river bank can further help to improve water quality.

Dew, snow and fog collection systems

Rainwater probably accounts for more than 99 per cent of all precipitation harvested directly for domestic use. Nevertheless, dew, fog and snow are also

37

exploited and, in certain arid localities, provide essential sources of water. Since rainwater utilization is the focus of this book, these other sources of water supply are dealt with only briefly below.

Dew collection

The potential for obtaining water through harvesting dew is limited and has possibly been overstated in the past due to a mythology which seems to have grown up around the practice. This may have resulted from a variety of anecdotes and references to the practice dating back to biblical times, such as the story about harvesting enough dew 'to fill a drinking cup' from a fleece spread on the ground overnight (Judges, Chapter 6, Verse 38). The construction of so-called 'dew ponds' in southern England, and enthusiastic if somewhat subjective investigations into their function in the early part of this century (Hubbard and Hubbard, 1905), also added to the confusion. Subsequent investigations confirmed that these ponds do not catch significant quantities of dew and were actually filled mainly by rainwater (UNEP, 1982; Pacey and Cullis, 1986).

In North Africa and the Middle East, rock mounds on hilltops, some over 2000 years old and known in some places as aerial wells, had been thought to function as dew harvesting systems (UNEP, 1982). An extensive investigation in the Negev desert in Israel where the structures are known locally as *teleiats*, revealed the mounds had nothing to do with dew collection at all, but rather were the result of clearing rocks from slopes to increase runoff for water-harvesting purposes (Evenari, Shanan and Tadmor, 1971).

Snow collection

In colder temperate and mountainous regions a substantial portion of the annual precipitation comes in the form of snow. This can be stored and utilized when needed, either by melting it indoors in winter or storing the snow melt in a reservoir for use in summer. In some parts of the world, such as Afghanistan and Iran, snow is packed into watertight pits in mountainous areas and the resulting meltwater is used the following spring and summer. The example shown in the illustration below (Figure 2.5) is from a remote village in Takhar Province, Afghanistan, where snow was collected in bags, carried by donkey and emptied into a communal system. The snow was compacted and, when filled, the pit was covered with earth to act as an insulator. When full, the approximately 300m^3 snow-storage system could provide drinking-water for a community of 10 families for up to 2 years, (UNEP, 1983).

In the snowy Tokamachi City in Niigata on the west coast of Japan, at least one householder has developed a system whereby snow sliding from the roof of the house is stored in a pit and the water subsequently used in spring (Higuchi, 1994). Although interesting, examples of single-purpose snow catchment systems around the world are relatively few. Many rainwater catchment systems in colder climates, however, depend on snow melt at the end of winter for a significant proportion of their annual inflow.

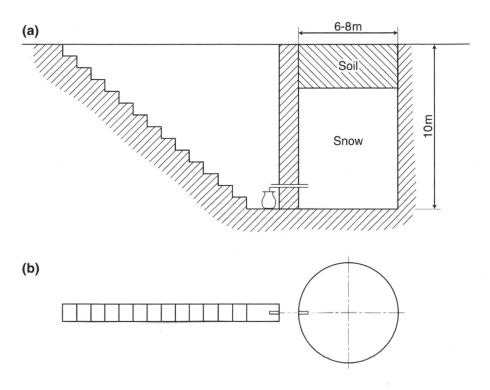

Figure 2.5 Snow collection system in Afghanistan.
(a) Cross section; **(b)** from above
(Adapted from UNEP, 1983, p.193)

(a)

6-8m

Soil

Snow

10m

(b)

Measurements by Ree (1976) in Oklahoma, USA showed that, while roof runoff from rainfall averaged over 90 per cent of rain gauge readings, roof meltwater runoff following snowfall was equivalent to just 50 per cent. Ree et al. (1971) also noted that drifting snow distorted readings of runoff from ground catchment systems.

On the North China Plain, Mou (1995) describes another way in which snow is utilized. It is collected from roads and courtyards and spread on fields to provide additional moisture to crops when the spring thaw arrives.

Fog collection
An innovative approach to the harvesting of water from the atmosphere for both domestic supply and ecosystem restoration has been the recent development of fog collection systems (Plate 2.4). The exploitation of fogwater is applicable in coastal desert regions, especially where mountains and prevailing winds ensure frequent fog occurrence. Locations experiencing such conditions include parts of Peru, Ecuador, Chile, Oman, Nepal, Namibia, South Africa, Hawaii, California, Mexico and the Canary Islands (Schemenauer and Cereceda, 1991).

During the past 15 years, there has been a major research and development effort in several countries, most notably Chile, Ecuador and Peru, supported by the Canadian agencies IDRC and CIDA and more recently by the European Union. Preliminary work focused on identifying appropriate sites and establishing the feasibility of fogwater utilization for domestic supply (IDRC, 1993). Having established the technical feasibility of fog collection, the next step was to test its viability in practice, so in 1987 a pilot project was initiated in El Tofo, Chile (Schemenauer and Cereceda, 1991, 1992 and 1993). The project involved the construction of 50 fog collectors located along a ridge line at 780m a.m.s.l. where a stratocumulus cloud deck was a common feature. The collectors consisted of 48m^2 (12m × 4m) double layer polypropylene mesh supported by treated wooden poles and galvanized steel wires. Fog droplets trapped on the mesh beaded together and dripped into PVC troughs from where the water flowed via pipes to a storage tank. The system's mean yield over three years was equivalent to 7200 litres/day or 3 litres/day for each square metre of collector surface area.

In 1992, the collector panel's total surface area was increased from 2400 to 3528m^2 and a 6km gravity flow pipeline was completed to the small village of Chungungo (population 330). The water was stored in a 100m^3 tank and reticulated to 89 households providing a supply of 30 litres/person/day. Socio-economic analysis to assess the cost and acceptability of fog collection systems compared with other alternatives was conducted (IDRC, 1993). When compared with the only available alternative water-supply option – that of trucking water from a borehole 34km away – it was found that the fogwater collection system could produce water 34 per cent cheaper, at a cost of US$3.2 per cubic metre delivered to the village. Several other social benefits of using fogwater collection were also identified by the study, including training benefits and an increased sense of self-reliance by the community. This study shows that fogwater collection has some promise as a source for domestic supply in regions of low rainfall where local conditions produce regular fog.

While the number of suitable collection sites are limited, and fogwater often requires treatment and reticulation over substantial distances in areas lacking other alternatives, it can provide a viable source. Fogwater collectors are also effective collectors of drizzle and fine rainwater and their utilization deserves wider consideration.

A related aspect, that of harvesting fogwater for revegetating arid coastal mountains, may nevertheless have greater potential. An ongoing applied research project in Peru is examining the potential for restoring the original *lomas* ecosystem by using artificial fogwater collectors to support the re-establishment of indigenous trees and shrubs (Falciai and Bresci, 1997). Once established, the vegetation should auto-capture fogwater itself and thus sustain its own further development. The project is still at an early stage but the initial findings seem promising. If successful, both the ecosystem and hydrological system in the area could be restored and local water sources would be revitalized.

In areas where both fog and rain contribute significantly to the total precipitation, the development of systems designed to collect both fogwater and rainwater are appropriate. Although very few, if any, combined systems of this type exist, their theoretical viability has been investigated (Schemenauer and Cereceda, 1993). Their analysis suggests that not only would systems designed to collect both rain and fog be viable in many localities, but that more consideration of the horizontal component of rainfall could help greatly to increase the yield of existing roof catchment systems. Where strong prevailing winds exist or where rain droplet size is small, appropriate modifications to roof catchment systems would be to align the slope of the catchment perpendicular to the prevailing wind. The exploitation of vertical walls and the addition of vertical panels on the top of the roof could, under these circumstances, lead to large increases in water yield.

Rainwater harvesting for domestic production

The focus of this book is mainly on rainwater catchment systems for domestic water supply; water harvesting for agricultural purposes, which is covered in detail by several other texts (Pacey and Cullis, 1986; Hudson, 1987; Reij et al., 1988) is generally excluded. The use of rainwater runoff for irrigating gardens and crops at household level does nevertheless merit a mention here (Figure 2.6). While it is beyond the scope of this text to discuss all of the various techniques available to the householder to concentrate runoff on to vegetables and other domestic crops, the following examples, nevertheless,

Figure 2.6 Runoff gardening techniques applicable in rural Africa: water conservation measures appropriate for households in Botswana.

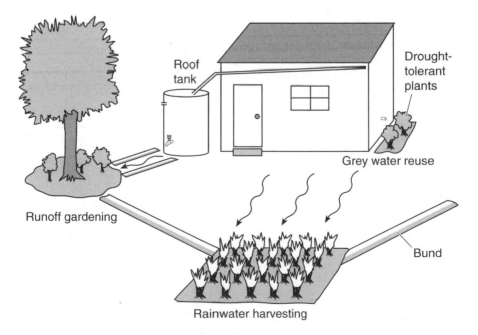

41

illustrate how rainwater can be collected and concentrated around the house and used to boost domestic food production.

Rainwater harvesting for subsistence agriculture
In the arid Province of Gansu in Central China a simple, cheap and highly effective approach to boosting the water availability for household vegetable production and subsistence crops has been developed, based on using plastic sheeting. Many families in this area have constructed small greenhouses by tying transparent plastic sheeting over a simple wooden framework. Around each a trench is dug where rainwater running off the plastic collects and can be scooped up to water vegetables inside. The plastic sheeting also reduces water loss within the greenhouse. The sheeting is also used in the fields, where it is placed on the ridges between the furrows to help concentrate rainwater runoff around the plants and reduce evaporative losses from the soil. Both of these techniques are illustrated in Plates 2.5 and 2.6.

Rainwater harvesting for domestic small stock
Since roof catchment systems may often not provide sufficient water to support the requirements of domestic small stock, it is simetimes worthwhile excavating and lining a simple ground tank at a point near the household where water normally flows. While the quality of this water will be poor, it should suffice for small numbers of chickens, goats, pigs or other smallstock which are often kept near the household. Care should be taken to fence any such tanks to prevent small children or animals falling into them. Ideally the tank should be covered to reduce evaporation and the risk of providing a mosquito breeding site.

Runoff gardening and permaculture
Runoff gardening is really just a scaled-down version of runoff agriculture and involves the use of bunds and micro-catchments to divert surface runoff on to small plots and trees. Some of the simple methods involved are illustrated in Figure 2.6. The use of stone and organic mulches around trees and other crops can help to maximize the effectiveness of runoff gardening techniques by helping to retain the water in the soil, once it has been absorbed, by reducing the rate of surface evaporative losses. Permaculture, the innovative and popular minimalist approach to sustainable domestic food production, embraces rainwater harvesting techniques as an essential component of the system (Mollison, 1992). In particular, the use of swales is advocated. These are shallow, level depressions designed to encourage accumulation of runoff during storms and its infiltration and storage in the soil.

Summary of key points

- Every rainwater catchment system consists of three basic components: a catchment surface, a delivery system and a storage reservoir.

Plate 2.5 *Irrigating vegetables with rainwater runoff from a greenhouse made of plastic sheeting in the mountains of Yuzong County, Gansu, China.* (Photo: John Gould, 1995)

Plate 2.6 *Growing sorghum using rainwater runoff concentrated by plastic sheeting between rows in the mountains of Yuzong County, Gansu, China.* (Photo: John Gould, 1995)

- There are three common types of system which may be used for collecting water for domestic supplies: roof catchments, ground catchments and rock catchments.
- Several types of delivery system exist for transporting water from the catchment to the storage reservoir, including gutters, glides, and surface drains or channels.
- Storage reservoirs include various types of surface and sub-surface tanks, rock catchment dams, earth dams, hafirs and sub-surface or sand dams in sand rivers.
- In some locations where conditions allow, dew, fog and snow can also be collected for domestic water supply.
- Household rainwater harvesting systems can also provide useful amounts of water for watering domestic smallstock, vegetable gardens and limited supplementary irrigation of rainfed crops.

3

Rainwater quantity: supply and demand

IN ORDER TO DETERMINE whether or not rainwater catchment systems are an appropriate choice of water supply in any given situation, it is necessary to estimate the potential rainwater yield to check that it can meet the required demand. The reliability of the systems along with technical, socio-economic and environmental considerations must then be compared with all alternative forms of supply. Technical considerations relating to the choice of design, construction method and materials are covered in Chapters 4 and 5. Issues relating to water quality are addressed in Chapter 6, and those relating to the socio-economic aspects of rainwater catchment systems are addressed in Chapter 7.

In this chapter, questions relating to the theoretical technical feasibility of rainwater catchment systems are examined. Namely, can a viable design supply sufficient water to meet the water demand in any given situation? It is important to remember here that rainwater catchment systems are frequently used in tandem with other water sources as supplementary, partial or backup supplies. The design of any system should therefore match its required function. This is especially true in situations of water scarcity, where rainwater may provide a vital backup supply during short periods of breakdown or disruption to the main supply. Rainwater is most often used as a partial supply, for example, for drinking, where other sources are less clean, or for toilet flushing where other sources are cleaner but more expensive. The water demand requirements placed on rainwater catchment systems in these situations will be quite different from where they are the primary or sole source of supply. Where rainwater is the main or only source of water supply the reliability of the system becomes of critical importance.

Several approaches to estimating rainwater supply exist and some of the key methods are discussed below. In addition to establishing the potential rainwater supply, it is also important to determine the water demand. Although estimating mean daily household demand may appear simpler than determining the rainwater supply, in reality, where supplies are not metered, getting a good estimate of demand is often difficult. Information on both of these are required to determine whether all, or only part of the demand can be satisfied and the storage capacity required. Most of the following discussion and examples relate to household roof catchment systems. Nevertheless, the principles and approaches outlined can in most cases be just as easily applied to larger-scale ground or rock catchment systems with only minor modifications, such as adjusting the runoff coefficient in any calculation.

Rainwater supply

Although rainfall is abundant globally, its distribution in both time and space is erratic. Developing rainwater catchment systems which can meet any given requirements depends, therefore, on careful design. The maximum yield of rainwater runoff from any system is dependent upon two variables: the rainfall amount and the size of the catchment area. In practice, the total yield will also be determined by the collection efficiency (runoff coefficient) and storage capacity of the system.

The actual amount of rainwater that can be supplied varies greatly, depending on the amount and distribution of rainfall, the size of existing or affordable catchment surfaces, and the volume of the storage tank. In cases where existing roofs are to be used, the catchment area is fixed and, for a particular location, the amount of rainfall cannot be changed. In these instances, the only variable the designer can use to influence the available rainwater supply is the volume of the storage tank.

In climates with abundant all-year-round rainfall, a small tank, sufficient to hold just a few days of rainwater supply, may suffice in providing water for domestic requirements for a significant portion of the year. In a recent analysis of household storage requirements in Uganda in areas where climatic conditions were favourable for rainwater use, it was found that surprisingly small storage tanks could meet water demand for a large part of the year (Thomas, 1998). The two locations, Mbarara and Kyenjojo, have mean rainfall of about 900mm and 1400mm respectively and both are in a region with two distinct rainy seasons. In a realistic scenario for a household roof catchment system, a mean water demand equivalent to 80 per cent of the mean rainwater runoff was assumed. Analysis of the data revealed that storage tanks with volumes equivalent to only four days of household water consumption could provide a supply for more than half the year. In order to provide a supply available for 97 per cent of the time, a tank storage capacity equivalent to around 64 days' consumption would be required. In semi-arid tropical climates with marked wet and dry seasons of up to six months or more, large tanks, able to store around half a year's water supply, may be required. Although designing a system to meet demand in such harsh semi-arid environments may seem challenging, actually estimating the mean long-term yield of systems is reasonably straightforward.

Rainfall data

In order to determine the potential rainwater supply for a given catchment, reliable rainfall data are required, preferably for a period of at least 10 years (Schiller and Latham, 1982a). Ideally, if accurate local historic rainfall data for the past few decades are available, a 20 or 30-year rainfall series is preferable, especially in drought-prone climates. Longer rainfall data series may, however, give a false picture of current rainfall conditions if regional climatic changes have occurred.

Rainfall data can normally be obtained from national meterological departments, the Ministry of Agriculture, universities, research stations and directly through the Internet. Care should be taken when selecting the best rainfall data source station as, in some areas, mean rainfall may vary markedly over short distances, especially in mountainous terrain. In such instances, the rainfall records from the nearest station may not necessarily be the most representative; for example, if the site of a new rainwater catchment system is on the drier leeward (rain shadow) side of a mountain range. It would be far better to use rainfall data from the nearest station with comparable conditions with respect to aspect and altitude, even if this was at some distance, than to use data from a closer station on the windward (rainy side) of the mountain range.

For a particular location, rainfall amounts can vary greatly over a period of years, so although mean annual or mean monthly rainfall data may be the easiest to obtain and apply for design purposes, it may not yield the best results. If the actual monthly or daily rainfall totals can be obtained for at least the last 10 years, or preferably longer, more accurate statistical, graphical and computer-based methods for determining the most appropriate design dimensions can be used. Some of these techniques are outlined later in this chapter.

In situations where system reliability is critical, a simple way to build in a degree of certainty into any design calculation for estimating the minimum amount of rainwater supply available is to use a minimum annual rainfall value in place of the more commonly used mean annual rainfall figure. This can be defined as required, but typically it might be taken as the minimum annual rainfall that will be exceeded 90 per cent of the time. Any system designed using this value for rainfall should meet at least minimum design expectations in nine years out of ten. This approach was adopted by Schiller (1982) and is shown in the simple graphical technique for calculating rainwater supply illustrated in Figure 3.2.

Domestic water consumption and demand
Worldwide, levels of domestic water consumption vary widely from less than 5 litres/person/day in many of the poorest communities in developing countries (Hofkes, 1982) to 1000 litres/person/day or more for the very wealthiest. While rich and poor alike may drink the same amount of water, the wealthy have cars to wash, gardens to water and swimming pools to fill. A detailed discussion of the issues related to these inequalities of water provision and the growing global problem of water scarcity are covered in the thought-provoking book *The Last Oasis* (Postel, 1992). While the above consumption figures may represent extremes, there are many millions with lifestyles which match them, especially at the lower end of the spectrum. Indeed, it is not uncommon in times of droughts or other crises for the per capita water consumption for the worst-off to fall well below 5 litres per day. At these low levels of water consumption, people are never satisfied with their lot and, inevitably, would prefer more water if possible. It is probably reasonable to assume that the minimum consumption level at which water demand starts to be satisfied is around 20 litres/person/day. This was the minimum target

supply level set for rural communities in developing countries by the United Nations during the IDWSS Decade. Within the context of rainwater systems design, a range for total demand of between 20 and 200 litres/person/day, depending on circumstances, is realistic. For most people, even with cars to wash or gardens to water, 200 litres is a generous quota, which, if used wisely and efficiently, can go a long way. Very few people, however, have roofs (or other catchments) large enough, or live in areas wet enough, to sustain supplies at this level. Often due to water scarcity, people are most concerned that rainwater systems should be able to meet at least essential purposes, including water for drinking, cooking and washing, either for short periods in the case of backup supplies, or year round in cases where rainwater is the main source of supply for these purposes. In this case an appropriate range for meeting essential demands would be from 15 to 25 litres/person/day.

Consumption levels will invariably be much higher in wealthy countries, even in remote rural locations. One survey of rural domestic water use in New South Wales, Australia, found that for households totally reliant on rainwater supplies, mean consumption ranged from 126 to 165 litres/person/day (Patterson, 1985). A maximum daily demand of 350 litres per person was occasionally recorded. In South Australia, the water department estimates that rural residents need around 89 litres/person/day. This includes water for a three-minute shower, toilet flushing, clothes washing, kitchen use and drinking, but is dependent on using water-saving devices such as low flow aerated showerheads and dual flush toilets (EWSD, 1987). In poorer countries and regions, water consumption is much lower. Surveys in rural Botswana have revealed that per capita water consumption in scattered isolated settlements and homesteads ranges from 8 to 20 litres per capita per day (Gould, 1985, 1995a). Generally, however, people are seldom satisfied with their daily water supply once it falls below about 15 litres per capita, and even well above this figure people can suffer considerable hardships.

In order to determine whether rainwater catchment systems are appropriate in any given context and what are the best dimensions for any design, a good starting point is to estimate water demand, usually using a survey or metered data. Often good data may not be available for any given community, in which case it will have to be collected. For an accurate determination of the demand, a detailed survey of a representative number of households is needed.

Domestic water demand includes all water used in and around the home for the following essential purposes:

- drinking
- food preparation and cooking
- personal hygiene (washing hands and body, cleaning teeth)
- toilet flushing (where flush toilets are used)
- washing clothes and cleaning
- washing pots, pans and other utensils.

Additional domestic water uses may include:

48

- watering gardens (trees, flowers, vegetables, etc.)
- watering animals (cats, dogs, chickens and small stock)
- washing vehicles (bicycles, cars, carts, etc.)
- water for construction (repairing mud walls)
- recreational uses (paddling pools).

In most areas, properly designed household roof catchment systems can normally meet domestic demand for essential purposes. Only in situations where rainfall is low or roof and tank size too small will systems routinely fail to meet basic domestic water needs. Few domestic catchment systems are able to meet total household water requirements including the additional uses listed above. Only if a large tank capacity and sizable roof or ground catchment areas are available in areas of higher rainfall, will this normally be possible. The quantities of water used will vary according to individual circumstances. For example, the type and number of any animals watered will depend on the amount of water available.

Watering gardens can require very large amounts of water, especially if the plants are dependent on regular watering for long periods. A small $10 \times 10m$ vegetable plot could easily require 500 litres per square metre each year, equivalent to 50 000 litres (50m³) – well beyond the capacity of most household rainwater catchment systems. Although rainwater supplies are usually insufficient for general garden watering, if after essential needs have been met surplus rainwater is available, some watering of plants may be possible. In such circumstances the limited rainwater supply needs to be used as efficiently as possible and targeted very specifically; for instance, watering only certain less drought-resistant plants during critical dry periods when they start to show signs of water stress. Watering of trees should be restricted to seedlings and then only while they are getting established. The use of a porous pot or large perforated tin placed in the earth next to the plant or seedling requiring supplementary water can help to reduce evaporation losses and get water directly to the root zone. The use of mulches around plants can also help to reduce evaporation losses. If substantial quantities of water are required for watering plants, construction of a ground catchment tank in the garden may be appropriate provided a suitable surface catchment is available or can easily be constructed. Other ways of increasing water supply to plants include runoff gardening and the reuse of waste water from baths, clothes washing or kitchen sinks. Even if waste water contains a small amount of detergent, it is normally not harmful to most plants and some even seem to thrive on it, e.g. banana and papaya. Some of these techniques of concentrating runoff and conserving water are illustrated in Figure 2.6. Ideally, any greywater should be applied direct to the soil around the root zone of the plants as this is cleaner and reduces any evaporative losses.

Estimating domestic water demand
Estimating household annual water demand may, at first, seem straightforward, i.e. multiplying mean daily water use per person by the number of

household members by 365 days. For example, if in a survey the head of a household reports that water use is 20 litres per person per day and that there are five members in the family, the simple calculation shown below might at first suggest an annual household water demand of 36 500 litres (36.5m³):

Demand = 20 litres × 5 × 365 days = 36 500 litres per year

In reality it may not be so straightforward. Further questioning may reveal that adults and children use different quantities of water and that seasonal water use varies significantly, with more water being used in the hottest or driest seasons. The number of family members staying at home may also vary at different times of the year, if some members work or study away from home. To try to take into account all such variables, household surveys need to be designed very carefully, and detailed information sought.

In the above example, if more detailed questioning of the householder revealed that water use fell to 14 litres per person during the cooler half of the year, making the mean daily consumption 17 litres per person, the calculation would have to be revised as follows:

Demand = 17 litres × 5 × 365 days = 31 025 litres per year

If further questioning revealed that the household consisted of two adults and three children, but one of the adults lived away from home for half of the year, the calculation would have to be revised again to:

Demand = 17 litres × 4.5 × 365 days = 27 923 litres per year

Even this final revision, which revealed estimated consumption to be far lower than originally suggested, may require further revision. If the absentee adult is away from home mainly during the period of highest consumption (hot/dry season) for instance, even this last calculation would be an overestimate. Further investigation may reveal other significant factors having a bearing on household consumption. For instance, small children will probably use far less water than older children. Although in this example the acquisition of further information about the household resulted in a downward revision of the demand estimate by about 23 per cent, in another instance it is just as likely that actual demand might have been much greater than first estimated.

The best estimates of household water demand will come from detailed surveys of many households where mean per capita consumption can be calculated on the basis of hundreds of responses. If a particular household appears to have a consumption level well above or below the mean, further detailed questioning may reveal an explanation for this. It is important to define domestic consumption carefully. Does it, for example, include water for irrigating gardens or watering chickens or small stock? Even with great care and attention to detail, estimates of water demand can be far off the mark. Often, this is because they measure actual consumption and not de-mand itself. If water shortages exist or access to water supplies are restricted by distance or cost, people may use less water than they would like. If an improved water supply (such as a rainwater tank or standpost) is provided, water consumption may increase. In a survey conducted in rural Botswana it was found that when rainwater tanks were introduced into remote rural areas, water consumption almost doubled (Gould, 1995a). It is, therefore, worthwhile asking householders if they are satisfied with their current quantity of water supply.

Where demand estimates are being used as the basis for designing rainwater systems, they should be treated with great caution, especially if the rainwater systems are the major or only source of supply. As a general rule of thumb, it is appropriate to 'over-design' systems to provide at least 20 per cent more than the estimated demand. While this may risk using available resources at below optimal efficiency, it is far preferable to under-designing the system and risking periods when the tank is empty. In situations where no other supplies are available, this safety margin may need to be further increased. In reality, however, people will tend to use rainwater more sparingly when water levels in household tanks get low. This informal rationing process is very important as it can significantly reduce the likelihood of the tank becoming completely empty and reduce the duration of any such system failures, when they occur.

Calculating potential rainwater supply by estimating runoff
The size of the supply of rainwater depends on the amount of rainfall, the area of the catchment, and its runoff coefficient. For a roof or sloping catchment it is the horizontal plan area which should be measured (Figure 3.1). The runoff coefficient takes into account any losses due to leakage, evaporation and overflow, and is normally taken as 0.8 for a well-constructed roof catchment system. Rainfall is the most unpredictable variable in the calculation since in many areas there is considerable variation from one year to the next. An estimate of the approximate, mean annual runoff from a given catchment can be obtained using the following equation:

$$S = R \times A \times C_r$$
$$\text{Supply} = \text{Rainfall} \quad \text{Area} \quad \text{Coefficient (Runoff)}$$

$$S = 500 \text{ mm/a} \times 200\text{m}^2 \times 0.8$$

$$= 0.5 \text{ m/a} \times 200\text{m}^2 \times 0.8$$

$$= 80\text{m}^3/\text{annum} = 80\ 000 \text{ l/annum}$$

$$= 0.22\text{m}^3/\text{day} = 220 \text{ l/day}$$

Where: S = Mean rainwater supply in cubic metres (m³)
      R = Mean annual rainfall in millimetres (mm/a)
      A = Catchment area in square metres (m²)
      C_r = Runoff coefficient

The actual amount of rainwater supplied may vary greatly from year to year, and also depends on the volume of the storage tank and the rate of water use.

Figure 3.1 Typical roof catchment system.
(Used in sample calculation)

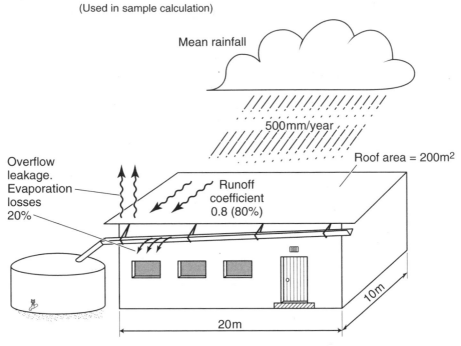

Runoff coefficient

The water runoff coefficient (C_r) for any catchment is the ratio of the volume of water that runs off a surface to the volume of rainfall that falls on to the surface.

$$C^r = \frac{\textbf{Volume of runoff}}{\textbf{Volume of rainwater}}$$

All calculations relating to the performance of rainwater catchment systems involve the use of a runoff coefficient to account for losses due to spillage, leakage, infiltration, catchment surface wetting and evaporation, which will all contribute to reducing the amount of rainwater that actually enters the storage reservoir.

For a well-constructed roof catchment, especially one made from corrugated-iron sheets or tiles, the runoff coefficient for individual rainfall events may often be over 0.9, i.e. > 90 per cent of rainfall collected (Ree, 1974). The long-term runoff coefficient for the system will, however, probably be less due to occasional but substantial losses resulting from gutter overflows during torrential storms or temporary blockages by debris such as leaves. Other factors which may occasionally reduce the collection efficiency of both roof and ground catchment systems is when precipitation occurs as snow or hail or is affected by very strong winds. For this reason it is appropriate to use a runoff coefficient of 0.8 as standard when designing roof catchment systems. This figure is also recommended in a recent guide produced in Australia on the use of rainwater tanks (Cuncliffe, 1998). Runoff coefficients for traditional roofing materials such as grass thatch and local clay tiles are generally lower than this, as are those for most ground catchment systems.

A major recent study in Gansu Province in China (Zhu and Liu, 1998) to determine the runoff coefficients of different local roof and ground catchment surfaces in areas with mean annual rainfall varying from 200 to 500mm came up with the following estimations:

Roof catchments
- Sheet-metal (estimate)   (0.8 – 0.85) – Note: for comparison and NOT included in the study
- Cement tile   0.62 – 0.69
- Clay tile (machine-made)   0.30 – 0.39
- Clay tile (hand-made)   0.24 – 0.31

Ground catchments
- Concrete-lined   0.73 – 0.76
- Cement soil mix   0.33 – 0.42
- Buried plastic sheet   0.28 – 0.36
- Compacted loess soil   0.13 – 0.19

These figures show the runoff coefficient for the particular catchment types that could be expected 95 per cent of the time (it may be less in occasional extreme-drought years). The higher figure in the range relates to catchments in areas with mean annual rainfall of between 400 and 500mm, while the lower figure is for areas receiving just 200 to 300mm. The long-term estimate of the runoff coefficient for sheet-metal roofs is included for comparison and was not part of the study. Metal roofs and gutters are too expensive for the poor Chinese peasants living in the study area.

Natural land surfaces will normally have runoff coefficients below 0.3 and these may even be as low as zero (Skinner, 1990). Massive rock outcrops used for rock catchment systems are the one exception and these may have runoff coefficients as high as 0.8, according to Lee and Visscher (1992).

Simple graphical technique to estimate rainwater supply
Another simple and straightforward method for estimating mean annual rainwater availability from catchments of different areas subject to different rainfall conditions is a graphical technique developed by Schiller (1982). All that is required are the necessary annual rainfall figures for locations representing the full range of rainfall conditions in any region or country, and a sheet of graph paper. Using the rainfall data, a set of curves (straight lines) can be drawn and a useful diagram for estimating rainwater availability per person for any given roof catchment in any part of the country is possible.

In the example shown in Figure 3.2, the rainfall range for Tanzania is 0 to 1000mm, represented by ten lines, one for every 100mm. Rather than use the mean annual rainfall, the minimum annual rainfall (defined as that which is exceeded 90 per cent of the time) was taken to ensure the design would be more reliable. The horizontal axis represents horizontal roof area per person and the right-hand vertical axis shows maximum (100 per cent) potential rainwater runoff. Since some runoff will be lost due to spillage and evaporation, the actual supply is likely to be significantly less than 100 per cent even given sufficient storage capacity. The left-hand vertical axis is thus adjusted to show the 80 per cent rainwater runoff volume; this is based on using a runoff coefficient of 0.8, as discussed earlier. The graph gives a realistic estimate of the potential supply, assuming a large-enough storage tank is provided so that no water is lost due to overflow. As an example, if a roof area of 10m² per person is used, which is equivalent to a family of five sharing a house with a 50m² roof, a potential annual rainwater supply of around 5.72m³ (5720 litres) per person could be expected, equivalent to over 15 litres per day. The result from this simple analysis shows that while rainwater may not be able to provide a total water supply for this particular household, it could provide an important supplementary source, equivalent to about a third to a half of typical household water consumption in Dar es Salaam. Even for much drier Dodoma, with only half the rainfall, a similar set-up would yield around 2.92m³ (2920 litres) per person/ year. This would provide a useful 8 litres per person daily and would be sufficient to meet all drinking- and cooking-water requirements.

Figure 3.2 Set of curves for determining rainfall availability in Tanzania
(Adapted from Schiller, 1982)

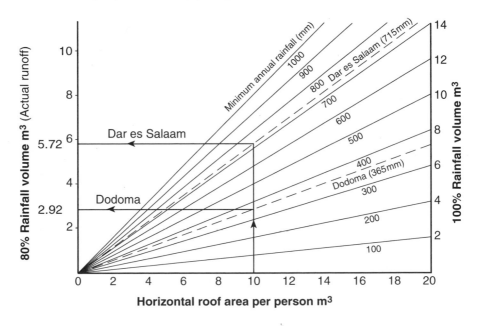

Techniques for determining storage tank size

Water storage capacity is required to balance out the differences between rainwater supply and household demand. If the rainwater supply exceeds demand in any given month, storage is needed to allow this water to be carried over and used in a future month when demand exceeds supply. For a rainwater system to provide a total year-round water supply, two conditions must be met. First, the total rainwater supply must exceed the total demand. Secondly, there must be sufficient storage capacity to allow enough surplus water collected in wetter periods to be carried over to meet the demand in drier periods. The storage capacity required in any situation, therefore, can be determined by balancing the inflows to the tank (rainwater collected) against the outflows (rainwater used).

Several techniques are available for calculating appropriate storage reservoir volumes, either for maximizing supply from a given catchment, or for meeting a required target demand. Using computer-based models, it is even possible to simulate the performance of any particular rainwater catchment system under different rainfall or water withdrawal scenarios. The results of any modelling exercise must always be treated with some caution, since the results will be only as good as the historic rainfall data fed into the model. Inaccurate assumptions regarding withdrawal patterns and even future local or regional climatic change may affect the validity of any predictions about the future performance of any particular rainwater catchment system. Nevertheless, when correctly applied, techniques for optimizing system design are a powerful tool which should be used if the risks of under-design or over-design are to be avoided, and some of the more common approaches are discussed below. Readers interested in greater detail for these and other methods should refer to the source references or visit the relevant websites listed in Appendix 3.

Dry-season demand versus supply
This is the simplest approach to system design but is relevant only in areas where distinct dry seasons exist. In this approach, the tank is designed to accommodate the necessary water demand throughout the dry season. The dry season is taken as the period during which there is no significant rainfall and hence no inflow to the tank is expected. If the daily household water demand is 100 litres and the dry season lasts for 120 days, a tank with a capacity of at least 12 000 litres would be required. While this method is easy to calculate and provides a rough estimate of storage volume requirements, it does not take into account variations between different years, such as the occurrence of drought years. The method also entirely ignores rainfall input and the capacity of the catchment to deliver the runoff necessary to fill the storage tank. If the method is used it is important that some crude estimate of the available roof runoff is made to ensure there is sufficient rainwater to fill the tank. This technique does, however, have some advantages. It can be used in the absence of any rainfall data and is easily understandable by the layperson. These points are especially relevant when designing systems in the remote areas of developing countries where obtaining reliable rainfall data can be difficult. Also, in seasonal semi-arid climates, with distinct wet and dry seasons, the introduction of rationing in dry years can greatly improve system

performance. To apply rationing effectively it is critical that the householder understands how best to apply it. In this case the householder might be advised that if the tank was less than half full halfway through the dry season (i.e. less than 6000 litres remaining in the tank), daily water use should be cut to half (50 litres/day). Once the level of water in the tank reaches a quarter, the householder could be advised that if they can reduce daily consumption to just 30 litres/day, the remaining 3000 litres in the tank will supply them for a further 100 days. In circumstances where the household was totally dependent on the rainwater supply, such a strategy would ensure that at least its essential water needs were met in all but the most extreme circumstances. While this method can be useful for giving a rough idea of the minimum reservoir capacity required to satisfy dry season demand, it is not recommended if other methods and the necessary rainfall data are available, as it does not consider rainwater-availability details.

Graphical methods
Another simple method which can be used to estimate the most appropriate storage-tank capacity for maximizing supply is to represent roof runoff and daily water consumption graphically. This method will give a reasonable estimation of the storage requirements, but daily or weekly data should be used for a more accurate assessment, especially for climates with year-round rainfall.

This approach is illustrated in Figure 3.3. The basic steps that have to be followed are:

● Plot a bar graph of mean, monthly roof runoff.
● Plot a cumulative roof-runoff graph, by summing the monthly runoff totals.
● Add a dotted line showing cumulative water use (water withdrawn or water demand).

In this case, the monthly roof runoff totals are what one might expect from a 100m² catchment in a semi-arid region with mean annual rainfall of 500 to 600mm and a five-month dry season. The storage volume needed is equivalent to the greatest difference between the two lines (rainfall supply and water demand). In this case it is 27m³ – typical of what might be required in a semi-arid seasonal climate. Note, however, that the cumulative water use of 45m³ for the year (equivalent to 123 litres per day) is significantly more than the volume of the tank, since a significant amount of water is removed from storage throughout the wet season while the tank is filling.

Although mean monthly data are easy to use, a more accurate graphical method involves the analysis of cumulative daily rainfall data. Figure 3.4 shows two graphs indicating cumulative roof runoff from a 100m² roof in two hypothetical locations with very different rainfall patterns. In both cases, the mean annual rainfall is 1000mm and a runoff coefficient of 0.8 is assumed. The roof runoff is shown as a cumulative total for each month (stepped line), while the water consumption is shown as the continuous line A-B assuming a regular consumption rate of 220 litres/day (80m³/365days). In this case, the line X-Y

Figure 3.3 Step-by-step graphical method to determine approximate storage requirement for maximizing rainwater supply.

(a) Mean monthly roof runoff (m³)

(b) Cumulative monthly roof runoff (m³)

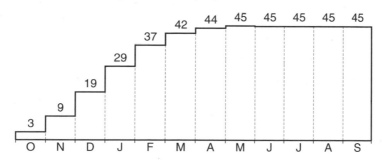

(c) Estimation of storage requirement

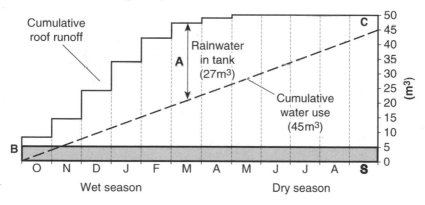

A	Storage requirement (27m³) - the minimum tank volume needed to satisfy water demand throughout the dry season, allowing for a small amount in reserve (**B**) in case the rains start late.
B	Residual storage (5m³) - rainwater remaining in the tank at the start of the wet season.
C	Residual storage (5m³) - rainwater remaining in the tank at the end of the dry season.

Figure 3.4 A graphical method to determine rainwater tank storage requirements for a constant water demand in two markedly different rainfall regimes

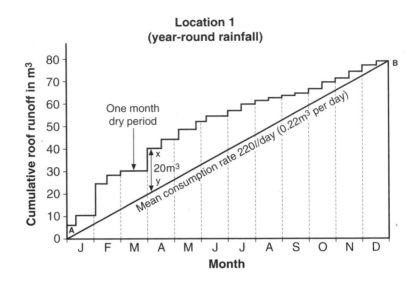

**Location 1
(year-round rainfall)**

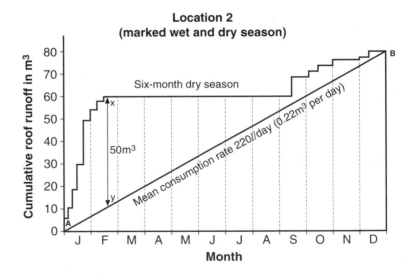

**Location 2
(marked wet and dry season)**

represents the storage capacity required in order to guarantee the maximum level of supply of 220 litres per day in a normal year. For Location 1, the longest dry period is only one month, but for Location 2 a six-month dry season is experienced. It is clear by comparing the two that a far greater storage volume is required to provide a constant year-round supply when there is a prolonged dry season; 50m^3 for Location 1, compared to 20m^3 for Location 2. Of course, since no year is 'normal', the supply will vary and may have to be rationed slightly in drier years, or severely during drought periods, if a continuous supply is to be maintained. If rationing is introduced during the dry season, or if alternative water sources can be used during this period, the storage requirement can be greatly reduced. In practice, in areas with low and very seasonal precipitation, rainwater is often used for drinking and cooking purposes only, and this greatly reduces both the storage requirements and the cost of the system.

Since climates with distinct wet and dry seasons require large storage capacities, which may be prohibitively expensive, it is worth investigating ways to reduce the storage requirements significantly by manipulating the demand strategy. The most effective approach is to use more water during the rainy season, and less during the dry season. In Figure 3.5, the storage requirements and system performance are shown for the same system, subject to three different demand scenarios: a) constant demand, b) demand exceeding supply, and c) rapid rainy season depletion followed by dry season rationing. For each graph, the greatest difference between the cumulative runoff (tank inflow) curve and the demand curve represents the minimum storage requirement.

For the sake of simplification, models often use an assumption of constant demand, as shown in Figure 3.5a. In practice, this may result in an unnecessarily high storage-volume requirement and, in any case, in reality, demand rates will be variable. The penalty for exceeding a given design demand rate over an extended period will be system failure, which is manifest by the tank becoming and remaining empty for some time, as shown in Figure 3.5b. Figure 3.5c shows the advantages of following a dual demand schedule, with higher depletion rates in the rainy season. When compared to the constant demand scenario in figure 3.5a, it can be seen that a smaller tank, 10m^3 compared to 15m^3, can sustain the same total annual level of supply (35m^3) if a variable demand strategy is adopted. In this example, it can be seen that a relatively small and simple manipulation in the demand strategy can lead to a significant reduction in storage volume requirement. By setting the wet season demand at only 25 per cent above the mean, and the dry season demand at 25 per cent below the mean, the storage requirement is reduced by a third. Although this is a hypothetical case, the rainfall pattern shown is typical of many seasonal tropical climates. This example illustrates that system efficiency can be influenced as much by careful compliance with rationing schedules by system users as by sophisticated technical design. The significant impact of rationing on system performance has been shown in a number of studies, particularly under seasonal or drought-prone climatic conditions (Perrens, 1982b; Gieske et al., 1995).

In order to take into account variations between years, the graphical method is most effective if at least 10 years of rainfall data are plotted. For drought-prone climates, plots of 20 years or more are advisable. Figures 3.6a and 3.6b show examples of 10-year records for two markedly different

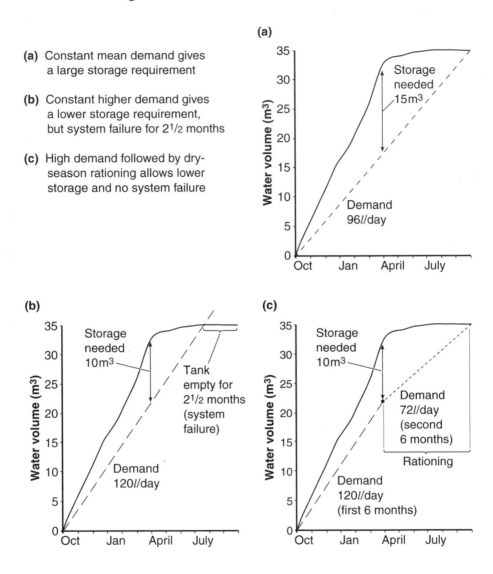

Figure 3.5 Cumulative supply graph for 12 months illustrating the effect on storage of three different demand scenarios

(a) Constant mean demand gives a large storage requirement

(b) Constant higher demand gives a lower storage requirement, but system failure for 2¹/₂ months

(c) High demand followed by dry-season rationing allows lower storage and no system failure

rainfall regimes, a seasonal drought-prone climate typical of the semi-arid tropics and a humid climate with rainfall all year. The difference in the storage requirement (tank volume) needed to satisfy the same constant demand is striking. To meet the same constant demand (35m³/year or 96 litres/day) a storage capacity of 70m³ is required in the drought-prone climate compared with just 15m³ under humid conditions. Again, while these examples are hypothetical, they are typical of many real situations.

Figure 3.6 Cumulative supply graph for 10 years illustrating the effect on storage of different rainfall regimes

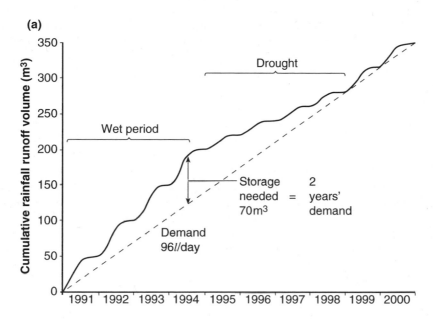

(a)

Drought

Wet period

Storage needed 70m3 = 2 years' demand

Demand 96*l*/day

(a) Variable climate (seasonal drought-prone)
    mean runoff = mean demand = 35m3/year
(b) Steady climate (rainfall all year)
    mean runoff = mean demand = 35m3/year

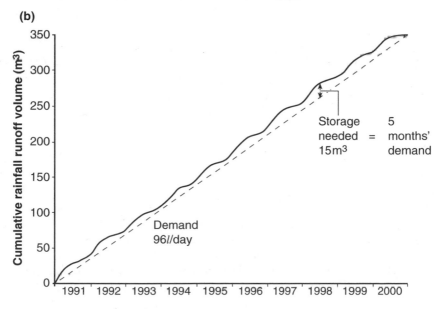

(b)

Storage needed 15m3 = 5 months' demand

Demand 96*l*/day

Mass curve analysis
The basis of the mass curve analysis technique is demonstrated in Figure 3.6. The method involves the identification of critical periods in the data where the difference between cumulative rainwater inflows and cumulative demand are at a maximum. This difference represents the maximum volume available for future use, and hence the necessary capacity required to maximize supply. The mass curve analysis technique was originally described by Rippl (1883) and has formed the basis of many subsequent adaptations. The method, which lends itself well to computerization, is described in any good engineering textbook dealing with hydrology.

For accurate determinations of the storage requirement needed for meeting a given demand with a certain probability, mass curve analysis can be used. The technique can further be extended to derive a dimensionless constant graph, which can be used to determine the performance of any system, subject to the same rainfall conditions used in the analysis. A detailed presentation of this procedure is beyond the scope of this text, but a clear and easy-to-follow explanation of both mass curve analysis and dimensionless constant analysis are given by Schiller and Latham (1982a).

Statistical methods
A number of statistical methods have been developed, which can be used in combination with other methods such as mass curve analysis to determine the reliability of supply or, in other words, the probability of system failure. One approach based on an analysis of the frequency of occurrence of minimum rainfall amounts for periods from two to 84 months in a 75-year record, was used by Ree et al. (1971). By applying standard statistical techniques, the minimum rainfall with a given probability can be determined for the various time periods. If the cumulative minimum rainfall values are plotted against time, a mass curve can be derived and mass curve analysis conducted.

Another approach, based on the deterministic and probabilistic processes of weekly rainfall data involving the application of Bayes analysis, is outlined by Fok et al. (1982). The lengthy calculations involved in all statistical approaches make the use of a PC (personal computer) essential.

Computer-based methods
The use of computer-based models allows great flexibility when producing output for system design since the model can be tailored to any particular system under given rainfall conditions. The format of the output can also be customized to requirements, and the performance of specific designs simulated under various demand scenarios. For example, the implications of introducing a dry-season rationing schedule such as that shown in Figure 3.5c could easily be tested using a long rainfall record. Due to their speed and flexibility, computers provide a powerful tool when simulating future rainwater supplies and anticipated storage requirements on the basis of past rainfall data.

The increasing power, affordability and user-friendliness of PCs make them an increasingly appropriate tool for system design. With worldwide Internet links it is also becoming easy to access information, and even download some software free of charge. One such software package is SimTanka which has been developed by the Ajit Foundation in Jaipur, India (Vyas, 1996). More information about SimTanka and how to download it can be found in Appendix 3. Interactive Windows-application software is user-friendly, flexible and could be widely used for system design (Scott et al., 1995). Another easy-to-use spreadsheet-based method for determining system design or performance is the 'Balance Method', where monthly tank inflows are balanced against demand in order to allow minimum tank volume requirements to be determined to meet a given demand (Burgess, 1996). While this method is more appropriate for seasonal climates if monthly rainfall data are used, the approach can easily be adapted to use weekly or daily data if required (for further details see Appendix 3).

Computer models can be designed in various ways but most are based on the principles of mass curve analysis (Schiller and Latham, 1982b; Latham, 1983; Perrens, 1975) or stochastic modelling techniques (Ahmed and Fok, 1982; Fewkes and Frampton, 1993; Gieske et al., 1995). Because the use of computer models removes all the laborious calculation, it is possible to also incorporate statistical analysis to determine the probability (reliability) of different levels of supply. This is useful, as systems can be designed to a given reliability specification, such as one failure per year or one failure every five years for any given demand schedule.

While computer models are becoming increasingly capable of mimicking the performance of real systems, they are only as good as the data used. Obtaining good-quality rainfall data in a format that can readily be used in any model will greatly reduce the time, effort and cost of any computer-based modelling exercise. As with other methods, an accurate and lengthy rainfall record is essential. A minimum of 20 years of rainfall data are preferable, especially in drought-prone areas. While mean monthly data can be used, weekly or daily records will give a more accurate prediction of system performance (Fewkes, 1995; Heggen, 1993). Where feasible these should be used, especially if they are available in a digital format that can be readily fed into a computer program. Normally, the data will need to be reformatted to meet the specifications of any particular program. Care should be taken to check the data carefully, so any missing or spurious values can be accounted for. Where rainfall records are short, it is possible to use computers for data simulation to extend the record. This may be convenient, but the resulting data will be no more accurate than the historical data on which they are based.

The application of computer models for tank-size determination has been attempted in many countries including Australia (Perrens, 1975, 1982a, 1982b), Botswana (Gieske et al., 1995; Gould, 1987, 1997), Canada (Scott et al., 1995), Kenya (Burgess, 1996; McPherson et al., 1984) and Thailand/Indonesia (Latham, 1984). While it is beyond the scope of this book to go into the specific details, further information relating to various modelling techniques is given in Appendix 3. The graphs shown in Box 3.1, taken from a free technical-advice booklet produced by the South Australia Water Corporation (SA Water, 1998), are a good illustration of the usefulness of the output from these models.

The sets of curves representing the range of annual rainfall values within the given region, provide an effective tool for estimating the most appropriate storage-tank capacity for any given roof area and target demand. Alternatively, the graphs can be used to determine appropriate water usage rates and the reliability (degree of security 80, 90 or 99 per cent) associated with any given roof and tank system. For those who really like to do it themselves there is even advice on how to use common computer packages, or write your own program to determine the performance of any roof catchment system (Box 3.2).

An extension of the standard programs for determining tank size and catchment area combinations for different demands and levels of security of supply involves the addition of an economic component. Such an approach was considered by Heggen (1982), who incorporated cost considerations by including marginal economic analysis in a computer simulation to demonstrate optimal system design. In another study by Wall and McCown (1989), a water budgeting program was used to analyse rainfall data from two contrasting stations in Kenya and Australia, and cost curves for determining the economic optima for different roof area and tank volume combinations were included in the analysis.

It should be borne in mind, however, that the tidy and uncomplicated world of the computer simulation can turn out to be very different from reality, where leaks or the pranks of small children can play havoc with the neat predictions of the most sophisticated computer model.

Although at the time of writing the Internet is still in its infancy, it certainly has the potential to make some of the facilities of world-class research centres available even at village level. To what extent these recent technological developments translate into real technology transfers that benefit those still on the global technological periphery remains to be seen. For readers who do have ready access to the Internet a list of useful websites is included in Appendix 3. This is only a small fraction of many thousands of sites related to rainwater catchment systems worldwide that are potentially available to anyone with Internet access. The number of sites and the amount of information available is bound to increase very rapidly during the shelf-life of this book, and the sites listed in Appendix 3 provide only a possible starting-point.

Deciding on rainwater catchment system dimensions

Any decision or advice given regarding the most appropriate dimensions for a rainwater catchment system will depend on a broad range of factors. These include rainfall amount and distribution, the demand schedule and rationing,

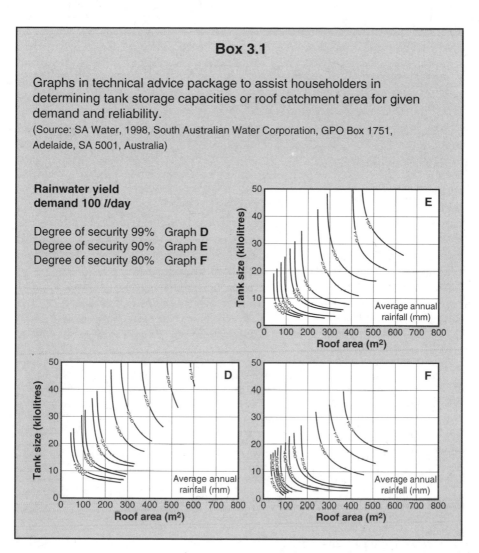

Box 3.1

Graphs in technical advice package to assist householders in determining tank storage capacities or roof catchment area for given demand and reliability.

(Source: SA Water, 1998, South Australian Water Corporation, GPO Box 1751, Adelaide, SA 5001, Australia)

Rainwater yield demand 100 l/day

Degree of security 99% Graph **D**
Degree of security 90% Graph **E**
Degree of security 80% Graph **F**

catchment area, and storage volume. Since the rainfall amount and distribution cannot be manipulated, any decision has to be based on the following:

- the affordability of different storage/catchment size combination options.
- the nature of the rainwater supply to the users (i.e. sole water source or supplementary supply)
- the water-demand pattern
- the householders' willingness to adopt and maintain a water-rationing strategy in times of water shortage.

In situations where only the rainfall parameters are fixed, models can be used to manipulate the system dimensions to satisfy other requirements, such as a minimum demand level, reliability, or even cost limits. If catchment areas are

65

Box 3.2

Technical advice on how to use common computer packages to determine appropriate system demand and reliability

If you have a computer with a spreadsheet-software package (e.g. Quattro, Lotus or Excel) or a programming package (e.g. Fortran or C++) you can do your own calculations:

1. Obtain monthly rainfalls for your location from the Bureau of Meteorology. (In South Australia, a long period – at least 50 years – of record is required to include major prolonged droughts). [*Authors' note: Shorter records of just 20 years may be appropriate in less drought-prone climates*].

2. Calculate the runoff, allowing for losses, e.g. evaporation from hot, wet roofs.

   $Q = max[0, \{A \times (P-B)/1000\} \times C]$
   where
   Q = monthly runoff (m^3)
   A = coefficient of runoff
   B = initial loss (mm)
   C = roof area connected to tank (m^2)
   P = monthly rainfall (mm)
   $A = 0.8$ and $B = 2$mm have been used in calculating the graphs in Box 3.1. If you have a tank already you can calculate your own A and B using measurements of rainfall and water volume in the tank before and after rain. (Average several measurements). If first flush devices are fitted, B may be larger.

3. Calculate the volume of water in the tank at the end of the month.
   $V_t = min [max \{(V_{t-1}+Q-D),0\},T]$
   where
   V_t = volume of water in tank at end of month t (m^3)
   V_{t-1} = volume of water in tank at start of month (m^3)
   Q = monthly inflow (m^3)
   D = monthly demand (m^3)
   T = tank volume (m^3)

   For the first month, assume that the tank is empty.
   If $V_t = 0$, then a failure is recorded.

4. Add up the failures and divide by the number of months in the period of record, to give a monthly time failure.
   Reliability% [or security(%)] = (1–failure) × 100

5. Change the demand by trial and error until you get the desired level of security.

Source: SA Water (1998), South Australian Water Corporation, GPO Box 1751, Adelaide, SA 5001, Australia

Note: For details relating to this and other methods see Appendix 3.

fixed, as is often the case for existing roof catchments, the other parameters can be altered and the impact modelled.

Any model will always rely on certain assumptions and data of variable quality. It is worth remembering that, while models can be powerful tools for predicting future system performance, they are often subject to a significant margin of error – and, on occasion, can be completely wrong. Human behaviour can be fickle, and assumptions regarding water-consumption rates or voluntary rationing are especially vulnerable to miscalculation. Despite the need for caution when applying the results of any modelling exercise, the benefits can be substantial. Provided good data are available, rigorous analysis is conducted, and there is reasonable compliance regarding water-abstraction rates and rationing, significant cost savings or improvements in system performance should result when appropriate designs are implemented.

Often the time and effort involved in undertaking detailed analysis to optimize a system design will not be worthwhile or cost-effective in the case of an individual system, especially if large quantities of rainfall data have to be processed. Local experience regarding the performance of existing systems is often the only guide available, along with simple calculations. These can often produce a quite acceptable result in terms of optimizing a system design. Where large numbers of tanks are being implemented in any project or programme, detailed analysis will often be worth undertaking as economies of scale become apparent. Even small improvements in system efficiency can often lead to very substantial cost savings when the construction of many systems is involved. Nevertheless, however sophisticated the analysis, useful results will ultimately depend on the quality of the data used. Any accurate estimation of rainwater catchment system performance, therefore, relies on the availability of good rainfall data, careful measurement of the horizontal (plan) area of the catchment surface draining into the tank or reservoir, and the determination of a realistic runoff coefficient.

Summary of key points

- Reliable rainfall data for a period of at least 10 years (longer in drought-prone areas) is ideally required to get an accurate estimate of the potential rainwater supply from a given catchment.
- Estimating household water demand must be done with care as demand may vary over time due to factors such as changes in consumption rates during different seasons. Worldwide, total daily water demand varies widely, but usually ranges from about 20 to 200 litres per person, essential daily water requirements for drinking, cooking and personal hygiene vary less, and 15–25 litres per person can normally suffice.
- Estimating the potential maximum supply of rainwater runoff is straightforward if good data are available. Simply multiply the mean annual rainfall by the horizontal catchment area and runoff coefficient.
- Runoff coefficients, when averaged over the long term, range from as high as 0.8–0.85 for a well-constructed corrugated-iron roof to 0.1–0.2 for a compacted soil surface.

- Several techniques are available for sizing rainwater storage tanks, and these include:
  - Dry season demand versus supply
  - Graphical methods
  - Mass curve analysis
  - Statistical methods
  - Computer-based methods
- Any decision regarding rainwater catchment system dimensions will depend on a range of factors, including the rainfall amount and distribution, the demand schedule and willingness to ration, and the affordability of the catchment/storage size options.
- Assumptions about future water-demand requirements and tank life will always mean that any predictions of a systems water yield or cost effectiveness should be treated only as a guide.

4

System components and design considerations

Selecting an appropriate tank design

FOR MOST RAINWATER catchment systems, the storage tank represents the single greatest cost. This is especially true for roof catchment systems where an existing roof structure provides, in effect, a free catchment area. The choice of a suitable tank design to match an existing catchment and local conditions is important, and careful consideration should be given to selecting the right one. As well as having the appropriate volume with respect to the catchment area, rainfall conditions and demand, it should have a functional, durable and cost-effective design. Field experience has shown that a universally ideal tank design does not exist. Local materials, skills and costs, personal preference and other external factors may favour one design over another. Nevertheless, there are a number of key requirements common to all effective tank designs and the list below, adapted from Latham and Gould (1986), summarizes these:

- a functional and watertight design
- a solid, secure cover to keep out insects, dirt and sunshine
- a screened inlet filter
- a screened overflow pipe
- a manhole (and ideally a ladder) to allow access for cleaning
- an extraction system that does not contaminate the water, e.g. tap/pump
- a soakaway to prevent spilt water forming puddles near the tank
- a maximum height of 2m to prevent high water pressures (unless additional reinforcement is used in the walls and foundations).

Other features might include:

- a device to indicate the amount of water in the tank
- a sediment trap, tipping bucket or other foul-flush mechanism
- a lock on the tap
- a second sub-surface overflow tank to provide water for livestock.

If rainwater catchment systems already exist in an area where tank construction is being planned or considered, it is important to take time to visit and inspect a few systems. The owners or users of the systems should be questioned regarding their assessment of their own tank designs. This process allows the advantages and disadvantages of different, locally produced designs to be compared and weighed against the sales pitch given by commercial manufacturers. The exercise will also provide some useful lessons, which may help to avoid potential future problems that might result from the selection of an inappropriate design.

Having established the required volume for the storage reservoir, it is also necessary to decide whether to opt for buying an 'off-the-shelf' commercially available tank or to construct the system on site. A number of factors are likely to influence this decision. These include the cost, durability, acceptability and appropriateness of the various options. Transport costs can also be high, especially where distances are large and roads are poor. Practical considerations are also important. For example, in many circumstances, such as in remote rural locations, $10m^3$ represents the upper capacity limit for tanks that can be constructed at central locations and transported in one piece to the required location. Plastic and fibreglass tanks, although expensive in some countries, are light and easy to transport (Plate 4.1). Metal tanks are also commonly delivered by road. Where delivery to remote locations is required, such as in Australia, costs can sometimes be reduced by nesting several progressively smaller tanks together, if covers can be detached. While delivery of small ferrocement tanks is possible if care is taken and road conditions permit (Plate 9.13), ferrocement tanks as large as $25m^3$ are delivered in some countries, for example New Zealand, although extreme care is necessary during loading and unloading.

There are some advantages in buying ready-made commercial tanks. They can be quickly erected at the site and be operational within days, compared to weeks or months for tanks requiring construction on site. Because commercial tanks are normally built in large numbers, they are subject to economies of scale and quality control. This can, in some cases, make them more durable and cost-effective than tanks built on site especially if levels of workmanship are suspect. Commercially available tanks do not require the availability of skilled labour, construction materials and an appropriate design. Since commercially made tanks, especially those requiring special equipment, such as for moulding plastic, are often produced only at major centres, transport costs to remote rural locations are often high. The other main disadvantage with commercial ready-made tanks is that they are normally more expensive than tanks constructed on site. This is especially the case in situations where free or low-cost labour and local building materials are available. The free collection of river sand and aggregate, for example, is common practice in many community self-help projects in developing countries. Systems designed and constructed by an individual householder or community can also be tailor-made to meet the specific local requirements. In the context of a community project, there are several other benefits to be derived from constructing systems on site. While unskilled voluntary labour may help to bring down system costs, the utilization of skilled paid labour from the community will provide employment. The involvement of the community in the construction of any water systems helps to develop skills and self-reliance. This also ensures the community is more likely to be able to operate, maintain and repair the systems properly in the future.

Plate 4.1 *10m³ plastic water tank being transported as part of a drought-relief programme in rural Botswana.* (Photo: John Gould, 1996)

Plate 4.2 *4.5m³ corrugated, galvanized-iron tank being used for supplementary supply at school housing in S.E. Botswana.* (Photo: John Gould, 1996)

Tank shape, dimensions and type

As a general rule, water tanks should ideally be cylindrical or spherical. This is because cylindrical or spherical shapes optimize the use of materials and increase the wall strength. Although some attempts at constructing spherical rainwater tanks from ferrocement and other materials have been made for tanks up to 2m³ in Fiji (Iddings, 1984), for larger surface tanks it does not seem practical. Another problem with spherical tanks is that they require some sort of stand for support. A good 'compromise' shape for strength and cost-effectiveness is the Thai jar (Figure 4.1). The jar shape gives maximum strength since the walls are curved in both vertical and horizontal directions, yet it requires no special stand. Although 'jumbo jars' up to 6m³ have been built, to construct larger surface tanks in this way would be very difficult so, for practical purposes, a cylindrical shape is the best compromise. This does lead to comparatively large stresses along the joint between the wall and the base, which must be strong enough to withstand this (Watt 1978).

The same principle is applied to housing in rural Africa, where most people build round houses because this shape is the most economical and practical. When cylindrical and cuboidal tanks, both with a height of 2m and a volume of 27m³ are compared, the difference becomes clear. The surface area of the cylindrical tank is more than 6 per cent smaller. Spherical tanks are even more efficient: a 27m³ sphere having a surface area 25 per cent smaller than a cube of the same volume.

Figure 4.1 Ferrocement Thai jar (2m³) – the curved shape gives the tank both strength and cost efficiency

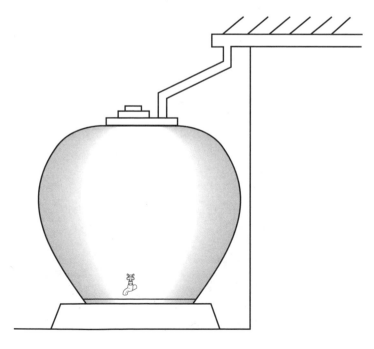

In the mid-1980s, a large, hemispherical, ferrocement ground-tank design was developed in Kenya, and has been replicated in Uganda, Rwanda and Botswana. While the standard design was for 80m³ tanks, some larger ones of over 100m³ were constructed. Initially, these reservoirs had flat or conical roofs. Subsequently, ferrocement dome roofs were developed (Figure 4.2). These allow water storage within the dome cavity, give the tank a very efficient overall shape, and increase the storage capacity from 80m³ to 90m³ (when compared with flat-roofed tanks).

As far as surface tanks are concerned, the cylindrical shape is by far the most common. To maximize the storage volume while minimizing the cost, the tank should be reasonably evenly proportioned. Tall tanks with narrow widths and very low tanks with large diameters require more materials and cost more per unit volume. There are, nevertheless, a number of other factors which need to be considered. Unless extra reinforcement is added, the height of water tanks for roof catchment systems should not exceed 2m. This is because the internal force of water against the tank walls increases with the depth of the water. If the height of a tank is increased, the reinforcement must be increased accordingly to prevent collapse. Since this book deals with simple methods of constructing water tanks, most of the tanks described are designed to hold water no more than 2m in depth. Where tanks exceed this limit, special attention should be paid to reinforcing the lower sections adequately and, if in doubt, expert advice should be sought. Another consideration is that the gutter inlet on the roof of a water tank must be at least 20cm below the roofing sheets to allow a sufficient gradient for the rainwater to run into the tank by gravity. For many single-storey buildings, where the gutter height is often little more than 2m above the ground, a tank with a total height of even 2m may not match the height of the inflow downpipes running from the eaves, especially if the tank is built on any kind of plinth or raised foundation.

Figure 4.2 Ferrocement dome roof on 90m³ sub-surface ferrocement rainwater storage tank
(Source: Nissen-Petersen, 1992b)

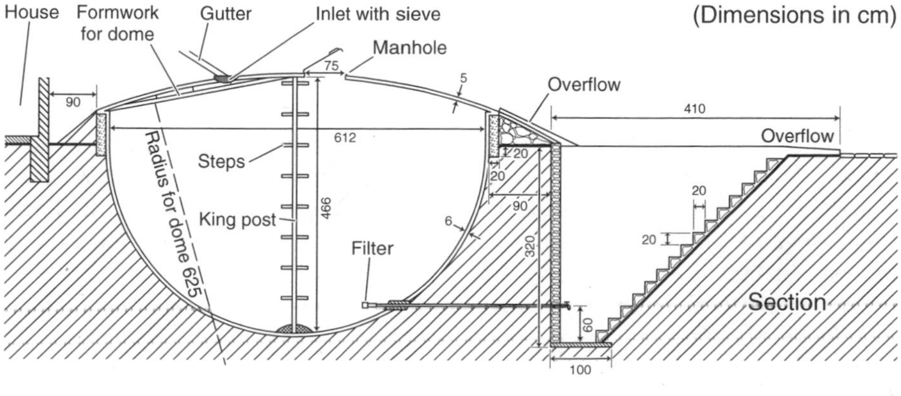

When deciding whether a surface or sub-surface tank is more appropriate, the following points should be considered. Although underground storage reservoirs are generally cheaper, some form of pump or gravity-flow connection to an excavated or lower-level tap stand is generally required to extract water. While substantial cost savings may be possible, particularly in the case of larger excavated tanks, other factors such as local soil conditions need to be considered. Where the sub-soil is rocky, excavation may not be feasible and, where it becomes waterlogged, there is a risk that a nearly empty sub-surface tank could start to float and rise out of the ground. The decision regarding the final choice of storage tank will depend on a wide range of factors, including the availability of materials and locally available labour skilled in tank construction. These issues are discussed below and a range of some of the possible design choices are described.

Cost effectiveness
The cost effectiveness of rainwater catchment systems is a crucial aspect of the technology since cost is frequently the determining factor when deciding to choose a particular technology. The high, initial capital costs required for rainwater catchment systems, particularly in more arid and seasonal climates where large storage reservoirs are required, further increase the need to ensure cost efficiency. Tank sizing and the selection of a tank with a suitable shape and dimensions are crucial in optimizing cost effectiveness. The choice of a durable design with a long life-expectancy and low maintenance costs is also critical. While a $1000 tank may initially appear a much cheaper alternative than a $2000 tank, if the more expensive one has a life expectancy of 25 years compared with 10 years for the cheaper one, the costs could be reassessed in terms of $2000/25 = $80/year versus $1000/10 = $100/year, respectively. In this case, the more expensive tank would seem to be cheaper over the long term. The use of discount rates which involve making assumptions regarding the declining future value of current funds upsets such simplistic analysis, as do uncertainties surrounding the actual life expectancies of different designs. Nevertheless, it is clear that two different designs cannot simply be compared at face value without taking other factors into account. The economic aspects of rainwater catchment systems are further explored in Chapter 7.

Availability and suitability of construction materials and skilled labour
In addition to the factors already discussed above, the availability of different raw materials is crucial to the decision regarding the eventual choice of tank design. Some of the specific criteria for different building materials, i.e. sand, aggregate and water are discussed in detail in Chapter 5. If costs, particularly transport costs, are to be minimized, it is essential that the tank technology chosen reflects the availability of the necessary, readily available raw materials for its construction. If key raw materials are not locally and cheaply available, it may be worth considering a ready made commercially available design, rather than substitute a critical building material with something less suitable.

The availability of suitably experienced and qualified labour for tank construction is vital if a project involves tank construction on site. Certain designs, such as ferrocement, require particular care and attention to detail which, if ignored, could eventually jeopardize a project. Examples of such problems are cited throughout this text with respect to the use of ferrocement in parts of Africa. If the necessary skills are not available in the project area, it is sometimes possible to develop these skills through training courses. Unless large numbers of tanks are going to be built, it may be difficult to justify any such major investment. It should nevertheless be recognized that investment in training and skills development may have many positive spin-offs for a community in a variety of areas unrelated to the project itself.

Siting of tanks
Several points need to be considered when selecting the specific site for a tank at any particular location. Key issues among these are the avoidance of any potential health hazards. Tanks should *never* be located near toilets or pit latrines. They should also, wherever possible, be located well away from any waste-disposal facility or other source of pollution or contamination which may threaten the quality of the stored water. Tanks also need to be carefully sited with respect to the possible damaging effect of soil erosion. Sites where substantial surface runoff may occur in storms should be avoided since this may undermine the foundations of the tank. If such sites have to be used, bunds and/or cutoff drains should be constructed to divert flood waters away from the base of the tank. Where possible, tanks should be located so they can collect water from as large a roof area as possible. This will often be the determining factor regarding the siting of the tank, e.g. between two buildings. Other factors worth considering when siting tanks include convenience of access to the users, and whether the tank blocks any walkways. Water tanks should be located at a minimum distance of 90cm from the wall of their roof catchments. If the distance is less there will be too little space for building the tank. If the distance is more, the down-gutters will require supports. If soils are unconsolidated, or where cylindrical-shaped sub-surface tanks are constructed, a greater distance may be required. If in doubt, a qualified civil engineer should be consulted.

Roof catchment system components

A typical roof catchment system consists of three basic sub-systems: a catchment area (a roof), a delivery system (gutters and downpipes) and a storage system (a tank). Each of these sub-systems may include additional components, e.g. a tap point as part of the storage system. Some of the types and features of roof catchment systems were introduced and discussed in Chapter 2. In the following sections, more detailed information about the nature and function of specific components is given.

Gutters and downpipes
Although gutters and downpipes are not the only method of delivering water from the catchment to the storage tank, they are by far the most common.

Other methods include the use of roof 'glides' as in Bermuda (Figure 2.2), and cement channels are common in parts of rural China (Figure 9.2) where the cost of metal fittings is considered prohibitive. Simple gutter troughs made of wood or sheet metal are a common technique used for simple, informal home-made systems in millions of poorer households across the developing world (Figure 1.5).

A carefully designed and constructed gutter system is essential for any roof catchment system to operate effectively. A properly fitted and maintained gutter–downpipe system is capable of diverting more than 90 per cent of all rainwater runoff into the storage tank (Ree 1976) even though the long-term collection efficiency is usually between 80 and 90 per cent, for reasons explained in Chapter 3. Gutters and downpipes can be made of a variety of materials: metal, plastic, cement, wood and bamboo. Typically, conventional off-the-shelf metal or plastic gutters and downpipes will cost between 5 and 15 per cent of the total system cost, depending on local prices and conditions. Those made from organic materials, although cheap and readily available, may not be so efficient and will require more frequent replacement. Another cheap alternative, which can be made to any shape and is good for circular houses, can be made by smearing plastic sacks shaped as required, with a cement slurry.

All too often, both individuals and projects overlook the importance of guttering. This frequently results in the runoff from only part of the roof area being utilized (Gould, 1991, p32). The authors have observed many examples in both Africa and Asia, where only a small fraction of roof area has been provided with guttering for directing runoff into large storage tanks. In other instances, gutters have not been erected properly and do not slope sufficiently in the direction of the tank, or have rusted through and not been repaired.

The gutter and downpipe systems are crucial to any rainwater catchment system, yet they are frequently the weak link which results in poor system efficiency. Broken gutters often lead to little or no water reaching the tank. Regular gutter maintenance is, therefore, essential; gutters and downpipes need to be thoroughly inspected; and minor repairs and cleaning conducted at least once a year. Leaves and other debris in the gutter must be cleaned out and overhanging branches should be removed where possible, as these not only drop leaves into the gutters, but provide ideal havens from which birds and small animals can defecate on to the catchment surface.

A common method for excluding leaves and other debris from the tank is to place a coarse, 5mm or smaller wire mesh over the top of a slightly raised downpipe inlet at the end of the gutter. If used, this must be checked regularly to ensure it is not blocked. A better alternative may be the use of a self-cleaning tank inlet or guttersnipe described below. The simplest and most efficient 'downpipe' consists of a straight and open extension of the gutter into the tank. In this system the gutter extension is called the down-gutter and replaces the downpipe. This design avoids water wastage because it does not reduce the speed of the inflowing water, and any debris is flushed away at the sloping inflow of mesh without causing a blockage (Figure 4.4). Many conventional 7.5cm downpipes include sharp bends which can slow down the inflow of water into the tank to such a degree that much water is wasted due to overflow during heavy showers. This type of downpipe is also easily blocked by small branches and leaves, thus stopping inflow completely. A downpipe should normally enter a water tank at the highest part of the tank to maximize the volume. In the ASAL Consultants tank designs with domes, the inlet is situated near the top of the dome in order to use the volume of the dome for water storage (Figure 4.2; Nissen-Petersen, 1992b).

Gutter and downpipe sizing

Gutter and downpipe sizing is a crucial element of the design of any system. Large quantities of runoff may be lost during heavy storms if gutters are too small and, therefore, overflow. As a general guide to gutter dimensions for catchment areas of different sizes, a useful rule of thumb is to make sure that there is at least 1cm^2 of gutter cross-section for every 1m^2 of roof area (Hasse, 1989). To avoid overflow during torrential downpours, it makes sense to provide a greater gutter capacity. The gutter must be of a sufficient size to discharge water to the tank without any overflow in the gutter. The usual 10cm (4")-wide half-round gutter is generally not big enough for roofs larger than about 40m^2. A 10cm^2 × 10cm2 gutter with a cross-sectional area of 100cm^2 can be used for roof areas measuring up to about 100m^2 under most rainfall regimes. For large roofs, such as at schools, the 14cm × 14cm V-shaped design described below, which has a cross-sectional area of 98cm^2, is suitable for roof sections up to 50m long and 8m wide. When installed with a steeper gradient than 1:100 and used in conjunction with splash-guards, V-shaped gutters can cope with heavy downpours without large and unnecessary losses due to gutter overflow, splash and spillage (Figure 4.3; Box 5.5). A gradient of 1:100 also ensures there is less chance of gutter blockage from leaves or other debris as these are more easily flushed out. Under ideal conditions, a properly designed and installed gutter and downpipe system with splash-guards can have a runoff coefficient in excess of 0.9 (90 per cent).

Downpipe cross-sections are sometimes smaller than those of gutters as it is assumed that since they are normally vertical, water will pass through them faster than through gutters. In roof catchment systems, however, downpipes should have similar dimensions to gutters. This is because the downpipes are often not vertical and usually act as channels to convey water from the end of the gutter into the tank.

Heggen (1989) undertook a detailed theoretical analysis of the hydraulic performance of gutters. The various factors affecting a gutter's capacity to carry runoff from the roof to the tank were examined. These included the gutter's length, cross-sectional area, shape, roughness, and slope. Additional factors affecting the ability of a gutter to cope with all the runoff during a storm were also considered, such as rainfall intensity and the roof width (from roof crown to eave) 'feeding' the gutter. A comparison of the performance of gutters of different shape, size and slope, collecting from different-sized roof areas was undertaken. Circular, trapezoidal and square-shaped gutters, with

Figure 4.3 Splash guards: useful as flow deflectors to prevent runoff over-
shooting the gutter.
(Adapted from Skinner, 1990)

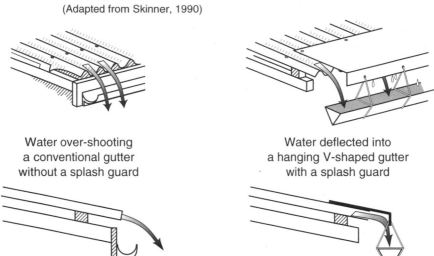

Water over-shooting
a conventional gutter
without a splash guard

Water deflected into
a hanging V-shaped gutter
with a splash guard

different cross-sectional areas (ranging from 25cm^2 to 628cm^2), set at three different slopes (0.01, 0.02 and 0.03) for gutter lengths of 5m, 10m, 15m and 20m each collecting water from roof widths ranging from 5m to 20m were compared. The theoretical carrying capacity of the three gutter shapes was calculated for all the different permutations of gutter size, gutter length, slope and roof width assuming a total roof area of 100m^2 subjected to a rainfall intensity of 20mm/hr. The results of Heggen's analysis revealed a number of interesting insights which are worth consideration when undertaking gutter design; these included:

- Increasing slope from 0.01 to 0.03 (1:100 to 3:100) increased potential water flow by between 20 and 100 per cent – this effect was especially prominent for smaller gutter sizes.
- Semi-circular gutters were the most efficient at conveying water.
- The rule of thumb of '1cm^2 of gutter cross-section per 1m^2 of roof catchment area' seems to apply under realistic conditions, i.e. a 20m-long gutter on a 100m^2 roof (20m × 5m) subjected to a storm with rainfall intensity of 20mm/hr.

While the findings from a general theoretical analysis are no substitute for location-specific practical experimentation and observation, they do provide a useful starting point, and allow a wide range of possible approaches to be modelled to help identify the most promising ones. Ultimately, the practical considerations and realities in the field will determine the design of the gutter and downpipe system. For example, gutter slope may be determined by tank height and roof length. As Heggen (1989) states: 'Proper design must combine sound hydraulic theory with achievable implementation'.

Splash-guards

During torrential downpours, large quantities of runoff can be lost due to gutter overflow and spillage (Figure 4.3). This is particularly a problem on long roofs where, due to the slope of the gutter, it may hang many centimetres below the eaves of the roof. To overcome this problem, a device known as a splash-guard, which was originally developed in Kenya, can be incorporated on corrugated-iron roofs (Nissen-Petersen, 1992c). Splash-guards consist of a long strip of sheet metal 30cm wide, bent at an angle and hung over the edge of the roof by 2–3cm to ensure that all runoff for the roof enters the gutter. The splash-guard is nailed on to the roof and the lower half is hung vertically down from the edge of the roof. This simple device, which can be manufactured on site, serves two purposes:

- The gutter can be suspended from the splash-guard instead of being fitted in gutter-brackets nailed to a fascia-board, which becomes redundant.
- The vertical flap of a splash-guard diverts all roof runoff into the V-shaped gutter hanging underneath it, preventing 'over-shooting' or 'under-cutting' of rainwater, which otherwise would lead to substantial losses.

Tank inflow – with self-cleaning mesh

Many contraptions have been invented as mechanical first flush or foul devices to exclude debris from entering storage tanks (Box 4.1 and Figure 6.1). The simplest involves the appropriate design of the tank inlet using a self-cleaning screen. This consists of placing the end of the downpipe or down-gutter about 3cm from the mesh screen in front of the inlet hole. The galvanized 5mm-mesh screen should slope at not less than 60° from the horizontal above the tank inlet (Figure 4.4). Objects larger than 5mm, such as stones, small branches and leaves, are pushed down the gutter and downpipe by flowing water until they strike the mesh. Here the debris will be caught and roll downward off the screen while the water shoots through the mesh into the tank. Any dust from a roof, which is finer than the mesh, will enter the tank along with the water, and settle at the bottom of the tank. Since dust lying on roofs is sterilized by prolonged exposure to sunshine and it will settle on the tank floor below the draw-off pipe intake, it should not affect water quality adversely once it has settled. Nevertheless, dirt and dust from the initial roof-wash at the beginning of a storm can be diverted from the inflow of the tank by lifting the end of the down-gutter out of the tank inlet and placing it on the roof for a few minutes; then the down-gutter can be replaced. Alternatively, the mesh inlet can be covered with a removable metal sheet to prevent the initial dirty runoff from entering the tank.

Guttersnipe

The guttersnipe is another very simple device for preventing leaves, insects and other debris from entering the storage tank (Figure 4.5) and it works along the same principles as the self-cleaning tank inlet. The guttersnipe sits at the top of the downpipe in a PVC housing at least 15cm below the gutter inlet,

Box 4.1
The myth of foul-flush diverter contraptions

In addition to the techniques shown above, numerous designs and references to various foul-flush diverters, sediment traps and filters can be found in books, manuals, articles and reports dealing with roof catchment systems. In the field, however, the reality is that most of these are rarely used. Those most likely to be found operating effectively are ones that are very simple to operate and maintain. Many of the more sophisticated and cumbersome examples, while providing some entertainment value at demonstration projects, have not been widely replicated in most parts of the world. The main problem is that these devices normally need regular inspection and maintenance in order to function properly. Without attention, many systems will get blocked and may even pollute the water in the tank (Vadhanavikkit et al., 1984).

The main types of system include various types of sediment traps and sedimentation devices which sit on the tank (Michaelides, 1989), different types of tipping bucket mechanisms (UNEP, 1983; Omwenga, 1984; Mollison, 1992), and different manual diversion devices. While some of the tipping bucket systems are quite ingenious, some need to be reset after each shower, or risk the next runoff going to waste. At the risk of continuing to perpetuate the myth of their widespread utilization, some examples of different devices are shown below and in Figure 6.1. Further discussion regarding the utilization of different systems and techniques for excluding debris from rainwater tanks can be found in Chapter 6. Systems should always be designed in a way that tries to ensure that water quality is protected as far as possible, irrespective of whether regular cleaning and maintenance of the system takes place.

Two examples of foul-flush contraptions more common in books than in the field

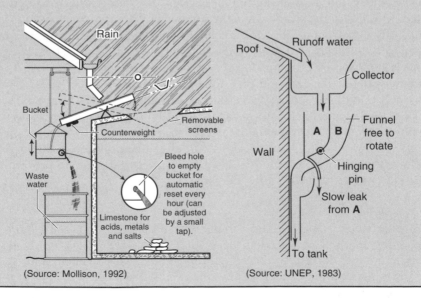

(Source: Mollison, 1992)   (Source: UNEP, 1983)

Figure 4.4 Self-cleaning tank inlet. (Source: Nissen-Petersen in SIDA, 1995)

(a) Side view

(b) Front view

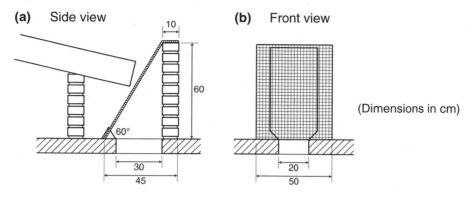

(Dimensions in cm)

(c) Gutter, downpipe (down-gutter) and screened inlet

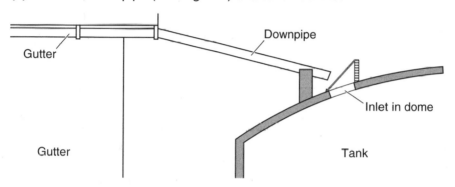

and consists of a stainless steel or copper-nickel mesh angled at 60° from the horizontal. This wire screen has 1mm gaps between the wires, and measures about 18cm by 9cm for a standard gutter. The screen allows water to pass through it, but excludes other material, which is washed off in a self-cleaning mechanism. The maintenance required involves cleaning the screen once a month to remove any algae which may accumulate. Tests have revealed that the use of guttersnipes may reduce bacteriological contamination of stored rainwater (Finch, 1994). A similar principle to the guttersnipe is employed in the filter collectors discussed in Chapter 9 (Figure 9.9).

Storage tanks
The storage tank is usually the most expensive component in any roof catchment system and choosing the most appropriate type is important. The choice of tank will depend on the range and price of locally available commercial options, and on the cost and availability of building materials. Some of the more common types of water tank are described later in this chapter. Construction methods for some of these are discussed in Chapter 5 and step-by-step procedures are given in Appendix 5.

Figure 4.5 Guttersnipe - A self-cleaning, coarse rainwater filter
(Source: Finch, H.,1994; TIRUC, 1994 p.336)

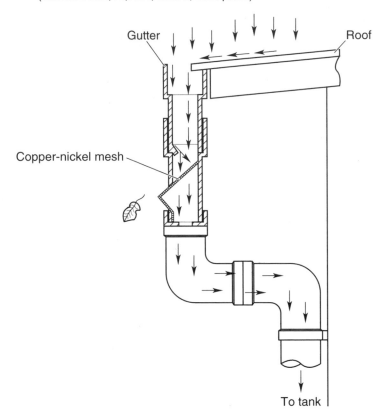

If saving money is a priority – as it usually is in developing countries – it is often best when constructing tanks to choose a design based on the use of local materials. This is usually the cheapest option as transportation costs will be lower. Local builders also generally know how to use these materials to the best advantage. For example, in regions with pebbles and stones it may be appropriate to use these as aggregate for building tanks out of concrete, either cast *in situ* or constructed from concrete blocks made on site. Where only fine sand or soil is available it is sometimes more economic to make tanks from bricks, local stone blocks, or compressed-soil blocks made on site than to use ferrocement (see Table 5.1). The use of rubble-stone blocks, for example, can reduce costs by up to 40 per cent as less cement, sand and aggregate is required.

If constructing ferrocement tanks in regions where only very fine sand is found, a builder will often be forced to use it, due to the expense of trucking in coarser sand from a distant source. To make up for the shortcomings of the fine sand, the builder will have to use a higher cement ratio, increasing the construction cost without increasing the strength of the tanks. While ferrocement has become popular in some parts of the world, it does have its

82

limitations – especially for larger tanks where it is sometimes wrongly considered a cheap and simple building technique. The requirements for ferrocement are availability of coarse, clean, well-graded sand and affordable reinforcement mesh, as well as local builders with excellent skills in the use of reinforcement, plastering and curing. Where these conditions exist, ferrocement is often appropriate, especially for smaller tanks. In many rural developing-country settings, however, it is often simpler and cheaper to build larger water tanks using locally produced burnt bricks or soil compressed blocks reinforced with barbed wire.

Tap point

Often the water tap on a tank is built into the tank-wall, where it is difficult to avoid seepage and impossible to draw water from that part of the tank situated below the level of the tap – a wastage of storage capacity called 'dead storage'. In other water tanks, the draw-off pipe is correctly placed in the concrete of the foundation, but the tap is raised to about 60cm above the floor of the tank to allow for a bucket to be placed under the tap (Figure 4.6). Again, this arrangement wastes a good portion of the tank volume on 'dead storage' – sometimes as much as 20 per cent of the tank volume. To avoid 'dead storage' in the lower part of water tanks, the tap must be positioned below the floor level of a tank (Figure 4.7). There are two ways of obtaining this; either the foundation of a tank can be elevated around 50cm above ground level, or the tap point can be situated below ground level. In the latter option, a lockable manhole can be placed over the tap and wastewater drained to a soak-away pit. An alternative and cheaper solution to avoid damage and tap misuse is to place an empty cooking-tin upside-down over a tap and put a lock across the bottom of the tin.

Wash-out pipe and sump

For privately owned tanks, a washout pipe will aid cleaning and should be included in the tank design. In East Africa, much discussion has centred on whether communal rainwater tanks, particularly at schools, should be equipped with a wash-out pipe. Proponents claim that a tank should not have to be cleaned manually by somebody climbing into a tank. Opponents claim that the gate-valve on a wash-out pipe is easily broken, for example, by schoolchildren, thereby wasting all the water in a tank. In addition, they say that money spent on a wash-out pipe and its gate-valve could be used for better purposes. A viable compromise solution is to use the draw-off pipe as a wash-out, as illustrated in Figure 4.7 and explained below.

To prevent dust, sediment and other debris on the tank floor from entering the draw-off pipe, this should be elevated 5cm above the floor by screwing a G.I. elbow and PVC nipple on to the inner end of the draw-off pipe (Figure 4.7). Although this arrangement creates a 'dead storage' of 5cm at the bottom of the water tank, it has three benefits:

● It prevents sludge on the tank floor from reaching the outlet tap, thereby protecting water quality.

83

Figure 4.6 'Dead storage' in the bottom of a water tank due to the wrong positioning of the watertap

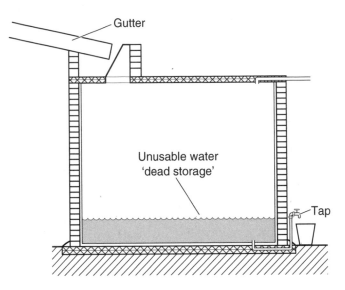

Figure 4.7 A draw-off pipe being used for tap point, sediment trap, moisture control and wash-out pipe

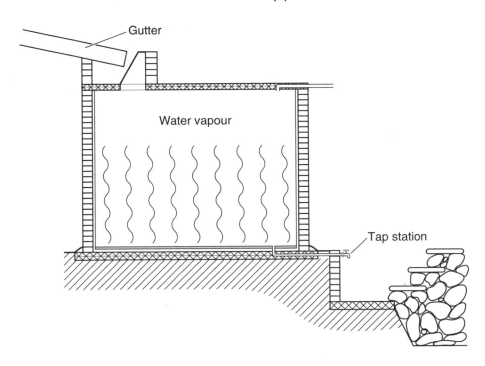

- It ensures water is retained even in an otherwise empty tank, keeping the tank interior moist and protecting the tank from cracking in hot weather.
- It allows the draw-off pipe to be used as a wash-out pipe; by unscrewing the nipple and tap, sludge can be removed through this outlet with a thick piece of wire.

While a 5cm protrusion of the draw-off pipe above the base of the tank may seem small, in larger tanks it still represents a significant volume of dead storage – over 1000 litres in a 46m³ tank. In arid regions where water is scarce it is better to clean the tank regularly than to increase the dead storage resulting from increasing the height of the draw-off pipe inlet above the base. In more humid climates, and especially where accumulations of organic and other debris (sludge) in the base of the tank is considerable, it may be appropriate to elevate the height of the draw-off pipe further above the base of the tank to avoid sucking up sediment, and thereby protecting water quality. If guaranteeing the highest possible water quality is critical, a floating suction fine filter such as the one being marketed in Germany and shown in Figure 9.9, can be used. This will always draw water from the cleanest part of the tank, and the design will keep the inlet above the base even if the tank is almost empty.

In some designs, a sump near to the wash-out pipe provides a useful aid when cleaning the tank, as do a manhole and internal ladder which allow access. While the inclusion of a simple internal ladder is always recommended, the inclusion of a sump is not. This is because a sump can create problems by weakening the floor and foundation of the tank. If it is included, extra reinforcement and particularly good craftsmanship will be required. Instead of including a sump, the floor of the tank should be sloped slightly towards the draw-off (wash-out) pipe providing a slightly lower area which can be used for the same job.

Water-extraction devices and other features

In order to withdraw water from the storage reservoir, some form of extraction device is needed. Normally, this will be some form of water tap or pump. Often in construction manuals this component is mentioned only in passing, or overlooked entirely. However, in common with gutters and downpipes, the extraction device is a vital link in the system. Broken or leaking taps all too often render systems useless for want of regular inspections and basic maintenance.

Taps   A properly functioning and well-maintained tap is a necessity for any surface catchment tank. A dripping or leaking tap can lose thousands of litres, quickly emptying most average-sized rainwater tanks. Taps are most vulnerable to breakage on communal tanks – particularly at schools, where they are frequently used and occasionally abused by the children. Since a 20-year life expectancy is a reasonable assumption for a well-constructed and maintained water tank, a durable tap with a good life expectancy should be fitted, especially on communal tanks. It is worth spending a little bit more for a good-quality tap which has a better chance of lasting. In some instances where

85

school and communal tanks are being used by large numbers of people, a lockable tap may be appropriate in order to control access and extraction rates from the tank. Alternatively, taps can be situated in a lockable chamber (as shown in Appendix 5). A responsible person, such as a water technician or teacher should be in charge of the key and should also inspect the tap from time to time to make sure it is not leaking. If it does leak, it should be fixed immediately. The authors have witnessed many hundreds of communal and school tanks, particularly in Africa, which are empty simply because of a broken or poorly maintained tap. While abuse and vandalism are sometimes the cause, poor initial construction and lack of maintenance is often also a factor. Sometimes tanks become empty simply because taps are left dripping or running. Self-closing taps can help to overcome this problem, although they are more prone to breakage and maintenance problems. Privately owned household tanks generally suffer few problems with tap breakage and maintenance. While this is partly due to lower levels of usage, it is also an interesting reflection of human nature.

Water pumps   Pumps tend to be used where water needs to be lifted from a sub-surface tank. The same principles apply to pumps as to taps, i.e. communal pumps are far more prone to breakdown than individually owned ones. The one major advantage that sub-surface tanks with pumps have over surface tanks with taps is that the former will not quickly empty if the pump breaks. In many situations, this fact alone is a good reason to consider using sub-surface tanks for communal supplies rather than surface ones. Pumps do, however, require careful operation and regular maintenance, which in many remote rural situations is often neglected, leading to system breakdowns. At least if the pump breaks it is still possible to extract water with a rope and bucket.

The most common type of pump used for extracting water from sub-surface tanks is the handpump. A variety of pumps designed for lifting water from shallow wells are appropriate, such as the Blair pump (Morgan, 1990). Other handpumps which may be suitable include various direct-action pumps, e.g. the rower pump and bucket pump. In some circumstances, it may be appropriate to use mechanically driven or electric pumps. The use of wind- and solar-powered pumps provides an environmentally benign alternative (Barlow et al., 1993; Kenna and Gillet, 1985). The high initial cost of purchasing commercially available windpumps or solar panels may make these less attractive. Cheaper do-it-yourself wind pumps can, however, be constructed from old oil drums and the like. Small electric and other motorized pumps are further alternatives where large quantities of water need to be raised to header tanks for distribution. In Kenya, one of the authors uses a 12-volt submersible pump running off a solar panel and car battery for this purpose; it costs about US$90 and can pump up to 300 litres per hour.

Rope and bucket   Extraction using a rope and bucket, although still common in many rural areas in developing countries, does risk secondary contamination of the stored water. This can be reduced to some extent by using a dedicated bucket and windlass to prevent the rope coming into contact with the ground.

Gravity systems   Where the point for supply is below the tank, it should be possible to supply the water using gravity, irrespective of whether a surface or sub-surface tank is being used (Skinner, 1990). In some cases, when extracting water from a sub-surface reservoir, a siphoning technique can be adopted using a plastic hose. The gravity flow extraction system – used with many large sub-surface hemispherical tanks in Kenya – using a staircase and tap stand (Figures 4.2 and 5.3) has proved very successful since its introduction in the early 1990s (Nissen-Petersen, 1992b). The excavated tap stand can also provide an additional 5m³ of crude open storage should the main tank overflow.

Tank overflow
Additional 'dead storage' will be created at the top of a water tank if the bottom of the overflow pipe is not placed at the maximum water level of the tank (Box 2.1). This means that in flat roofs made of reinforced concrete, the overflow pipe should be concreted into the base of the roof to avoid dead storage. In domes being used for storage, the overflow can either be placed at the level of the inlet for guttering, which determines the maximum water-level, or the gutter inlet can also be used as the overflow. In any case, the overflow should be situated vertically over the tapstand to force water overflowing to fall on to the concreted tap-point excavation, from where it is drained to a soak-away pit without eroding the base of the tank (Figure 4.8).

Manhole and internal ladder
Access into a roofed water tank is gained through a manhole, which should be placed near the highest point of the tank roof. The cheapest and simplest way of making a manhole is to use a wash basin made of plastic as a formwork placed in a hole cut in the reinforcement in the tank roof. To make the manhole cover, fill the basin with a 5cm-thick layer of concrete, and insert a rounded piece of weldmesh with a bent iron bar to function as a handle. Once in place, the remaining part of the roof is concreted. After a week of curing, lift the manhole out of the basin by using the handle embedded in the concrete. Then remove the plastic basin and replace the manhole into the seat made in the tank roof by the basin (Figure 5.9c). Alternatively, manhole covers can be made of sheet metal. A tight fit is recommended to prevent lizards, insects and other animals entering the tank. An internal ladder can easily be included in any design, with a central pillar supporting the roof. This can be made by installing a 10cm-diameter PVC pipe with a reinforcment rod and five 50cm lengths of 20mm (¾") G.I. pipe inserted at equal intervals before filling the PVC pipe with concrete (Figure 4.2).

Descriptions of selected rainwater-reservoir designs

Surface tanks

Ferrocement jars and tanks   Ferrocement water jars owe their origin to one of the oldest and smallest types of rainwater storage container, the traditional

Figure 4.8 Overflow into tap stand with drain

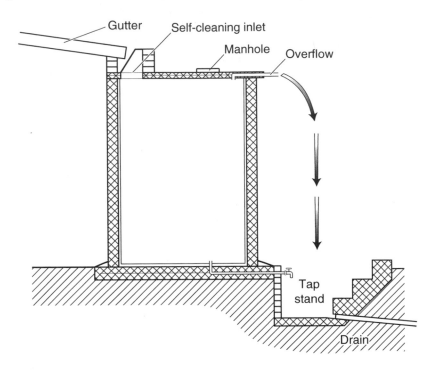

glazed-clay water jars of South-east Asia, which can hold about 200 litres. These have been used in Burma and Thailand for centuries and are still used today. In the early 1980s, larger jars – with volumes of between 1000 and 2000 litres – made from ferrocement were introduced in Thailand, and the production of the jars was later subsidized by the Thai government. These large rainwater jars have become extremely popular and it is estimated that more than 12 million jars are in use today. Details of the construction procedure for these jars can be found in Chapter 5, and the case-study of Thailand in Chapter 9 contains more background information about the programme as a whole.

In 1995, a larger jar with a volume of 2500 litres and built of ferrocement was introduced by UNCHS during training courses on the construction of the jar and gutter in three zones of Burma (Myanmar). The ferrocement-jar technology has also been adopted in parts of Cambodia, Laos and elsewhere in South-east Asia. A number of jars have even been built in Kenya (Appendix 5) and elsewhere in East and Southern Africa, but they have not been adopted anywhere to the extent they have in Thailand.

Ferrocement was first developed by a Frenchman, Joseph Monier, who displayed flower pots made of ferrocement in Paris as early as 1867. The technology has been used in a variety of constructions, including boat building. Its use in water-tank construction is a relatively recent phenomenon and really took off only in the 1950s and 1960s. While the technology has been adopted widely in some developed countries and regions such as New Zealand and Arizona (Watt, 1978), its high labour input really makes it most appropriate in countries with cheap skilled labour. In the 1980s and 1990s, the use of the technology for tank construction spread rapidly in Asia, especially in north-east Thailand, and parts of India and China. Although it is technically possible to build surface tanks with volumes of 100m^3 or more, most of the tanks built in South, East and South-east Asia have been less than 12m^3 in volume. Although many larger surface ferrocement tanks have been built in East and Southern Africa, their success has not been as universal as in Asia. This stems from a variety of reasons, in particular, problems with the level of skills and workmanship on some projects (Gould, 1998).

Ferrocement tanks have sometimes been promoted as a low-cost technique requiring only limited skills. In fact, considerable skills are required, both for the correct installation of the reinforcement and in mixing the plaster. The ever-increasing costs of weld mesh, chicken mesh and galvanized wire have also meant that, in many places, ferrocement tanks now cost much more than some alternatives, such as water tanks built with bricks and blocks. On the positive side, cracks in ferrocement tanks can be repaired fairly easily (Hasse, 1989), and leaks can be sealed by coating the interior of a tank with sealants and bonding agents (Enyatseng, 1988).

Brick and block tanks   A wide range of brick and block-tank designs has been developed, and construction methods are described by several authors including Hasse (1989), Morgan (1990), Vadhanavikkit et al. (1984) and Nissen-Petersen (1998a). In colonial East and Central Africa times, most rural settlers relied on roof catchment tanks built of concrete or quarry blocks for domestic water supply. Using the same approach as the settlers, one of the authors built a 10 000-litre and a 23 000-litre water tank from concrete blocks at Wanza farm, Kibwezi in 1977. The tanks are still functioning after more than 20 years, and a description of the construction technique is given in Nissen-Petersen (1982). Many local farmers and business people in Eastern Kenya also built water tanks of burnt bricks as this was the cheapest material. Unfortunately, most of these tanks have cracked due to one or more of the following reasons: insufficient reinforcement, poor plastering, or using a square rather than a circular design. In 1995, circular and correctly reinforced and plastered burnt-brick tanks were built during training courses in Burma by UNCHS. As a result of the simple construction technique and low-cost material, these tanks quickly became popular. This improved design is now also being promoted in Kenya and Uganda (Appendix 5).

Two water tanks were built of compressed soil/cement bricks using a mixture of one portion of cement to 20 portions of soil, compressed in a hand-powered press at Friends World College at Machakos, Kenya, in 1983. The tanks were cheap to build and are still functioning well after 15 years without maintenance. A similar technique has also been used in Thailand, where large numbers of tanks have been built using this approach in the Khon Kaen Province (Vadhanavikkit et al., 1984).

The use of interlocking blocks for water-tank construction has been tried in a number of countries around the world, including Thailand and Kenya. An English firm, Parry & Associates, is marketing 12V-battery or solar-powered machinery for making interlocking pre-cast concrete blocks, using a vibrating mould, for the construction of water tanks with volumes of 9.5m³, 14.5m³ and 18.5m³, without reinforcement. The tanks are able to withstand the pressure of water without reinforcement as long as they are no higher than 160cm. Beyond that height, the tanks must be reinforced. Although the use of inter-locking blocks appears attractive, they have several drawbacks in a rural setting, such as importing the machinery and its mould, maintaining the ma-chinery, and obtaining spare-parts. Furthermore, as blocks get broken during transportation on rural roads, the machinery has to be moved from site to site.

Reinforced-concrete tanks The main drawback with conventional reinforced-concrete tank designs is that they are expensive. Nevertheless, these seemingly 'over-designed' tanks can be extremely durable. Large cisterns built in rural Ghana under German administration in around 1910 were still reported to be functioning in the 1970s by Parker (1972), and on Belau in the Pacific (W. Caroline Islands) many large rainwater cisterns built under Japanese mandate between 1924 and 1941 were reported still to be in use in the early 1980s (Romeo, 1982; O'Meara, 1982). In New Zealand, con-crete tanks constructed as early as 1914 were observed to be still functioning well in 1998. While conventional reinforced-concrete construction techniques may often be inappropriate in developing countries due to their high cost, in areas where aggregate is abundant, it may be worthwhile adapting it into a more affordable method. In the late 1970s, the Diocese of Machakos in Kenya trained some builders in the construction of water tanks built by pouring concrete between two circular forms made of corrugated-iron sheets. The tank is reinforced with barbed wire laid as a spiral in the moist concrete. The trained builders, assisted by local residents, constructed a demonstration tank at each location in the district. Thereafter, the residents borrowed the form-work and built their own tanks. By the mid-1980s, more than 6000 tanks of this type had been built by the residents themselves, with no financial assis-tance. The tanks were built in three sizes: 4m³, 5.4m³ and 13.5m³, and con-tinue to be built today. A design-drawing for an adapted version of the technique for a 5m³ tank is described in Appendix 5, and the original design is described in a manual produced in English and Swahili by the Diocese (De Vrees, 1987).

Metal tanks Corrugated galvanized-steel tanks have been popular for much of the twentieth century but, although they are still used widely around the world, their success-rate has been somewhat mixed (Plate 4.2). Three factors influence their durability: the quality and thickness of the metal used; the level of protection provided for the tank, e.g. protective paint; and the quality of construction and level of exposure to saline or acidic water and atmospheric moisture. Life expectancy for these tanks can vary from less than two to more than 20 years. Clearly, the tanks are not appropriate in coastal environments or in any situation where saline or 'aggressive' acidic water will be mixed with any stored rainwater. In areas with 'acid rain' due to atmospheric pollution, metal tanks are also best avoided. In other situations, tanks should last for between 5 and 8 years, even without external painting, if they are erected properly on treated timber boards on top of a brick plinth. The tank's life may also be extended by painting both the inside and soldered joints with special paint (Hasse, 1989). Since these paints produce toxic fumes, a breathing mask should be worn. To avoid storm damage – being blown away when empty – the tank should be fixed to the plinth with steel ropes or strong fencing wire.

Probably the most common type of rainwater tank in the world is the recycled 200-litre oil drum (Plate 4.4). The only real advantage it has over other systems is that it is available almost everywhere and is generally afford-able in even the poorest communities. Oil drums are, however, generally much too small to provide storage for more than a few days' water supply. Except in areas with heavy regular rainfall all year round, oil drums can provide, at best, only a useful supplementary supply. Nevertheless, while an oil drum may have only 10 per cent of the storage capacity of a $2m^3$ Thai jar, or just 1 per cent that of a $20m^3$ tank, it can still collect and store ten times the amount of water held by a large bucket. When one considers that people, especially women and children, in many of the world's poorest regions still carry several buckets of water many kilometres every day, then the benefit of even one or two oil drums for rainwater collection can be appreciated. Every time a drum is filled, the effort and time required to carry 10 large buckets of water is saved.

Compared with larger tanks, oil drums have several limitations. Apart from their small size, they do not come with taps or covers and, if these are not provided, the rainwater will inevitably become contaminated. Open drums also provide breeding-sites for various disease-carrying insect vectors, such as mosquitoes (see Chapter 6). After some time, the drums start to rust, dis-colouring and contaminating the rainwater. The use of oil drums does, however, indicate a desire and real felt need to utilize rainwater, and is a good precursor for any rainwater-tank implementation project.

Corroded and leaking oil drums can be repaired by coating their interior with a 2cm layer of 1:3 cement mortar and coated with Nil. Even new oil drums can be treated in this way to extend their life expectancy and to help keep the water clean and palatable. As well as numerous oil drums, the authors have also seen several examples of old fuel-storage tanks with vol-umes of up to $20m^3$ being used as rainwater tanks. Obviously, the use of containers once used for storing potentially toxic liquids could be hazardous and, where no alternative exists, great care should be taken to ensure the container is thoroughly cleaned out before being used for water storage. Even then, drinking this water is not recommended.

Plastic tanks Moulded plastic tanks have become popular in recent years and, due to improved processes to stabilize plastic against deterioration

Plate 4.3 *2m³ plastic rainwater tanks being used as the main source of water supply at a household at Charteris Bay, near Christchurch, New Zealand.* (Photo: John Gould, 1998)

Plate 4.4 *An oil drum; probably the world's most common type of rainwater-storage container at a household in eastern Kenya. Note the under-utilized roof catchment area.* (Photo: John Gould, 1984)

resulting from exposure to UV (ultraviolet) light, these tanks are much more durable than they used to be. They are, however, relatively expensive and their durability beyond 10–15 years is still unknown. In Southern Africa, tanks ranging from 1 to 10m³ are becoming very widespread. Because plastics are light and flexible, they can be easily transported, even on very bad roads (Plate 4.1). Plastic tanks up to 25m³ have been developed relatively recently and, in some places, are becoming increasingly cost-competitive with other alternatives, e.g. in New Zealand (Plate 4.3). This is not, however, the case everywhere; in East and Central Africa, plastic tanks cost up to four times as much as those constructed on site by local masons. To prevent plastic tanks being blown away by strong winds when empty, they must be properly secured.

Other tank types Fibreglass tanks are also expensive when compared to tanks constructed on site, but are popular in some parts of the world especially for storage volumes of 20m³ or less. Manufacturers claim the minimum life expectancy of 25 years, and the fact that tanks can be easily relocated, as a major advantage. Being light, they are also easy to transport and can be repaired if damaged. In contrast to fibreglass, high-density polyethylene (HDPE) 'Aquadam' tanks, common in Southern Africa, are one of the cheapest types of water tank but are difficult to repair. Field experience has shown that their durability is often limited and they need to be shaded from extended exposure to strong sunlight. Hundreds of 7m³ Aquadam tanks were installed in remote parts of rural Botswana as part of the ALDEP programme but use of the tanks was discontinued after some years due to their poor long-term performance. In common with plastic and metal tanks, fibreglass and PVC tanks are very light when empty and need to be secured against strong winds.

Surface rainwater tanks have also been made of various other materials including wood, bamboo, fibre-reinforced cement and natural-fibre polymer resins. None of these are recommended for widespread replication. Wood tanks are not very common as they tend to be expensive, but are found in parts of the United States, Canada, New Zealand and Northern Europe. Some manufacturers claim very long life expectancies of 80 years or more if an ongoing maintenance programme is adhered to. In Hawaii, tanks built using treated redwood timber are the preference among the most wealthy tank owners as they are considered the most aesthetically pleasing design.

Cement tanks using bamboo, sisal fibre and basketwork 'reinforcement' were enthusiastically promoted during the early 1980s, but failed to stand the test of time. Although these designs, which were championed as a low-cost alternative to ferrocement in both South-East Asia (bamboo) and East Africa (sisal and basketwork 'reinforcement'), they were simply not durable. Termites, bacteria and fungi attacked any exposed 'reinforcement', leading to cracking and even bursting. The construction of these tanks, which was once hailed as a major development in appropriate technology, has now, with a few minor exceptions, been generally discontinued.

Another design which failed to take off was based on a natural-fibre laminated polymer resin (Dorfman and Valentijn, 1993). Tank manufactured using an inflatable mould was a technique which was actively promoted in Central America in the early 1990s, but seems to have failed to achieve broad acceptance and be widely replicated. While widespread replication of any particular tank design depends ultimately on an effective awareness-raising and promotion strategy, ultimately, a good tank design will sell itself, and a bad design will always fail as knowledge of its poor performance spreads.

Sub-surface tanks
One approach to constructing sub-surface tanks is to build a surface tank in an excavation which is then back-filled. This buried tank approach has been described using a 40m³ ferrocement tank design constructed in Zimbabwe (then Rhodesia) as a demonstration (Watt, 1978; Pacey and Cullis, 1986). This approach, however, defeats the main advantage of sub-surface tanks, that of being able to build a cheaper tank using less material due to the support provided by the surrounding soil.

Ferrocement hemispherical tanks Large 90m³ hemispherical sub-surface ferrocement tank designs, as illustrated in Figures 4.2 and 5.3, originated in Kenya in 1978 (Nissen-Petersen, 1982). However, smaller cylindrical sub-surface ferrocement tanks with volumes ranging from 6m³ to 60m³ were built in Botswana from the late 1970s onwards (Maikano and Nyberg, 1980; Gould, 1985). The construction of sub-surface ferrocement tanks seems to have its origins in the New Hebrides Islands in the Pacific, where a number of smaller tanks with volumes of 22.5m³ were built in the 1970s (Calvert and Binning, 1977). These tanks included a ferrocement dome roof cast on a soil mound and then lifted on to the tank. This technique was later tried elsewhere, even for surface tanks, but the weight of the ferrocement dome made it difficult, and impossible for larger tanks. Eventually, methods for casting the dome roof directly on to the tank were developed using flattened oil-drum templates supported by a wooden framework (Nissen-Petersen, 1992b). While this approach is good on projects where many tanks of standard sizes are being constructed, it is less appropriate in cases where single tanks or few tanks of varying sizes are being constructed. In such cases the construction of flat roofs would be better (Chapter 5).

Before the development of ferrocement dome roofs, many larger sub-surface ferrocement tanks had roofs made of corrugated-iron sheets supported by wooden poles. Due to the deterioration and rotting of the wood, the water quality was affected and the roof supports eventually collapsed. The ferrocement dome roofs can easily support the weight of 20 men or the odd stray cow! Before the ferrocement dome roof was developed, there were a number of reports of livestock falling into both covered and uncovered tanks.

Excavated water cellars (*Shuijao*) In large areas of Central and Western China, the windblown loess soils are ideal for the construction of excavated rainwater tanks. These thick layers of silty soil have also been excavated to provide 'cave dwellings' cut directly into exposed hillsides. Due to the low permeability of the loess soil, traditionally excavated tanks in Gansu Province were lined with local red clay and could hold water very effectively (Zhu and Wu, 1995). This clay-lining process was difficult and time-consuming and, in recent years, ferrocement linings have been used instead. Typically, these tanks have capacities of between 15 and 20m³ and often one or two tanks will provide a family's main source of water. In areas with more sandy soils, a 15cm concrete tank wall and base are used to line the excavation. Since the mid-1990s, hundreds of thousands of new systems have been introduced through the '1–2-1 project' in Gansu Province; for further details of this project and designs see Chapter 9.

Other sub-surface tanks   Several other sub-surface tank designs have been developed and widely adopted around the world. The use of bricks and con-crete blocks has been adopted in situations such as in western Botswana, where sandy soils have precluded the use of ferrocement (Whiteside, 1982; Gould, 1985). In Bahia, north-east Brazil, large numbers of tanks with vol-umes up to 40m³ have been built using a 20cm-thick double layer of burnt bricks, on which a layer of lime-mortar plaster was applied. To waterproof the tank completely, a cement-slurry layer was added in between two layers of lime mortar. This technique is described in detail by Gnadlinger (1995a, 1995b, 1993). Another type of cistern used in the area is found in Casa Nova county, where uncovered hand-dug tanks have been excavated directly into the soft micaceous rock. Over 1000 of these systems, known locally as *caxio*, have been constructed using only simple tools. The reservoirs with volumes of 70m³ or more are usually at least 4m deep and have vertical walls to help reduce evaporation. They are generally surrounded by a wooden fence to keep animals and children away.

Another approach to constructing sub-surface reservoirs is to line excava-tions with various liners. While the use of butyl rubber and polythene sheeting to line tanks can be quite effective, it is not cheap, and the durability of the tanks is limited due to damage caused by roots, rodents and sunlight. The life expectancy of polythene-lined tanks is even less – usually just a couple of years. A very cheap alternative to cement is to line sub-surface tanks using powdered anthills, mixed with a little cement, lime and sand, followed by two coats of bitumen. About ten of these tanks were built in Mutomo in eastern Kenya in the mid-1980s, and recent reports suggest that a couple are still holding water.

Communal systems

Although the focus of this book is on domestic rainwater systems at the household level, larger communal systems also play an important role in meeting domestic water needs in many rural areas. Some of the key design issues of these larger communal systems are discussed below. Detailed designs and construction procedures are not included in this text; however, relevant references are provided for interested readers.

While it is widely recognized that effective initial design is essential to the success of any system, equally important are proper operation and maintenance. Whereas the individual householder has a vested interest in the careful operation and maintenance of a roof catchment system used exclusively by his or her family, effective operation and maintenance are far more difficult to ensure in a context of communal ownership. In the case of the communal systems described below, the key to effective operation and maintenance involves protecting the catchment and reservoir from pollution and erosion. This requires adhering to a regular schedule of inspection, as well as undertaking repairs and sediment removal when necessary.

Rock catchment systems   Rock catchment systems can vary greatly in size, with volumes ranging from less than 20m³ to several thousand cubic metres or more. Rubble-stone masonry dams built with the assistance of self-help labour can provide highly cost-effective water supplies. Dam walls can range from 2m to 6m in height and from 10m to 60m in length. The walls can be straight or be built in sections as V-shaped or trapezoildal structures (Figure 4.9a). Dams should be constructed where natural depressions, gullies or hollows are found on or below exposed rock outcrops where depressions can provide free storage capacity after soil and vegetation have been removed. The key to successful rock catchment system design is the selection of an appropriate site. While aerial photos and aerial surveys can be used for general appraisals, a field survey done with local people who know the area is usually the most effective way to identify the best sites. The following summary checklist is adapted from one developed by Lee and Visscher (1992) to highlight the main siting factors which need to be considered:

- Dams should be built at sites that produce a relatively high depth to surface area ratio to minimize evaporation losses.
- Rock surfaces should not be fractured or cracked, so causing leakage losses.
- Dam foundations must be solid impermeable rock with no soil pockets or fracture lines.
- There should be no erosion in the catchment area.
- Location must be convenient for the user group.

Preparation of the site is important and all vegetation and loose soil should be removed from the rock catchment surface. Any cracks or fissures in or around the dam foundation and reservoir area should be filled with mortar. Detailed designs and construction procedures are provided by Nissen-Petersen (1990a, 1998b) and Lee and Visscher (1992).

Sand river storage   There are two basic types of sand river storage system in which water is stored in the voids between sand particles. These are subsurface dams and sand dams (Figure 4.10) and are often referred to as groundwater dams. Sub-surface dams are constructed of either soil or rubble-stone masonry from a key trench excavated into the floor of soil or murram under the sand to the surface of the sand in riverbeds, with nothing protruding above the sand level. These dams can be built in almost any seasonal water course

96

Figure 4.9 Rock catchment system, showing three different designs using straight wall sections
(Adapted from Nissen-Petersen, 1990)

a) Single wall built across a small rock valley

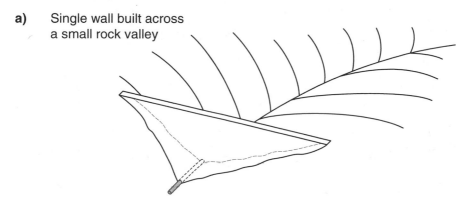

(b) V-shaped dam wall built in rock depression or basin

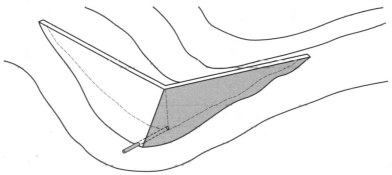

(c) Trapezoidal U-shaped dam built on a continuous slope

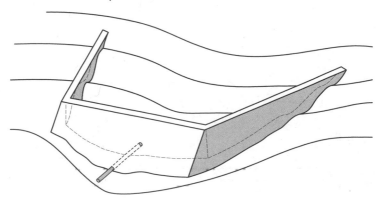

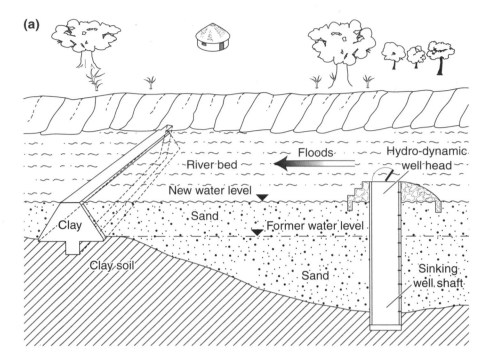

Figure 4.10 **(a)** Sub-surface dam built of clay soil with hydro-dynamic
well head.
(Source: Nissen-Petersen,1997)

(b) Stone-masonry sand dam built in multiple stages with
river-intake.
(Source: Nissen-Petersen,1997)

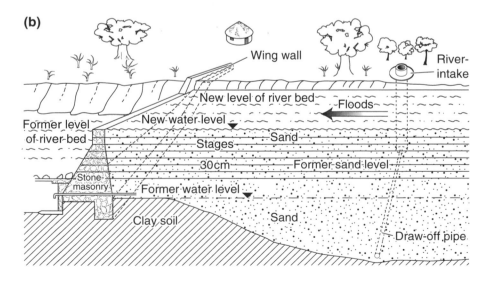

with at least a metre of sand. Over the last two years farmers at Makueni in Eastern Kenya have proved that they can build sub-surface dams of soil successfully, and at no cost except their own labour.

Sand dams are built of rubble-stone masonry or concrete from a key trench and foundation dug into a river bed floor of soil, murram or bedrock without fissures beneath the sand. Sand dams protrude above the sand level in riverbeds and, therefore, must have a wide foundation and wing-walls built into the river banks to withstand the force of flash-floods. These dams are built in stages of 30cm above the sand level for the purpose of trapping coarse sand and water brought by flash-floods. Sand dams may be built several metres high during rainy seasons, thus enlarging the sand and water storage to many thousands of cubic metres. The dams require high banks on each site of the sand-river because they will raise the sand and water level. Sand dams also require catchment areas which produce coarse sand from eroding rocks and heavy flash-floods capable of transporting many tonnes of sand to the dam reservoirs. Sand dams are so site- and design-specific that only engineers with experience in sand-dam construction can build them successfully. All too often, sand dams are found to be malfunctioning or damaged beyond repair.

Water is extracted from a sub-surface dam in two ways; either a hand-dug well is sunk in the deepest part of the sand reservoirs and equipped with a hydro-dynamic well-head capable of withstanding flash-floods, or water can be drawn from a river intake built as a hand-dug well in a river bank near the deepest part of a sand reservoir (Figure 4.10). A perforated PVC pipe drains water from the sand into the river intake. Water can be extracted from sand dams as described above, or it can be gravitated downstream through a galvanized-iron pipe passing through the foundation of a sand dam. It has to be equipped with a filter to keep sand out of the end of the pipe that is situated in the buried sand reservoir. At the downstream end of the pipe, an underground tap stand can be constructed and closed with a steel door to prevent flash-floods from doing any damage. The correct siting of both types of dam is important for minimizing the construction work and maximizing the storage capacity of sand rivers. Good potential dam sites include:

- locations on ephemeral (seasonal) sand river (dry river bed) which is periodically flooded during a normal rainy season
- river beds comprising coarse sand, as this has large voids for maximum storage of water – the finer the sand the less water it can store
- sites free of boulders, fractured or saline rocks. If calcrete deposits are situated in or upstream of a reservoir, its water will be saline or brackish
- locations where existing water-holes remain for at least a month after the rains.

Water found in water-holes is trapped in the sand due to an underground dyke of clay, murram or impervious (watertight) rock rising up from the river floor under the sand somewhere downstream of the water-holes. Such dykes are the best potential sites for dam walls because they minimize construction works and provide a watertight and partly 'free' reservoir in the depressions where water-holes are found upstream of the site.

For further discussion and design and construction details for the above systems consult the following references: Nissen-Petersen (1982, 1986, 1990, 1996 and 1999 in press), Nilsson (1984) and Lee and Visscher (1992).

Earth dams and hafirs   Earth dams do not produce water that is generally suitable for drinking without some form of treatment. Nevertheless, these systems do provide an invaluable source of water in many arid and semi-arid regions, where they provide water for livestock, washing and, in the absence of any alternatives, drinking and cooking as well. If a hand-dug well is constructed immediately downstream of the dam wall, seepage from the dam will recharge the well, and the water quality withdrawn from it will be far better than that in the reservoir. Typically, small earth dams may have volumes ranging from $500m^3$ to $10\,000m^3$, with straight or curved walls up to 100m long and 8m high (Figure 4.11). On hillsides, curved dams known as curved hillside dams are constructed, while elsewhere straight embankment dams are built across seasonal water courses (Nelson, 1985). Unlike larger earth dams, these can normally be designed by a local technician, and constructed and maintained by the community with very low capital and cash input. The main problems associated with these systems are sediment accumulation, erosion and evaporation. The key strategy for overcoming or reducing these problems is a careful initial site selection. The following checklist of siting factors for small earth dams is adapted from Lee and Visscher (1992) and Nissen-Petersen (1990), who also provided design details. Small earth dam sites should be situated:

- where people and livestock are in need of water and where the community has implemented soil-conservation measures on any cleared land in the catchment area of the dam
- on public land with a public access road for the members of the community and users of the dam
- in a natural depression or gully to enhance water-storage capacity
- where the type of soil limits seepage and is capable of carrying the weight of the dam wall
- where runoff from rains on the catchment area can fill the dam reservoirs at least once a year
- there are no anthills, pits, sewage outlets, saline or calcereous soil.

The most suitable sites for a straight embankment dam are normally found at points where small seasonal water courses widen over flatter ground. Where a natural depression already exists on sloping ground, a curved hillside dam may be built. It is essential that the dam foundation is watertight and no seepage occurs, and that the construction is robust enough to ensure stability. A well should be constructed for water abstraction downstream of the dam wall and the reservoir area fenced. Two spillways should be constructed to minimize the risk of overtopping. The reservoir dimensions should be proportional to the size of the labour force and the community's enthusiasm for the

100

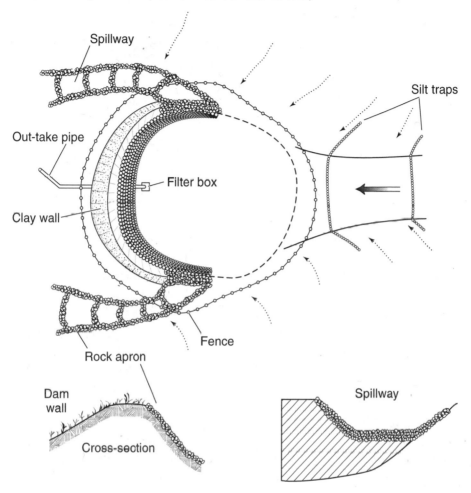

Figure 4.11 General design for an earth dam with curved walls
(Source: adapted from Lee and Visscher, 1992)

project. Any soil erosion in the catchment area should be checked with soil-conservation measures such as check dams in the inflow channel.

Hafirs are common water sources in large parts of central Sudan, but are also found elsewhere in Africa and around the world. These reservoirs are surrounded by embankments made from the material excavated from them, normally by machinery (Figure 4.12). Hafirs store rainwater runoff and are larger than earth dams, typically having volumes ranging from $15\,000\text{m}^3$ to $250\,000\text{m}^3$ (Gaddal, 1991). Hafirs usually have a guard who ensures that animals and people do not enter the water. As in the case of earth dams, siltation and erosion of the embankments are the main problems. To overcome this, they must be maintained through repair programmes and periodic de-silting. Although heavy machinery is often used for de-silting, a UNICEF programme

Figure 4.12 Mechanically excavated sump and contour hafirs in Sudan
(Source: adapted from Robertson, 1950)

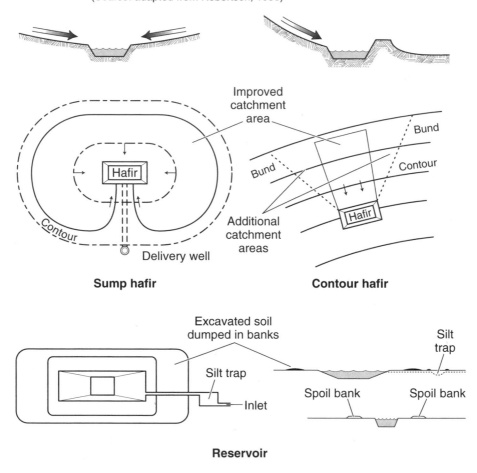

Sump hafir

Contour hafir

Reservoir

in Kordofan in the mid-1980s clearly demonstrated that, for smaller hafirs at least, manual de-silting was practical and could be done for a small fraction of the cost of using heavy machinery (Dodge and Zelenika, 1987).

Summary of key points

- Essential requirements for an effective rainwater storage tank include:
  - a functional and watertight design with a solid, secure cover
  - a screened inlet, overflow pipe and a covered manhole
  - an extraction system which protects water quality, and a soakaway
  - a maximum height of 2m (unless additional reinforcement is used).
- Cylindrical or Spherical tanks, e.g. the Thai jar, are stronger and more cost-effective – using less material than square (cuboid) tanks.

102

- The availability of suitable materials and skilled labour are important factors when deciding on the selection of a particular tank design.
- Care should be taken when siting tanks to avoid risks from pollution sources or damage by erosion.
- Gutters are often the weak link in any rainwater catchment system; they must be appropriately sized, properly erected around the whole roof area, and fitted with splash-guards if necessary.
- Many reservoir types are suitable for rainwater storage, including: surface tanks made of ferrocement, bricks/blocks, reinforced concrete, metal, plastic, fibreglass and wood; sub-surface tanks made using ferrocement, concrete, brick and traditional clay linings; and communal rock catchment dams, sub-surface dams built of soil, sand river dams, earthdams and hafirs.
- Most common designs, if properly constructed with good-quality materials and good workmanship, are effective. The use of organic 'reinforcement' such as bamboo, sisal fibres or sticks (in basketwork) as a substitute for steel reinforcement and wire is *not* recommended for the construction of water tanks.

5

Materials and construction techniques

WORLDWIDE, THE VARIETY of rainwater tank is enormous. There are thousands of ways to construct a household rainwater tank and most well-tried methods found in good texts and manuals will, if followed properly, give a satisfactory result. Clearly, it is not possible to describe all the methods here. The purpose of this chapter, therefore, is to focus on some fundamental principles and practices essential to ensuring the successful construction of durable, watertight tanks. Every method has its own advantages and disadvantages and the appropriate choice of design and construction technique will depend on local conditions. The emphasis here is on tank designs that reduce costs without unduly compromising the quality and durability of the final product. Although in richer countries high labour costs often make 'off-the-shelf' water tanks competitive, in poorer countries it is usually cheaper to build tanks on site; several successful designs relevant for implementation in poorer rural areas are described in detail in Appendix 5. All of these designs have been developed by Erik Nissen-Petersen in Kenya and have been widely field-tested and refined over many years. They are all durable, cost-effective and, with the assistance of trained builders, can be constructed almost anywhere. One other design, the Thai jar, is also described in detail later in this chapter due to the phenomenal success it has enjoyed in South-east Asia and the potential appropriateness of the design (in a modified form) in other parts of the world. With all designs, it is necessary to adapt them to local conditions. A comparison of the 2m^3 Thai jar design with the modified 3m^3 ferrocement jar design (Appendix 5) adapted for Kenyan conditions, is a good example of this (Plates 5.1 and 5.2). Although much of the material in the following sections is based primarily on experiences from Africa and South-east Asia, most of it has a broader relevance.

There are numerous other texts and manuals describing water-tank construction methods and any reader interested in constructing water tanks should try to compare a number of designs by referring to other relevant texts, design manuals and design drawings (see Appendix 4 for further details). An excellent introduction to ferrocement water-tank construction is given by Watt (1978). Although this concise text is slightly dated, it covers very well the basic principles, practice and theory behind this technique. Detailed step-by-step descriptions of ferrocement and brick tank construction techniques using different approaches to those described here are given by Hasse (1989) and Morgan (1990). A series of manuals and photo-manuals for the construction of a range of surface and sub-surface

104

Plate 5.1 *Woman wrapping wire around first layer of mortar during construction of 2m³ 'Thai Jar', Khon Kaen, Thailand 1986.* (Photo: John Gould)

Plate 5.2 *Wire-reinforced 'African Jar' being given second and final layer of mortar in Kibwezi, Kenya 1997.* (Photo: Erik Nissen-Petersen)

ferrocement, brick and block tanks, earthdams, rock catchments and gutter installations have also been produced by one of the co-authors, Nissen-Petersen (1992a, 1992b, 1992c, 1999 in press).

While it is important, when deciding on which design to adopt, to compare and contrast different available options, it is vital to avoid designs that have proved to be unsuccessful in the past. Several texts and manuals, especially those written during the 1980s, advocate and provide design drawings for cement tanks with bamboo, sisal fibre and basketwork reinforcement. As already mentioned, the use of organic reinforcement failed to produce durable tanks and should be avoided.

Problems such as cracking and leakage in water tanks are often attributed to poorly selected materials, bad workmanship, or both. Potentially, the cause of these problems can often be overcome with proper training and supervision, but these are also sometimes lacking. Some artisans seem to regard the building of water tanks and installation of gutters as simple jobs for which, as builders, they are automatically qualified. Few will admit that they do not know how to construct water tanks properly and instead they will assure a client that he will get 'the best water tank ever seen' if only *they* are given the contract. In reality, many tanks constructed by individual building contractors (in Kenya at least) have suffered leakages due to insufficient reinforcement or badly applied concrete and mortar. The result has been that many tank-owners regret having wasted money on constructing a rainwater tank and the technology as a whole gets a bad name.

The following sections, therefore, are aimed specifically at builders, designers and potential tank-owners; for builders, to provide guidance regarding the selection of materials and application of construction techniques; for designers, to give a practical insight into the construction of water tanks to assist them in drawing up clearer plans and instructions; and to potential tank buyers to help ensure they get good value for money. The materials and methods recommended have proved to be effective during two decades of application in the field. For definitions of some of the terms used in this chapter, refer to Box 5.1.

Materials

Construction materials often make up a significant proportion of the cost of rainwater systems. If locally available materials can be used for little or no cost, major savings can often be achieved. In Box 5.1, commonly available raw materials are listed. In each case, their potential uses – along with the water structures they may be used to construct – are indicated. When deciding on a particular design, it is always important to consider the cost and availability of materials. The quality of the construction materials is a critical factor influencing the quality of the completed tank. If in doubt over the quality of any the materials being used, these should be tested; this can usually be done using simple methods, some of which are described below.

Box 5.1

Definitions of cement-based mixtures and construction techniques

All water tanks require the use of cement, including tanks made of metal, plastic or fibreglass, because they need concrete foundations. Definitions of various types of materials made from cement and used for tank construction are as follows:

Concrete is a mixture of cement, coarse sand, crushed stones (aggregate) and water.

Reinforced concrete is concrete that is reinforced with steel bars, weld-mesh or BRC (British Reinforcement).

Mortar is a mixture of cement, sand and water *without* crushed stones.

Nil is a cement slurry made from mixing cement and water, which can be used as a substitute for waterproof cement.

Brick-masonry is the term for using mortar to build with burnt bricks.

Stone-masonry is using mortar to build with regular dressed stones and blocks.

Rubble stone-masonry is the term for using mortar with uncut, or undressed, rubble stones and rocks.

Ferrocement is mortar reinforced with weld-mesh, BRC mesh, chicken mesh, G.I. wires or barbed wire.

Pointing is the process of finishing joints in brickwork or masonary with mortar and concrete.

Curing is the process of assisting the hardening of mortar by keeping it moist (see graph below).

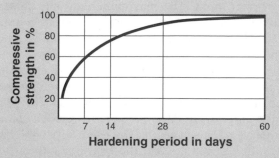

Graph showing the relationship between compressive strength and curing (hardening period).
Source: AED/Irrigation and Drainage, Ministry of Agriculture, Kenya (1990)

107

Table 5.1 Locally available materials for construction works

Raw materials	Potential processed products	Potential construction uses
Clay soil	Burnt bricks Dam walls	Water tanks Earth dams Sub-surface dams Hand-dug wells
Loamy soil	—	Earth dams Sub-surface dams
Sandy soil	Compressed soil blocks	Surface water tanks
Fine sand	Compressed soil blocks and cement bricks	Surface water tanks
Coarse sand	Ferrocement	Water jars Surface and sub-surface water tanks
Gravel/pebbles	Concrete Concrete blocks	Surface and sub-surface water tanks Sand dams Rock catchment systems
Rubble stones	Rubble stone blocks Rubble stone-masonry	Surface and sub-surface water tanks Rock catchment dams Sand dams
Boulders/rocks	Rubble stone-masonry	Sand dams Rock catchment dams Hand-dug wells

Note: This table is designed to assist in determining the types of rainwater catchment system structures which might potentially be built using local materials.

Sand The quality of sand also influences the strength of concrete and plaster. Sand collected from roadsides and slow-flowing water courses is unsuitable because it consists of fine sand particles and silt which will shrink and crack in water tanks. The maximum allowable content of silt in sand for cement mixtures is 8 per cent by volume. The silt content of a sand sample is found by filling a transparent plastic container or bottle half water and half sand. Shake the bottle vigorously and leave it to settle for three hours. Then measure the height of sand and the height of silt over-laying the sand in the bottle. If the height of silt is more than about 1/12 (8 per cent), then the silt content is too high for the sand to be mixed with cement. In dry and windy regions it is possible to remove some of the silt from the sand by throwing the sand up in the wind. The lighter silt particles will be carried away by the wind, while the heavier sand particles will fall to the ground. Coarse sand – with particles measuring 1 to 4mm – is the most suitable sand for concreting foundations and flat roofs on water tanks. Coarse sand can be found near the outer bends of sand rivers where water has a higher velocity which carries away the finer sand. Finer sand is suitable for mixing mortar for plaster. Before being mixed with cement, sand should always be sieved and all organic materials removed because grass straws or tiny branches will function as drainage pipes in water tanks when they have rotted away.

Cement   Portland cement is a powder – normally sold in paper bags weighing 50 kg and with a volume of 37 litres – which is made of:

60–65% lime	(CaO)
18–25% silica	(SiO_2)
3–8% alumina	(Al_2O_2)
0.5–5% iron oxide	(Fe_2O_3)
0.5–4% magnesium oxide	(MgO)
0.1–1.5% potassium oxide	(K_2O)
0.1–1.0% sodium oxide	(Na_2O)
2–3% sulphate	(SO_3)

Cement becomes plastic a short time after contact with water. After a couple of hours, a chemical reaction will stiffen, or set, the cement to a stone-hard material which bonds well with aggregate, iron and steel – provided it is cured for a minimum of three weeks. Cement loses strength during prolonged storage and gets spoiled if stacked directly on a concrete floor or kept in a moist place. Cement intended for the construction of water tanks must be fresh and stacked on timbers. Cement which has clumps should be rejected; it does not help to break up the clumps, as the strength of the cement will have been lost. To prevent cement from clumping during long storage, the cement bags should be turned upside down once a week. The application of cement could be much improved if the producers would print 'users' instructions' for builders on their bags of cement, just as some lime manufacturers do – and almost everybody else producing manufactured goods.

Aggregate   Crushed stones, also known as aggregate or ballast, are used for making concrete. The crushed stones should measure between 8 and 32mm, have a rough surface for good bonding and be extremely hard. Porous, soft or easily weathered stones should not be used as they will produce concrete of low quality. As with sand, the crushed stones must be free of lumps of silt, soil and organic materials.

Water   Some textbooks advocate that water mixed with cement should be of a quality comparable with drinking-water. While this may be ideal it is often not compatible with the realities in rural Africa and elsewhere in the developing world where women carry drinking-water from distant water sources. Practice has shown that dirty water can be used for mixing and curing cement with hardly any negative effects. However, saline and brackish water (containing salt) cannot be used for reinforced concrete and ferrocement. If the water tastes salty it is probably too saline.

Reinforcement   For most of the tanks described in this text, the reinforcement is provided by weld-mesh (gauge 8), BRC (No. 65), galvanized 3mm wire, barbed wire (gauge 12.5), twisted 12mm iron bars, and chicken mesh (25mm). Some of the designs described elsewhere require the use of steel reinforcement rods with diameters ranging from 6mm to 20mm (Hasse, 1989; Morgan, 1990). While these undoubtedly increase the strength of the tank, they will also increase the cost significantly. Furthermore, they need to be properly interlocked to stop them sliding in the concrete, and their use requires careful supervision. A summary of the reinforcement requirements and concrete mixtures for the tanks described in this chapter is given in Table 5.2.

Whitewash In tropical and hot arid climates, water tanks should be whitewashed to make external surfaces more reflective and reduce the effect of solar heating. High temperature build-up in the structure during the day, followed by cooling at night will cause structural tensions, due to expansion and contraction, especially in empty water tanks. In addition, correctly mixed whitewash seals minute cracks in plaster, and whitewashed water tanks look much more attractive. A good weather-resistant and sealing whitewash has been found to consist of one part of cement mixed with 10 parts of hydrated (powdered) lime. A cheap whitewash, excellent for outdoor use can be made from:

> 52kg clean white lime;
> 7kg salt dissolved in hot water;
> 4kg rice pounded and boiled to a thick paste; and
> 0.7kg glue.

These should be 'well mixed and brought to required consistency by addition of hot water, then allowed to simmer over a fire for a few hours; then strained and put on hot' (Longland, 1936).

Site preparation and transportation of materials
The construction site should be cleared of all vegetation, loose soil and rocks. If possible, tanks should be located away from big trees, or the trees cut down. All the materials and tools required should be transported to the site before construction starts. Lorries for transporting soil, sand, cement and other building materials are expensive and vulnerable to breakdowns on bad roads in rural areas. Tractors with trailers are much stronger and versatile. Although they are slow, tractors tend to suffer fewer breakdowns than lorries. In very poor rural communities where tractors may be too expensive, or not easy to hire, ox-carts or donkey-carts can be used. Bicycles and wheelbarrows are also useful for local transportation of materials.

In situations where other convenient water sources are absent, it should not be forgotten that considerable quantities of water are needed for construction and curing, and this may need to be transported to the site at added expense. When completed, tanks should be filled with at least some water to aid the curing process. In arid environments during the dry season, rainfall cannot be relied upon to fill the tank so additional water may also need to be transported for curing purposes.

Construction techniques

Mixing mortar and concrete

When constructing water tanks it is essential to adhere to a few basic yet critical rules with respect to correct mixtures and applications of concrete and mortar. These include:

- mixing cement, aggregate and water properly, and not adding too much water
- applying the mortar or concrete within a maximum of half an hour of mixing
- curing cement work properly by keeping it moist and under shade for at least three weeks after its application.

By neglecting these rules, the strength and waterproof properties of the concrete and mortar are much reduced. For example, if the curing process is stopped after seven days, the cement will have only about 50 per cent of its potential compressive strength (Box 5.1).

The amount of water used has to be judged carefully and should be kept to a minimum. The mortar should never be so wet that it spreads out like porridge, but rather have the consistency of mashed potatoes. The mortar must be moist, not wet – water should never be visible in the mixture and it should not look shiny.

A common problem is that, for some unknown reason, builders like to apply water to cement/sand mixtures before the two components are properly mixed. This bad habit results in:

- extra work for the builders because they still have to turn over the cement and sand which becomes heavier when wet
- poor mixing of cement and sand, leading to further mixing after being handed to a plasterer – giving extra work
- weaker concrete and mortar, because cement starts losing its strength half an hour after it has been mixed with water
- more extra work to keep the mortar and concrete moist and in the shade because it has been mixed too early.

Clearly, it is important that water should not be added to cement until everything is ready for the mortar and concrete to be applied. Unfortunately, many builders neglect all these considerations; they mix enough mortar in the morning to last throughout the whole day, often leaving the mortar exposed to sunshine. When the mortar sets after a couple of hours, more water is added, thereby making the mortar weaker. When the mortar has hardened in the afternoon, it is hacked into pieces and water added again so that it can be beaten into a paste. Given such practices it is perhaps not surprising that many water tanks leak, even when builders claim 'we applied a very thick layer of mortar'!

The usual, but incorrect, way of mixing (batching) mortar and concrete is to work on the assumption that a wheel-barrow has the same volume as a bag of cement. Since wheelbarrows typically have a volume about one-third bigger than a bag of cement, this method results in making a weaker mixture than required. To obtain the correct mixture, a gauge box should be used for measuring the ratio of sand and crushed stones. The good news for builders is that gauge boxes also make handy seats and tables during tea-breaks. A gauge box is required for each of the two recommended cement to sand ratios for building water tanks, namely 1:3 and 1:4 (see Box 5.2), as the ratios are based on volume of material, not weight. The correct procedures for mixing mortar and concrete are shown in Box 5.3 and Box 5.4, respectively.

Application of concrete
Concrete is used for constructing the base slab and flat roofs for water tanks. The concrete, 1:3:4 (cement:sand:aggregate) is not mixed until the foundation, the draw-off pipe and the reinforcement mesh are complete. If hardcore (rubble stones) is backfilled in the excavation to provide a foundation in areas with unconsolidated soils, care should be taken to ensure that the stones will not press into the tank floor when it is loaded with many tons of water. Care should also be taken not to allow any water on to the soil in the excavation before placing the concrete, as contact with wet mud would damage the concrete. Compact the concrete and reinforcement together well in order to get air bubbles out of the concrete. Any air and water left in the concrete will create voids (when the water evaporates), making the concrete weak and porous.

Use of lime
Adding a small amount of lime to the cement mortar has a number of advantages. It makes the mortar more workable and the final plaster more waterproof, as any micro-cracks are filled through a self-sealing process. For plaster, a ratio of one part cement, one-third part lime and five parts sand is appropriate. For mortaring bricks a ratio of one part cement, one-third part lime and four parts sand is better. Using lime also helps to strengthen the bond between bricks and blocks in brick tanks. In some places, lime is cheaper than cement and can help to reduce overall costs.

Waterproof cement
Magical powers seem to be attached to waterproof cement by some builders, who are sometimes careless when building water tanks because 'the waterproof cement will seal everything'. The fact is that waterproof cement dries too quickly in hot and dry climates, thereby making fine cracks in the sealing coat of water tanks. A better and cheaper solution to waterproofing is a material called Nil which is made by mixing cement with water to form a thin paste (cement slurry). Nil is applied to the final layer of plaster with a square steel trowel on the same day as the plaster is applied.

Construction of cement water jars
The construction of wire-reinforced cement jars deserves a specific mention due to the phenomenal success of the Thai jar programme in which many

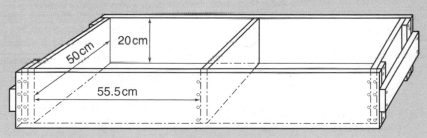
millions of 1m³ to 2m³ rainwater tanks, known locally as water jars, were constructed (Plate 5.1). Details of the programme are discussed in the Thailand case-study in Chapter 9 but it is appropriate here to outline briefly the construction methods used. With such a large programme, a variety of approaches to building the jars evolved. Volumes ranged from less than 0.25m³ to more than 5m³, the vast majority of the tanks had capacities of 1m³ to 2m³

Box 5.3

Mixing mortar

(1) Make a mixing platform of bricks, flat iron sheets or timber. If this is not possible, make a hard area and remove loose soil, grass and roots.

(2) Place the gauge box, 1:3 or 1:4 depending on the required mixture, on the platform. Fill the box to the rim with sand.

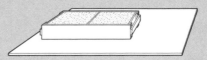

(3) Lift up the gauge box, which is easy because it has no bottom. Pour a bag of cement on to the sand.

(4) For the first time, turn the heap of sand and cement into another heap on the platform – without water.

(5) For the second time, turn the heap back to its original position, again without water.

(6) For the third time, turn the heap back to its other position, without water.

(7) For the fourth time, turn the heap back to its other position, without water.

These turnings will have given the mixture a uniform grey colour which is the sign of proper mixing. The time has now come to add water – but, please note – only to that part of the mixture which will be used within half an hour. Do not add more water than is absolutely necessary to make the mortar workable, because the lower the water content, the higher its strength. The remaining part of the mixture must stay dry, and under cover to avoid wind blowing the cement away, until it is mixed with water just before the mixture is to be applied.

Box 5.4

Mixing concrete

The first part of the procedure for mixing concrete is identical to mixing mortar. However, since a larger volume may be required, several boxes of aggregate and bags of cement may be necessary. Again, avoid mixing more concrete than can be used up within half an hour, otherwise the strength of the concrete will deteriorate.

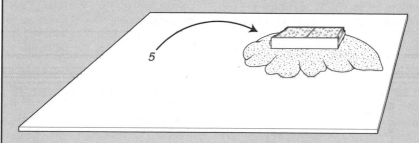

(8) For 1:3:4 Concrete (continuing from the mixing mortar described in Box 5.3, steps 1-7).
Level the flat heap of mixed sand and cement.
Place the 1:4 gauge box on the heap and fill the box with the required volume of crushed stones.

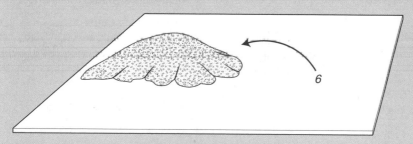

(9) Now pour water on the crushed stones lying over the sand/cement mixture, while simultaneously turning over all three components: sand/cement, crushed stones and water, to make concrete.

Do not add more water than is absolutely necessary to make the concrete workable, because the lower the water content of the concrete, the higher its strength.

Table 5.2 Recommended mortar/concrete mix, thickness and reinforcement

Tank components	Reinforcement	Mortar/concrete* mixture and thickness	Finishing coat
Foundation	BRC mesh No 65 or weld-mesh gauge 8	1:3:4 13cm	1:3 + Nil 2cm
Wall of ferrocement	BRC mesh 65 or weld-mesh gauge 8. Chicken mesh. G.I. wire 3mm	1:3 6cm	Interior: Nil Exterior: 10 lime to 1 cement
Wall of burnt bricks and soil-compressed blocks	Spiral of barbed wire gauge 12.5 wrapped around the wall and spaced 5cm at lower half and 10cm at upper half	1:5:1/3 lime for mortar joints and internal and external 2cm-thick plaster	Interior: Nil Exterior: 10 lime to 1 cement
Wall of blocks (concrete, rubble stones)	Spiral of barbed wire gauge 12.5 wrapped around the wall and spaced 5cm at lower half and 10cm at upper half	1:4 for mortar joints and internal and external 2cm-thick plaster	Interior: Nil Exterior: 10 lime to 1 cement
Wall of concrete *in situ*	Spiral of barbed wire spaced 10cm in concrete	10cm-thick wall 1:3:4 Joints 1:4 2cm internal plaster 1:3	Interior: Nil Exterior: 10 lime to 1 cement
Flat roof of concrete tank	Weld-mesh gauge 8	1:3:3 10cm-thick roof slab	Exterior: 10 lime to 1 cement.
Dome roof of ferrocement tank	BRC No. 65 with Chicken mesh or Weld-mesh No. 8 without Chicken mesh	1:3 5cm thick	Exterior: 10 lime to 1 cement

* Mortar and concrete mixture ratios for cement: sand:aggregate or lime

to 2m³ and were built along similar lines. In every case, one of three types of formwork (mould) was used:

- stuffed hessian sack
- clay-plastered brick mould
- bamboo mats attached to a steel frame.

Each method has its own advantages and drawbacks. The use of the hessian sack (or gunny bag) is in many ways the simplest and seemingly the most convenient approach. While sand is the most common material used to fill the sack, other materials can be used such as sawdust, rice husks, grass or even dried cow dung. While the use of a sack mould is very effective for smaller jars up to 1m³, it becomes harder to maintain the necessary shape and rigidity when used for larger jars.

The brick mould is made from about 90 bricks constructed in the shape of the jar, using mud both as a temporary mortar between the bricks and plaster to give a smooth external shape to the formwork. Light wire can be used to hold each layer of bricks in place before applying the external mud plaster.

The use of a frame made from 9mm-steel rods (or wood) and covered with bamboo or straw mats is the quickest formwork to erect. The framework consists of several sections which can be quickly assembled and dismantled. Although the framework-mould system is the most expensive, in common with the other form-works, multiple reuse makes them all very cost-effective. Whichever type of formwork is chosen, the construction procedure uses a 1:3 cement: river sand mortar follows more or less the same sequence (Figure 5.1):

1. A circular, 1m-diameter 4–6cm-thick base plate is poured into a circular metal ring mould on a sheet of strong paper in two layers; between these layers, eight 1.4m lengths of 1mm-steel wire are arranged like the spokes of a wheel, each overlapping the base by 20cm on each side.
2. When the base has hardened after 24 hours, the mould is placed on the base and a temporary mud 'mortar' made from mixing non-organic soil with water is applied to give the mould a smooth finish and facilitate its removal once the mortar has set.
3. A cement slurry (Nil) is carefully applied around the base–wall joint.
4. Two concentric metal ring moulds for the lip of the jar opening (internal diameter 65cm, 8cm high, and 5cm thick) are placed on strong paper on the top of the formwork.
5. A 1cm layer of mortar (1:3) is then applied evenly, starting with the top of the tank; then continuing with the lower half from the base upwards.
6. Sixteen, vertical 1mm reinforcing wires are then attached to the wire ends protruding from the base and attached to a wire ring placed around the opening. A 1mm wire is then wrapped around the jar in a single spiral containing about 20 loops, each about 8cm apart (Plate 5.1).
7. The tap should then be placed in the wall about 10cm above the base and the second 1cm-thick layer of mortar (1:2¾) applied.
8. Next, the jar lip should be completed and, when the mortar has set, the ring moulds removed. The inner mould can be used to cast a cement cover in which a hole should be left for the downpipe.
9. Finally, a red-coloured slurry which can be mixed with cement is applied and, once dry, the tank is covered with polythene and cured for at least two weeks.

Due to its efficient shape and very thin walls, the material requirements for the jar are surprisingly small. Three bags of cement (50kg each), ¼m³ of sand, 1.5kg of wire, 0.3kg powdered colour, one tap and short PVC pipe, and a steel lid or lid handle for a cement cover. It is the low labour and material costs for the jar, along with simple and affordable payment mechanisms, which accounted for the enormous popularity of this design in Thailand.

117

Figure 5.1 Constructing a 2m³ wire-reinforced cement Thai water jar

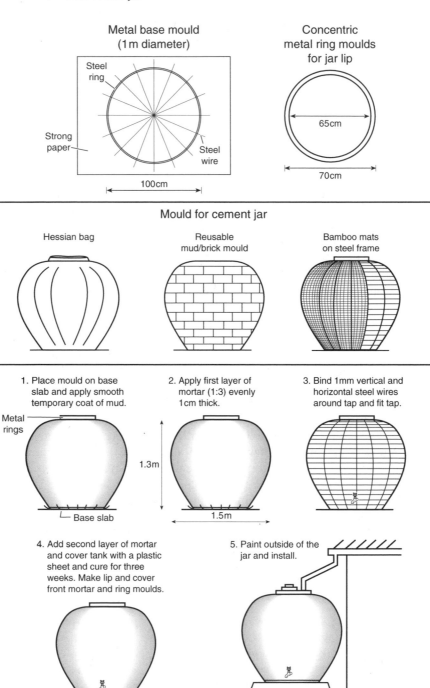

Metal base mould
(1m diameter)

Steel ring

Strong paper

Steel wire

100cm

Concentric metal ring moulds for jar lip

65cm

70cm

Mould for cement jar

Hessian bag

Reusable mud/brick mould

Bamboo mats on steel frame

1. Place mould on base slab and apply smooth temporary coat of mud.

Metal rings

Base slab

1.3m

2. Apply first layer of mortar (1:3) evenly 1cm thick.

1.5m

3. Bind 1mm vertical and horizontal steel wires around tap and fit tap.

4. Add second layer of mortar and cover tank with a plastic sheet and cure for three weeks. Make lip and cover front mortar and ring moulds.

5. Paint outside of the jar and install.

It should be noted that constructing jars with such thin (2cm) walls takes considerable skill and experience, something many Thai builders have certainly acquired during the construction of 10 million jars since the early 1980s. Even in Thailand, however, some observers have reported that levels of workmanship vary considerably (Latham, 1984). The construction procedure for a larger 3m³ water jar modified to suit African conditions and with a thicker wall is described in Appendix 5. The fact that this design has been adopted both outside Thailand, and now with modifications outside Asia, is a testament to its success (Plate 5.2).

Construction of above-ground rainwater storage tanks
There is no formal definition or distinction between a rainwater tank and jar. In fact, a rainwater jar is a type of tank. To avoid any confusion in this chapter, however, jars are considered as rainwater storage reservoirs with capacities of less than 4m³, even though a few larger jars have been constructed. Tanks are considered to be storage reservoirs with capacities of 4m³ or more. In Appendix 5, step-by-step construction procedures for the following tanks, along with drawings and bills of quantity, are given: Ferrocement Jar (3m³), Concrete-in-situ Tank (5m³), Burnt Brick Tank (10m³), Ferrocement Surface (11m³), Ferrocement Surface (23m³), Ferrocement Surface (46m³) and the Hemispherical Sub-Surface Tank (90m³). Some general points regarding the construction of the main components of rainwater tanks with volumes ranging from 4m³ to 90m³ are discussed below.

Foundation and floor A solid foundation is essential as this carries the weight of the tank and its water. A suitable site therefore must not contain any ant-hills, old latrines, waste pits or tree stumps. The site must also be at least 10m from trees to avoid their roots seeking under the tank for moisture and thereby breaking up the foundation.

The circular site for a water tank is drawn on the ground; the radius should be 15cm longer than the external radius of the tank. There should be a distance of 90cm between the tank and the house from where rainwater will be harvested. If the distance is less than 90cm there will not be enough space to build the tank; and if the distance is longer, extra support for the down-gutters will be required. The marked site is excavated to a depth of 15cm, or until solid soil is reached, and made level using a spirit level on a straight edge. Weld-mesh No.8 or BRC mesh for ferrocement tanks are tied together with overlaps of 20cm and cut into a circular shape having a radius 5cm shorter than the excavation. This is to ensure that the mesh will not come into contact with soil once it is concreted into the foundation. The mesh can be cut using a hacksaw or a chisel.

The draw-off pipe is made of a 90cm length of 18mm (3/4") galvanized-iron pipe with threads at both ends. A socket is screwed on to the outer end and an elbow and PVC nipple fitted to the inner end of the pipe. When the draw-off pipe and reinforcement are made ready, and there is time to complete concreting the foundation in one day, concrete with a ratio of 1:3:4 can be mixed.

Failure to concrete a foundation within one day produces a weak foundation which may leak or even crack. Concrete is mixed as explained in Box 5.4 and compacted on to the dry soil in the excavation in a 7cm-thick layer. Water should *not* be poured on the soil before laying out the concrete because mud may enter the concrete and weaken it. Lay the reinforcement and draw-off pipe on the concrete. The outer end of the pipe should protrude 30cm from the concrete and the nipple at the inner end should be blocked with paper to avoid concrete blocking it. The second 6cm layer of concrete 1:3:4 is then compacted on to the reinforcement and the underlying concrete. The final surface of the concrete must be roughed to make a good bond to the 2cm plaster that will be applied to it when the walls have been completed. The foundation must be kept moist and covered with plastic sacks or polythene to ensure good curing for obtaining maximum strength.

Tank walls The tank walls should be cylindrical in shape as these are stronger and better at taking the loads exerted by the water pressure than rectangular walls, and they are also preferable since they provide a more economical design. The reinforcement of ferrocement-tank walls is tied to the reinforcement of the floor before the foundation is concreted, while for other types of tanks the reinforcement of the wall and floor is not connected.

For the designs described in this book, the wall height does not exceed 2m, as beyond this limit the higher water pressure may cause the tanks to crack or even fail, unless additional reinforcement is used. The height of the successful concrete ring mould *in situ* design widely used in Machakos, Kenya sometimes exceeds 2m, but this is compensated for through additional reinforcement.

Brick and block tanks When building walls of bricks and blocks for water tanks, it is important that both horizontal and vertical joints are filled with mortar 1:4, otherwise water will seep through the wall and make moist spots on the outside of a tank. To ensure that the vertical joints between bricks and blocks are placed on the middle of the underlying block or brick for obtaining maximum strength, lay out a circle of bricks or blocks on the foundation without mortar, with such spacing that no brick or block is cut to fit into the circle.

Immediately thereafter, waterproof joints are made by dipping each brick or block in water just before it is laid upon the mortar. Each brick or block is pushed forwards and backwards until it settles into the mortar. Simultaneously, the brick or block is kept at its correct level and place. The common trick of putting a small stone under a low corner of a block is almost certain to lead to a leakage in a brick or block water tank.

Bricks and blocks in walls should be sprinkled with water just before plastering for bonding. There is a tendency when applying plaster to the wall to try to apply one thick layer which then falls off in patches and is repaired by throwing dry cement on to the patch. This is another certain way to cause leaks in water tanks. The right way to apply plaster is to throw a thin coat of mortar 1:3 on to the inner wall and then a thin coat of 1:4 on the outer wall while the first coat settles, and so on until the required thickness of plaster has been reached. The surface of each coat of plaster, except the final one, is made rough to make sure there is good bonding between coats.

For simplicity and maximum strength, walls built of burnt bricks, or blocks made from compressed sandy soil and cement, rubble stones, concrete or lava are reinforced after they have been built to their final height. The reinforcement consists of a spiral of barbed wire, gauge 12.5, which is wrapped tightly around a tank and nailed on to it to keep the wire in position (Plate 5.3). The barbed wire is first wrapped around the base of a tank three times, thereafter the wire continues rising in a spiral spaced 5cm until the middle of the tank is reached. From there the spacing is 10cm between the wraps of barbed wire until the top of the tank. The reason for having a closer spacing at the lower half of a tank is due to the water pressure being highest there. After the wire is in place, the tank should be plastered inside and outside. It is also possible to incorporate the barbed-wire reinforcement within the wall between each layer of bricks or blocks. While somewhat more complicated and reducing the strength, it does mean that external plastering can be avoided although the joints must be sealed with pointing.

Plaster on the walls of water tanks must not be allowed to dry or be exposed to sunshine for the first three weeks, otherwise the plaster will turn whitish and the process of hardening and waterproofing will stop. The hardening process cannot be revived, no matter how much water is applied to the wall. The process of keeping the mortar wet is called curing. This is done by covering the walls with polythene sheeting or plastic sacks, which must be properly secured against the walls using sisal strings (Plate 5.4). Water is poured between the wall and the sacks or polythene morning and evening for three weeks. The external wall can be made weather-proof with two coats made of 1 part cement to 10 parts lime.

Ferrocement tanks   Reinforcing walls built of ferrocement is different from the procedure for brick or block tanks described above, because the main reinforcement of a wall, a cylinder of BRC mesh No. 65, is concreted into the foundation. The basic stages of the construction of an 11m³ surface tank are shown in Figure 5.2. The same basic stages apply for larger, common 23m³ and 46m³ versions of the same tank. The BRC cylinder is kept exactly vertical by wires attached to pegs hammered into the ground. Thereafter, chicken mesh, 2.5cm × 90cm, is wrapped tightly around the BRC cylinder and tied to it by twisting the chicken mesh on to the BRC with an end of bent wire. Do not use binding wire for tying the chicken mesh to the BRC, because the ends of the tiny wires may stick through the plastering and create leaks. Now wrap a 3mm galvanized wire (G.I.) tightly around the base of the BRC cylinder four times; thereafter, continue upwards in a spiral with a spacing of 5cm on the lower half of the tank and 10cm on the upper half of the tank. Upon reaching the top horizontal wire in the BRC mesh, wrap the G.I. wire six times along it and tie it with binding wire. This is the ring beam for making the dome self-supporting. Although the dome is truly self-supporting if constructed as described above, experience has shown that poor workmanship will create

Plate 5.3 *The addition of barbed wire reinforcement to a rubble-stone tank being constructed in Kilowezi, Kenya.* (Photo: Erik Nissen-Petersen)

Plate 5.4 *A 23m³ ferrocement tank covered with a polythene sheet while being cured at a primary school in Kanye, Botswana in 1995.* (Photo: John Gould)

Figure 5.2 Stages of construction for 11m³ ferrocement water tank

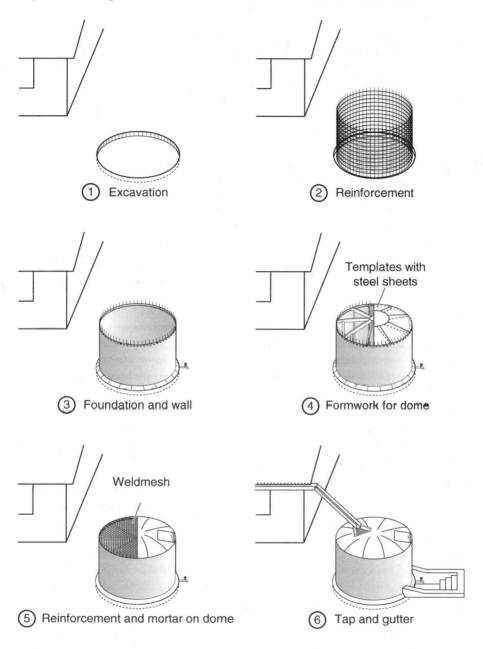

① Excavation

② Reinforcement

③ Foundation and wall

④ Formwork for dome

Templates with steel sheets

Weldmesh

⑤ Reinforcement and mortar on dome

⑥ Tap and gutter

leakage along the joint between dome and wall, thus rendering the dome unsuitable for water storage. It is wise, therefore, to support the dome with a central pillar which can also function as a permanent ladder in the tank. The pillar is easily and cheaply made of a PVC pipe, as described earlier. For a detailed step-by-step description of the construction of 11m³, 23m³ and 46m³ surface ferrocement tanks, refer to Appendix 5.

Concrete in situ *tanks*   Concrete (1:3:4) is cast into concentric corrugated-iron ring moulds and reinforced with spiral turns of barbed wire (gauge 12.5) not more than 10cm apart. The concrete is left to set and next day the mould is removed from the first ring and installed on top of it, and the process repeated. When the wall is completed, its interior side is plastered with mortar 1:3 plus Nil, while the outside is whitewashed with one part cement to 10 parts lime. Several thousand tanks of this type have been successfully constructed in the Machakos district of Kenya, where standard designs for tanks with capacities of 4m³, 5.4m³ and 13.5m³ have been used (de Vrees, 1987). Design drawings and a step-by-step description of the construction procedure for a similar tank with capacity of 5m³ can be found in Appendix 5.

Tank roof or cover

The roofs of water tanks play a crucial role with respect to both the quantity and quality of the stored water. The tank roof has two vital functions. First, it prevents evaporative losses which, in dry tropical regions, can account for very substantial water losses. Second, it reduces the risk of contamination by preventing insects, reptiles and birds entering the tank, or allowing algal growth which would render the water unsuitable for drinking. Large tank roofs, if specially designed, can even provide additional catchment area in their own right, such as in locations where water is very scarce and the main catchment area is limited. They can also provide additional storage capacity as in the case of the ferrocement dome described below. Various roofing options are available, including flat roofs built of reinforced concrete and domes constructed of ferrocement. Materials for the two types of roofing cost about the same amount. The advantage of a dome is that it can be used for storing water, thereby reducing the size and cost of its tank. The advantage of a flat roof is that it requires less skill to construct.

During the last 20 years there have been several attempts to simplify the construction and reduce the cost of tank roofs. In the 1970s, many tanks in East and Southern Africa were roofed with corrugated-iron sheets nailed on to timber coated with wood preservative. Unfortunately, the timbers gradually became rotten due to moisture evaporating from the stored water and many roofs caved in after about five years. A similar fate was suffered by ground tanks covered by using conical sisal pole frames. In the early 1980s, domes were built by tying trapezoid sheets of BRC mesh together and sewing plastic bags to the underside of the mesh. Thereafter, the mesh was placed on the tank and mortar pushed lightly on to the mesh without any compacting. The plastic bags prevented mortar from falling into the tank. After curing the dome for a few days, the plastic bags were removed and the underside of the dome was plastered from within the tank. This is a difficult task since mortar falls into the eyes of the builder and it is very hot and humid inside the tank. Many builders found this difficult and did not cover the internal reinforcement adequately with mortar, risking moisture corroding the exposed reinforcement and domes cracking or collapsing. A cone-shaped roof was promoted as a viable compromise between a flat roof and a dome in the mid-1980s, and some people are still using this design. The cone is built of mortar reinforced with chicken mesh over a formwork of Sisal poles which allowed for proper compaction of mortar against the formwork. Unfortunately, after some years these cones tend to crack and collapse due to uneven stress distribution.

Ferrocement dome roof   Finally, in the late 1980s, a proper dome roof was developed and constructed by compacting mortar against reinforcement on a solid and reusable formwork (Figure 5.6, and Plates in Appendix 5). The formwork is made of metal sheets from old oil drums or scrap car bonnets supported by a timber structure. These timber props, 8 or 12 of which are required depending on the size of the tank, are supported in the centre of the tank by a 10cm-diameter concrete-reinforced PVC pillar (or kingpost). The resulting framework of equidistant timber props radiate from the centre to the tank's rim like the spokes of a wheel. These timber props, which can be made on site or preferably in a workshop beforehand can, along with the formwork metal sheets, be reused many times. The curved shape of the timber props is dictated by the radius of the domes, and details for the tanks described is shown in Appendix 5.

Several thousand of these domes have been built successfully during the last decade without any technical problems. The domes are made of a 5cm-thick layer of mortar 1:3. Reinforcement of domes may consist either of BRC mesh covered with chicken mesh or sheets of weld-mesh without chicken mesh (Appendix 5), the latter being the cheapest method and, therefore, recommended. The mesh is cut into trapezoidal sheets which fit over the formwork of the dome. The sheets are then tied together with binding wire and a place cut for the manhole. Mortar is compacted on to the reinforcement and formwork while the mesh is being lifted and shaken to get a good bond between the mesh and the mortar.

The curing of a dome is done by covering it with large sheets of polythene laid on the dome just after completion of plastering. The polythene sheet is covered with soil to prevent wind from blowing it off. Water evaporating from the voids in the mortar will condense on the underside of the polythene and drip on to the mortar, thereby keeping it moist and under cover without adding any water. One should not walk on a dome until it has been cured for one week to avoid cracking the mortar. The formwork for the dome can be removed after seven days of curing, but the central pillar remains. The joints between the floor, wall and dome or roof, are made watertight for all types of water tank by pressing mortar 1:3 into the internal joints using a large bottle to make round and watertight corners (Figure 5.9c), while the external joint between the foundation and wall is sealed by a 5cm-high and 15cm-wide triangular apron made of 1:3 mortar.

Although dome roofs are self-supporting due to the ring beam around their base, poor workmanship can result in fine cracks along the base of domes allowing leakage and preventing water storage under the dome. By placing a pillar in the middle of a water tank to support its dome, pressure on the ring beam can be reduced. Using a pillar has the following advantages:

- It supports the formwork for building a dome, thus eliminating the need for a temporary centre-post to support the formwork.
- It supports a dome, thereby preventing cracks along the ring beam of a dome, thus making the dome suitable for storage of water.
- It can provide access if steps for a ladder are incorporated.

The simplest way to make a pillar-cum-ladder is to use a 10cm-diameter PVC pipe. This should be filled with concrete (1:3:3) with a length of 12mm twisted iron bar as reinforcement. The pillar can be made to function as a ladder by inserting short lengths of G.I. pipes into the PVC pillar before it is filled with concrete. Holes for the steps are burnt in the PVC pipe by heating one end of a G.I. pipe over a fire. Caution should be exercised at this point as toxic fumes will be produced. The manhole should be placed near to the pillar to assist access.

Flat reinforced-concrete roof Flat roofs on water tanks of reinforced concrete are made in a similar way to the foundations, i.e. by casting two layers of concrete (each 5cm thick) with BRC or weldmesh reinforcement in between them. A flat timber formwork is used made from 15cm × 2.5cm (6" × 1") planks supported by wooden props. It is also important to cure the concrete properly for a minimum of three weeks. The formwork may be removed after 10 days of curing. The roof is not plastered as the second layer of concrete should be smoothed to give a good finish, but it should be coated, along with the walls, with 1:10 cement/lime whitewash.

Since flat roofs, unlike domes, are not self-supporting, it is necessary to support the roof with pillars. For tanks with diameters up to 3m, a single central pillar should suffice. Roofs on larger tanks of 20m³ or more will also require reinforced-concrete beams for support. As a rule of thumb, beams should have a height of 15cm, a width of 10cm and be spaced a maximum of 1.2m apart. Beams are made of concrete (1:3:3) and reinforced with four lengths of 12mm twisted iron bars. Pillars can be spaced up to a maximum of 2m apart under the beams, Figure 5.8.

Construction of sub-surface rainwater storage tanks
Tanks built partially or totally beneath the surface can be made by making a hemispherical (bowl-shaped) excavation in consolidated soil (Figure 5.3, Plate 5.5). A reinforced-concrete ring beam is constructed around the rim of the excavation, on top of which a wall can be constructed of stones or blocks to raise the edge of the tank 60cm above the surface (Figure 5.3, Plate 5.6). The ring beam should be reinforced by wrapping eight rounds of barbed wire around it. Two layers of plaster of 1:3 mortar are next applied on successive days. The first layer is 1cm thick and is applied straight on to the excavated soil surface and kept moist. The second layer, 2cm thick, is applied on to the

126

first coat the following day and kept moist while barbed wire is nailed to the plaster in a spiral starting from the centre of the tank with each loop spaced 20cm apart (Plate 5.6). A second set of barbed wire is nailed from the rim down over the wall and across the centre of the tank (like spokes of a wheel). The wire is spaced 30cm at the top of the rim and protruding 30cm so that it can later be tied to the weldmesh in the dome.

Chicken mesh is then nailed over the reinforcement of the barbed wire in the tank and covered with a 3cm plaster of mortar 1:3 with Nil. A ferrocement dome should then be constructed as outlined above, and is described in detail for a 90m³ sub-surface tank in Appendix 5 and shown in Figure 5.3.

There are a variety of other ways of building sub-surface rainwater tanks, and the technique used will vary depending on local soil conditions. Where soils are unconsolidated (loose and sandy) a more expensive plastered-brick construction may be best, such as that developed for conditions in the Kalahari desert in Botswana (Figure 5.4a). Another design developed in Botswana under the ALDEP scheme, and used for tanks with volumes ranging from 2 to 30m³, simply involves laying a concrete base in an excavation, lining it with chicken wire and applying three layers of mortar (Figure 5.4b). A corrugated-iron or ferrocement dome cover should be added to complete the construction.

In central China, on the loess plateau, different kinds of excavated water tank have been developed. Here, traditional bottle-shaped clay-lined water cellars (*shuijiao*) with volumes of up to 30m³ have been in use for more than a thousand years (Zhu and Liu, 1998). Recently, many of these have been upgraded by being lined with cement mortar. Others have been replaced or complemented with a range of new 15–20m³ designs, including a cylindrical concrete-lined cistern and the concrete shell design illustrated in Figure 5.5. In this design, the loess soil is first excavated to the level of the concrete tank cover, which is then cast *in situ*. The soil beneath is then excavated and removed through the opening, and the base constructed and, finally, the walls plastered.

Tap station The dimensions of the tap station will vary with different tank designs. In the case of sub-surface tanks where water is to be withdrawn by gravity from an excavated tap station, the depth of the tank and level of the draw-off pipe will dictate the depth of excavation needed for the tap station. For surface tanks, the main consideration is that there must be ample room underneath the tap for a large bucket. Normally 50cm would be the minimum gap, and so the excavation needs to be at least 60cm deep to give space for a 10cm concrete slab. Assuming a 15cm brick wall by the tap, a minimum floor width of 85cm and three steps 20cm wide by 20cm high, the excavation for the tap station must be at least 1.7m long and 1m wide.

Construction tools and survey instruments
A list of all the essential tools for tank construction is given in Appendix 5. Tools such as collapsible ladders, sand sieves, gauge boxes and formwork for domes and flat roofs can all be made on site provided the skills, tools and materials are available (Figure 5.9a and Box 5.2).

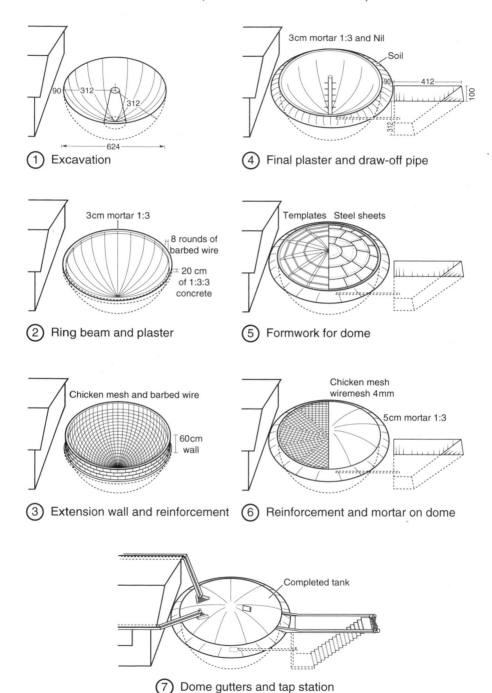

Figure 5.3 Stages of construction for 90m³ hemispherical sub-surface ferrocement tank (Note: dimensions are in cm)

① Excavation

② Ring beam and plaster

③ Extension wall and reinforcement

④ Final plaster and draw-off pipe

⑤ Formwork for dome

⑥ Reinforcement and mortar on dome

⑦ Dome gutters and tap station

Plate 5.5 *Women excavating a tap station for a 90m³ sub-surface barbed-wire-reinforced ferrocement tank in eastern Kenya.* (Photo: Erik Nissen-Petersen)

Plate 5.6 *Reinforcement of a 90m³ sub-surface ferrocement tank using barbed wire in eastern Kenya.* (Photo: Erik Nissen-Petersen)

Figure 5.4 Brickdome and ferrocement sub-surface tank designs from Botswana. (Source: Gould, 1985)

(a) Brickdome design

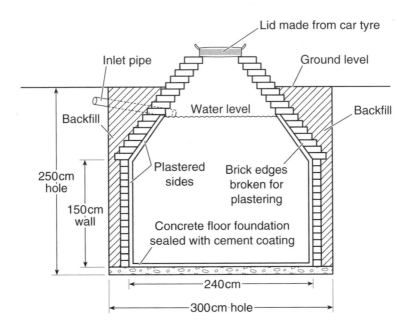

(b) Ferrocement design

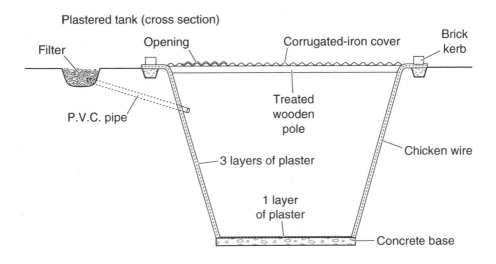

Figure 5.5 Sub-surface rainwater tank designs from Gansu Province, China (Source: Yuan and Benjing, 1997)

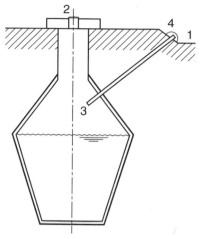

(a) Cement-lined cellar

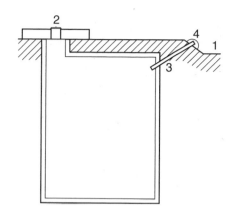

(b) Thin cement shell

1. Sedimentation chamber

2. Cover

3. Inflow pipe

4. Coarse inlet filter

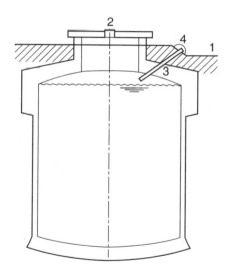

(c) Concrete shell

Conventional instruments for surveying and setting out corners and heights for water structures, such as theodolites, are expensive to buy and difficult to borrow, especially in the rural regions of poorer countries. However, such instruments and equipment are not essential for small-scale projects and it is often possible to improvise very successfully. Instead of using a theodolite,

Figure 5.6 Two domes being built of ferrocement on solid and reusable formwork made of timber and metal sheets reclaimed from old oildrums or scrap car bonnets.

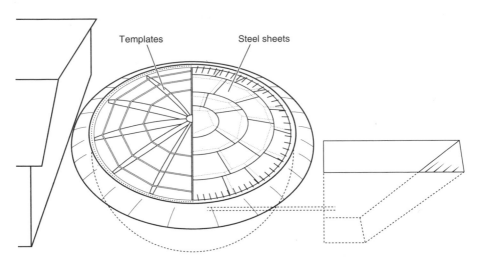

A 90m³ ferrocement sub-surface tank.

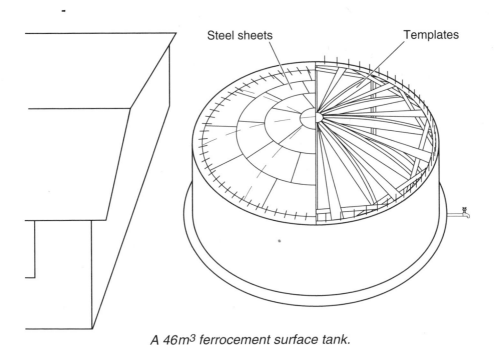

A 46m³ ferrocement surface tank.

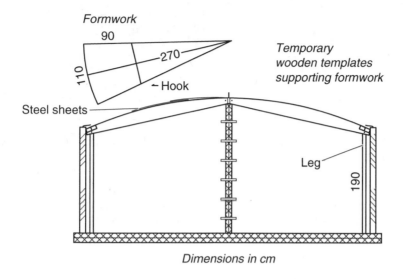

Figure 5.7 The centre pillar provides support to formwork and dome, as well as acting as a ladder allowing access to 46m³ ferrocement tank

Formwork

90

270

110

Hook

Temporary
wooden templates
supporting formwork

Steel sheets

Leg

190

Dimensions in cm

Figure 5.8 Pillars and beams — built of concrete — for flat roofs

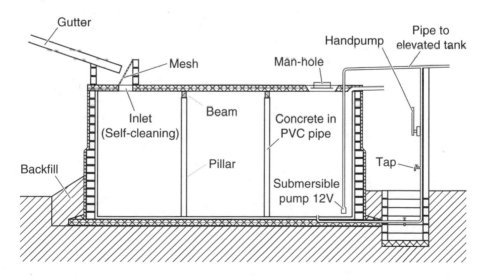

Gutter

Pipe to
elevated tank

Handpump

Mesh

Man-hole

Inlet
(Self-cleaning)

Beam

Concrete in
PVC pipe

Backfill

Pillar

Tap

Submersible
pump 12V

use 30 metres of any thickness of transparent hosepipe. The hosepipe can be used for transferring exact levels between two or more points at intervals of the length of the pipe by holding up both ends of the hosepipe and filling it with water. The water levels at each end of the pipe will be exactly horizontal (Figure 5.9b).

*Figure 5.9***(a)** Collapsible ladder and sand sieve

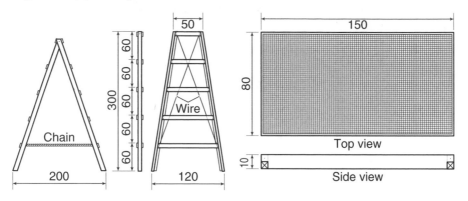

*Figure 5.9***(b)** A hosepipe filled with water for measuring horizontal levels. A circular hosepipe for measuring horizontal level, contour lines and gradients

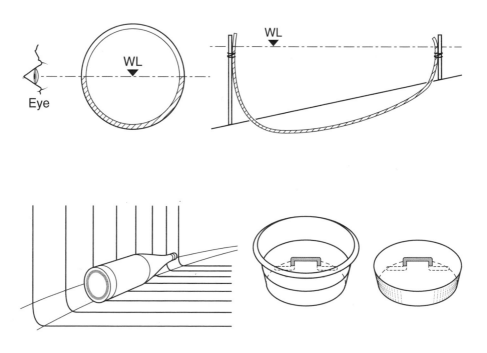

*Figure 5.9***(c)** Examples of simple improvisations. Using a glass bottle to smooth a tank's wall–base joint and using a wash-basin as a man-hole cover mould

Where a gradient of 1cm for every 100cm length is required for gutters gradients, the procedure is as follows:

Tie the hosepipe to the corner of the roof near the tank and the other end of the hosepipe to the corner of the roof farthest from the tank. Fill the hosepipe with water until the water level reaches the edge of the roof at the corner farthest from the tank. Measure the length of the roof in metres, say 25m. Now measure 25cm down from the water level near the tank and draw a builder's line from this point to the water level in the far end of the hosepipe. The line will slope 25cm over 25m, which is 1cm gradient per 100cm.

A similar, but simpler, levelling instrument can be made by bending a transparent hosepipe, about 100cm long, into a circle and half filling it with water. Lift the circular hosepipe to eye level so that the two water levels are at exactly the same height. By looking ahead of the two water levels, a horizontal line is projected far ahead, perhaps to the other side of a valley. This simple instrument is very useful for laying out contour lines and can also be used for measuring gradients, Figure 5.9b.

Ingenuity is essential when constructing systems in remote developing regions, and simple ideas can help to save significant costs. Two further examples of such improvisations are illustrated in Figure 5.9c: the use of a glass bottle for smoothing the final plaster along the wall–base joint, helping to ensure it is watertight; and using an old plastic wash-basin as a mould for the manhole cover.

Tank repair
While the need to repair tanks can be reduced by careful selection and testing of materials, good workmanship and regular maintenance, eventually all tanks may need to be repaired.

The possibilities for repairing leaking tanks depend on several factors, including:

● being able to locate the point of leakage
● the type of tank
● the size of the leak
● whether the leak is above or below the level of water still in the tank.

Although locating a leak may sound like a trivial problem, in sub-surface tanks this can often be the main obstacle preventing remedial action. Usually, locating leaks in the walls of surface tanks is straightforward – unless these are in the tank floor. Repairing ferrocement tanks is relatively easy and is described in detail by Hasse (1989) Nissen-Petersen (1992d) and in Appendix 6. These methods involves chiselling out the damaged area around the leak, wetting the whole area thoroughly to make it moist, and applying new mortar (with the same cement:sand ratio as the original). A coat of Nil can be applied the next day and the patch covered with plastic sheeting and cured for at least three weeks.

Some types of tank, such as plastic and metal tanks, are much harder to repair. One approach that can be adopted is to try to find an appropriate watertight plastic or rubber liner if the prospects of a successful repair seem slight. A common technique used in parts of Africa for rejuvenating corrugated-iron tanks is to line them with cement or ferrocement.

In most tanks, small leaks are generally much easier to repair than large ones. Hasse describes two ways to seal small leaks in ferrocement tanks even while they still contain water. The first method involves the use of rapid-setting cement. This requires chiselling out the hole, which should be enlarged until it is at least 10mm across. The wire reinforcement should be visible and, ideally, the enlarged hole should be in the shape of a swallowtail. The rapid setting cement should be added to water in a tin, stirred with a stick and then moulded in the hand until it has a plastic consistency. Provided the material is not out-dated it will become warm in the hand and then harden rapidly. Before this occurs a piece of the appropriate size should be forced into the hole with a thumb. A small piece of timber (slightly smaller than the hole) and a small hammer should be quickly used to press the plug firmly into the hole before the cement sets. Two people and fast work are normally required for this procedure. It is worth doing a test first and being thoroughly prepared. The second method requires the application of sodium silicate to the leak after first sanding down the wall around the leak. Sodium silicate is a clear viscous liquid which hardens on contact with air. This can be applied to a leak, provided water is not gushing out under pressure. While these techniques often succeed for small leaks, even if they fail they will not jeopardize more serious attempts to rectify the problem.

Construction and position of gutters and gutter brackets

The proper construction of gutters is crucial. All gutters and downpipes should direct water towards the tank and not go to waste. Preferably, gutters should slope towards the tank and down-pipe entrance with a slope of not less than 1 in 100 (1cm per metre) and ideally 1 in 50 (2cm per metre). The gutter must be placed 3cm inwards from the edge of the roof to catch the back-drop of water from light showers. The gutter brackets must be strong enough to ensure they do not bend due to the weight of water and pressure of wind. The distance between brackets should not normally exceed 100cm for square and triangular gutters made of gauge 26 or thicker iron sheet. It is important to remember that, when full of water, a 14 × 14cm V-shaped gutter will have an extra load of nearly 10kg/m, so securing the gutter properly is absolutely essential.

It sounds rather simple, but experience shows that the correct installation of gutters causes frustration for many builders. Problems encountered include:

- Gutters or down-pipes blocked with debris when their gradient toward a water tank is so low, or is so uneven, that it allows debris to settle, thus creating a blockage.
- The gradient of gutter slopes away from the tank, thereby letting gravity pull the water to the wrong end of the gutter.

- Gutters are not fixed right underneath the eave of a roof, which allows water to 'over-shoot' or 'under-cut' the gutter.
- The distance between gutters and the eaves of roofs is made so deep in order to gain a sufficient gradient on the gutter that water 'over-shoots' the gutter.
- Normal semi-round gutters tend to flatten after some time, thereby allowing spillage.
- Gutters or down-pipes become disconnected.

These problems are easy to overcome on small roofs, but the difficulties increase with larger roofs at schools and public institutions. Rural African schools with uneven roofs and no fascia-boards were, in the past, nightmares for builders until a new type of gutter was developed in 1985 – the V-shaped gutter with splash-guard (Box 5.5, Nissen-Petersen, 1992c). In addition to the technical advantages described below, the V-shaped gutter and its splash-guard also raises the runoff co-efficient significantly. To date, more than 150 000m of the V-shaped gutter with splash-guard have been installed in eight African countries.

The V-shaped gutter and its splash-guard can be installed on roofs using only a tin snip, pliers, hammer, a builder's line, a transparent hose and a collapsible ladder, while making the gutters requires a 2m-long U-shaped iron bar and a mallet made from a piece of timber. The gutter is bent into its V-shape with three corners of 90 degrees to gain maximum strength and water transporting capacity. It can be made and fitted completely without soldering. The even gradient of 1cm per 100cm gives the runoff water such a high velocity towards its tank that it prevents overflow due to blockage by debris, which is flushed out. The gutter can also function as a down-pipe, by continuing from the roof straight into the inlet of a water tank. This increases velocity and helps to prevent blockages.

The gutter-hanger is made by bending 2mm G.I. wire around a few nails along the profile of a gutter, thus costing less than gutter brackets. The hangers keep the V-shaped gutter in the correct position below the eave and suspends the gutter with adjustable wires to the splash-guard, which facilitates an even gradient, no matter how uneven a roof might be. For a detailed step-by-step description of the construction process, along with a bill of quantities, the reader should refer to the photo manual by Nissen-Petersen (1992c).

While the use of hanging gutters with splash-guards is particularly appropriate for use on long uneven roofs at schools and institutions, especially if facia boards are absent, several other types of gutter and construction method are available which are appropriate for small household systems. Examples of some of these are shown in Box 5.6.

Summary and key points

- To ensure that tanks are durable, good-quality, clean, construction materials which meet required specifications must be used.

Box 5.5

V-shaped gutters and splash-guards
Standard design (Nissen-Petersen 1992c)

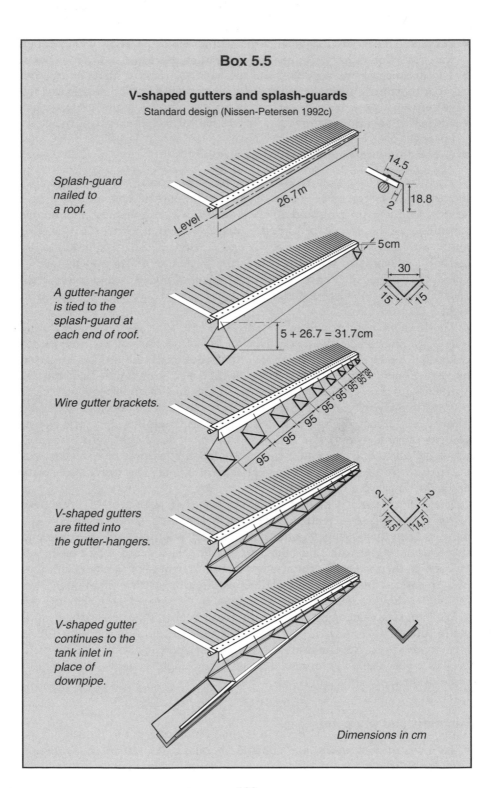

Splash-guard nailed to a roof.

A gutter-hanger is tied to the splash-guard at each end of roof.

Wire gutter brackets.

V-shaped gutters are fitted into the gutter-hangers.

V-shaped gutter continues to the tank inlet in place of downpipe.

Dimensions in cm

Box 5.6

Examples of different gutter systems

Gutter attached to facia board

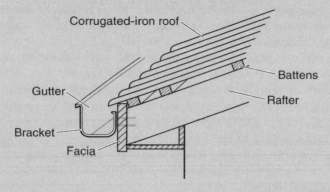

Corrugated-iron roof

Battens

Gutter

Rafter

Bracket

Facia

Thatched roof with gutters attached to overhanging eaves

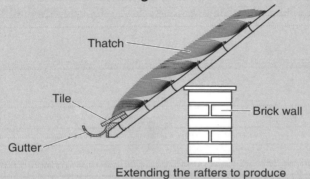

Thatch

Tile

Brick wall

Gutter

Extending the rafters to produce
an overhanging eave

Gutter attached on board fixed to wooden wall post
(Pacey and Cullis, 1986)

Wooden rafter

Gutter made
from boards
120mm wide
× 20mm thick

Wooden wall post

- Proper mixing of mortar and concrete is essential for good water tank construction. Poor selection of materials, poor mixing and poor workmanship are common causes of problems in completed water tanks.
- Construction of the 2m^3 wire-reinforced cement 'Thai Jar' can be achieved using any of three types of formwork; a hessian sack, a clay brick mould or a steel frame with bamboo mats.
- A solid foundation is essential for surface rainwater tanks and this can also double up as the tank floor. A 13cm reinforced-concrete slab cast in two layers on the same day is normally sufficient.
- Tank walls can be constructed in several ways, including using bricks, blocks or concrete poured *in situ*, and ferrocement.
- The failure of tank roofs made of corrugated iron supported by treated timber led to the development of the ferrocement dome, constructed using a metal-sheet formwork supported by a wooden frame.
- Proper construction of gutters is essential and these must slope evenly towards the tank. For long roofs, hanging V-shaped gutters with splash-guards are useful for reducing any loss due to runoff over-shooting or under-cutting gutters.
- For a detailed step-by-step description of six surface tanks ranging from 3m^3 to 46m^3, and a 90m^3 ferrocement sub-surface tank, see Appendix 5.

6

Rainwater quality issues

Rainwater quality

THE QUALITY OF rainwater used for domestic supply is of vital importance because, in most cases, it is used untreated for drinking. The issue of water quality is a complex and sometimes controversial one, mainly because rainwater does not always meet WHO drinking-water standards (the definitive global water-quality standard) especially with respect to bacteriological water quality. The same, however, is also true for many improved rural water sources in much of the developing world (Morgan, 1990, p77 and p253). Only where water is being provided to larger settlements is systematic treatment and water-quality monitoring common, and even here water-quality standards vary considerably. For most smaller and remoter settlements, especially in developing countries, treatment is both impractical and often unrealistically expensive. For such settlements across the world, the emphasis remains on providing and maintaining any sort of improved water source as hundreds of millions still remain unserved.

It should be borne in mind that just because water quality does not meet some arbitrary national or international standard, it does not automatically mean the water is harmful to drink. In the 1980s, drinking-water-quality guidelines more appropriate for rural conditions in developing countries were proposed and widely adopted (Lloyd, 1982; Ockwell, 1986; Morgan, 1990). These less strict guidelines allowed water with mean *E.coli* counts of up to 10 per 100ml to be accepted for drinking. This compares to the WHO recommended limit of 0 per 100ml (WHO, 1993). When the quality of stored rainwater samples are judged according to this less rigid but more realistic criterion, the number of rainwater supplies with water acceptable for drinking is greatly increased.

Compared with most unprotected traditional water sources, drinking rainwater from well-maintained roof catchments usually represents a considerable improvement, even if it is untreated, and normally it is quite safe to drink. In answer to the question 'Is rainwater safe to drink?' the official policy of the Australian government (National Environmental Health Forum) can be summarized by the following statement from Cunliffe (1998):

> Providing the rainwater is clear, has little taste or smell, and is from a well-maintained system, it is probably safe and unlikely to cause any illness for most users.

Only for immunocompromised people, such as the very young, very old, cancer patients, diabetics, organ transplantees or HIV-positive individuals is disinfection through boiling recommended before consumption.

The quality of water in ground catchment tanks, however, is generally low due to contamination of the catchment area by children and animals and is not recommended for drinking unless it is first boiled or filtered (Gould and McPherson, 1987). The water extracted directly from ground tanks is, however, suitable for most non-consumption purposes without treatment.

People who are used to drinking water with small amounts of bacteriological contamination tend to build up a resistance to this and generally suffer no ill effects (Riddle and Speedy, 1984). A visitor who is used to drinking only pure or treated water may, however, suffer from diarrhoea (gastroenteritis) or even dysentery when drinking the same water. Although a bout of diarrhoea may not be a pleasant experience, for healthy adults it is not normally a serious condition. In small children, however, severe diarrhoea, if untreated, can be life-threatening and kills millions of under-5s every year, particularly in Africa and South Asia. For this reason alone, water-quality considerations have to be taken very seriously. Nevertheless, targets need to be realistic and achievable, and an incremental approach to improving water quality is often the most appropriate. It is generally better to make small improvements even if these do not result in official standards being met immediately because, when water quality improves, health benefits are likely to result, especially if hygiene-education programmes are run in tandem.

Morgan (1990), in his useful text *Rural Water Supplies and Sanitation* based on experience from Zimbabwe, provides the following sound advice regarding an appropriate approach to addressing the issue of water quality:

> At the present time, the most practical approach to the problem of improving and maintaining the quality of water delivered in rural water-supply schemes is not to impose a set standard, but to insist on adequate measures of sanitary protection which significantly improve the quality of water, compared with traditional sources that might have been taken otherwise.

This principle should be applied to all domestic rainwater catchment systems, especially in developing countries, where systematic monitoring and treatment of rural water sources is seldom possible.

Ultimately, the goal everywhere should be to ensure that rainwater supplies are safe and meet the highest possible standards. A number of recent studies show that, even in several developed countries, such as the USA, Canada and Australia, they are far from reaching this situation (Waller, 1984; Lye, 1992a,b; Crabtree et al., 1996; Cunliffe, 1998). Perhaps it may be appropriate in a few countries where general water-supply-quality standards are already very high to extend these to rainwater supplies, at least where systems are for communal use. For most countries, however, it would be inappropriate and, in some cases, may actually be counter-productive to do so. The danger of imposing standards is that in the absence of better alternatives, millions of water sources worldwide could potentially be condemned because they do not meet WHO or some other standard, depriving millions of people of their best existing water sources.

The reality in much of the developing world today is such that even where water supplies meet WHO standards at source, they are normally contaminated during collection and transportation to the household (Falken-mark, 1982). The water may be further contaminated in the home through transfer to another storage container, or even contamination from the drinking vessel (Wirojanagud et al., 1989). While this secondary contamination problem should never be used as an argument for not trying to achieve the highest possible water quality at source, it does put the issue of water-quality standards into context, and highlights the crucial importance of hygiene education.

Sources of rainwater contamination

Rainwater is generally a very pure form of water, having resulted from the process of distillation (evaporation and condensation). Nevertheless, cloud droplets do react with other atmospheric constituents such as carbon dioxide and naturally occurring oxides of sulphur and nitrogen. This results in natural rainwater being slightly acidic, normally in the range of pH5 to pH6, with the most commonly accepted value being pH5.6. Natural releases of sulphur dioxide into the atmosphere during volcanic activity, such as the eruption of Mount Pinotubo in the Philippines in 1991, can lead to local increases in rainfall acidity. This effect has also been noted in Hawaii, as has the influence of the ocean leading to elevated chloride and sulphate content in rainwater (Dugan et al., 1984). Despite these influences, human activity rather than natural processes are by far the main cause of atmospheric rainwater contamination.

Numerous man-made atmospheric pollutants exist, of which the most prevalent and damaging to rainwater quality are sulphur dioxide (SO_2), nitrogen oxides (NO and NO_2) and various hydrocarbons, which together are the principal causes of anthropogenic acid rain (Pickering and Owen, 1994). The combined effect of these result in rainwater in the most industrialized regions of the world, such as Northern Europe and the eastern United States being in the range pH4 to pH5, with values sometimes falling to pH3 or less for short periods. Acid rain is also becoming an increasing problem in several other rapidly industrializing regions of the world, most notably in parts of Brazil, India, China and South-east Asia. These areas are all primarily dependent on coal-based economies which, along with their already large populations, are growing rapidly. Given these trends and the rising expectations in these regions, it seems likely that rainwater quality, along with many other environmental-quality indicators, will continue to decline for some time to come.

In most industrialized urban areas, the atmosphere has often been polluted to such a degree that the rainwater itself is unsafe to drink (Thomas and Greene, 1993). In the US drinking rainwater within 48km of urban centres is not recommended (Grove, 1993). Heavy metals such as lead are potential hazards, especially in areas of high traffic density or in the vicinity of smelters (Yaziz et al., 1989; Thomas and Greene, 1993). Organic chemicals such as organochlorines and organophosphates used in biocides can also contaminate rainwater. Although serious atmospheric

143

contamination of rainwater is normally limited to urban and industrial locations, studies in the north-eastern United States revealing the presence of pesticides and herbicides in rainwater do give some cause for concern (Richards et al., 1987).

Atmospheric pollutants can be transported very great distances before being washed out in the rain. Evidence of this was graphically revealed during the Chernobyl disaster in 1986 when radioactive isotopes, such as caesium-137, were carried over 2000km to Wales, northern England and eastern Sweden, before being washed out by rainwater and causing serious long-term contamination of soil and vegetation. Although, in the medium term, prospects for improved atmospheric and rainwater quality in heavily industrialized regions appear bleak, in theory, with sufficient emphasis and resources invested in pollution-control measures, it should be possible to improve both air and rainwater quality everywhere. Through the processes of precipitation, which wash out pollutants, the atmosphere is actually self-cleaning and once pollution sources are removed, air quality rapidly improves.

Despite the numerous examples of atmospheric pollution cited above, in much of the world, and especially in rural and island locations, the levels of contamination of natural rainfall are low. The main source of contamination of rainwater normally occurs after contact with the catchment surface (roof or ground) and during subsequent delivery and storage.

Chemical quality of stored rainwater
Several studies examining the chemical constituents of stored rainwater have found that it generally meets WHO, EPA or similar drinking-water-quality standards for a broad range of parameters, with only a few exceptions (Scott and Waller, 1987; Wirojanagud et al., 1989; Michaelides, 1989). These included slightly elevated levels of zinc and manganese exceeding guideline levels in only a few cases but, in any case, not posing a significant health risk. Some concerns regarding rainwater acidity do not relate to any direct threat posed by low pH values but are due to the indirect effects of this more 'aggressive water'. When pH is depressed, rainwater becomes more aggressive in leaching out metals and other constituents from storage tanks, taps, fittings and sludge deposits on the tank floor. In Hawaii, these are sources of lead and other metals found in storage tanks as a result of acidic rain resulting from volcanic gaseous releases (Fujioka, 1998 – personal communication). Evidence from Ohio, in an area with serious atmospheric pollution and acidic rainfall, suggested that elevated lead and cadmium levels in cistern sediment and water posed a potentially serious health risk (Sharpe and Young, 1982). Investigations in Halifax, Nova Scotia also revealed high lead concentrations in runoff water collected from an old roof with considerable amounts of lead flashing from rainwater with pH4 (Waller and Inman, 1982). Evidence of the potential health dangers of excessive lead levels in stored rainwater comes from a study in Port Pirie, an industrial port in South Australia and the location of one of the world's biggest smelters (Body, 1986). This study

revealed a correlation between blood lead levels in children under seven, and lead in tank waters, one source of which, it was suggested, may have been highly leaded roof paint. The effect of acidic (pH3) water and leaf litter in the tank was also shown to increase the rate of dissolution of lead from tank sludges by up to 50 times.

There has been considerable debate regarding the influence of cement and ferrocement tanks on water quality, especially when they are new. Although elevated pH (alkalinity) and high calcium content of tank waters have been observed in new concrete tanks (Thurman, 1993), these have not been at levels hazardous to health. In some cases they have even compensated for acidic rainfall, making tank waters less aggressive and corrosive to metal fittings (Sharpe and Young, 1982). In a major survey of ferrocement jars in north-east Thailand, some villagers complained of a cement taste (Hewison and Tunyavanich, 1990). It has sometimes been suggested that cement tanks should not be used until they have been thoroughly cured (Michaelides and Young, 1984), although how practical this might be in reality will vary greatly depending on local circumstances.

Clearly, in certain circumstances such as in areas of severe air pollution or where lead-flashing, lead-based paints or other potentially toxic building materials have been used, chemical contamination of rainwater can pose a health threat. Under normal circumstances, however, serious chemical contamination of rainwater is rare. Nevertheless, extra vigilance may be advisable with respect to very old roof catchment systems, which may have been constructed at times when building codes and regulations relating to the use of lead-based paints, lead fittings and other hazardous materials were far more lax than today.

Bacteriological quality of stored rainwater
Faecal bacteriological contamination of rainwater is not inevitable, and a number of studies have revealed that properly constructed roof catchments with well-maintained tanks can yield high-quality water. In most cases, this water is safe, potable and usually meets or almost meets strict international drinking-water standards (Waller and Inman, 1982; Gould and McPherson, 1987). This is especially true when measures such as tank cleaning and the use of foul-flush diverters are undertaken (Yaziz et al., 1989; Michaelides, 1986, 1989). Several other detailed investigations in the 1980s nevertheless raised some concerns when they revealed that in many instances stored rainwater does not meet WHO, EPA or other similar standards with respect to one or more bacteriological water-quality indicators (Fujioka and Chinn, 1987; Haebler and Waller, 1987; Krishna, 1989). While these findings do not in themselves imply the water is unsafe to drink, they did prompt further investigations which focused on determining both the sources and implications of any contamination, as well as examining possible measures to protect rainwater sources.

In north-east Thailand, where several million people use household rainwater jars, a major study of rainwater quality was conducted by Wirojanagud et al. (1989) to examine the extent, route and cause of bacteriological, pathogenic and heavy metal contamination. Samples from roofs and gutters showed faecal coliform to faecal streptococci ratios of less than 1 (FC:FS <1) suggesting that the contamination was of non-human origin (animals and birds). In the same study, bacteriological analyses of water from 189 rainwater tanks and jars revealed that only around 40 per cent met WHO drinking-water standards. Water samples from 100 in-house storage containers in the same households revealed that almost 90 per cent failed to meet the standard. Almost half had high FC:FS ratios >4, implying that serious, secondary faecal contamination of both animal and human origin was occurring. Poor general levels of hygiene and sanitation were also observed. This, along with the fact that a third of villagers reported they did not wash their hands after using the latrine or before preparing food, was clearly a contributory factor to contamination. Nevertheless, harmful pathogens were detected in none of the jars and in only 2 (0.6 per cent) of the rainwater tanks. Those found included *Salmonella group C* and *Aeromonas hydrophila*, associated with diarrhoeal diseases in humans. The more regular cleaning of the ferrocement jars may have accounted for the absence of pathogens and lower counts of indicator bacteria. Despite these findings, the study still concluded that, potentially, rainwater is the safest and most economical source of drinking-water in the region. This was because, in general, contamination was only slight compared with traditional sources and had no major health implications. Improvements in the hygienic collection and handling of the rainwater, sanitary practices and the use of disinfection techniques where necessary were recommended to improve the situation.

Investigations in Hawaii have indicated that the source of the high levels of total coliform, faecal coliform and faecal streptococci found in stored rainwater samples may be wind-blown soil particles and that they are not indicative of serious contamination of human faecal origin (Fujioka et al., 1991). When a sample of coliform-free water was poured on to a roof and the runoff collected and tested, high levels of total coliform, faecal coliform and faecal streptococci were found, even though no obvious evidence of contamination was visible on the roof. On the basis of these findings, it has been proposed that *E. coli* or faecal coliform should be used as indicator bacteria for stored rainwater since, unlike total coliform and faecal streptococci, *E. coli* specifically highlights human faecal contamination. A drinking-water standard for cistern water of 10 faecal coliforms/100ml was suggested as appropriate, as this would encourage treatment and mitigation rather than encouraging rainwater sources to be abandoned altogether.

Rainwater-quality standards
In 1993, bacteriological water-quality standards for potable rainwater were formally proposed by Dr J. Hari Krishna, following a technical meeting with Dr Roger Fujioka and Dr Denis Lye at the US Virgin Islands, Water Resources Research Institute (Krishna, 1993). It was recommended that standards should be achievable and less stringent in tropical regions and developing countries. Faecal coliforms were proposed as the most appropriate indicator

of cistern water quality and the following three-tier classification was suggested as a useful guide to cistern water quality originating from rooftop runoff:

Class I   0   : faecal coliforms/100ml
Class II   1–10   : faecal coliforms/100ml
Class III   > 10   : faecal coliforms/100ml

In this classification, Class I represents the highest and ideal water quality, Class II represents water of marginal quality, and Class III represents water unacceptable for drinking purposes.

Rainwater quality and health
Proving direct links of causation between water quality and health can be notoriously difficult, especially when contamination levels are low. There are many references to pathogens including *Salmonella, Clostridium, Cryptosporidium, Giardia, Legionella-like spp.* and *Campylobacter* having been isolated from rainwater samples (Chareonsook et al., 1986; Lye, 1992b; Fujioka et al., 1991; Wirojanagud, 1989; Crabtree et al., 1996; Cunliffe, 1998). Papers citing proven links to disease outbreaks, however, are rare. One of the best documented cases records an outbreak of gastrointestinal illness including diarrhoea, headaches, fever and vomiting among 48 adults and children from a group of 88 (73 of whom were children) at a rural camp in Trinidad, West Indies (Koplan et al., 1978). The probable cause of the outbreak was postulated as *Salmonella arechevalata* contained in animal or bird excrement on the camp roof and washed into the rainwater tank, water from which was used for drinking. When tested, however, only one out of 128 faecal samples from birds, reptiles, small mammals and amphibians yielded a positive test for salmonella – that from toad faeces. Despite the limited direct evidence of the presence of salmonella pathogens, (none was actually isolated from the tank) the roof supplying the tank was overhung by branches harbouring large numbers of birds. The roof was covered in both fresh and dried faeces and the link between bird and animal excrement and salmonella is well-established. In his conclusions, Koplan noted that the lack of previous reports linking disease outbreaks to roof-collected water may be in part because most systems serve individual households, where similar incidents are less likely to be reported and drawn to the attention of the authorities.

While very serious, it should be realized that both the above salmonellosis outbreak in Trinidad, and the correlation between high levels of lead in children's blood and rainwater-tank waters reported from Port Pirie, are isolated and rare incidents. They do, nevertheless, provide an important warning regarding the potential hazards associated with drinking rainwater from poorly maintained or suspect sources.

It has been postulated that another possible cause of adverse health conditions associated with the exclusive use of rainwater may result from its low mineral content (Neri et al., 1984). Although there is some debate over whether or not all mineral requirements can be met from dietary sources alone, Neri argues that minerals in drinking-water may make a significant contribution. Neri reports that Russian studies have shown that drinking only distilled or weakly mineralized, desalinated water may result in adverse health conditions, such as increased urinary excretion. The possibility of similar effects from prolonged exclusive consumption of rainwater deserve further investigation.

The link between rainwater storage and mosquitoes has also been extensively researched; a clear link exists between the presence of mosquito larvae and rainwater-storage containers (Kolsky, 1997). Where containers are open or lack secure covers or screens, they are far more vulnerable to infestation. While in some parts of the world, mosquitoes represent only a public nuisance, there is particular concern in tropical areas where they are vectors of serious diseases such as malaria, yellow fever, dengue fever and filariasis. Several approaches to mosquito control, outlined in detail in Box 6.1, have been tried with some success. These include the addition of small amounts (5ml per 1000 litres) of domestic kerosene, and various forms of biological control such as using fish and dragonfly larvae to consume mosquito larvae (Corbet, 1986; Campbell, 1993). Although insecticides such as DDT are sometimes sprayed on open water breeding sites, these should *never* be applied to rainwater stored for consumption.

Protecting water quality

Good design, operation and maintenance
The best initial step to protecting water quality is to ensure good system design and proper operation and maintenance. As Cunliffe (1998) aptly puts it, 'collection of rainwater involves *low* maintenance, *not no* maintenance'. Apart from occasional tank cleaning and keeping the gutters clear. In some situations sludge may build up on the tank floor and if re-suspended particles can contaminate the water. Sludge, while normally not a problem, can harbour micro-organisms and accumulations of lead in some circumstances. It is possible to remove sludge without removing all the water in the tank by using an inverted funnel and a simple syphoning technique.

In rural areas, particularly in developing countries, rainwater is generally clean and pure before reaching the ground. It is also in these areas that rainwater from roof catchments is most commonly used for drinking. Common sources of rainwater contamination result from: dirt and faeces (mainly from birds and small animals) on the roof surface, leaf debris and organic material being washed into the tank, and animals, insects and birds drowning in the water. Field observations and bacteriological examination of roof-tank samples in Botswana have shown a clear link between high faecal coliform and faecal streptococci counts, and excessive pigeon excrement on roof catchments. The best way to protect the water quality, therefore, is to minimize these and other sources of potential contamination, especially from heavy metals.

Box 6.1
Mosquito breeding and control

The three main groups of mosquitoes and their associated diseases are *Aedes* associated with dengue and yellow fever, *Anopheles* with malaria and *Culex* with filariasis and extreme nuisance. Larvae from members of all three groups may be found in tanks containing stored rainwater, especially in tropical regions. It is the *Aedes* group, and particularly *Aedes aegypti*, the vector responsible for transmission of dengue and yellow fever, which is most commonly found in water storage containers, both large and small, in and around the house. While evidence suggests that covering containers can significantly reduce the prevalence of mosquito larvae in the water, it is difficult to prevent the problem completely.

In a survey of 150 households in three villages in Khon Kaen Province, Thailand, *Aedes* mosquito larvae were present in all of them. They were found in 95 per cent of small, indoor, clay storage containers, in 32 per cent of all rainwater jars and 4 per cent of rainwater tanks (Chareonsook et al., 1985). Hewison and Tunyavanich (1990) reported that villagers complained of increased mosquito infestation in north-east Thailand following the widespread introduction of ferrocement water jars. While this may have been due to the increased availability and presence of water in the village, it also seemed to be much worse where containers were not covered. To reduce the problem significantly it was recommended that all containers, large and small, and both inside and outside the house, must be covered and screened with some form of mesh. In Queensland, Australia, a survey of 1349 premises revealed that rainwater tanks provided important breeding sites for immature *Aedes aegypti* mosquito larvae (Tun-Lin et al., 1995). A study conducted in two villages in south-east Nigeria, where all households use rainwater stored in earthenware pots around the house, revealed the widespread presence of *Aedes aegypti* mosquito larvae. In this case, the vector was associated with the transmission of yellow fever, and between 53 and 76 containers per 100 households were found to be infested during the wet season (Bang et al., 1981).

Various approaches to mosquito control can be used. The addition of small amounts of domestic kerosene (5ml per 1000 litres) works well, but can give the water an unpleasant taste and may not be suitable for tanks lined with plastic. [Note: Commercial or industrial kerosene should *not* be used]. Various forms of biological control, such as keeping fish and dragonfly larvae in the tanks to consume mosquito larvae, have also been tried with some success (Skinner, 1990; Corbet, 1986). While biological control may be a useful and effective tool at specific locations over limited time periods, the best guarantee against preventing mosquitoes from laying eggs in rainwater jars, tanks or other water storage containers is to make sure they are inaccessible. To exclude mosquitoes, containers must be tightly covered and any openings properly screened with fine nylon or metallic mesh. Nevertheless, regular inspection is also essential to alert users to potential problems and should prompt immediate action when necessary. Leaving rainwater tanks, jars and in-house water storage containers unscreened or uncovered in areas where malaria, dengue or yellow fever are endemic is to court danger.

It has been clearly demonstrated that, if careful measures are taken, roof catchment tanks can provide rainwater clean enough to drink (Michaelides, 1986, 1989, Figure 6.2). To achieve this, certain design features must be incorporated and other criteria met. These include:

- A clean impervious roof made from non-toxic material is essential. Lead roofs should be avoided, as should any covered with lead-based paint.
- The roof surface should be smooth and any moss, lichen or other vegetation removed, including branches from over-hanging trees, since these provide sanctuary for birds and access for rodents and other animals to the catchment surface, where defecation could contaminate the rainwater runoff.
- Taps or draw-off pipes on roof tanks should be at least 5cm above the tank floor (more, if debris accumulation rates are high); this allows any debris entering the tank to settle on the bottom where, provided it remains undisturbed, it should not adversely affect water quality. Alternatively, if available and affordable, a floating filter outlet can be used (Figure 9.9c).
- A coarse filter and/or foul-flush device should intercept water before it enters the tank, to remove dirt and debris (See Figure 6.1).
- Wire or nylon mesh should cover all inlets to prevent any insects, frogs, toads, snakes, small mammals or birds entering the tank.
- If birds persist in perching on the catchment, bird scaring and other physical measures (or the services of a cat) may be required.
- The tank must be covered and all light must be excluded to prevent the growth of algae and micro-organisms.
- Tanks, gutters, screens and all system components should be inspected and cleaned annually, if possible. A tank floor sloping towards a sump and washout pipe can greatly aid tank cleaning. A well-fitting manhole to allow access is essential. (See Figure 6.2).
- Water should not, if possible, be consumed directly from the tank without treatment for the first few days following major rainfall.
- Water from other sources should not be mixed with that in the tank.

Immediately following heavy rainfall, the quality of water in the tank may be lowered due to any debris washed into the tank or stirred up from the bottom, which may take some time to settle out. It is appropriate, therefore, to avoid drinking water directly from the tank for a few days. Contrary to popular myth, however, rather than becoming stale with extended storage, rainwater quality usually improves. This is because bacteria and pathogens gradually die off during the first several days of storage (Watt, 1978; Michaelides, 1986, 1989; Skinner, 1990). For this process to occur, however, it is essential that both light and organic matter are excluded from the tank. Any light getting into the tank will allow algal growth, and organic matter will provide nutrients enabling bacteria and other micro-organisms to survive. In such situations, the stored water may become stale and unpalatable. Measures to exclude both light and organic debris (leaves, moss, etc.) such as covers and screens will

Figure 6.1 Examples of different types of first flush and foul flush diverter

(a) Automatic foul-flush system, Togo, 1987
(Source: Lee and Visscher,1990)

(b) Simple pivot system, Kenya
(Source: Omwenga,1984)

(c) Movable downpipe system
(Source: Waterlines, 1984 Vol 3(1))

(d) Foul-flush device used widely in Thailand
(Source: Latham,1984a)

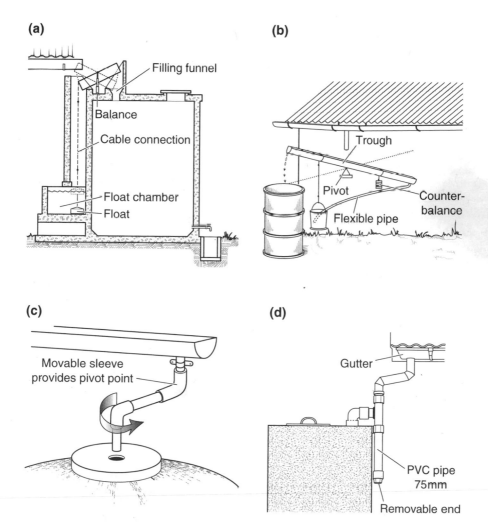

Figure 6.2 Idealized tank design incorporating water-quality-protection measures

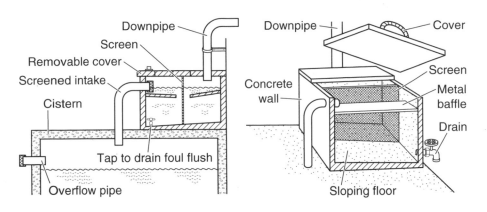

Two views of foul-flush diverter box
(Source: World Bank, 1982)

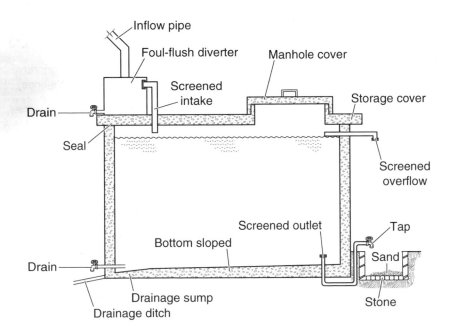

Design incorporating water-quality-protection measures
(Source: Adapted from Michaelides, 1984)

also help to keep small mammals, reptiles, frogs, birds and insects out of the tank. Even with the best efforts, some matter and small organisms will get into tanks from time to time, so regular inspections and occasional cleaning and maintenance are essential. If all reasonable measures are taken, however, the water quality should not deteriorate, and because the stored water is normally cool, clear and sweet, it is often preferred to other sources.

Foul-flush and filter systems

Although not absolutely essential for the provision of potable water in most circumstances, when effectively operated and maintained, foul-flush and filter systems can significantly improve the quality of roof runoff. If poorly operated and maintained, however, such systems may result in the loss of rainwater runoff through unnecessary diversion or overflow, and even the contamination of the supply. In poor communities, where the provision of even a basic roof tank represents a substantial upgrading of the water supply, the addition of a relatively elaborate foul-flush mechanism to the catchment system would add unnecessary expense and complication to the system and could even risk jeopardizing its effective use. In some locations, where roof surfaces are subjected to a significant amount of blown dirt and dust, or where particularly good-quality water is required and proper operation and maintenance can be guaranteed, a foul-flush system can be very effective. In a study by Yaziz et al. (1989) water-quality analysis of the initial 'foul-flush' runoff from both a tile and galvanized-iron roof in which the first, second, third, fourth and fifth litre of runoff were sampled, revealed high concentrations of most of the pollutants tested in the first litre, with subsequent improvements in each of the following samples, with few exceptions. Faecal coliforms, for example, ranged from 4 to 41 per 100ml in the first litre of runoff sampled but were entirely absent from samples of the fourth and fifth litres. The study also revealed that the rainfall intensity and number of dry days preceding a rainfall significantly affect runoff quality, with higher pollution concentrations after long dry periods. Based on these findings, the minimum volume of foul-flush ('first flush') which should be diverted for an average-sized 'Australian' house was recommended by Cunliffe (1998) to be between 20 and 25 litres. Numerous ingenious devices have been developed and many of these have been reviewed by Michealides and Young (1984). Some examples of different devices are shown in Figures 6.1 and 6.2. About 250 of the automatic foul diverters shown in Figure 6.1a were installed in a project in Togo in the mid-1980s. While half of these systems were still functioning well after three years, many villagers chose to block them open for some reason (O'Brien, 1990).

The simple operation and maintenance of rainwater catchment systems is one of the most attractive aspects of the technology. The amount of maintenance required by a basic, privately owned household roof catchment system is limited to the annual cleaning of the tank, regular inspection of the gutters and downpipes, and the removal of any leaves, dirt or any other matter. In seasonal climates, where roof surfaces may become dirty and dusty in the dry season, the cleaning or sweeping of the roof before the first major rains may be advisable. A more convenient method of cleaning the catchment surface is to detach the downpipe from the tank before the start of the first major downpour, to allow the initial rainfall to wash the roof and allow the first flush to run to waste for several minutes until the roof is clean. Roof tanks with tipping buckets, sediment traps or foul-flush mechanisms may require more attention. Some tipping bucket first flush systems need to be reset after each rainfall event; failure to do this may result in future runoff running to waste.

Although widely cited in the literature on rainwater catchment systems (Pakianathan, 1989; Michealides, 1989), in reality the use of foul-flush devices is limited. This is especially the case in most developing countries, where finding working devices beyond the confines of appropriate technology demonstration projects is quite rare. Exceptions do, however, exist, such as in north-east Thailand, where the first flush diversion system, shown in Figure 6.1d, was fitted as standard to thousands of tanks. Nevertheless, even here, lack of regular cleaning of the devices has been a problem, rendering many ineffective. Where such devices are used, sometimes due to lack of proper operation and maintenance they actually end up doing more harm than good, either by diverting useful runoff away from the tank to waste, or even causing contamination of the stored water they are supposed to protect.

Based on this experience, it is recommended that if any kind of foul-flush or first flush device is to be considered, it should be extremely simple, and should not require regular operation and maintenance. Examples include:

- self-cleaning gutter snipes sold commercially in Hawaii and elsewhere in the US (see Figure 4.5)
- self-cleaning inlet mesh (see Figure 4.4)
- sedimentation chambers requiring only occasional cleaning (see Figure 6.2)
- movable downpipes for diverting the runoff from the season's first downpour (see Figure 6.1c).

The last device is appropriate in regions with distinct wet and dry seasons; cleaning the catchment and delivery system, flushing away dust and other debris which may have accumulated in the dry season. Although the authors have observed well-maintained and effectively operated foul-flush devices in the field, these tend to be the exception rather than the rule.

Hygiene education and monitoring
Since the problem of secondary contamination of rainwater supplies has been highlighted in several studies (Wirojanagud et al., 1989; Gould, 1985; Pinfold et al., 1990), hygiene education and monitoring of the condition and maintenance of systems, along with sanitary practices, are essential if rainwater supplies are to fulfil their potential and provide clean water. In the absence of hygienic water practices, attempts to ensure high water quality will be futile. This point was emphasized by McKenzie (1981) in relation to

remote water projects in the Eastern Highlands of Papua New Guinea. Any project involved in improving water provision, including rainwater systems, must have a hygiene-education component. Since roof catchment systems provide a water source at the point of consumption, there is less opportunity for secondary contamination to occur. Private ownership of systems also makes it easier to encourage people to clean the systems and better sanitary practices.

One problem with rainwater catchment systems in rural areas in developing countries, where they are used as the main source of drinking-water, sometimes occurs during the dry season or in droughts when the tanks become empty. At this point people often have no choice but to revert to traditional contaminated sources, thus exposing themselves to increased health risks. Careful rationing of rainwater supplies and reserving it for drinking and cooking could help to reduce this problem. Further discussion of these and other health issues can be found in Chapter 7.

Treatment of stored rainwater

Treatment of stored rainwater makes sense only if it is done properly, and if hygienic collection and use of the water will ensure it does not suffer from re-contamination. There are several types of treatment possible, the more common being chlorination, sand filters, boiling, and exposure to sunlight.

Chlorination

Chlorination of the water, either in the tank or after extraction, can be an effective way to purify the water, but it must be conducted with care. The chlorine can affect the taste of the water and over-application could cause problems. These factors can sometimes make chlorination somewhat impractical in remote rural locations. Since chlorine is available in different forms and local brand names can confuse this further, if uncertain, it may be best to seek advice from the local public health or environmental health authority. In the Virgin islands, people are recommended to add ordinary house-old bleach (5.25 per cent sodium hypochlorite) twice monthly, with doses of 40ml per 1000 litres. The Western Australia Environmental Health Service gave the following advice on their Internet website (http://www.public.health.wa.gov.au) in 1997:

Chlorination procedure If you suspect water in your tank is contaminated, it should be treated by adding swimming pool calcium hypochlorite (60–70%) or sodium hypochlorite (12.5%). The initial dose to treat the contamination should be 7g of calcium hypochlorite or 40ml of sodium hypochlorite per 1000 litres of water in the tank at the time of treatment. The water should be stirred and left to stand for at least 24 hours to allow the chlorine taste and smell to dissipate. It is important that the chlorine used is not stabilized. To maintain a safe water supply after the initial dosage, 1g of calcium hypochlorite or 4ml of sodium hypochlorite per 1000 litres should be added to the rainwater tank weekly and allowed to stand for a minimum of two hours. The water will be safe to drink provided the chlorine smell is not too strong. Note: Stabilized chlorine (chlorinated cyanurates) should *not* be used.

It is important to mix the chlorine in a plastic bucket *in the open air* before adding it to the tank. Mix it thoroughly with the tank water. *Do not pour water onto chlorine. Always add chlorine to water. Avoid skin contact and store in a cool, dark place out of reach of children.* To ensure that sufficient chlorine has been added, the water is normally tested for a chlorine residual using a simple colour-coded testing kit – normally a chlorine residual in the range of 0.2– 0.5mg/litre should be maintained.

Use of filters

Sand filters provide a cheap and simple method to purify water, and can be used in the home (Morgan, 1990). Such a filter can provide 50 litres of water per day – enough for the drinking and cooking needs of a small family. They do, however, require careful operation and maintenance to ensure they continue to work effectively. Although all that is required to make a filter is a clean 200-litre oil drum or cement jar, a tap and a short length of polyethylene hose – along with a supply of readily available clean river sand, gravel and, sometimes, charcoal – they are not widely used. This is unfortunate because, if more widespread, they could have a dramatic effect on reducing the global incidence of water-borne diseases. With respect to rainwater catchment systems, they would be especially appropriate for purifying lower-quality water from ground catchment systems, or for improving the quality of roof water runoff.

Boiling

Although boiling water thoroughly for two to three minutes normally ensures it is free from any harmful bacteria or pathogens, it is not always a practical option. Boiling requires a lot of energy which, in areas where fuel is scarce or expensive, may be a problem, and waiting for the water to cool is also tiresome. In parts of rural Gansu, in central China, these problems have been overcome to some extent by using low-cost solar dishes to boil the water, which is consumed mainly as hot tea (Plate 9.7). A variety of cheap solar cookers are available and could be used where water quality is suspect (Stone, 1994).

Sunlight

Another way to kill many of the harmful bacteria in water is to put it in clear glass or plastic bottles and place it in direct sunlight for several hours. This technique, originally pioneered by Professor Aftrim Acra at the American University of Beirut in the early 1980s, has undergone extensive subsequent field tests. The process works in two ways: bacteria and micro-organisms are killed both by exposure to direct radiation and, if heated sufficiently, by water temperatures exceeding 70°C. This latter effect can be increased by painting half of the bottle black to increase solar radiation absorption. When done correctly, Solar Water Disinfection (SODIS) can reduce coliform levels by 99.5 per cent in up to 97 per cent of samples (Wegelin and Sommer, 1998). To be effective, the water should not be too turbulent or excessively contaminated. The solar decontamination of water is most effective when the water is fully oxygenated, so leaving some air in the bottles and shaking the bottle occasionally will help speed up the process (Reed, 1998). Although exposure to sunlight is very effective against *E. coli* and other pathogenic bacteria, it is less effective against pathogenic human enteric virus (Fujioka, 1998 – personal communication).

Other treatments
Several other treatments have been proposed and are used locally in some parts of the world. These include various chlorine substitutes, such as Microdyn, a colloidal silver compound used widely for water disinfection in Mexico (Owen and Gerba, 1987). Another recent development is the use of a copper sulphate pentahydrate bound to a non-toxic carrier and marketed under the name Ecol2000. The manufacturer claims this is cheaper and easier to use than chlorine, much less is required, and that the treatment becomes effective after just 30 minutes and lasts for 30 days. It is also tasteless, non-toxic at the recommended dosage, and cheaper than chlorination. It should be noted that copper sulphate itself is potentially toxic in water and treatment should always be conducted with great care. Another technology consisting of a solar-powered ultraviolet unit is able to process 1.5 litres of water per minute. The unit developed by Professor Otto Joklik (1995) was evaluated on rainwater cistern water in Hawaii and found to be 99.9 per cent effective in removing indicator bacteria (Fujioka et al., 1995).

Personal observations   A large amount of research has been conducted into rainwater quality and much has been written on the subject. Nevertheless, it is worth bearing in mind the following general observations. Since accounts of serious illness linked to rainwater supplies are few, it would appear that slight contamination of roof runoff from occasional bird droppings on the catchment surface does not represent a major health risk. Both authors have drunk rainwater collected from numerous roof catchment sources all over the world for over 20 years and have never suffered any ill effects. That said, it is always worth inspecting any tank thoroughly before consuming rainwater from it, and, if in doubt, don't!

Summary of key points

- While rainwater quality will not always match WHO or national drinking-water standards, when compared with most unprotected, traditional water sources, rainwater from well-maintained roof catchments usually represents a considerable improvement and is generally safe to drink without treatment.
- Rainwater from ground catchment systems is not recommended for drinking unless first boiled or treated.

- Except in heavily urbanized and industrialized areas or regions adjacent to active volcanoes, atmospheric rainwater is very pure and any contamination of the water usually occurs after contact with the catchment.
- A degree of chemical and microbiological contamination of roof rainwater runoff is inevitable, but this will not generally cause a problem if the roof, gutters and storage tank are properly maintained and regularly cleaned and inspected.
- Reports of disease outbreaks linked to roof water sources are rare. A few cases of gastrointestinal illnesses linked to large quantities of bird or animal droppings on the roof have been reported, and appropriate measures should be taken to reduce any risks.
- The chemical and physical quality of stored rainwater is normally high. Care should be taken to avoid any possible sources of lead or other heavy metals, e.g. from lead flashings or lead-based roof paints.
- Rainwater tanks can provide breeding sites for mosquitoes, which in some areas act as vectors for diseases such as dengue fever, yellow fever and malaria. It is therefore essential that any openings to the tank are fully screened.
- To protect water quality, good system design, operation and maintenance are essential. Water quality will generally improve during storage, provided light and living organisms are excluded from the tank, and fresh inflows do not stir up any sediment.
- The use of filters and foul-flush diverters can further improve the rainwater quality. Further treatment through boiling, exposure to sunlight or ultra-violet radiation and chlorination can be undertaken if there are concerns over the water quality.

7

Social, economic and environmental aspects

IN COMMON WITH any technology, it is vital when considering the appropriateness of rainwater catchment systems not to view it purely from a narrow technical perspective. The importance of considering not only the technical appropriateness of water projects, but also their broader suitability in terms of economic, environmental, health and social factors is not a new concept, and the reasoning behind this approach was clearly spelt out in a seminal ITDG paper by Pacey et al. (1977). Nevertheless, while the relevance of this broader approach is widely recognized, it is frequently not fully applied in practice. The evidence for this is widespread and the rusting remains of water pumps and other equipment from recent schemes, much of which was technically sound and may have worked perfectly well on better managed projects, still litter many developing countries (Mather, 1996).

Experience has shown that where only a narrow technical focus is adopted, many projects have failed. The reasons for the failures are varied. Sometimes the high cost of the systems prevents continued implementation and replication once donor funds for the pilot project have dried up. At other times, communal systems fail because responsibility for the management, maintenance and repair of the system has not been clearly defined. According to the UNDP/World Bank Water and Sanitation Programme Report 1994–5:

> This is often the result of the extensive involvement of government personnel, rather than local decision-makers, in decisions related to the location, construction, operation and maintenance of community facilities.

A key factor in project success is community involvement at every stage from inception to long-term maintenance and operation. Involvement in planning and construction phases will not only help to build skills and a sense of self-reliance within communities, but also prepare the community better for any future maintenance or repair work (Plate 7.1).

Social and political considerations

Social, cultural, health, gender and broader political issues are usually relegated to a secondary position behind economic and technical aspects when rainwater catchment projects are being planned and designed, and sometimes they are overlooked altogether. This is a serious problem because they are crucial elements and can greatly influence the success of a project. Numerous examples of project failures exist, and donors and NGOs can sometimes be

159

Plate 7.1 *Community involvement in the construction of a sub-surface dam in eastern Kenya.* (Photo: Erik Nissen-Petersen, 1997)

just as blind as government departments to the community's desires. One particularly clear-cut case was a major donor-initiated household rainwater tank implementation project at Kilifi on the Kenyan coast in the early 1980s (McPherson et al., 1984). The project involved the provision of durable, centrally manufactured high-quality $6m^3$ ferrocement rainwater tanks to poor rural households (Plate 9.13). While the concept was sound, as the villages clearly needed improved water sources and the technical quality of the water

160

tanks was excellent, the programme foundered due to lack of community involvement. The implementing agency's failure to engage the community as a full partner in the project led to several flawed assumptions. To start with, it was assumed that recipients of the tanks could afford to pay for them and that they understood the contracts they were required to sign. These committed householders to repayments – after a two-year grace period – to cover the cost of the tank plus an additional 6.5 per cent per annum interest charge. It was also assumed that participating villagers would purchase and install gutters and downpipes. The long-term plan was that after an initial input from the donor, money from the loan repayments would fund further tank construction and the project would become self-sustaining.

Problems with the project became apparent very early on. Many house-holders either could not afford, or did not understand that the whole roof area of their house required gutters, and many just put short lengths of guttering up close to the tank. Few participants took very seriously the contracts they had signed. This was hardly surprising perhaps, considering that in many traditional African cultures, the distinction between a loan and a grant (gift) is not very clear-cut. The collection of loan repayments became very difficult and very expensive and the funding base for the project quickly dried up. The lessons here, of not involving the community fully as equal partners in the planning and implementation of the project, are obvious. Clearly, the capacity of the community to participate in this project was poorly understood by the donor, who adopted a top-down management approach. Ultimately, this not only produced little benefit to the community, but may actually have under-mined the community's self-confidence and willingness to engage in future self-help projects.

The above example illustrates that both an ability and willingness to pay for at least a portion of the project costs is important if individuals and commu-nities are to become active partners in any initiative to implement a rainwater catchment system. Where communities are very poor, and system costs are beyond their reach, there also needs to be a willingness by donors and govern-ments to contribute as well. The best projects often have support at all levels, as was illustrated in the successful Thai jar programme (Wirojanagud and Vanvarothorn, 1990) and, where possible, mechanisms should be developed to enable users to pay for systems themselves (Gould, 1989). It is, however, essential that the institutional, administrative and managerial aspects of the project are properly organized, as well as those directly concerned with imple-mentation. A realistic funding strategy is essential and, where communities are poor, various fundraising or income-generating activities need to be con-sidered. These, along with the use of revolving funds, are discussed in more detail below.

Social issues
Social issues relate to the needs, perceptions, desires, beliefs, experience and existing practices of the community. For any rainwater catchment system project to succeed, whether at a single household level or across a whole

161

region, it must address a real felt need within a community and be socially acceptable. Furthermore, not only should it be affordable, but people must be willing to pay for it.

The *actual* quality or quantity of any rainwater supply is often less significant to the popularity of a project than that perceived by the local community. To some extent perceptions can be changed, especially if they are ill-founded. This can be done through various awareness-raising and public education campaigns. Before embarking on any campaign, it is essential to understand the community's current perceptions and practices by undertaking some form of social assessment. Perception of water quality provides a good example of why the social dimension must be taken into account. If people do not perceive current unsanitary practices relating to the collection and storage of water as unhealthy, even if great technical effort is put into providing cleaner water at source, this will probably be of little benefit due to subsequent secondary contamination of the water before consumption.

The social structure, organization, and administrative and leadership capacity within a community are also important factors influencing the prospects of any communal water project. In communities where there is a history of communal co-operation, a new project involving the shared use and maintenance of a communal rainwater tank at a school or other public building is more likely to succeed than in a community with no such history. There is, however, no guarantee that a history of communal co-operation will necessarily ensure the success of such a project. Evidence suggests that the successful operation and maintenance of shared rainwater schemes is the exception rather than the rule, while privately owned systems are invariably much better managed.

In Kenya, the tradition of *harambee* (to pull together) on community self-help labour was popularized after Independence, and it has greatly assisted many villages with the affordable implementation of rock catchment dams, earth dams and sand river storage systems. Another traditional funding mechanism which has provided a useful means of funding household roof catchment systems is the use of revolving funds, discussed below.

Cultural issues
Cultural issues relate to the customs and belief systems of any society, cultural or ethnic group, and these often have a bearing on how water is used. Religious beliefs usually provide the foundation of any culture's particular view of water, and almost without exception rain is perceived as a 'gift from God' – a fact observed in a recent review of the evolution of religious and scientific thought relating to rainfall by Heggen (1997). The significance given to the religious and cultural dimensions of rainwater utilization in some societies should not be underestimated. A complete volume of the proceedings of the 8th IRWCS Conference in Iran is devoted to religious and cultural aspects of water and rainwater use from an Islamic point of view. Clearly, any rainwater projects need to be sensitive to the belief system in any society, although, fortunately, in most there are few taboos relating to rainwater collection and use.

162

Cultural factors also relate to other influences, such as personal preferences. The way different cultures perceive the taste of rainwater may vary, depending on local diet and the water sources from which they are used to drinking. For example, a villager in Botswana may consider rainwater to have a 'sweet' taste compared to the 'salty' groundwater they are used to, while a villager in China used to drinking mineral-rich water from a limestone aquifer may consider the rainwater to be 'flat' and tasteless. In some parts of the world, mud, bark, leaves and other 'flavourings' are sometimes added to rainwater to *improve* its taste (Pacey and Cullis, 1986).

Health issues

The impact of improvements in water supply on health is not as clear-cut as is sometimes supposed. While improvements in water provision are normally linked to improvements in health, a direct causal link cannot necessarily be drawn. Certainly, little evidence exists in the literature showing significant health impacts even following substantial improvements in drinking-water quality (Esrey et al., 1990). This may be because other factors such as water handling and hygiene practices can have a significant impact on degrading water quality even if it is clean at source. Feachem (1988) has also noted that there are several other interventions, which often occur simultaneously with improved water-quality provision, that are likely also to have a positive impact on the health status of a community. These include improved sanitation, immunization programmes, the promotion of breast-feeding, and better domestic hygiene. Feachem supports the growing consensus view among researchers that improvements in the water quantity available may be more important to health than improvements in either water quality or sanitation. Although recognizing that no adequate studies exist, Feachem also suggests that even with combined water, sanitation, and hygiene education improvements, reductions in the incidence of diarrhoea may only be around 35 to 50 per cent.

The limited impact of water and sanitation improvements in eliminating diarrhoeal diseases seems to be borne out by data from rural Thailand. Despite an increased access to safe water, from about 25 per cent in 1981 to 77 per cent in 1990 (mainly as a result of the widespread introduction of millions of 1–2m³ rainwater jars), and increased access to latrines from 42 to 63 per cent over the same period, north-eastern Thailand has not seen any great reduction in diarrhoeal diseases (Hewison, 1996). The apparent failure of water supply and sanitation improvements to make a major impact on key rural health indicators may in part be a problem with interpreting the available data. In reality, the situation may only *appear* not to be improving due to much better health-status reporting systems. Whatever the reality, Hewison suggests that the cement jar programme should be considered a success in development terms, even if its direct impact on health is unclear. Another aspect of the problem is the re-contamination of drinking-water after its collection from the tank (Wirojanagud et al., 1989).

Rather than being overly concerned with trying to address the quality of stored rainwater at the source, Pinfold et al. (1993) suggest that it is more realistic and cost-effective to make incremental improvements. In north-east Thailand this process has already begun with the addition of taps, covers and mosquito screens to most jars, along with efforts to encourage improved water handling and hygiene practices. The full importance of health and hygiene education programmes to support the successful implementation of the rain-water tank programmes often lags a few years behind the construction and implementation of the hardware, as was the case with the Thai jar programme (Tunyavanich and Hewison, 1990).

Another important health issue relating to rainwater supplies is that, in seasonal climates, they often dry up during the dry season or in drought periods, if people have no alternative, they will revert to unimproved traditional water sources, exposing themselves to greater health risks (Plate 7.2).

Gender issues
In developing countries, gender issues are of particular significance with re-spect to rainwater catchment systems due to the direct impact these systems have on the lives of many rural women (Thoya, 1993). A well-designed roof catchment system can liberate women from the onerous task of carrying tens of tons of water every year from distant sources (Plate 9.14). Yet, despite this,

Plate 7.2 *Women and children collecting water from a sand river bed in eastern Kenya.* (Photo: Erik Nissen-Petersen, 1997)

women have often been overlooked when it comes to the planning, design and construction phases of rainwater catchment system implementation projects. The situation is slowly changing and there have been some excellent women's self-help projects, such as in Kenya (Kingori, 1995; Simmonds, 1993) and the Philippines (Salas, 1989), where the involvement of many female civil engineers in rainwater projects is becoming commonplace. Given these changes, the continuing exclusion of women from technical training programmes and construction in many parts of the world seems both surprising and unwarranted, particularly given the fact that women are key actors in the development process and are often fully involved in related activities such as house construction and repair.

In many situations, such as that found at a project in Karagwe, Kagera Province, Tanzania, family finances are controlled by the male who is considered the *de facto* head of household. Decisions such as whether or not to spend limited household income on a costly item such as a rainwater tank tend, in these circumstances, not to favour women (Simmonds, 1993). Men may be reluctant to pay for a tank as the benefit to them may be perceived to be minimal, since the water is delivered to the household by the women and children anyway (Plate 7.2). The only obvious solution to this problem is to find ways to raise the status of women within the society and educate/sensitize the men about both gender issues and the importance and benefits of an improved water supply.

Although the benefits to women of household rainwater catchment systems are self-evident, concern has been raised by various commentators (Salas, 1995). The fear is that by designing rainwater projects with the sole purpose of alleviating women from the burden of water collection, one may be inadvertently stereotyping them as 'domestic water gatherers', and this might ultimately be counterproductive to women's empowerment. Clearly, the introduction of a rainwater catchment tank into a household should not be a substitute for greater awareness and equality with respect to gender roles and issues.

Political issues
Politics is found at every level, from the household, village committee, district offices, and regional council, to national ministry, bilateral agency and international organizations; and can influence the prospects of any project. A conducive political climate locally, nationally and internationally can result in a project receiving both grassroots and external support, critical for its success. Conversely, political conflict, whether within the village water committee or between the national government and a bilateral donor government can result in support for a rainwater project quickly evaporating.

Influencing policy- and decision-makers
While a centrally planned top-down approach to small water project implementation seldom works, it is also rare to find flourishing grassroots initiatives which have not received some support or encouragement from an external agency. Clearly, some form of partnership is needed, for while the community

165

knows what it wants and understands the local conditions and situation best, the government or donor has easier access to the resources and technical expertise the project may require. Where strong support from above meets vigorous grassroots initiatives, the outcomes can be impressive, as can be seen in the 1–2-1 project in China, discussed in Chapter 9.

Winning the hearts and minds of policy- and decision-makers is often a vital first step towards ensuring the appropriate choice of technology and level of intervention necessary to ensure a successful project. Often it is not just villagers who have to be persuaded about the potential benefits of an unconventional technology, but senior officials in government and donor organizations. While these influential individuals may not be directly involved in project implementation, a 'green light' from them can signal the flow of funds to enable a project to receive the subsidy or initial injection of funds it might need to become viable.

In order to convince policymakers to allocate limited public funds to domestic rainwater collection, it may be necessary to demonstrate that such an investment produces wider tangible gains beyond the household itself. Ray (1983) suggests that these broader benefits may include the cost-effectiveness of schemes compared with public piped supplies, the employment-generation opportunities through small-scale tank-construction enterprises, and increased self-reliance leading to reduced dependence on welfare, for example famine relief. Improved water provision may also help lead to better health and reduced demands on government health care resources. These benefits all have the potential to reduce demands on public funds, and thus provide a valid basis for any request for central funding either from a regional or national level.

Rainwater catchment systems such as large-scale ground catchments, rock catchments, sand river storage, water harvesting and runoff gardening can also provide an important benefit in terms of resource conservation. This explains the growing interest in combined soil and water conservation schemes in recent years. The specific benefits derived from harvesting and storing runoff include flood control, erosion control, groundwater recharge, and reduced sedimentation rates in lakes and reservoirs (Ray, 1983). These all provide particularly good reasons for investments using public funds.

Community participation, partnership and empowerment
The traditional view of community involvement in water projects has often been that since *they* (the community) will benefit, *they* should contribute materials and labour, so that *they* feel the project belongs to them. While a degree of community participation is probably better than no participation at all, if it is limited to such a subsidiary role in a paternalistic relationship with an external agency, it may actually do more harm than good. The track record of community participation has been mixed, sometimes working well, especially where it is conducted in communities with a tradition of self-help activities, for example *harambee* projects in East Africa. In other cases, the approach has singularly failed, and usually for very good reasons. One

common problem, for example, is that villagers' motivation to voluntarily work is undermined by government or donor food-for-work or paid labour projects in the same area (Tharun, 1995).

To improve the success rate of community participation, over the years an approach that involves the community, either as an equal partner with an external agency or ideally in a dominant role, gradually evolved to become one. In the latter case, the external donor or NGO simply acts as a project facilitator and eventually withdraws altogether (Lugonzo-Campbell, 1989). Ideally, a proactive, self-confident community will be able to construct, operate and maintain its own water systems on a sustainable basis. In reality, such total community empowerment is rare and normally requires the dual conditions of a united community with a strong democratic leadership. Where such a situation does prevail there is also a risk that the community may come into conflict with government officials used to a top-down approach to water systems implementation, who may feel their authority is being undermined.

What is essential is that the community feels in control over its own destiny and is actively engaged in every dimension of the project right from the outset, including the initial formulation and planning of any scheme. This involves in-depth dialogue between all the stakeholders in any project: community, government, NGOs and donors. An example of this approach with respect to a rainwater harvesting project is Turkana, Kenya, where the local community identified its priorities and took full control over project administration (Cullis and Pacey, 1991).

Awareness-raising and user education
In localities where rainwater collection has not previously been widely practised, any attempt to introduce the technology will first require a campaign to raise awareness about it. This can be done in various ways, including the construction of demonstration tanks, holding public meetings, newspaper reports and radio announcements. In places where the technology is already familiar, awareness-raising activities may relate to different aspects of the project. If affordability is an issue, alerting the public to available funding mechanisms might need to be the key message. Where improved health is a fundamental project objective, which it invariably is, then hygiene education will need to be promoted in tandem with rainwater tanks. In Kenya, women's groups – who have built over 2000 15m³ household tanks in the Catholic Diocese of Nakuru – would be addressed by a health officer once construction was complete. This enabled the groups to receive advice on safe operation and maintenance practices, including the draining of stagnant water away from the tanks (Kingori, 1995). The link between clean water and good sanitation is also significant here, as improvements in one without the other are unlikely to bring about substantial improvements in health (Erskine, 1995).

Socio-economic constraints
When rural dwellers in developing countries are questioned about household rainwater catchment systems, those with systems inevitably express

satisfaction with them provided they are functioning properly. Those without normally express a desire to acquire a system and invariably cite cost as the main factor preventing acquisition. While this is generally true, it is not always the case and often there are competing priorities to balance. In many instances, households may have money, but not the substantial amount (with respect to local incomes) required to purchase a tank outright. For this reason, many rainwater tank projects have started to flourish only when they have found mechanisms, such as some of those discussed below, which allow householders to acquire and pay for their own tanks.

Economic considerations

Economic analysis and economic comparisons can become notoriously difficult when applied to water, particularly with respect to scattered, rural rainwater supplies. Water is not like most commodities because, without it, we die. It is unlike air, however, as it is generally no longer available as a free good. The difficulty with the economics of rural water supplies is brought about by the fact that there is usually an inverse relationship between the cost of supply on the one hand and ability to pay on the other. While it becomes increasingly expensive to provide supplies to smaller and remoter settlements and homesteads, the economic opportunities for the respective householders decrease at the same time.

Economic analysis is also complicated by the need for assumptions about discount rates and system life expectancies which depend on somewhat arbitrary assumptions that can significantly influence the apparent costs. Even if the real system cost can be established, the absolute amount has little meaning unless quoted in context. A US$100 system may not sound too expensive to an average Westerner, yet this may represent a year's income to a rural African. Comparisons of system costs between different times and different countries are also difficult because of the combined influence of exchange rate fluctuations, inflation, purchasing power variations, and the inclusion or exclusion of the cost of administrative overheads, self-help labour, local materials, transport or technical advice.

Another important economic consideration that is sometimes overlooked relates to the time and energy involved in collecting water. White et al. (1972) try to put a cost to time and energy spent so that this can be included in the total system cost, allowing different systems to be compared. In the case of roof catchment systems, the water supply is next to the house, so the time and energy cost reduces to near zero. While the value of the time saved may be small in the case of poor rural communities, the benefits in terms of improved quality of life and livelihoods will often be dramatic. Freed from the daily drudgery of water collection, women can devote more time to child care, food production and other activities. They might even earn an occasional well-deserved rest, an activity which, while of no economic significance, will be highly valued by most over-worked rural women. In many parts of the world, children, particularly young girls, may be deprived of education due to the need to assist their mothers with essential daily chores such as water and fuel collection. The time savings associated with the implementation of roof tank supplies may be sufficient to allow at least some children to attend school – a benefit hard to quantify in purely economic terms.

Costing rainwater supplies
Given the above constraints relating to economic analysis and cost comparisons, it is not surprising that there is considerable variability within the literature about true system costs and how they compare to other technologies. The picture is complicated by the fact that the relative costs of different types of system vary from place to place, and the costs of most communal systems are subject to significant variations based on economies of scale. Despite these complications, the following generalizations based on findings by Omwenga (1984), Pacey and Cullis (1986), Lee and Visscher (1992), and Gould (1996) can be made about rainwater catchment system costs:

- Initial per capita capital costs are relatively high compared with alternatives (such as shallow wells, protected springs, tubewells) where available.
- Recurrent (running) costs are low, especially when compared to boreholes and piped schemes.
- Ground tanks are generally cheaper per cubic metre of storage than surface tanks.
- Systems are normally subject to economies of scale which makes storage costs per cubic metre decrease as storage tanks become larger. This favours communal systems over private systems when compared purely in terms of cost.

Any comparison between rainwater catchment systems and other water supply technologies should be undertaken with caution. One is seldom comparing like with like, as the nature of the provision differs with each type of technology. Nevertheless, such an analysis is normally required in order to get a grip on the relative costs of different options. First, an up-to-date cost breakdown of all viable technology options should be done. This will involve a detailed bill of quantities, accurate information regarding skilled and unskilled labour requirements, transport costs and institutional and administrative costs (e.g. for project planning, designing and monitoring).

Because the cost of tanks varies so widely from place to place and time to time, there seems little point in reproducing the sort of table found in many texts on the subject, which shows cost comparisons of different tank types, in different places and at different times. The absurdity of such comparisons is perhaps best illustrated by the following facts. In 1994, a small 200-litre household rainwater tank cost as much as US$400 ($2000/m^3) in Tokyo, Japan, or about 100 times the equivalent cost per unit volume of a 1.4m^3 ferrocement tank in neighbouring rural China which was selling for the equivalent of less than $30 ($20/m^3) in 1997! By 1998, the Japanese tank had actually become almost 40 per cent cheaper in dollar terms due to a weakening Yen/US$ exchange rate and near zero inflation in Japan. Considering that the Yen is a relatively stable currency by international standards, this only reinforces the difficulties with making an international comparisons of different tanks, at different times and in different places.

By way of illustration of a more useful means of comparison, Table 7.1 shows the costs of several types of system including labour and material inputs, all costed at the same time in 1997 at the same place, Kenya. From the table, the economies of scale associated with large tank volumes are clear. Drawing up a table of this type is a useful starting point for doing any local comparison of options. It does, however, have its limitations and tells only half of the story. This is because a number of key items of information, needed to give a more accurate picture of the actual cost of the water the system can provide, are missing. These include the expected life of the tank, the expected frequency with which the tank will fill, and the discount rate.

If we leave aside the issue of discount rates for a moment and focus on the other two issues, we can see the significant influence these can have on the

Table 7.1 Comparison of different rainwater tank and other water-scheme costs in Kenya (August 1998) given to nearest US$ equivalent

Tank or reservoir type	Tank volume (m^3)	Cost[1] US$	Cost/m^3 US$/$m^3$
Plastic tank	4.6	580	126
Corrugated-iron tank	4.6	340	74
Water jar* (ferrocement)	3	150	50
Concrete *in-situ* tank*	5	300	60
Brick tank*	10	500	50
Ferrocement tank*	11	550	50
Ferrocement tank*	23	750	33
Ferrocement tank*	46	1200	26
Sub-surface ferrocement tank*	90	1900	21
Rock catchment dams	50	500	8
Sub-surface reservoir	—	—	0.25–1
Hand-dug well	—	320–1160	3–12
Piped water scheme		4000	12

[1] Cost includes materials and labour only – US$1 = Ksh60 (August 1998).
* Cost of formwork is not included here – Details in Appendix 5

Table 7.2 Cost of rainwater tanks in US$/m³ assuming expected tank life scenarios of 10, 20 and 30 years under arid, semi-arid, semi-humid and humid conditions

	Expected tank-life scenarios		
	Pessimistic 10 years	Realistic 20 years	Optimistic 30 years
Annual rainwater supply in tank volumes	*Cost of Water[1] US$/m³*	*Cost of Water[1] US$/m³*	*Cost of Water[1] US$/m³*
× 1 (Arid)	2–12	1–6	0.66–4
× 2 (Semi-arid)	1–6	0.5–3	0.33–2
× 5 (Semi-Humid)	0.4–2.4	0.2–1.2	0.13–0.8
× 10 (Humid)	0.2–1.2	0.1–0.6	0.06 – 0.4

[1] Assuming tank cost in the range US$20–120 per m³

actual cost of water in Table 7.2. In this table, the actual price range for each cubic metre of water supplied over the life of the tank is calculated assuming three different tank-life expectancy scenarios, an optimistic (30 year), a realistic (20 year), and a pessimistic (10 year) tank life. The amount of water the tank is able to supply is a function of the annual rainfall, the size of the catchment, and the rate at which water is withdrawn from the tank. In an arid environment, with erratic rainfall and limited catchment area, the annual supply may be equivalent only to the tank volume – in a drought it could be even less. More typically, even in semi-arid environments such as Botswana, it is not unrealistic to expect a well-designed system to yield about twice its own storage volume of water annually. In semi-humid and humid conditions, especially where a small tank is fed from a large catchment, a yield of 5 to 10 times the storage volume is not unrealistic. These four situations are shown in Table 7.2, and in each case the cost range for the water is shown in US$/m³. For simplicity, the range of rainwater tank storage costs is taken as US$20/m³ to US$120/m³; this approximately encompasses the cost range shown in Table 7.1 for surface tanks.

The results in Table 7.2 illustrate that even given an identical tank design, a 30-fold variation in the cost of water could result simply due to climatic/runoff influences and differing assumptions about tank life expectancy. If discount rates are also added to the equation, a further set of assumptions is needed which adds additional complexity and increases the overall cost differentials still further.

Lee and Visscher (1992) proposed costing systems based on an Equivalent Annual Cost (EAC) basis similar to that shown for the three tank life expectancy scenarios shown in Figure 7.2. Their approach did not simply take the tank cost and divide it by the life expectancy in years, but incorporated a discount rate to take into account the interest over the remaining debt. To calculate this they proposed the following formula to calculate the EAC:

$$EAC = C \times \{r(1 + r)^n\} / \{r(1 + r)^n - 1$$

Where:

EAC = Equivalent Annual Cost
C   = Initial capital Cost
n   = Expected Tank Life
r   = Discount Rate

In their calculations they chose an EAC of 30 years, which seems somewhat optimistic, especially for systems constructed and operated under the difficult conditions in rural Africa. Perhaps not surprisingly, they found the gap between the costs of rainwater catchment systems and shallow wells was less than that estimated by other researchers.

Cost–benefit and cost-effectiveness analysis

While cost–benefit analysis can be conducted on rainwater catchment projects, and indeed have been in the past (Parker, 1973), often such analysis turns out to be purely an academic exercise due to the complexities involved and the uncertainties of many of the assumptions required. It is also difficult to put a monetary figure on the value of the time saved. Some ideas and guidance as to how this can be done, along with a detailed illustration of cost–benefit calculations for rural water supplies is given by Churchill et al. (1987). Due to the difficulties of translating many of the social benefits of rural water projects into monetary terms, a more appropriate technique is required. Cost-effectiveness analysis is one such technique and requires quantifying project costs and benefits, but not having to put the benefits into monetary terms (Freeman et al., 1979). For example, the cost effectiveness of a free text-book distribution project might be expressed as follows: Reading ability scores were increased by X points for each Y dollars spent. This approach allows for comparisons and ranking of potential projects by donors or governments according to the magnitude of their impact relative to their costs. While cost-effectiveness analysis is useful when comparing similar projects with comparable outcomes, it is of little use when comparing the cost effectiveness of substantially different projects. What is often more crucial than such theoretical analysis, is whether systems are affordable and if people are willing to pay for them. If people are willing to pay but the system costs are too high, then some kind of funding mechanism will be required, as discussed below.

Affordability

Affordability is a key constraint on many household rainwater-tank initiatives. There are literally hundreds of millions of households throughout the poorer regions of the world that could benefit substantially from the installation or upgrading of a roof catchment supply, but for whom the costs are prohibitive. A clear indication of this is given by the numerous homes at which rainwater is collected using inadequate technology: pots, pans, buckets and old oil drums, and limited or no guttering.

Although it is true that many households have relatively limited resources when compared to the high cost of roof catchment systems, almost all households do have some resources at their disposal which could be invested in systems. Even if ready cash is not available, households will normally have some surplus labour capacity which could be used to assist in the construction of a system. Many households will also have access to freely available local materials such as sand, stones and boulders which can be used in construction. In a survey of five African countries, Lee and Visscher (1990) estimated that community contributions of this type accounted for between 10 and 40 per cent of project inputs. Most households also own some livestock or small-stock, one or two of which can sometimes be sold to raise the necessary funds. In a survey by Simmonds (1993) in a poor village in Karagwe, Tanzania, the following sources of income available to householders, from which contributions towards rainwater tanks could potentially be made, were identified:

- surplus cash crops (coffee and beans)
- goats and chickens (in 60 per cent of households)
- surplus vegetable production (one woman raised US$100 from a 10m² plot)
- preparation and sale of the local 'brew' generating regular monthly incomes of around US$10
- cattle-keeping (sale of one beast could pay for a rainwater system).

In Karagwe, annual income generation averaged around US$150 per household, yet despite the ability to pay for a locally made 1.2m³ cement jar ($30), there was a lack of willingness to pay more than $1/month, especially among poorer villagers. A fall in coffee prices at the time of the survey may have been partially responsible for this. Another factor in this instance was male control over income-generating activities, while women were the ones collecting the water. The women walked, on average, 15km daily to collect five buckets (100 litres) from a saline water hole. While it may seem strange that, given such circumstances, there is not a greater willingness to pay for water-supply improvements, it should be remembered that poor households have many competing demands on their limited resources. These will include purchasing food and medicine, school fees, clothes, shoes, etc. Another obstacle which may have been relevant here is that when a new technology is being introduced, there is often considerable reluctance to invest large sums of money in something whose reliability is unknown.

An incremental approach to implementation has advantages in situations such as that in Karagwe. Initially, demonstration tanks might be constructed to convince the community that the technology is a worthwhile investment. Once interest has been aroused, small tanks should be constructed during a pilot project. Small tanks will be more affordable and reduce the financial risk to participating households. With small tanks, extra tanks can be added when resources permit, and failure of one tank is less disastrous if another functioning tank is available.

Loans and subsidies
Experiences with loans and subsidies for rainwater catchment systems have been very mixed. Some schemes, such as that at Kilifi in Kenya discussed

earlier in this chapter, failed dismally while others, such as some of the community projects based on revolving loan funds and income-generating activities discussed below, have been resounding successes.

It is important that where loans are made they are set at realistic levels. Before any loan scheme is embarked upon, it is essential that the following conditions exist:

- The loan recipient wants the loan, understands the loan conditions and is willing and able to make the repayments.
- The loan recipient is willing to enter into a formal legal contract regarding the loan.
- The recipient is willing to comply with any loan conditions, such as provision of a down-payment, local materials and voluntary labour.
- There must be some non-financial controls to encourage repayments such as those used by Bangladesh's Grameen Bank, where group pressure helps to ensure timely repayments of loans.

In many instances, subsidies are both appropriate and necessary in bringing rainwater catchment systems within reach of the rural poor. However, where they are available they should be used with care. A 100 per cent subsidy is seldom appropriate. By contributing towards a rainwater system, a householder not only signals a desire to acquire it, but also secures some ownership of it. High levels of subsidy are normally unsustainable and limit the size of the population that can be reached. They also set an unsatisfactory precedent and may encourage dependency. While it has been argued in some quarters that subsidies are inappropriate, this position risks depriving the rural poor of improved water supplies indefinitely, and furthermore many urban supplies are already subsidized.

Where tools are scarce in a community, one of the best forms of subsidy can be the provision of tools, which may subsequently be used for other projects as well as training and skills development, especially where these also have broader applications. Alternatively, tools can be made available to the project by an external agency on short-term loan. Where tools are available within the community there are several advantages to using these. These include engendering a greater sense of self-reliance, showing what can be done with the community's own resources, and helping to promote long-term sustainability.

Revolving funds and income-generating activities
Revolving funds work in the following way. A group of households agrees to make a small regular monthly contribution to a central fund. For example, if 12 households each agree to contribute US$10 per month, $120 can be raised. The amount raised each month should be sufficient to pay for at least one tank. Each month a tank can be constructed (with the lucky recipient being selected through a lottery, vote or other agreed method). After one year a total of $1440 will have been raised and 12 tanks constructed, one for everyone in the group. Members of the group are also expected to provide labour

and collect materials for construction. This approach has been especially successful in Kenya, which has a tradition of such schemes (Lee and Visscher, 1992; Kingori, 1995). In communities that are very poor, larger groups may be needed, with longer contribution periods or alternatively a higher level of subsidy to the project by a donor or government.

The Diocese of Machakos self-help programme (de Vrees, 1987) for building $4m^3$, $5.4m^3$ and $13m^3$ *in situ* concrete tanks at households initially provided a generous direct subsidy to community groups. In 1986, after 1500 tanks had been constructed, this subsidy was removed but the demand for tanks did not diminish. The groups consisted of 50 members contributing about US$2.5 each per month over a 25-month period, with two tanks being built each month. The groups were required to register with the Diocese Office. The Diocese administered the funds and organized delivery of cement, formworks and some materials, as well as a trained artisan to build the tank. They also trained one member of the group in tank construction. The groups were required to meet the following conditions before work commenced:

- pay for three tanks in advance
- provide one person to be trained in tank construction
- provide all local materials, e.g. sand, aggregate and hardcore
- provide food and accommodation for the diocese artisan.

Revolving fund schemes have also been used to a lesser extent in Asia to fund household rainwater projects. In Thailand, the government became involved in the 1980s and was initially asked to pledge seed money to set up funds in all participating villages. In addition, further funds were requested for training, tools and formworks. Initially, some revolving funds were established where villagers formed groups and standard contributions of around US$4 per month were made. However, as the project took off and gained widespread support, government funds became more readily available and this began to stifle grassroots community-based revolving fund and implementation initiatives. During 1986 alone, the project was able to construct approximately 1.7 million $1-2m^3$ jars in north-east Thailand (Wirojanagud and Chindapraisirt, 1987). The project developed at such a frenzied pace that revolving funds were seen by many as too slow and cumbersome a mechanism to fund the rapid implementation of systems. In the event, the programme evolved in a different way to that envisaged. Wirojanagud and Vanvarothorn (1990) explain that, in many cases, districts provided construction materials, tools and training while people contributed labour to construct their own jars under supervision from experienced technicians. In other cases, groups of villagers were paid to make jars at construction centres; these were then transported to households, and sometimes the construction was sub-contracted directly to small-scale jar-making factories. Increasingly, it seems the private sector took over production as it was able to produce jars at ever-lower prices due to economies of scale. The government at local, regional and national levels remained a major donor to the project, funding construction to the tune of almost 1.6

billion baht (US$ 64 million) through the Rural Job Creation Programme during the 1980s.

In Indonesia and the Philippines, loans and income-generating activities have been a more popular method of fundraising than the use of revolving funds. At the Dian Desa rainwater tank project in Jogjakarta, project recipients were each given two she-goats along with a tank. When the goats produced kids (usually four), two were sold to assist with the loan repayment, two were retained by the household, and the original pair of she-goats were passed on to the next tank recipient (Aristanti, 1986). A similar approach was adopted using the raising of piglets in Capiz Province in the Philippines during the late 1980s (Appan et al., 1989). Here, other income-generating activities such as cooking, dressmaking, tailoring and compost-making were also encouraged. Several hundred ferrocement tanks were constructed at both projects as a result of the funds generated through these various activities, of which animal rearing was the most productive.

Environmental considerations

Environmental considerations encompass two different aspects of rainwater catchment systems implementation. The first is the environmental feasibility of the project at any particular location, and the second its environmental impact.

Environmental feasibility
Environmental feasibility is dependent more than anything else on the amount and pattern of precipitation in the area. As has been discussed earlier, usually some form of rainwater (fog, water or snow-fed) supply is possible in most localities. To what extent rainwater systems can compete with other alternatives will depend on the specific rainfall conditions at the locality. For some types of project, including rock catchments, ground catchments, earth dams, hafirs, sand river storage and water harvesting for plant production, other environmental factors such as local geology, soil conditions and hydrology may also be important.

Environmental impact
The second aspect involves the potential environmental impact of the systems. Generally, the environmental impact of rainwater catchment systems for domestic supplies are minimal. Even larger-scale ground catchment and rock catchment systems for communal supplies tend to have positive rather than negative environmental impacts, e.g. reducing storm runoff and hence soil erosion and flooding problems in an area. Some concern has been raised in the past that groundwater recharge may suffer in areas where widespread rainwater catchment is practised. While this is possible in theory, there are two important facts which should counter any concern. First, generally speaking, the total area from which rainwater is harvested is usually only a small fraction of the total area on to which rain falls in any particular locality.

176

Second, much of the rain that reaches the ground runs off towards the sea and does not contribute to groundwater recharge.

In most cases, small-scale rainwater catchment initiatives designed primarily for supplying domestic water should not require environmental impact assessments (EIA). In some instances, however, larger-scale schemes such as a series of sand river storage projects, which could impact downstream water users, may need some form of environmental assessment.

Summary of key points

- Experience has shown that projects that are not socially appropriate will fail just as surely as those that are not economically or technically appropriate. For rainwater catchment systems projects to succeed, they need to adopt an integrated and holistic approach which goes beyond only technical details and economic feasibility.
- The best approaches will marry first-rate appropriate technology and design with good workmanship and a socially and environmentally acceptable implementation strategy.
- In any community rainwater project, consideration must be given to social aspects including socio-economic, cultural, health, gender and local political issues.
- Economic considerations are crucial when making comparisons between various alternative types of supply. Mechanisms for assisting households to pay for systems include the use of subsidies, loans, revolving funds and income-generating activities.
- Environmental issues and impacts of any project should always be considered, although in the case of most rainwater systems for domestic supply, impacts tend to be minimal.
- Successful community project implementation depends on effective administration, organization, management, financing, training, operation, maintenance and evaluation.
- The key to long-term success in rainwater (or other) projects is the motivation of the community and its total integration into every aspect of the project from inception to evaluation.

8

Project implementation

Principles and pre-conditions

THERE IS NO single prescription that can be followed when implementing any particular rainwater catchment system project. The implementation strategy will vary depending on the type and scale of the project, the technology used, and the nature of the community involved. Despite these differences, there are some important common principles which apply to all projects. Although the following discussion focuses primarily on community initiatives in poorer countries, many of the principles and approaches can be applied universally, subject to modifications to fit local circumstances.

Rainwater catchment systems and the broader development process
The implementation of domestic rainwater catchment systems' 'hardware', e.g. tanks, gutters, etc., in any development project normally represents just one component of a broader effort to achieve a number of development objectives. For this reason, Andersson (1989, 1990) states that 'water-supply development must be put in the context of total development in communities'. Ideally, a rainwater tank implementation programme in a poor community lacking adequate water supplies will not only improve the immediate water situation but also lead to a whole range of 'software' benefits to the community. These might include:

- improved health and improved hygiene awareness and practices
- development of new skills and employment in the community
- development of capacity in project planning, implementation, management, operation and maintenance
- development of experience in democratic community leadership and organization
- development of capacity in financial management and fundraising
- a growing sense of self-esteem, self-confidence and self-reliance among individuals and the community at large.

All too often, project success is measured predominantly in terms of the successful implementation of the technical hardware, with less attention being given to social development. This is partly because social benefits are less obvious, harder to measure, and less easy to demonstrate as evidence of a successful project. Thailand's rainwater tank implementation programme in the 1980s provides a good illustration of this phenomenon. This programme, and in particular the widespread introduction of the household wire-

reinforced cement water jars, was almost universally recognized as a development success story. This was due both to the rapid rate of implementation and
to the extent to which replication of the project spread throughout the country. While the achievements of the programme in Thailand are undeniable, a
more careful evaluation reveals that it was not quite the unequivocal success
that is generally assumed. Although the millions of household rainwater systems implemented in the course of the programme have been widely appreciated, the broader impact of the project with respect to rural development in
general has been less spectacular. For example, the involvement of the community in setting up revolving funds and implementing and managing projects
was much less than initially envisaged (Wirojanagud and Vanvarothorn,
1990), and the health and hygiene impacts were limited (Hewison, 1996). A
more detailed discussion of the project including these issues can be found in
the case-study on Thailand in Chapter 9.

Project sustainability
To ensure the sustainability of any rainwater project, it is essential that the
community is fully engaged at every stage. Lee and Visscher (1992) suggested
the several key elements needed for a sustainable project. These include full
community involvement in:

- identifying their most serious water-related problems and potential
  solutions
- decisions based on informed choices between viable alternatives
- sharing local knowledge and experience regarding social, economic and
  environmental conditions, and to use this when designing the project
- training both for system construction and system management
- selection, siting and construction of rainwater catchment systems
- developing and running a workable financing mechanism to ensure the
  project is sustained and costs are recovered
- evaluating the project and then redesigning it where necessary.

Hewison (1996) states that 'sustainability should be the principal criterion for
evaluation of any rural water programme'. He goes on to suggest that while
this may initially mean slower progress, eventually coverage will be higher
and cost governments less.

There is also a growing realization in many parts of the world that projects
based on existing technologies and community-based institutions are far more
likely to succeed and be sustained than those based on models imposed from
outside. This is especially so where new institutions, e.g. community-based
management committees, compete with or are replaced by existing ones. It is
often better to upgrade existing technologies and institutions where possible,
especially where these have potential and/or long track records. In India the
recent realization that highly effective rainwater catchment systems are still
operating in almost every part of the country, despite the competition of
modern water-supply technologies, has led to a revival of interest in traditional water harvesting technologies and management practices (Agarwal and

Narain, 1997). The recent success of the 1–2-1 project in China, discussed in Chapter 9, also supports this assertion. The project, based on upgrading traditional sub-surface water cellar designs, has been very well received and widely replicated by the local communities that have been actively involved in the improvement of their own existing rainwater systems. Since many traditional rainwater schemes have been operating successfully for centuries, if not millennia, it is not surprising that these should remain sustainable after upgrading using modern techniques and materials.

Institutional and human resource development
For projects to be sustained, to flourish, and to be widely replicated, it is essential that effective and supportive institutions exist. It is also important that the necessary local human resources are available to ensure the institutions continue to function effectively once any external agency assistance is withdrawn. Institutions comprise any agreement between people, whether formal or informal, and include laws, contracts, and regulations as well as sector organizations, educational establishments, NGOs, and communities themselves. It is widely believed that the failure of many water projects in the developing world can be attributed to systematic deficiencies in the institutions responsible for policymaking, project design, and management (Alaerts et al., 1997). Strengthening these institutions through institutional capacity-building, of which human resource development is a key component, is therefore vital to the long-term sustainability of any project. According to Austin et al. (1987), 'institutional development refers to the organization, management, financing, staffing, training, design, construction, operation, and maintenance of any water [and wastewater] programmes and facilities'. While 'human resource development relates to the human resources needed to carry out these activities and includes training, management and planning, as well as the creation of organizations that will supply the personnel'.

While individual village-level water project initiatives may succeed in the short term, their long-term sustainability may be severely tested in the absence of the appropriate institutional development at all levels. It is also unlikely that widespread replication of appropriate technologies and community-based implementation strategies will be achieved in the absence of supportive institutions at higher levels, even if isolated project success may be possible. These institutions include sector policies, sector plans and budgets, advisory and support services to assist with the technical, financial and management aspects of community projects, and training opportunities. Lee and Visscher (1992) suggest that successful projects depend on a long-term commitment by government; this requires the support of high-level decision- and policymakers. To ensure this support, it is often necessary to explain and convince senior government and aid officials of the benefits of using appropriate technologies, such as rainwater systems and the advantages of community-managed implementation strategies. Seminars, short meetings and training courses, video presentations, newspaper articles, and the use of other media are all effective ways to reach and persuade key officials.

Measures and features of successful projects

In order to measure effectively whether a project has been successful or not, clear and realistic aims and objects need to be drawn up to provide a yardstick against which project success can be measured. In Box 8.1 the importance of establishing an appropriate aim or goal for the project is illustrated, using two hypothetical examples.

Experiences of rainwater projects from around the world, particularly in rural parts of the developing world, reveal a number of the features common to the majority of successful projects. These include the following:

- Most successful projects have started small and grown slowly (at least initially). This allows for the testing, development and modification of both

---

Box 8.1
Measuring project success

Measuring the success of any project involves first comparing the final outcome with the original aims and objectives of the project to see if these have been achieved. For a project to be truly successful, the aims and objectives need to be ambitious, while remaining realistic. For example, the following two aims, (a) and (b) could be for the same project:

(a) to construct 100 household roof catchment systems in a water-short village.
(b) to provide an adequate, clean, sustainable village water supply through the implementation of 100 roof catchment systems in a community-managed programme with the long-term goal of improving health and livelihoods in a water-short village.

Clearly, (a) is far less ambitious than (b). The significant point here is that the initial aim and objectives of a project will affect its ultimate impact. While two projects with the above aims might each be initially deemed as successes, after a period of 10 years the situation might look very different. Obviously, a finely worded set of initial project goals containing all the right buzzwords – 'sustainability', 'community managed', 'improving health and livelihoods' – is of little value unless concrete steps are taken to make these happen. Nevertheless, a project with very limited goals and a narrow, purely hardware-based technical focus may be doomed to failure from the outset.

A truly successful rainwater project will be one that produces both hardware and software sustainability over the long term. Not only will the project meet the specific objectives of providing clean, convenient water supplies, but it will have a broader impact. It will result in strengthening the community's capacity to manage and plan its own development, through the development of the necessary skills, human resources and institutions. The project will leave the community more self-confident and self-reliant, and ready and enthusiastic about embarking on other projects. While in reality few projects will ever quite measure up to this ideal, it is important to set ambitious goals and at least attempt to move towards these in an incremental way. Even some project 'failures' can often teach us valuable lessons, which help in avoiding similar problems in future.

the system design and implementation strategy based on constant re-evaluation.

- Successful projects are generally associated with communities where a real 'felt need' for water has been expressed and where this figures very highly in the development priorities for the locality.
- Successful projects are generally planned, implemented and run predominantly with the input of local people. Projects set up by people foreign to an area with little local input are rarely sustainable. Outsiders may, however, act as important catalysts to stimulate project initiation.
- Projects where the community contribute funds, labour and ideas generally expand and endure, while those supported entirely with external funding are seldom sustained.

Responsibilities of implementing agencies and recipients

The majority of projects, other than individual initiatives at household level, involve a partnership between individual community members and government, donors, and/or NGOs. For such a partnership to succeed, it is essential that the community is fully involved in every aspect of the project, including planning, administration, management, financing, training, construction, operation, maintenance, repair and evaluation. It is also crucial to the success of any project that from the outset, the various stakeholders involved have their specific roles and responsibilities clearly defined.

Project types: household, institutional, community, regional and national
Project types will vary depending on the type of technology used. A small household roof catchment system varies greatly from a large community rock catchment project. The overall scale of implementation will also have a bearing on every aspect of a project even if the technology is the same. For example, the installation of roof catchment tanks can be either an entirely private initiative at a single household or part of a national programme. We can categorize projects according to their scale of implementation as follows:

- *Household level:* These are the smallest projects and are undertaken by individual families at the household level. They are generally private initiatives financed entirely by the householder. This type of project, usually involving the installation of a roof catchment tank, is common throughout the world, especially among wealthier households in developing countries and most households using rainwater in industrialized countries. Occasionally, such initiatives are motivated by subsidies and technical information provided by government or other agencies (see Australia and Germany casestudies in Chapter 9).
- *Institutional level:* Systems built at schools, clinics, and other public buildings are often funded by the institutions (or indirectly by government), and their use is usually restricted to members of the institution. The effectiveness of these systems normally depends on the extent to which they are

managed by the institutions and whether any individual takes responsibility for them.

- *Community level:* These are projects conducted at the village or neighbourhood level and there are two types: First, projects which involve the sharing of a communal source such as water from a rock catchment dam or large ground catchment system, as well as systems constructed at public buildings for general use. Second, projects where individual systems are built through joint community action. Both types can involve a partnership between the community and the government or an NGO.
- *Regional and national level:* These are major projects covering whole regions or nations and often running over many years. They may be restricted to certain sectors of society, e.g. schools or small village populations, and they can take on different forms of involvement. Some projects at this level may provide only a small grant or other subsidy and some technical advice; others may be fully involved in every aspect of implementation. Normally these large-scale projects will include the involvement of several government departments and often donors, NGOs and the private sector. Large-scale projects of this type in Botswana, Thailand and China are discussed in Chapter 9.

Role of external agencies

Any external partner agency (government, donor or NGO) involved with a rainwater catchment system project at community level has a number of key responsibilities:

- First, they must be able to guarantee that the design being promoted is appropriate, i.e. it is safe, durable, and cost-effective.
- Second, they must ensure that they will meet any obligations made with respect to the project. To clarify these obligations and responsibilities, a written contract drawn up between the partner agency and the recipients is important.
- Third, the partner agency must ensure that all sectors of the community are fully involved in the project, especially marginalized groups such as women, the poor, and any disadvantaged minorities.

From the community's point of view, government, donors and NGOs are usually all considered to be external agencies. To reduce the barriers created by such perceptions, representatives from these organizations should engage with the community, visiting frequently and giving support especially during the initial phase of any project. This should not only help to increase understanding about the project by agency representatives, but also assist in cementing the partnership between the community and external agency.

The roles of donors, government, and NGOs in project implementation are often (but not always) quite distinctive, and sometimes all three will work together with the community, especially on larger projects. While it is possible for projects which include multiple stakeholders to succeed, there is a major risk that in such situations they will be held back by excessive bureaucracy and consultations. For example, where a local community-based NGO assists a poor community to approach a local government department for technical assistance and the national office of a donor for small-scale financial assistance, things may work well. In a situation, however, where several tiers and sectors of government, e.g. water, health, and construction at district, regional, and national level become involved, things quickly become complicated. This is especially true if donors and NGOs with their own local, national and international decision-making structures are also involved.

Sometimes donors and NGOs may be quite influential in persuading governments to adopt a more participatory approach with communities in project implementation. This situation occurred in Tanzania, both with the HESAWA project supported by SIDA (Andersson, 1990), and other developments in Dodoma supported by WaterAid (Jarman and Johnson, 1996). In this case, following consultations with donor organizations, the government adopted a National Water Policy advocating a community-based approach to rural supplies.

Government has a special further responsibility with respect to system designs and levels of workmanship. This is especially relevant in situations where the private sector becomes actively involved with system implementation. Through building codes and legislation designed to protect the public, the government has powers to set minimum standards. These may relate to the quality of materials used or the certification of builders or designs. The legal powers and potential to regulate builders vary a lot, and in most developing countries, especially in rural areas, enforcement of regulations is often effectively absent altogether. Nevertheless, there is sometimes a real problem as poor-quality construction by unscrupulous contractors exploiting unwary clients often results in rainwater catchment systems failing. Donors and NGOs can influence the situation through training and helping to raise awareness in the community. There are also opportunities for a degree of self-regulation within the private sector itself. Ultimately, though government is best placed to put controls in place and set minimum standards to protect the public, the challenge remains to ensure that these are set at appropriate levels and are enforced. For this process to be effective, good government at both local and national level are essential, as are the will and resources needed to succeed.

Role of communities and individuals
The success of any project that relies on a partnership between a community and an external partner agency depends on individual community members meeting their agreed obligations with respect to the project. These may include involvement in any public meetings relating to the project and establishing a water committee to manage its planning, implementation, operation and maintenance. The community may also provide agreed inputs of voluntary manual labour, local materials, and money. Formally registering with the project and entering into a legally binding contract can be a useful means of clarifying a recipient's responsibilities and confirming their commitment to meeting these. Another implicit responsibility of participating individuals is that they will work

in good faith both with the partner agency and other community members to ensure successful project implementation. Invariably, however, due to the diversities of interests, opinions and agendas present in all communities, conflicts often arise. If these cannot be resolved satisfactorily through compromise and arbitration the project will suffer. External agencies can sometimes assist communities by acting as arbitrators in any conflicts or disputes.

Once the rainwater system hardware is in place, it is normally the responsibility of the community or individual householders to ensure that proper operation, maintenance, and repairs are carried out. Many systems fail or fall short of their potential after some years because the community fails to meet its responsibilities. This is particularly common with respect to communally shared rainwater catchment facilities. Common problems include a failure to repair and maintain gutters and downpipes which become blocked and broken, reducing inflow into the tank. Tanks are also often neglected with leaking taps, cracks, broken screens, and covers not being repaired. The failure to conduct regular inspection and cleaning of systems is also common. These problems will normally lead to a reduction in both the quantity and quality of water a system can provide.

The failure of the community to maintain systems properly often stems from the fact that clear lines of responsibility for addressing and paying for repairs have not been put in place. While this is straightforward for individual household systems under private family control, where individuals have a direct vested interest in maintaining the system, it is more complicated with shared communal systems. A common problem is that where a community has not been sufficiently involved in a project, it looks to the donor, NGO or government agency that installed the system to repair and maintain it. Clearly, it is essential that the role of the community in the long-term operation and maintenance of systems is agreed between all stakeholders at the start of the project, and financial mechanisms to pay for maintenance and repair are put in place and properly managed.

Role of the private sector
In many parts of the world, the private sector has played an important role in the implementation of rainwater catchment systems. Household and community rainwater tank construction lends itself well to private sector involvement, as Layton (1987) observed in Papua New Guinea. It has also been suggested that:

> development agencies should encourage commercial marketing of tanks as the most effective way of extending or replicating their use whilst continuing to assist poorer families (Pacey and Cullis 1986).

Often, trained and experienced builders who have learned their skills on government- or donor-funded projects set up as small-scale entrepreneurs. These small enterprises generally service those individuals in the community who can afford to buy rainwater systems outright, although they are sometimes sub-contracted by government or donors to assist on projects.

Private sector involvement in rainwater catchment system implementation takes place in a variety of ways. In many richer countries, the private sector may be the only agent implementing systems. This may be done either by assisting clients with the delivery and installation of ready-made systems, or by constructing and assembling systems on site. A key aspect of the private sector involvement in rainwater catchment system implementation is that it introduces an element of competition which can help to drive prices down. This was certainly the case in Thailand where increasingly fierce competition by the private sector in the 1980s and early 1990s drove the price of the 2m^3 wire-reinforced cement jar down to between US$20 and $25. This made commercial jars both affordable to the masses and competitive with jars built through self-help initiatives, thus greatly speeding the overall rate of implementation. At the same time, however, this would have discouraged the community's own initiatives and may have been detrimental to achieving broader development objectives. The Thai experience is rather unusual as, generally, the poorer households, especially in developing countries, cannot afford the services of the private sector. In many cases, the private sector will service only the better-off sectors of the community, leaving the government and donor agencies to focus exclusively on assisting the poorer, more disadvantaged sectors. Increasingly, governments and donors around the world are contracting the private sector to assist with rainwater tank implementation, as occurs in Thailand.

The emergence of dynamic private sector involvement in rainwater catchment system implementation following a government- or donor-sponsored project is often a strong indication that the project has been successful. If people are prepared to pay hard cash for systems, they must clearly be fulfilling an important need. Private sector involvement provides the opportunity for the replication of designs introduced by the original project. If subsidies or other financing mechanisms are available, the private sector should also be able to service the needs of poorer members of the community.

The involvement of the private sector can sometimes create problems, especially if many small-time, unregulated contractors are competing in a limited market. The risk is that to cut tank prices, corners will be cut regarding with the quality of the materials used and workmanship. Another problem is that sometimes the private sector will 'poach' builders and artisans trained by government agencies or donors. This can seriously undermine progress on projects while new builders have to be recruited and trained. To avoid this, government agencies, donors, and NGOs must draw up appropriate contracts and offer realistic levels of remuneration and other benefits.

Choice of technology and implementation strategy

Technical, socio-economic and environmental feasibility
An essential starting point when considering the potential for the use of rainwater catchment systems in any domestic water-supply project is to

determine its technical, socio-economic, and environmental feasibility. Some of the specific approaches involved in technical assessment, such as determining the household water demand, the potential rainwater supply, and determining various aspects of system design are outlined in Chapters 3 and 4. Issues relating to social, economic, and environmental feasibility, including questions of culture, gender, health, affordability, financing and environmental impact are discussed in Chapter 7. A checklist of the points that need to be considered when assessing the appropriateness and viability of any rainwater catchment systems project is given in Box 8.2. In most poorer and disadvantaged communities, many of these preconditions may not be met. This does not mean that any project should not proceed, but rather that more time and resources may be required, particularly with respect to social mobilization work.

Box 8.2

Checklist for assessing appropriateness and viability of a rainwater catchment system project

The following pre-conditions are desirable:

- Technical Feasibility
  - Rainfall and catchment area must be sufficient to meet demand.
  - Design should be appropriate.
  - Skills or training potential must be available locally.
- Social and Economic Feasibility
  - A real felt need in the community for better water provision.
  - Designs should be affordable and cost-effective.
  - The community should be enthusiastic and fully involved.
  - Experiences with previous projects should have been positive.
  - Existence of social cohesion (not conflict) essential.
- Environmental Feasibility and Health
  - The project should have an acceptable level of environmental impact.
  - The project should be designed to enhance the environment.
  - The project should improve both the quantity and quality of water available and have a positive impact on the health of the community.
- Alternatives Considered
  - All reasonable alternative means of water provision should be investigated.
  - Consideration should be given to using more than one alternative in combination.

- Traditional and Current Practices
  - Consideration should be given to any traditional rainwater harvesting practices.
  - Existing approaches to rainwater utilization and possible upgrading should be investigated.

Considering alternatives

When considering the possibility of using rainwater catchment systems for domestic supply, it is important to consider both the advantages and disadvantages of the technology (see Box 8.3) and compare these with other available options. In many instances, other sources of supply may be more appropriate if they are cheaper, more reliable, and can produce sufficient high-quality water. The types of supply that may provide more appropriate alternatives in small communities in developing countries are described in numerous texts, including the following: Feachem and Cairncross (1978), Kerr (1989), Morgan (1990) and Pickford (1991). These cover a range of technologies, including shallow wells, protected springs, river intakes, tubewells, handpumps and gravity supplies which, frequently, are developed in preference to rainwater collection. In some instances, the decision regarding the technology choice may be obvious. Sometimes rainwater catchment systems are selected in the absence of any other viable alternative. Although trucking or piping in water supplies from distant sources are always potential alternatives to rainwater collection, these are extremely expensive options. Usually, a number of viable and potentially affordable options may exist and a choice has to be made on the basis of a complex process of comparing the costs and benefits of each. Ultimately, it is crucial that it is the community members themselves who make an informed choice regarding any alternatives based on the best information available.

In many cases the most appropriate mix of alternatives may involve a combination of technologies. There are many instances where rainwater catchment may not provide an appropriate supply on its own, but if used in combination with another water source, the two may provide the cheapest and most effective form of supply. For example, in eastern Botswana many rural households depend on both purpose-built household roof catchment systems and deep boreholes for their water supplies. Since the boreholes are very expensive to construct and operate, many households will share these supplies and may have to rely on sources several kilometres from their homes. Borehole water is collected using donkey carts or other vehicles and is then stored in the household rainwater tank. In this way, families have the advantages of both a supply at source provided by the rainwater tank, and a reliable and abundant water source provided by the borehole.

Real felt needs of the community

In any project with the objective of improving water supplies to individual households or communities, it is vital that an overall assessment of the 'real felt needs' of the project recipients is undertaken. The importance of this step cannot be overstated and the success of a project can often depend on it. This is especially the case where substantial community inputs in terms of time, labour, materials, and money are involved. It must be remembered that even where the level of water provision is inadequate, poor communities may have several other pressing priorities competing for their limited time and resources. For example, if at a particular point in time, a community's livelihood

Box 8.3

Advantages and disadvantages of rainwater catchment systems for domestic supply

ADVANTAGES

1. **Convenience**
   Provides a supply at the point of consumption.

2. **Good Maintenance**
   The operation and maintenance of household catchment systems are under sole control of the tank owner's family.

3. **Low Running Costs**
   These are almost negligible.

4. **Relatively Good Water Quality**
   Better than traditional sources, especially for roof catchment.

5. **Low Environmental Impact**
   Rainwater is a renewable resource and no damage is done either to the environment or to future supplies through its introduction.

6. **Ubiquitous Supply**
   Rainwater collection is always a water-supply alternative wherever rain falls.

7. **Simple Construction**
   The construction of rainwater catchment systems is simple and local people can easily be trained to build these by themselves; this reduces costs and encourages community participation.

8. **Flexible Technology**
   Systems can be built to almost any requirement. Poor households can start with a single small tank and add more when they can afford it.

DISADVANTAGES

1. **Expensive**
   When compared with alternative water sources, where these are available, the cost per litre for rainwater is frequently higher.

2. **Supply is Limited**
   Both by the amount of rainfall and size of catchment area.

3. **High Initial Cost**
   The main cost of rainwater catchment systems is almost wholly incurred during the initial construction, when a considerable capital outlay is required.

4. **Unattractive to Policymakers**
   Rainwater projects are invariably far more cumbersome to administer than single large projects, e.g. a dam.

5. **Supply is Susceptible to Droughts**
   Occurrence of long dry spells and droughts will adversely affect the performance of RWCS.

6. **Water Quality Vulnerable**
   The quality of rainwater may be affected by air pollution in the vicinity of certain industries. Contamination from animal or bird droppings, insects, dirt and organic matter can also be a problem.

is threatened by a pest outbreak or acute soil-erosion problem, which is reducing the production of food or cash crops, finding a solution to this will be the main priority. In such a context, trying to interest a community in improving its water supplies will probably meet with little enthusiasm.

One way to determine whether there is a 'real felt need' for rainwater catchment technology is to see if any individuals in the community are already using the technique (Skinner, 1990). If they are, even if using only basic technology, e.g. oil drums, then clearly a real need is being demonstrated. In some communities, awareness of the potential health benefits of improved water supplies may be very low. In such instances, it may be appropriate first to embark on a programme of health education before entering into any dialogue with the community regarding the potential for a rainwater catchment project.

Issues of domestic livelihood

Although livelihood is sometimes narrowly defined as 'earning a living', a broader definition of domestic livelihood is pertinent here which encompasses a state of family well-being. In this state, a household is able to meet its own needs using both its own and external resources. Pacey and Cullis (1986) discuss at length the issue of 'perceiving needs and understanding livelihoods' with respect to rainwater harvesting. In their analysis of the issues, a number of key points are emphasized. These include the following:

- Families depend on various sources to support their livelihood, including market production (e.g. agriculture or paid employment), home production (e.g. water collection, food preparation and child care), and resource transfers (e.g. inheritance or welfare handouts). These sources of support may be subject to both time and resource constraints which rainwater supplies can, to some extent, alleviate.
- Over-enthusiasm for favoured techniques may lead to their promotion based purely on their technical or environmental effectiveness, with the question of whether they represent the most efficient resource use being forgotten.
- Rainwater collection can provide both water for survival and water for production (e.g. small-scale irrigation).
- Where water is used purely as a domestic water supply, it is difficult to undertake economic analysis by comparing benefits and costs. Real benefits may include improved health, reduced time spent collecting water, and hence more time spent on productive activities such as agriculture or child rearing.
- It is a mistake to think that improved domestic water supplies must be justified purely in terms of increased production. Domestic work and 'home production' must be allocated a real economic value, based on economic opportunities foregone as a result.

Because of the difficulties in assessing the real costs and benefits of household rainwater systems, detailed economic analysis can be extremely complex and uncertain, and before it is undertaken its usefulness should be questioned. Apart from the difficulties of quantifying 'home production' benefits, system costs are often uncertain due to the need for imprecise assumptions regarding discount rates and system life expectancies, as discussed in Chapter 7.

Economic considerations

While detailed economic analysis may be difficult, for reasons discussed in Chapter 7, economic issues can obviously not be ignored. To be viable, systems must be affordable and within the range of investment costs of other similar types of development in the local water and sanitation sector.

There is a danger that decisions regarding project implementation strategies based purely on the findings of economic analysis may also result in inappropriate approaches being adopted. This is because as Ray (1983) points out, the economics of household rainwater catchment systems throws up a number of paradoxes. These include the fact that:

- Economies of scale provide a financial incentive to build large, shared, communal tanks rather than individual household systems. Experience shows, however, that individual household systems are both more convenient and almost invariably better managed and maintained than shared facilities.
- Economies of scale would also seem to provide a financial incentive to build fewer larger tanks, e.g. one $12m^3$ tank will use less material and normally be cheaper than three $4m^3$ tanks. In reality, however, people may find they simply can not afford to pay for a larger system in one go. Acquiring a number of smaller tanks over a period of time not only spreads the cost but also reduces the risk of system failure. If one of three tanks cracks or bursts, at least two will continue to function. In fact, some smaller tanks can work out to be surprisingly cheap per unit volume due to the lower requirements for reinforcement, e.g. the Thai jar (see also Table 7.1).
- Rainwater catchment systems are often appropriate in poor marginal areas suffering water scarcity and economic difficulties. Ironically, the regions and population groups – e.g. the rural poor in water-scarce localities – who stand to benefit the most from household rainwater catchment systems, are also the ones with least ability to pay.

While project experience from around the world has unequivocally demonstrated the advantages of individual, privately owned systems over communally shared facilities, a communal approach to implementation has many advantages. This has been clearly demonstrated by the use of revolving funds and self-help initiatives amongst women's groups in Kenya (Thoya 1995). In this case, the pooling of communal resources to raise funds for construction was an essential prerequisite for successful projects, even though the tanks themselves were constructed at individual households. For many types of projects such as rock catchment dams, hafirs, or large-scale ground catchment systems which are communal in nature, extra care and effort may be needed when developing management strategies. Aspects such as system maintenance and repair, for example, must be organized to ensure they are undertaken properly.

Capacity of individuals, community and partner agencies
Before embarking on any community project, it is vital to assess the capacity
of the project beneficaries to engage in the project. This will depend on the
resource requirements needed from them in terms of money, time, management inputs, and skills. Clearly, any project designed with a major cost-
sharing element included is unlikely to succeed if the recipients do not have
the means to meet their financial commitments. In such circumstances, two
options are available: either the project must be redesigned to make the
systems affordable to recipients even if this means compromising the level
of supply, or means have to be found to increase recipients' ability to pay,
such as through income-generating activities or revolving ('merry-go-
round') funds.

The extent to which individuals and the community at large will be prepared to commit time, labour, and money to a project will depend on their
enthusiasm for the project. If the enthusiasm can be generated for a viable
project, lack of skills in construction or project management need not necessarily be an obstacle to successful implementation if these can be addressed
through adequate training initiatives. Indeed, most successful projects include
a major element of capacity building within the community. This normally
results in much broader development benefits than those resulting purely
from the implementation of rainwater catchment systems hardware.

While it is common to scrutinize project beneficiaries to determine their
capacity to engage in any project, it is less common to scrutinize the external
partner agency's capacity to succeed. Many projects fail because the partner
agencies lack experience, human resources, or awareness and understanding
of the needs of the local community. Any donor or community needs to be
confident that any partner agencies involved with project implementation
have the capacity and experience to succeed.

Project initiation, implementation and evaluation

The implementation strategy for any successful project involves a partnership
approach in which both parties will have different things to offer (Lee and
Visscher, 1992). For example, the community may provide local knowledge
and contribute to project management and operational inputs, as well as
providing labour and local materials to help keep down costs. The partner
agency will normally offer technical and organizational know-how related to
the technology alternatives. It may also advise on the construction and maintenance implications of different options as well as providing financial support
and/or assistance in establishing financing mechanisms for the project. Furthermore, the partner agency will usually support training activities and provide support if unforeseen problems arise.

Implementation stages
The key stages in any rainwater catchment system project implementation
strategy include the following:

Identification The first stage in project initiation involves the identification of both appropriate project partners and appropriate technologies. Identifying partners may involve a donor, NGO, or government agency approaching a community that needs assistance with improving water provision, and opening a dialogue with them. It is preferable, however, that it is the community itself that organizes itself, identifies the specific issues with which it needs assistance, and seeks out partners. When a community approaches a donor, NGO, or government agency, a number of pre-conditions favourable to a successful project will already be in place; namely, the community has a 'real felt need' for water-supply improvements, it is prepared and motivated to do something to improve its situation, and it is willing, as a community, to work with an external partner agency. However, once the partnership is formed it is essential that the community remains engaged as an equal partner throughout the project planning, design and implementation stages. Eventually the community should take over responsibility entirely for the operation and management of any rainwater systems constructed. The other component of project identification is to identify the most appropriate technology and construction techniques. Layton (1987) suggests that the most appropriate rainwater harvesting technologies are those where local labour is used for construction, the materials and techniques are familiar to local people, and local materials and manufactured components are used.

Project management and administration Once a partnership has been formed between a community and a donor, NGO, or government agency, it is essential that an effective management structure is quickly put in place to ensure efficient administration of the project. This organizational structure should include substantial community representation and involvement. Where organizational structures exist in a community, these should be used. If they exist but are not functioning well, they could be strengthened. A village development committee, for example, if well respected and representative of the community, may form a useful core group to work with team members from an external partner agency.

Planning and design The planning stage will include technical, socio-economic, and environmental assessments as well as any surveys to collect relevant information. A more detailed understanding of the perceived needs of the community may be needed at this stage. Detailed social surveys, public meetings, and interviews are some of the methods through which the community's goals and desires may be clearly ascertained. Once these are clear, various technical-design options and implementation strategies should be discussed with the community.

At this critical planning and design stage it is vital that any community representatives (e.g. a water development committee) working with an external partner agency *do* represent the views of the whole community and are accountable to it. While community members may not be qualified to assess the technical merits of two different tank designs, they may have strong opinions or preferences based on experience or cultural beliefs, which may

193

strongly influence the popularity of a particular design within the community. Often very basic factors, such as the timing of projects, may be crucial to their success and here inputs from the community are critical. Chindaprasirt (1995), for example, comments on problems encountered during short, village-level training programmes in north-east Thailand inappropriately timed to take place in the rice-planting season. Clearly, if the community is fully involved in the project planning process, such conflicts are easily avoided.

Financing   Project-financing strategies will depend on the financial resources of the community. Where project beneficiaries are in a position to pay for the full cost of systems, they should be required to do so. Since few people will be in a position to make an outright payment in full, assistance may be needed by the community to establish revolving funds or credit facilities to assist with financing systems.

While contributions of free labour and local materials can help to keep costs down, a subsidy from a donor or the government will be required where project beneficiaries are too poor to pay the full system costs. The financial contribution from the beneficaries should also relate to their ability to pay. Where this is limited, the establishment of income-generating projects, as discussed in Chapter 7, should be considered. This has a secondary benefit since the greater the inputs and involvement of the community, the more they will feel they own the project, increasing its chances of being sustained and replicated.

For a project to be sustainable, it must have the capacity to pay for its operation, maintenance, repair, and, ideally, future replacement costs. To do this, it is vital that everyone is clear about who is responsible for this. If it is the householder's own responsibility, as will normally be the case with domestic systems, this must be made clear from the outset. For communal systems, it will normally be necessary to set up a water committee to manage the project and oversee the collection and expenditure of any funds.

Training   Training should not be limited simply to transferring specific skills such as the construction technique for a particular system. Instead, training should be part of a broader attempt to build capacity within the community to initiate, plan, implement, and manage a whole range of development projects. Training for rainwater catchment systems implementation should include the development of competence in some or all of the following areas:

- survey and evaluation of potential sites for rainwater catchment systems
- simple design techniques and technology selection
- appropriate construction methods and techniques
- selection of suitable, locally available building materials
- operation, maintenance and repair of systems
- project management and administration (including the administration of funds)
- project assessment and evaluation.

For larger-scale projects, training and institutional development will not be limited to individual communities but will take place at a variety of levels. In north-east Thailand, for example, a major, self-help participatory training initiative for small-scale water-resource development was conducted using a project-casework approach (Tharun, 1995; Chindaprasirt, 1995). This involved more than 700 training courses between 1987 and 1989. The training was conducted at three levels: district technicians and officers; village technicians; and villagers. The training modules consisted of three main components:

(a) planning and decision-making
(b) technical skills
(c) training of trainers.

All trainees, including 675 village technicians and 14 000 villagers, undertook modules (a) and (b), whereas only the district technicians and officers also undertook module (c).

Construction Communities should be fully engaged during the construction phase, and while their voluntary labour provides a valuable input it is essential that they are not involved simply in the capacity of providers of free labour. On-the-job training is an important component of grassroots capacity-building and, during the construction process, members of the community should be trained and gain skills that can be put to work both during later phases of the project and, ideally, also for other future development initiatives. To ensure that both the level of training and the quality of construction and workmanship remain high, it is vital that any trainees from the community are properly supervised.

On-the-job training during the construction phase can be formalized through an accreditation system, whereby certificates may be awarded to community members on the successful completion of a given number of rainwater systems. Such tangible evidence of skills transfer can provide an important motivation for community members to become enthusiastically involved in projects, even on a voluntary basis. If accreditation offers any prospects for future employment, the motivational effect will be further enhanced.

In the past, construction has often been viewed as a predominantly male occupation. While it is true that in some cultures heavy physical labour is predominantly undertaken by men, in many others women have traditionally been involved in construction. There is really no reason why women should not be involved in the construction phase, at the very least as team members, and there are several advantages to this. The more familiar women are with the rainwater catchment systems at household or community level, the more able they will be to maintain and repair them. In many parts of the world, women head households, often in the absence of men who may be absent for a variety of reasons such as working as migrant labour. Hence, it is important that women are able to operate, maintain, and repair systems effectively.

Operation, maintenance and repair Regular inspection, cleaning, maintenance, and occasional repairs are essential for the long-term success of any rainwater project. Clear guidelines should be provided on how to do this during the project's implementation stage, and systems must be designed to encourage these practices (see Chapter 4). Gutters, downpipes, catchment surfaces, and tanks need to be checked frequently and cleaned out from time to time. The speedy repair of leaking taps or minor cracks will reduce water losses and minimize repair costs. In practice, such tasks are frequently not done effectively or in good time because clear guidelines of responsibilities have not been discussed. In the case of communal systems it is particularly important that the community is clear as to who is responsible for undertaking these tasks.

Evaluation, monitoring, improvement and replication   No project will ever be perfect and a thorough evaluation at the end of the first round of implementation will invariably, with the benefit of hindsight, produce a number of valuable lessons. In order that the community also learns from any mistakes, it is essential that it is also fully involved in any evaluation exercise. Armed with the findings of a comprehensive evaluation, the community and any external partners should be in a position to make improvements to any part of the project that are deficient. This could involve changes to the design, construction methods, financing, management, training and even the evaluation exercise itself. This ensures that future replication of the technology, both within the community and beyond, benefits from any lessons learned. Even after the evaluation, any follow-up work, and replication have taken place, it is worthwhile monitoring the project through inspection of systems every few years to ensure that the technology and its maintenance, repair, and the overall project management continue to be sustainable, and that no systematic problems arise.

Addressing obstacles to project implementation

No rainwater catchment systems implementation project will ever be entirely problem free. There are inevitably obstacles to implementation which can slow down and sometimes jeopardize a project completely. In circumstances where the pre-conditions for implementation are good (see Box 8.2), the community is fully involved, and the technology and implementation strategy are appropriate, most obstacles can normally be overcome.

Obstacles to implementation
A wide variety of obstacles to successful project implementation exist, and these can be identified at every level from the local community to the international donor. Such obstacles include:

- a lack of willingness by individual community members to participate in a project due to a lack of understanding about the technology, or scepticism regarding its appropriateness. This concern is often well founded, based on past bad experiences.
- pressure from funding partners to adopt a certain technology causing the project to be inflexible, unresponsive to community needs, results oriented and time bound.

- an unsustainable Western-based 'hardware'-oriented top-down approach to implementation, which relegates the community's role to one of providers of free labour and materials.
- opposition to a community-managed approach based on simple appropriate technologies from engineers and decision-makers, many of whom have been trained along Western lines to implement conventional technology on government-run projects.
- a lack of enthusiasm from politicians and policymakers, who often prefer more prestigious large-scale projects, e.g. dams and pipelines, which may result in greater short-term rewards in political and 'other' terms for this small minority.
- difficulties for engineers and other government personnel in accepting and adapting to their new roles as facilitators of self-help initiatives using simple appropriate technologies, which are often considered incompatible with their status (Andersson, 1989, 1990).
- political obstacles which may result when a switch from a policy of 'free government provision of water to all' to one of self-help provision occurs, as was the case in Tanzania. Such a change also requires government to admit to the failure of its previous policy and approach (Andersson, 1989, 1990).
- the undermining of self-help programmes by government- or donor-funded projects in the same vicinity offering free systems, remuneration for labour inputs and other benefits (Tharun, 1995).
- special problems may surface when an innovative method such as a community-based participatory approach is introduced for the first time. It takes time and careful explanation to persuade decision-makers, engineers and technicians of the merits of the new approach. The process is slower than conventional strategies and requires patient dialogue between all the stakeholders; this can lead to frustrations and personality clashes (Tharun, 1995).
- the missing of appropriate opportunities for engaging the energies of the private sector by external funding organizations. Pacey and Cullis (1986, p82) suggest that because of their 'public service traditions' many aid agencies 'are reluctant to form a relationship' with local commercial enterprises or teach entrepreneurial skills to builders on training courses.
- conflicting priorities within the community, and between the community and the partner agency.
- an overlapping, conflicting or poorly defined role for government and, sometimes, other partner agencies at national, regional, district, and local levels.

Overcoming obstacles to implementation
Sometimes rainwater catchment system projects may have high potential in technical, economic, and environmental terms but the community lacks awareness and motivation to participate in a project. There may be good reasons for this and these should be investigated through a comprehensive social assessment. However, in some cases resistance to a project may be

overcome simply by engaging the community and raising awareness about the benefits and cost-effectiveness of the project, while simultaneously allaying any concerns. Often, community resistance can be overcome by conducting a pilot project; this also gives the implementing agencies time to develop a partnership with the community and together plan and design the project in a way that the community embraces. At this stage, several different approaches may be adopted to change a community's perception of a project. Some of these are outlined by Lee and Visscher (1990) and include the following:

- engaging community members in dialogue concerning the merits of rainwater catchment vis-à-vis other systems
- the use of local media such as radio, newspapers, posters, and community representatives to communicate the principal benefits of any project
- organizing trips for community members to visit any similar projects in neighbouring regions with similar climatic and socio-economic conditions
- constructing demonstration units at schools or other public buildings and introducing the technique to schoolchildren in a way that results in outreach to their families.

In addition to motivating communities, it is important to raise awareness and educate engineers and decision-makers about the benefits of community-based approaches using appropriate technologies. There is also a need to convince government and other external partner agencies about the benefits of this approach both in terms of cost-effectiveness and sustainability. The task of changing the entrenched practices and attitudes of both engineers and governments is often left to national or international NGOs and more enlightened donor agencies working in the water sector. Gradually, changes are starting to take place in many countries as governments, communities and aid agencies re-examine their roles (Mather, 1996).

In Tanzania, partnerships have been formed between government and external agencies such as SIDA, and with the communities themselves (Andersson, 1990). These have slowly helped to address a crisis in rural water provision brought about by the old 'top-down' approach to implementation. Although rainwater catchment systems are only one of a range of appropriate technologies that are being implemented through the new community-based initiatives, the Tanzanian experience does show that conventional government approaches can be radically changed.

Replication and technology transfer

Local and regional project replication

Another important measure of project success is where widespread, self-sustaining replication of rainwater catchment systems occurs (Gould, 1991). While such instances tend to be rare, there are several examples of this phenomenon around the world, of which the Thai jar programme, which began in north-east Thailand and spread throughout the country and across

198

some borders, is the best known. At a local level, the continued success of the Machakos concrete ring design in Kenya and its wider utilization in other parts of the region is another important example.

Technology transfer: regionally and globally
An effective way to transfer technologies between regions or countries is for the key individuals involved with the project implementation from one region to visit an ongoing project in the other. Ideally, they should work side by side with 'experts' who should then provide support for them when they return home and apply what they have learned.

It has long been recognized that the transfer of technologies between developing countries – South-South technology transfer – makes more sense than North-South transfers of technology. In the case of domestic rainwater catchment systems, much of the exchange of ideas and technologies during the last few decades has been predominantly between the countries of the South. For example, there have been a number of projects in Africa which have been based on the use of the Thai jar and other ferrocement tank designs developed in South-east Asia. When technologies and technological ideas are transferred, it is always necessary to adapt both the designs and implementation strategies to local conditions. Failure to do this will often result in disappointment with the technology.

During the last two decades some important developments with respect to information transfer about rainwater catchment systems have occurred. In 1982, the hosting of an international conference on rainwater cistern systems set the stage for what was to become a regular biennial conference series. Conference venues have included, in chronological order, Hawaii (1982), US Virgin Islands (1984), Thailand (1987), the Philippines (1989), Taiwan (1991), Kenya (1993), China (1995), Iran (1997) and Brazil (1999). Since 1993, the conference title has been changed to the *International Conference on Rainwater Catchment Systems* to broaden its scope to include rainwater harvesting for agriculture and systems that do not rely on rainwater storage exclusively in tanks. In conjunction with, and to support, the conference series, the International Rainwater Catchment Systems Association (IRCSA) was formed in 1991. In 1993, the IRCSA took over the publication of *Raindrop* which had originally been started by the USAID-funded WASH (Water, Sanitation and Health) Project in 1988. The development of the Internet, allowing the publication of electronic journals, manuals, design drawings, guidelines, and other relevant information has led to a rapid growth in the rate of international information exchange. While this technology is not yet widely available at village level, it probably soon will be, allowing even greater opportunities for technology transfer in the future.

Summary of key points

- Successful community rainwater projects can result in a broad range of benefits in addition to improved water supply. These include improved health, employment opportunities, development of new skills, and capacity in project planning, implementation, management, operation and maintenance. They can also result in a growing sense of self-esteem, self-confidence and self-reliance in the community.

- Most successful rainwater projects:
  - start small and grow slowly (at least initially)
  - are associated with communities with a real 'felt need' for water
  - are planned, implemented and run predominantly by local people
  - are projects where the community contribute funds, labour and ideas.
- Apart from household initiatives, most projects involve a partnership between community members, government, donors and NGOs. For this to succeed, the community *must* be fully involved in all aspects, including project planning, administration, management, financing, training, construction, operation, maintenance, repair, and evaluation.
- When assessing the viability of any rainwater catchment project, it is important that all alternatives should first be investigated as well as the technical, social, economic and environmental feasibility of the project.
- Rainwater projects often face many obstacles, especially in developing countries. If the project is viable and the community engaged and motivated, these can often be overcome.
- The replication of rainwater catchment systems technologies, both locally and globally, is ultimately the best measure of project success.

9

Case studies

THE FOLLOWING CASE STUDIES from Australia and New Zealand, Botswana, China, Germany, Japan, Kenya, Thailand and the United States represent a cross-section of the countries around the world where rainwater catchment systems are being utilized for domestic water supplies. A number of other benefits of rainwater utilization are also touched on in some of these case studies. For example, the significance of rainwater collection in Japanese cities relates as much to its benefits in flood control and the provision of emergency water supplies for fire-fighting and consumption following natural disasters, as it does towards providing an alternative water supply.

Since rainwater is collected and used for domestic supplies so widely, many other countries could also have been included in this chapter had time and space permitted. For some countries, detailed accounts of rainwater-collection activities may be found elsewhere, such as for Brazil (Gnadlinger, 1995a, 1995b), India (Agarwal and Narain, 1997), Iran (Aminipouri and Ghoddousi, 1997), Honduras (Brand and Bradford, 1991) and the Philippines (Villareal, 1989).

Australia and New Zealand

Australia

Due to its arid climate and the widely scattered nature of its rural population, rainwater catchment is widespread in much of the Australian outback. Australia's population is just 18 million, of which more than 90 per cent reside in major towns and cities around the coasts. Rural areas are very sparsely populated and the provision of reticulated supplies for remote farmsteads is uneconomic. Groundwater sources are also expensive to develop, besides these are frequently unreliable or unsuitable on grounds of quality. According to Perrens (1982) and the Australian Bureau of Statistics (ABS, 1994), around one million people in rural Australia rely on rainwater as their primary water source. The popularity of 'hobby farm' and 'lifestyle block' developments on the urban fringes has also increased the need for self-sufficient water supplies in recent years. Rainwater catchment systems are often the most cost-effective or only option, even on the urban periphery. Furthermore, a growing level of environmental awareness may also have contributed to popularizing more sustainable lifestyles involving greater self-reliance in water, energy and food supplies (Mollison, 1991). In many urban areas too, the use of rainwater supplies fits in well with state government policies on water conservation. In the city of Adelaide, the capital of South Australia, rainwater tanks are popular due to the poor quality of the water from the city's main water source, the Murray river (Hoey and West, 1982). Although rainwater catchment systems are especially widespread in South and Western Australia, from where examples are cited below, the use of roof runoff for domestic supply is common in many parts of the country. Use in rural areas varies from 30 to 85 per cent depending on the region, and approaches 100 per cent in some areas (Heyworth et al. 1998). There is some concern over the quality of the rainwater as many systems are not maintained as well as they should be. While the health risk may be minor for most people, vulnerable groups such as the very old and very young are more likely to suffer ill-effects. A major study into the risks associated with drinking rainwater is currently ongoing in South Australia (Heyworth – personal communication, 1998).

Ground catchment systems
Rainwater has long been an important source of water in rural Australia, and many of the early systems were designed and constructed by the farmers themselves. As early as the 1920s, however, applied research into and field-testing of innovative systems was undertaken by the Victoria State Rivers and Water Supply Commission, which built two experimental 990m^2 'iron clad' ground catchments. These each supplied a 175m^3 concrete and bitumen lined and covered storage reservoir. The systems were constructed on sloping land using 26 gauge GI sheets, which were also used to cover the tanks, at Drytank and Cabbage Tree Hill in the mallee country in north-west Victoria, and were described by Kenyon (1929). These demonstrations were half-size versions of a system designed to provide the total water needs of a small sheep station including six people, 150 sheep, 10 horses and two cows. In the proposed full-scale system it was envisaged that roof runoff from the house, sheds and the tank roof would also be collected to give a total catchment area of 2340m^2 supplying a 325m^3 reservoir. It was estimated that this could meet a constant demand of 450m^3 per year. Kenyon even simulated the performance of the system using the previous 51 years' actual local rainfall data and showed that the system never ran dry. At a cost of £480 in 1929, however, the system would hardly have been affordable to most small private sheep farmers.

In the 1950s, a much cheaper solution was developed in the form of the 'roaded' catchment (Laing, 1981). These were based on the principle that a well-constructed highway, even if unsealed, should shed rainwater quickly and efficiently. Roaded catchments are built in a similar way using heavy mechanical graders to shape and compact the surface. A series of parallel cambered 'roadways' are prepared and linked through a network of drainage ditches and channels, which divert runoff into an excavated open reservoir (Figure 9.1a). By smoothing out the land depression storage, evaporation and infiltration losses are reduced by water quickly flowing into storage tanks. Compacting the surface or first covering it with a layer of clay can further decrease infiltration losses. Catchments sizes typically range from less than two to over 40 hectares. In areas with rainfall of 300–400mm, the proportion that can be harvested varies from between about 25 and 40 per cent.

Several thousand of these systems have been constructed, especially in Western Australia where they are common on commercial farms for stock

Figure 9.1 **(a)** Roaded catchment in Western Australia
(Source: Hudson, 1987)

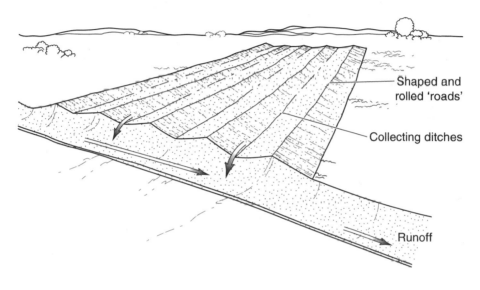

(b) Flat batter dam in Western Australia
(Adapted from Hudson, 1987)

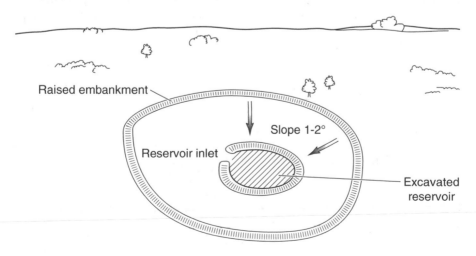

watering. Many are also used for domestic supplies for farms, villages and small towns (Hudson, 1987). Replication of this technique has occurred to a limited extent, with results from experimental systems in both Texas and Arizona indicating performance levels similar to those in Western Australia (Hollick, 1982). In areas with sandy soils, such as in the southern coastal area of Western Australia, roaded catchments do not work well. Here the presence of underlying clay and a mean annual rainfall of around 400mm have allowed the development of another system, the 'flat batter dam' (Hudson, 1987; Laing, 1981). These circular or square catchments are graded to slope at 1–2° towards a central reservoir, the excavation of which provides clay which is spread to a depth of 0.1m over the catchment, yielding runoff efficiencies of up to 40 per cent (Figure 9.1b).

The South Australian Rainwater Tank Promotion Campaign

In 1981 the government of South Australia initiated a Rainwater Tank Promotion Campaign, and Hoey and West (1982) reported that many new tanks were purchased following major newspaper publicity and advertising by local tank manufacturers. The scheme is still ongoing and, although it offers no financial incentives, it provides free technical advice and information on rainwater tank sizing, installation and maintenance to householders. A regularly updated booklet and other materials, provided free of charge by the scheme through SA Water, contain this information (SA Water, 1998). The booklet also includes easy-to-use graphs for assisting individuals in making accurate assessments of the most appropriate storage tank capacity for their needs in different parts of the state (Box 3.1). It even gives easy-to-follow directions for developing a simple computer model of any roof catchment system, giving users the option of determining the demand rate and level of system reliability that best suits them (Box 3.2). The benefits of soft rainwater for washing hair, clothes and 'making a really good cup of tea' are also highlighted. The material also deals with some of the problems associated with rainwater supplies such as the nuisance of mosquito larvae and gives advice on dealing with them by adding a teaspoon of kerosene or using an approved larvicide. Information on the use of interconnected rainwater and mains supplies to ensure the continuity of the supply even in times of drought, and the use of different foul flush mechanisms, is also provided. The State Health Commission also provides detailed guidelines on how to avoid contamination of rainwater supplies and maintain the quality of the water stored in the tank (South Australian Health Commission, 1995).

Technical support and advisory services

South Australia has led the way in actively promoting rainwater catchment systems and providing free, easily available information covering all aspects of rainwater use and water conservation (McLaren et al., 1987; SA Water, 1998). Other states and the federal government have, however, also developed resources to assist and advise householders. For example, the Health Department of Western Australia provides various relevant leaflets, including one on

204

how to ensure stored rainwater is kept safe to drink (Health Department of Western Australia, 1996). They even have this information on their website at http://www.public.health.wa.gov.au In the past much of the relevant information has been dispersed in numerous reports and information leaflets. A recent publication 'Guidance on the use of rainwater tanks' has helped to consolidate this into a slim volume (Cunliffe, 1998).

New Zealand

Rainwater collection is widely practised throughout rural New Zealand (Plates 9.1 and 9.2) which, like Australia, has a widely scattered and sparse rural population. Climatically, New Zealand is very different from her arid neighbour, being generally more humid. Despite being criss-crossed by major rivers and having excellent groundwater conditions in some areas e.g. the Canterbury plains, New Zealand also has many areas where fresh water is scarce. Reasons for this include a lack of surface water in some areas underlain by volcanic and limestone strata, and poor-quality groundwater due to high iron content or coastal saline intrusions in other places. Rainwater collection is especially widespread in Northland, a 300km-long peninsula north of Auckland, due partly to the high iron content of the groundwater in many places. Here, and in many parts of the country, farmsteads collect rainwater for domestic purposes and will typically have at least one rainwater tank of around 20m³. These tanks are generally supplied from commercial outlets and a variety of types including concrete, plastic, metal and ferrocement are popular. Ferrocement tanks have been made commercially in New Zealand for many years and Watt (1978) discusses their construction in detail. Tanks with capacities of up to 25m³ are commonly made centrally and delivered by lorry. In recent years, moulded plastic tanks have become popular, competitive with and comparable in cost to ferrocement or concrete tanks (Plate 4.3). The long-term durability of plastic tanks is unknown, although some come with a 20-year guarantee. The durability of ferrocement and concrete tanks is good, with one concrete tank built near Wanganui in 1914 still in good shape in 1998. Other localities where rainwater catchment systems play a critical role in providing water supplies are on many small peninsulas and off-shore islands, e.g. Whangaparaoa peninsula near Auckland, which has the highest concentration of rainwater tanks in the country, and Waiheke Island in Auckland's Hauraki Gulf where most of the 8500 residents depend on roof water for their potable supply. In a large number of New Zealand's numerous national and regional parks and forest reserves, many overnight huts and rest facilities rely on roof tanks, e.g. Nelson Lakes National Park.

Technical advice and information regarding the design, implementation and maintenance of water quality in domestic rainwater systems, although available from some district councils, is not as accessible or detailed as in Australia. Several anecdotal reports by professional tank cleaners suggest that tanks are not always maintained as well as they should be, and unscreened outlet pipes and poorly secured lids have sometimes allowed animals and birds to enter tanks. Although New Zealand has no indigenous mammals,

Plate 9.1 *Typical household roof catchment system used for all domestic water supply, Kakatahi, Wangunui District, New Zealand. (Photo: John Gould)*

Plate 9.2 *A 2m² roof catchment provides sufficient water to fill a 900-litre tank for handwashing at toilet facilities at Gillespies beach on the humid west coast of the South Island, New Zealand.* (Photo: John Gould, 1997

imported exotic species have overrun certain parts of the country. An estimated 80 million possums, for example, now outnumber the human population by more than 20 to 1. There have been several reports of possums drowning in tanks, as well as hedgehogs, rats, birds and even a pet dog. Such incidents can obviously create a serious health risk, as can droppings from these and other species on the catchment surface. Direct evidence of the effects on health are rare. One recent report by Simmons and Smith (1997) traced gastrointestinal symptoms suffered by a family of four over a 10-month period to *Salmonella Typhimurium phage* type 1. The family lived at a beach-side house and used a roof tank as a drinking-water source. Although *Salmonella* could not be isolated from a cat which frequently defecated on the roof, possums and occasionally rats clambered over the roof, which was overhung by bush. Seagulls were also thought to have perched on the roof from time to time. In response to these reports a survey of water quality of 125 roof tank systems is now being undertaken by Auckland Healthcare in collaboration with the New Zealand Occupational and Environmental Health Unit, Auckland University.

Botswana

Botswana is a semi-arid landlocked country with a population of just 1.5 million (1996). Water resources are extremely scarce in many parts of the country, 85 per cent of which is covered by deep Kalahari sands blanketed by desert scrub but devoid of any surface water. Although groundwater does occur at depth in some places, it is often saline. Despite the scarcity of water, the mean annual rainfall ranges from about 250 to 650mm and rainwater catchment is practised widely in rural areas.

A significant amount of research and development into rainwater catchment systems for domestic supplies in Botswana has taken place over the last 30 years (Gould, 1985, 1987, 1996). This began with Intermediate Technology Development Group's well-documented work in the 1960s (ITDG, 1969). Progress in implementing appropriate rainwater systems nationwide has, however, been slow and the full potential of these systems is yet to be developed. The diamond-based economy has enabled government to develop expensive conventional borehole and reticulated supplies in some areas, while many scattered remote settlements elsewhere depend on traditional sources or distant private boreholes, often several kilometres away.

In towns and villages, most roof catchment systems are commercial plastic or corrugated-iron tanks, although ferrocement and brick tanks are also found at some institutions. The large storage requirements necessitated by the seasonal and erratic rainfall regime mean that tanks are expensive, not only due to their size but also because of the high cost of materials and transport. In dry seasonal climates such as Botswana, large catchment areas are also required and, where roof areas are small, ground catchments are often more appropriate. The main disadvantage with ground surface catchments is the fact that the quality of water is poor compared with roof catchments and, if not treated, is generally unsuitable for drinking.

In rural areas only a few wealthy cattle owners are in a position to purchase appropriately sized rainwater catchment systems outright. Normally, poorer people and communities rely on some form of subsidy for rainwater systems. Three different initiatives, all initially joint ventures between government and donors to implement and promote rainwater collection in rural Botswana, are described below.

The ALDEP rainwater tank programme
The Arable Lands Development Programme (ALDEP) administered by the Ministry of Agriculture supports the largest rainwater tank construction scheme in Botswana. The programme makes a rainwater tank package available to needy small farmers. Between 1979 and 1991 over 700 10–20m³ sub-surface brick and ferrocement tanks were constructed in remote rural areas (Gould, 1996). Most of these used traditional threshing floors or compacted surfaces as catchment aprons (Figure 2.1). These systems provide an invaluable water supply to farmers in remote districts throughout the rainy season.

Although the ALDEP tanks were originally designed to provide water for draught animals in the 'lands areas' to allow early ploughing at the start of the rainy season, invariably people used the water for domestic purposes, including drinking. These ground catchment systems used traditional mud/dung threshing floors as catchment areas and, as with most ground catchment systems, the quality of the water was very poor due to contamination of the catchment area by excrement from small children and animals. In response to this problem, the Ministry of Agriculture developed a new design involving a raised 40m² corrugated-iron sheet catchment area and a 7m³ plastic polyethylene tank (Visscher and Lee, 1991). From 1991 to 1995, more than 200 ferrocement and imported 7m³ polyethylene surface tanks connected to 40m² purpose-built corrugated-iron roof catchments were constructed (Plate 9.3). Leakage problems and the limited durability of the cheap, imported polyethylene tanks resulted in a return to the original ferrocement sub-surface design. Trials have also recently taken place with 11m³ ferrocement surface tanks similar to the design developed in Kenya and introduced through training courses in 1994–95 (see Appendix 5).

The total number of tanks built under the scheme is now well over 1000. Farmers throughout Botswana owning fewer than 40 head of cattle can participate and they receive an 85 per cent subsidy from the government towards the US$1200 roof/tank system (1995 prices). Despite this generous assistance, some farmers find the 15 per cent down-payment, averaging around $150, prohibitive and the project remains under-subscribed (Gould, 1996).

One proposal is to introduce a combined roof and ground catchment system, with a 5m³ surface roof catchment tank for providing drinking and cooking water and a 15m³ ferrocement sub-surface ground catchment tank for collecting larger quantities of lower-quality water for other purposes (e.g. watering plants and animals, washing, etc). A computer modelling simulation suggests that this design (Figure 1.1b) could provide most of the rural

Plate 9.3 *A newly constructed 11m³ ferrocement tank connected to a purpose-built 40m² corrugated-iron 'ALDEP' roof catchment (and replacing a 7m³ polyethylene tank) near Kanye, Botswana.* (Photo: John Gould, 1996)

Plate 9.4 *A 46m³ ferrocement tank replacing a leaking 4.5m³ corrugated-iron tank at a primary school in Moshaneng, Kanye, Botswana.* (Photo: John Gould, 1995)

household water needs in much of the country (Gieske et al., 1995; Gould 1996).

Rainwater collection from a Kalahari pan

An innovative project pioneered by the Rural Industries Innovation Centre (RIIC) in the small 'remote area dwellers' settlement of Zutshwa (population approximately 250) utilizes runoff from the side of a pan. Pans (also known as salt pans when filled with evaporite deposits) are wind-eroded depressions, common in the Kalahari, which occasionally temporarily fill with rainwater. At Zutshwa pan, located 65km south-west of Hukuntsi in Kgalagadi District, low walls have been constructed to divert rainwater runoff from a fenced area on the side of the pan into three sub-surface tanks. The existence of rills and gullies leading down the relatively steep sides of the pan provided the evidence of surface runoff which led RIIC, in conjunction with the community, to construct three $68m^3$ cement-lined brick tanks (Figure 2.3). During its first season of operation, the tanks were full by mid-February and considerable losses were incurred due to overflow. Prior to the construction of the rainwater catchment system, water had been trucked in from Hukuntsi at a cost of around US$90/$m^3$. By direct comparison, the $205m^3$ of rainwater collected in the three full tanks would have an equivalent value of $18 450. At a total cost of about $27 000 (Petersen, 1993) the construction of the system seems easily justified. One problem associated with the system is that the water contains very fine particles which remain permanently suspended giving the water a turbid milky appearance. A number of methods for dealing with such turbidity, including the use of natural coagulants, are currently being considered. A year after the completion of the project, a pipeline was constructed from a borehole 10km away where a sophisticated reverse osmosis system was installed to remove dissolved salts. While this system has the potential to provide virtually unlimited clean water to the three standposts serving Zutshwa's 250 residents, many questions have been raised regarding the appropriateness and sustainability of such a comparatively high technology system. Indeed, when one of the authors visited Zutshwa in July 1994, the standposts in the settlement were dry, as the diesel pump had broken for the second time since its inception. As a result, people were again using rainwater as the only alternative source.

School roof catchment tanks

Roof catchment tanks are a common sight at primary schools in villages throughout Botswana. Surveys conducted by the Botswana Technology Centre have revealed that about half the 800+ primary schools in the country possess tanks, most of them being of the corrugated-iron variety, provided by the Government (Gould, 1996). Since these have an average life expectancy of only about five years, many schools have leaking tanks. Despite having average roof areas of around $1300m^2$, the average number of roof tanks is just over two, the average volume of the tanks totalling just $12m^3$ per school. This is only around a tenth of the volume required to ensure that most of the available rainwater is captured. Despite the poor performance of their roof catchment tanks, the majority of schools in Botswana are keen to have more tanks.

A recent pilot project undertaken jointly by the Botswana Technology Centre and Rural Industries Innovation Centre has pioneered the construction of large ferrocement roof catchment tanks with volumes of 23m^3 and 46m^3, at schools and clinics in rural areas, similar to those currently being constructed in Kenya (Plate 9.4). One 46m^3 tank when full could provide three litres of water per day for more than 30 days to up to 500 pupils and staff in the dry season, and for longer in the rains. To date, the design seems to be performing well and may be incorporated in standard designs in the future. The cost of the water, assuming a 15-year tank life expectancy, is around US$6/m^3 (Gould, 1996).

Conclusions
Despite a long-running interest in rainwater catchment systems in Botswana and the development of some innovative technologies, rainwater remains an under-utilized resource. In Gaborone, the capital, water is now pumped from reservoirs up to 350km away at considerable expense. Considerable potential exists both for developing rainwater catchment systems as primary sources of supply for many remote rural households (Figure 1.1b), and as supplementary sources in larger settlements (Plate 4.2).

China

Due to China's vast and varied nature there are many different contexts in which rainwater is used for domestic supply (Li Lijuan and Guoyeu, 1997; Bo, 1993). In the arid central and western regions, such as in Gansu, Ningxia, Qinghai, Shanxi and Shaanxi, absence or shortage of good-quality ground and surface water on the loess plateau, and the mountainous nature of the terrain, make rainwater collection the preferred water source in many areas. In the foothills and mountains surrounding the North China Plain, the absence of readily accessible water sources in some areas make roof and surface rainwater catchment systems an attractive alternative (Liu and Mou, 1993). China also has many island and coastal environments where seawater intrusions are causing goundwater to become increasingly saline, e.g. Zhejiang Province and Jiangsu Province. In many of China's fast growing mega-cities, the pressure on water resources is increasing rapidly, resulting in the severe over-exploitation of many conventional sources such as groundwater. Beijing is facing a major water crisis early in the twenty-first century if solutions to its growing water scarcity are not found soon. Shanghai is suffering from severe subsidence problems and an increased threat of flooding in some areas; in part this is due to the over-exploitation of groundwater. By reducing pressure on urban water resources and by retaining runoff, domestic rainwater catchment systems could, if used in sufficient numbers, help reduce some of these problems (Mou and Wang, 1997). In many urban areas, rainwater harvesting techniques are already increasingly being used to recharge groundwater. Interest in rainwater utilization, which in China is viewed in a holistic way, is therefore growing. Evidence for this includes the fact that China hosted the 7th International Rainwater Catchment Systems Conference in 1995 and has since held national conferences with international symposia annually. The proceedings of the international conference held in Beijing provide a useful overview of some of the broader aspects of rainwater utilization in China (Mou et al., 1995). Over 50 papers (in English) out of a total of about 130 deal with a variety of applications of rainwater utilization in China for agriculture, groundwater recharge, restoration of degraded land, flood control and water supply.

China has a very long history of domestic rainwater use, probably stretching back to the first development of fired clay pots in Gansu Province around 6000 years ago. Examples of domestic rainwater catchment systems in almost every type of environment can be found in China, from humid to arid, and from mountainous interior to coastal plain. While it is impossible in a few pages to give a detailed overview of the numerous rainwater catchment systems, projects, and activities taking place in China, the following three local examples will provide an insight.

Gansu Province
In the mountainous rural areas to the west of Lanzhou, in the arid Gansu Province in Central China, water has always been in short supply. The lack of rain, averaging just 300mm per annum, has been a major development constraint in this region, resulting in it being one of the poorest in China. The central and eastern parts of the province on the loess plateau are worst; here, grain yields average only 1.5 tons/hectare and mean per capita incomes are less than US$70 per year (Zhu and Wu, 1995). Traditionally, farmers in this region, many of whom live in caves cut into the fine loess soil, have excavated rainwater tanks, known locally as *shuijiao*. These bottle-shaped underground tanks dug into the loess were traditionally lined with clay to make them watertight (Figure 1.4b). Although these tanks have capacities of 30m^3 or more, in past drought years they have often dried up, forcing people to trek great distances down to river valleys often 1000m or more below to collect water. In response to this, the Gansu Institute for Water Conservation started researching and piloting techniques for upgrading traditional rainwater catchment systems. It was estimated that 20m^3 of storage was required by a family (five people with one animal using 80 l/day) to see them through the eight-month dry season (although 15m^3 would suffice for up to 10 months of drought if stricter rationing was applied (i.e. 50 l/day). By 1992, new tiled catchments, concrete-lined courtyards, cement channels and upgraded cement-lined *shuijiao* water cellars had been developed, demonstrated, and piloted, and were being widely replicated (Figures 5.5 and 9.2).

Generally, tanks with capacities of 15m^3–20m^3 were installed to collect runoff from combined roof and courtyard catchment areas of between 80 and

212

Figure 9.2 Typical rural household roof and courtyard catchment with underground *shuijiao* water cellar. Note also *shuijiao* using runoff from the road, Gansu, China
(Courtesy of Zhu Qiang)

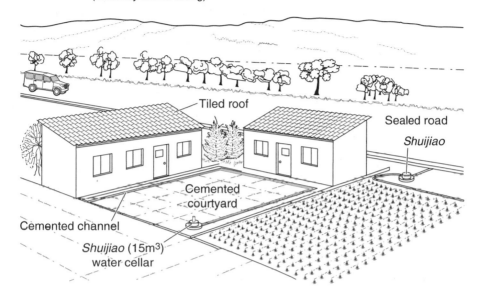

200m². Tiled roofs replaced traditional thatched roofs and, where no thatched buildings existed, tiles were laid temporarily on specially constructed earth slopes so that rainwater could be harvested immediately (Plates 9.5 and 9.6). The tiles would later be transferred to build roof catchments once suitable buildings had been constructed. The use of metal roofing sheets – or even metal gutters and downpipes – was beyond the means of most householders in the region. Instead of metal gutters hung beneath the eaves, cement channels were constructed on the ground to assist in diverting runoff from roofs and concreted courtyards into the tanks. The underground tanks had cement covers, and simple handpumps were used for extracting the water. The government provided about half of the project funds to subsidize each farming household by providing US$50–65 for cement. The remaining funds and inputs, equivalent to about 60 per cent of the full cost, came from the farmers, sometimes assisted by bank loans and the community. The farmers provided labour and local materials such as sand and gravel for construction (Zhu and Wu, 1995). Despite some concerns over bacteriological contamination of the stored rainwater, most is drunk as tea, sometimes boiled using solar cookers as in Plate 9.7.

In 1994–95 a very severe drought forced the local government to intervene and truck water at huge expense to help the worst-affected areas. Despite the severity of the drought – the worst for 65 years – those households with new rainwater systems survived without government assistance. In July 1995 the government extended the project to cover the whole region in order to

Figure 9.3 Example of one of several upgraded water-cellar (*Shuijiao*) designs, Gansu, China
(Courtesy of Zhu Qiang)

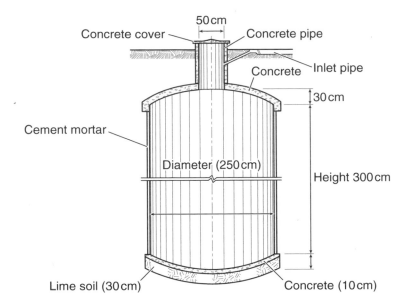

develop a more permanent solution to help address the water problem through comprehensive upgrading of all traditional *shuijiao* systems. The extended scheme, known as the 1–2–1 Project, targeted areas with rainfall between 300 and 500mm in seven prefectures: Baiying, Dingxi, Lanzhou (Yuzhong County), Lingxia, Qinyang, Pingliang and Tianshui (Yuan and Benjing, 1997). The scheme provided households with one tiled catchment area, two cemented 15–20m³ sub-surface tanks (water cellars), and one field with plastic sheeting covering ridges to concentrate rainwater runoff on to a cash crop planted along the furrows. Each family was provided with sufficient sheeting to cover a field of about 0.6 mu (400m²) for maize, cotton or vegetable production. The sheeting effectively doubled rainwater infiltration to the root zone, thereby boosting agricultural productivity. By 1997, more than 1.2 million people had benefited from this project, which has successfully boosted the self-reliance and self-sufficiency of about 240 000 rural households.

In parallel with the development of rainwater supplies for domestic consumption, the Gansu Institute for Water Conservation has also been researching and piloting techniques for utilizing rainwater for irrigating fruit trees, vegetables and other food and cash crops. The methods employed include those described above and in Chapter 2, involving the use of plastic sheeting for concentrating runoff from the surface or greenhouses (Plates 2.5 and 2.6).

Another approach has been to collect rainwater runoff from purpose-built cement ground catchments, store the water in a series of *shuijiao* sub-surface

214

Plate 9.5 *Typical tile roof and cemented courtyard catchment system with cemented channels leading to underground tank* (shuijiao) *in Yuzhong mountains, Gansu, China.* (Photo: Zhu Qiang/Wu Fuxue, 1995)

Plate 9.6 *Purpose-built tiled slope catchment with cemented channels leading to underground tank* (shuijiao) *in Yuzhong mountains, Gansu, China.* (Photo: Zhu Qiang/Wu Fuxue, 1995)

215

Plate 9.7 *Use of solar cooker to boil (and sterilize) rainwater – more than 55 000 were distributed in Gansu, China.* (Photo: John Gould, 1995)

Plate 9.8 *Purpose-built cemented pavement with underground tanks (shui-jiao) for irrigation in Yuzhong mountains, Gansu, China.* (Photo: John Gould, 1995)

tanks, and siphon water down-slope to irrigate crops using simple pipe or drip irrigation systems (Plate 9.8). Pilot schemes have shown that schemes can generate up to US$250 per mu ($3750 per ha) and investments can be recouped within two years (Zhu and Wu, 1995). Examples of such a system from Yuzhong County are shown in Plate 9.8.

Zhejiang Province

Unlike the farmers in poorer parts of Gansu, those in Zhejiang Province, which lies in the coastal region south of Shanghai, are relatively well off. Rainfall is plentiful, averaging 1200–1600mm per annum, and two crops per year can be harvested. Although many rural households have surplus income and can afford 'luxuries' such as washing machines and TVs, in many areas, such as that around Yuyao City, poor groundwater conditions due to seawater intrusion in coastal areas, water pollution and dry summers, make water supply through conventional methods difficult. In response to the poor water conditions, many householders have either purchased ferrocement tanks or, where finance permits, have incorporated large concrete cisterns into their houses when constructing them. In 1997 there were about 20 small entrepreneurs in Yuyou County (Population 850 000) constructing small, two-ring, cylindrical, thin-walled (2cm) ferrocement tanks, typically with volumes of 1–2m^3, at a purchase price of about US$20 per m^3.

Many of the better-off farmers in the region have recently constructed new houses which are typically three or four storeys high. Rectangular reinforced-concrete rainwater tanks with volumes around 6 to 12m^3 are often constructed on the top floor or attic, and the rainwater supply is connected to a standard plumbing system for toilet flushing and other domestic purposes, including drinking. In some cases a dual system is operated where an external piped connection also exists. Some concerns over water quality has led to an active research programme in the region to develop household filters to address bacteriological contamination (Bo, 1993; Guangen et al., 1997).

Hebei Province – Yuanshi County

Yuanshi County is a region typical of north China, with undulating hills in the west and a sloping alluvial plain in the east running up to the Taihang mountains. The terraced lower slopes of these mountains are characterized by intensive, mixed semi-subsistence agriculture based on wheat, maize, bean and vegetable production. The area has a continental, monsoonal, semi-arid climate, with temperatures ranging from a summer maximum of 42°C to a winter minimum of -25°C. The mean annual rainfall is 589mm and its distribution in time and space is highly variable. Because of frequent droughts and the growing water shortage, local people have started adopting rainwater harvesting techniques as an important means of addressing the problem, and for promoting development in general. Although rainwater utilization has a long history in Yuanshi County, interest had waned and the technology is now

217

being popularized again. According to Mou (1995) the whole county has more than 2000 schemes for collecting and storing rainwater, such as dams, ponds, pools, water cellars, and *dangwas* (shallow wells). The total storage capacity of all the schemes is about 100m³ (equivalent to about 25 per cent of the total rainfall). The main techniques for domestic rainwater utilization are as follows:

Water-jar wells   This is a traditional method of rainwater utilization in the Taihang hills of north China. The well (underground tank) usually has a diameter of 1.5–3 metres, a depth of 4–6 metres, and has a circular or square shape. It is composed of the well floor, a wall and a semi-circular cover. The well is built using mixed soils, bricks and concrete. Its wall has a 0.2–0.3m-thick seepage-proof layer. There is a circular inlet in the wall for rainwater collected from tiled roofs and courtyard. The water-jar well is used mainly to supply water for agricultural production, domestic use and animals.

Water tanks   These are circular or square in shape and are a widespread traditional method for storing surface rainwater runoff in this area. They are usually around 2m deep, and have storage capacities from about 50 to several hundred cubic metres. In the hills they are built in rock with mud linings to prevent seepage, while on the plain they are built using a three-soil mix.

Roof tank systems   Roof catchment systems are a method of rainwater utilization available to every family in the area. From the roof, via the collection trough (channel), the rainwater enters a concrete underground storage tank, typically with a volume of 6m³. In the past it used to provide water for washing clothes, irrigation and water for pigs. Due to the current lack of water resources, further improvements of the catchment system have allowed its use for supplying drinking-water for human consumption.

In a recent assessment of the rainwater resources of Yuanshi County, it was found that only about half of the rainwater resources which could easily be used and developed are at present being utilized. As the water-resource shortage increases, the growing water crisis is certain to deepen in the region and a greater emphasis on tapping the potential of under-utilized rainwater resources is likely to emerge in response. In anticipation of this, a pilot project in 1994–95 assisted about 50 households with installing rainwater catchment systems in Yuanshi County. Each consists of a roof and courtyard surface catchment area of about 100m³, and a 5–6m³ sub-surface cement rectangular tank and handpump. To save on costs, no wire reinforcement or metal gutters were used. Typically, total costs were less than US$100 (Mou, 1995). A line of bricks laid on the sloping roof directs water into a plastic downpipe and into the tank. The systems were effective and greatly appreciated by the recipient households, which provided labour and certain materials for construction. By 1997 the construction of these new 'water cellar' catchment systems, incorporating a sedimentation chamber and simple filter to improve water quality, had spread to 30 counties, benefiting an estimated 70 000 people (Lijuan and Guoyou, 1997).

Germany

Rainwater catchment systems for non-potable supply

In Europe, Germany is leading the way in encouraging the widespread utilization of rainwater catchment systems both for domestic supply and other purposes. Due to serious industrial air-pollution problems in many parts of the country, and concerns over contamination by bird droppings and other dirt on the roof, drinking rainwater is not recommended. Interest in household rainwater collection, therefore, focuses mainly on non-potable uses such as garden watering, toilet flushing and use in washing machines (Figure 9.4; Meemken, 1994). Apart from reducing demands on potable water supplies, household rainwater systems used in combination with seepage wells can bring about a broad range of benefits. These include decreasing pressure on stormwater drains, sewers and water-treatment plants, reducing flood risks and recharging groundwater. A number of recent publications discuss these and related issues, such as planted roofs and other rainwater-runoff retention techniques, in detail (König, 1996, 1998; Geiger and Dreiseitl, 1995).

In Germany, an integrated 'ecological' approach to rainwater utilization is being adopted; championed by a recently formed Specialist Association for Rainwater Utilization (*fbr*) (see Appendix 2 for details). Throughout the country, interest is growing and Hamburg, Bremen, Berlin, Münster,

Figure 9.4   Typical rainwater collection system In a German household. Overflow connection to seepage well saves on rainwater drainage, charges and recharges the groundwater.

Note: Drinking rainwater is not normally permitted. (Source: Meemken, 1994)

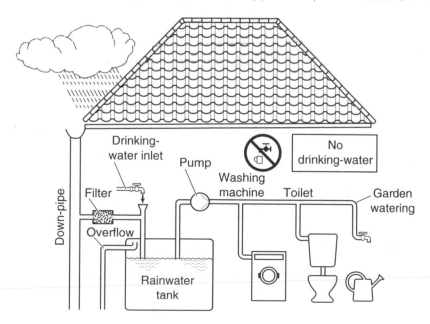

Zweibrücken and Osnabrück are just some of the cities where rainwater utilization is actively encouraged. Numerous small towns and rural municipalities are also promoting the technology. While most systems are purchased privately by individual householders from commercial manufacturers, local government often plays a crucial role in encouraging the spread of the technology, both by making regulations and providing subsidies.

In Osnabrück, for example, subsidies of DM1000–2000 (US$600–1200) are available for installing household rainwater tanks. An additional DM5/m^2 ($3/m^2) is payable annually for any roof area draining into a tank connected to a seepage well on the premises (Wessels, 1994; Fig. 9.5). Thus, apart from this direct subsidy for system construction, households make savings both with respect to their water bills and, if equipped with a seepage well, to their water drainage charges. Wessels calculated that the cost of constructing a rainwater utilization system would be around DM6000–8000 ($3700–5000) for a new house, and DM8000–10 000 ($5000–6000) for an existing house (1994 prices). The recovery time for a payback on the investment would be between 12–15 years with a subsidy from the city, or 16–19 years without it. If householders were prepared to construct all or part of the systems themselves, however, very significant savings could be obtained.

Figure 9.5 Double-chamber sub-surface rainwater tank for non-potable household supply, and seepage well for recharging groundwater, Osnabr ck, Germany
(Source: Wessels, 1994)

1. Coarse filter
2. Inlet pipe
3. Filter wall built of bricks
4. Suction pipe
5. Pump
6. Water meter
7. Emergency water-supply inlet
8. Garden tap
9. Overflow
10. Toilet

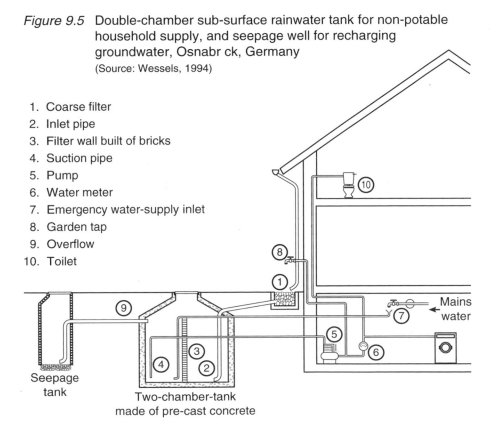

Figure 9.9 Three types of rainwater filter currently available in Germany
(Source: WISY AG, 1998: Oberdorfstrasse 26, D-63699,
Kefenrod-Hitzkirchen, Germany)

(a)   **(b)**

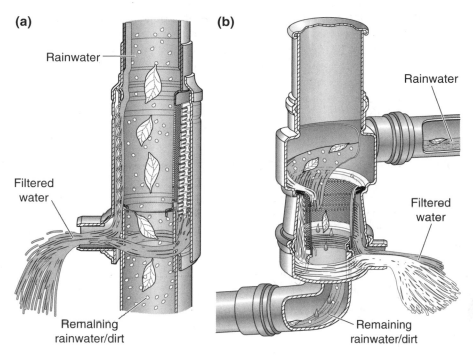

These filters are both largely self-cleaning

(a) Filter collector diverts 90 per oent of rainwater to a storage tank through a 0.17mm stainless steel mesh filter

(b) Vortex fine filter diverts 90 per cent of rainwater runoff from roof areas of up to 500mm^2. Made from environmentally compatible polyethylene

(c) A floating fine suction filter ensures that water is pumped from the cleanest part of the tank

221

According to Wessels (1994), concerns over the possible negative health effects of rainwater utilization led to some opposition. The Federal Office of Health, for example, initially objected to its use as an emergency potable supply, for washing clothes, personal hygiene and even for toilet flushing, due to possible risks of infection or allergic reactions. Long-term investigations by the health offices in Hamburg and Bremen, however, have yielded positive results with respect to the use of water for washing purposes and have confirmed that rainwater sources do not present a health risk.

In response to concerns over water-quality systems, some innovative design features have been developed. For example, a double chamber design, where part of the system acts as a sedimentation chamber and the porous brick wall separating the two chambers effectively acts as a filter, has been successfully piloted in Osnabrück (Figure 9.5; Wessels, 1994).

Private companies such as WISY, based in Kefenrod in Germany, are also playing an important role in promoting rainwater use by developing pumps and filter devices to improve water quality (see Appendix 2 for contact details). WISY has developed a simple filter system which can be attached to a standard household downpipe. Under conditions in Germany (assuming a mean annual rainfall of 650mm/year), this can divert and filter 90 per cent of the runoff from a roof area of up to 200m^2 (Plate 9.9a). A larger vortex fine filter can cope with runoff from roof areas of up to 500m^2 (Plate 9.9b). A floating fine suction filter for ensuring that the water pumped from the tank is extracted from the cleanest part of the tank and is free of particulates has also been developed (Plate 9.9c).

Another company, MALLBETON, a manufacturer of concrete tanks and filters, based in the Black Forest, is marketing a tank design which manages any overflows (König, 1998). This is done by constructing the top half of a sub-surface tank from a porous concrete ring, which allows water to gradually seep into the ground. While this reduces the volume of water available, it does make householders eligible for waivers on their rainwater drainage fees. These fees are already applied to householders and businesses in about 25 per cent of Germany. The charges that are levied on each square metre of roof area and sealed surroundings can be substantial. For example, annual current rates are DM2.54/m^2 (US$1.50/m^2) in Munich and DM3.08/m^2 ($1.80/m^2) in Bonn (König, 1998), so waivers often provide significant savings.

The recent interest and promotion of household rainwater collection both by local government and the private sector in Germany is providing a model which other densely populated industrialized countries, especially in Europe, may choose to follow.

Japan

Rainwater supplies on small islands
Rainwater collection has a very long history in Japan and much evidence of some of the traditional systems can still be found on many of the country's

outlying islands, especially those in the Pacific and Japan Inland Sea. On the Izu and Ogasawara island chains, which stretch due south for over 1000km from Tokyo Bay, reliance on rainwater supplies is very high. Most of these islands are volcanic and 13 are populated with communities of between 200 and 10 000 people. Rainfall on the islands is regular and ranges from around 2000 to 3000mm per year. On the islands of Toshima (population 300) and Aogashima (population 200), rainwater provides the only water source. A detailed description of the well-developed rainwater supply systems on both islands is given by Kaneko et al. (1992).

Aogashima did once have a natural freshwater pond from which people drew their water, but this was destroyed by a volcanic eruption in 1785, after which the islanders constructed a small artificial pond to collect and store rainwater. Only nearly 200 years later did the island get a modern rainwater collection facility complete with a slow sand filter and reticulated distribution system. The system, installed in 1979 and enlarged in 1985–86, comprises a 19 250m^2 cemented ground catchment area and total storage capacity in six covered reservoirs of 6480m^3. The storage capacity is equivalent to just 100 days' average supply, but the system can supply up to 120m^3 per day.

Toshima is a classical-shaped, conical, steep-sided volcanic island with an area of 4km^2, and is slightly smaller than Aogashima. There are no rivers or springs on Toshima and the groundwater has a high salinity. Historically, water supply was a major problem for the population, who traditionally collected rainwater from trees by binding ropes around their trunks to divert runoff into large earthenware jars, and more recently from household roof catchment systems still used today. In 1960 a concrete paved road was constructed, which was designed to divert rainwater runoff from its 32 300m^2 area into a 6000m^3 rubber-lined open storage reservoir. An asphalt sheet surface catchment of 4000m^2 was added in 1977 and, in 1988, a second new facility (linked to the first by a pipeline) was constructed on the other side of the island. This plant included another 2000m^2 asphalt-covered catchment and an additional 8200m^2 of storage in covered reinforced-concrete reservoirs and a rapid sand filtration unit capable of supplying 80m^3 of high-quality drinking-water daily. The catchment surfaces were prepared by first clearing all vegetation and removing tree roots and covering the surface with high-strength polypropylene sheets to prevent penetration by plants. Finally, the special asphalt and rubber polymer strips (2m wide) were laid and sealed together using a propane burner. The strips were anchored in concrete at the top and bottom of the catchment and a collection channel was constructed. While some deterioration was evident, the catchment was still operating effectively nearly 15 years after installation. The main disadvantages with the systems cited by Kaneko are the high cost of both the initial installation of the systems and the repair work required following typhoon damage. While the volumes of the rainwater supplies on the two islands may appear high in relation to their populations, both receive large numbers of visitors from the mainland, especially during the summer season.

On Mijakejima in the Izu island chain, more than half of the households (around 2000 people) use their own household roof catchment tanks for supplementing domestic supplies (Murase 1987, Plate 9.10). Although the island does have some alternative water sources, including a freshwater pond in a volcanic caldera, and treated piped water is available, people prefer the taste of rainwater. In 1983 a major volcanic eruption and resulting lava-flow destroyed many houses and the main school on the island. The disaster also put the island's treated piped-water supply out of action for a month. Despite these hardships, people did not evacuate the island but simply used their rainwater tanks as a backup supply. This action provided inspiration to local government officials from Tokyo's Sumida Ward to embark on a major rain-water initiative in the city, in an effort to mitigate the potential impacts of future natural disasters by making decentralized backup water supplies available.

Many other examples of rainwater collection for domestic supply can be found on Japan's numerous offshore islands. In the Japan inland sea, for example, rainwater collection is again being practised at both private house-holds and public buildings on many islands including Nakajima and Uoshima (Minami et al., 1992). Rainwater collection is also common on some of the 48 inhabited islands which make up Okinawa Prefecture, which stretches south from Japan towards Taiwan.

Rainwater utilization in cities
In Asia, Japan is leading the way with regard to the utilization of rainwater in urban contexts, and subsidies are increasingly being used to encourage the adoption of household rainwater collection for non-potable uses. According to Murase (1998), local government authorities from all over Japan, repres-enting 79 municipalities and six prefectures, have now joined forces and formed a council promoting rainwater utilization. Since most of these repres-ent urban constituencies, their efforts are mainly focused at ways to improve rainwater use in large towns and cities. Among the local government author-ities that already provide loans or subsidies for installing rainwater systems are Sumida City, Takamatsu City, Toyota City, Kamakura City, Kawaguchi City, Kagoshima City and Okinawa Prefecture.

While in rural areas rainwater collection is normally done primarily for water supply, in large Japanese cities rainwater collection at households and public buildings is done for several other reasons as well. These important secondary functions include improved flood control, reduced river pollution, countering over-exploitation of groundwater and associated subsidence problems, and making substantial cost savings on drainage infrastructure (Murase, 1994; Fok, 1994) and others (TIRUC, 1994). The Tokyo International Rainwater Utiliza-tion Conference, TIRUC (1994), was the first major meeting ever devoted exclusively to examining rainwater utilization in the context of modern urban development. This large meeting and associated exhibition attracted over 8000 people and generated a lot of interest in many aspects of rainwater utilization, including rainwater for domestic supplies. In August 1998 a meeting of Jap-anese local government authorities (the Rainwater Utilization Forum for Local Government and Citizens) attracted over 1500 participants.

Plate 9.10 *Household roof catchment system, Miyake Island, Japan.* (Photo: Makoto Murase)

Plate 9.11 *8000m² roof catchment at Kokugikan Sumo Wrestling Stadium, Tokyo, Japan.* (Photo: Makoto Murase)

The role of rainwater cisterns for fire protection and emergency water supply are also of particular significance to the Japanese. Firestorms following the Great Kanto Earthquake of 1923 killed more than 100 000 people in Tokyo. In 1995 a major earthquake in Kobe killed around 5000 people and, since few rainwater cisterns existed in the city, provision of clean water supplies became a major problem. To help alleviate the situation, the Tokyo-based group People for Promoting Rainwater Utilization donated a hundred 200-litre water tanks. The impact of the quake provided an important lesson regarding the urgent need to develop multi-purpose storage tanks in order to help people to overcome disasters in big cities (Minami, 1995). The benefits of small, decentralized rainwater catchment systems and solar power units during future earthquake, tsunami, flood or other natural disasters afflicting urban Japan would be immense. The siting of individual reservoirs in every building not only provides an emergency water supply, but can aid fire-fighting when mains supplies are ruptured. These systems can also be used as backup supplies for dry spells, droughts, or periods of mains supply break-down.

The Japanese have also constructed some very large roof and ground catchment systems in several cities to assist in reducing local flood problems, to decrease dependence on mains supplies, to reduce water bills, and to provide a backup emergency supply. In Tokyo there are over 500 large systems of this type now in use (Murase, 1998); one of the best-known being that at Kokugikan, the main sumo wrestling stadium, where water from the 8400m^2 roof is stored in a 1000m^3 reservoir in the basement and used for toilet flushing and cooling the building (Plate 9.11). Sofia University also has an interesting rainwater catchment facility designed in combination with the utilization of solar energy to reduce the overall environmental impact of the institution (Hayama, 1994). There are many other interesting examples of large-scale systems elsewhere in Japan, such as the Izumo Dome in Izumo City where rainwater runoff from the huge dome and surroundings with a total catchment area of 13 200m^2 are stored in two storage tanks with a total volume of 270m^3. The annual savings in water bills from this system has been estimated to be around 1.8 million yen (about US\$14 000) (Takeyama and Minami, 1995).

Kenya

Rainwater catchment systems are better developed and more widely utilized in Kenya than in any other African country. Although there is a long tradition of rainwater collection in some areas, such as along the coast where traditional purpose-built *djabia* ground catchment systems have been used for many centuries (Biamah et al., 1993), elsewhere in the country most of the rainwater schemes are relatively recent. In the last few decades numerous new roof, ground and rock catchment technologies have been developed using a wide variety of designs and implementation strategies (Bambrah et al., 1993). There are several reasons for the popularity of rainwater collection in Kenya. Key among these is the absence of easily accessible surface and groundwater sources in many areas, such as Eastern Kenya, and the failure of conventional borehole and piped water systems to meet the needs of the rural population. Another important factor is that many communities possess the motivation, organization, and resources (i.e. skills, local materials and money), to implement systems with only limited external technical assistance. It is difficult to estimate the total number of systems present in the country but, as a result of several major programmes over recent years, there are now thousands of schools with large rainwater tanks, several hundred rock catchment schemes, and numerous individual household systems. Whereas just 20 years ago the number of Kenyans using rainwater supplies could be counted in thousands, today it probably runs to over a million (if not millions), and the number of rainwater users is still increasing.

Rainwater catchment systems are found throughout the country in both arid and semi-arid districts such as Baringo, Isiolo, Kitui, Laikipia, Machakos, Marsabit, and Samburu, as well as in humid districts including Embu, Kajiado, Kisii, Kiambu, Kilifi, Kirinyaga, Murang'a, Meru, Nyeri, Nyandurua and South Nyanza (Bambrah et al., 1993; Wamani and Mbugua, 1993). Rainwater designs developed in Kenya have also been widely disseminated elsewhere in Africa, e.g. Uganda, Tanzania, Ethiopia, Rwanda, Namibia and Botswana. Due to the wide variety of local climatic and geological conditions in Kenya, many different types of system have evolved to suit these local environments. In the semi-arid areas of eastern Kenya, large surface and sub-surface tanks with volumes of 20–120m³ are popular, especially at schools due to the large roof catchment areas available. In more humid areas along the coast, in parts of the Rift Valley and in western Kenya, smaller, household 2–5m³ wire-reinforced cement jars and tanks are common, and can supply a substantial portion of the domestic water requirements from even quite small roof areas. The type of system chosen is governed to a considerable degree by the nature of the landscape. The presence of massive inselbergs, for example, provides an opportunity to build rock catchments, as in Kitui District, while sand rivers allow for the construction of sand or sub-surface dams. Where roof and ground tanks are to be constructed, the design and construction methods will be dictated to some degree by the availability of local building materials. The presence of aggregate (ballast) may favour concrete designs as in Machakos, while in other places the presence of rubble-stone blocks will favour designs using these. Elsewhere, burnt bricks, compressed-soil blocks, concrete blocks and ferrocement are also used. Examples of some of the designs commonly used in Kenya are shown in Appendix 5. Commercially available plastic tanks are also available in major centres but these are typically about three or four times the price of tanks constructed on site. Galvanized corrugated-iron tanks are cheaper than plastic but lack durability compared to brick and ferrocement tanks.

The development of appropriate, affordable and durable designs and implementation strategies has been a long evolutionary process. Many lessons have been learned and many initially promising designs have had to be abandoned. The *ghala* basket design, for example, in which a basketwork frame made from sticks was plastered with mortar, turned out to lack durability due to rotting or termite attack of the organic frame (Plate 9.12). Although

227

thousands of these tanks were constructed in the late 1970s and early 1980s with the support of donors such as UNICEF and ActionAid, the technique has now been largely abandoned due to the need to repair the tanks regularly. Experiments with the use of sisal fibres as a substitute for wire reinforcement by the Catholic Diocese of Kitui also failed to produce durable tanks. Even the use of treated wooden poles to support corrugated-iron sheets or other covers have generally failed to stand the test of time and led to the development of the durable ferrocement dome. In other instances failures have been due not to inadequacies in the quality of the design or construction, but to flawed implementation strategies, usually as a result of insufficient involvement of the recipient community. The failure of the household ferrocement tank project in Kilifi District on the coast was described in Chapter 7. This example provides an important reminder that projects fail most often for non-technical reasons, since, in this case, the centrally made tanks were technically sound (Plate 9.13). Despite the past failures, it is on the basis of the lessons learned from these that many thriving projects have subsequently been built, and details of some of these projects are cited below.

Diocese of Machakos household concrete roof tank programme
This project began in the late 1970s but was formally launched in 1983 with the present design (de Vrees, 1987). Although originally co-ordinated and initiated by the local Catholic Diocese Development Office, the project, which covers the whole of Machakos district, has now become self-reliant. Initially a third of the cost of the tanks was covered by the local Diocese Development Office, with the remainder paid for by the group members using a revolving fund. Although the subsidy is no longer available, this has not prevented the project expanding as the benefits have been recognized. The recipients of tanks provide materials and unskilled labour to help to reduce costs. The project is now virtually completely self-financing, and more than 6000 tanks of between 4 and 13.5m^3 have been constructed. The tanks are built of concrete, compacted in a double-ring mould of corrugated-iron sheets and reinforced with rounds of barbed wire. The floor and cover are made of concrete reinforced with weld-mesh. The Diocese, however, still provides the community with new moulds to replace old ones worn out after being used for about 20 tanks. The success of this tank programme has been largely due to the following reasons:

- Effective revolving-fund groups were set up for raising finance.
- The cost of the tanks and gutters is affordable by most families in this district.
- Sand and aggregate are freely available from sand-rivers near to most homesteads.
- The only alternative to rainwater harvesting is transporting water over distances of 10 to 20 km with donkey carts.
- The local Wakamba people have a well-defined social system for assisting each other with self-help activities.

Plate 9.12 *Example of Ghala basket tank constructed in 1983 in North Kitui, Kenya.* (Photo: John Gould)

Plate 9.13 *Centrally made 6m³ ferrocement tanks constructed in the early 1980s in Kilifi District, Kenya.* (Photo: John Gould)

Box 9.1
Rock catchments in Kitui

The following reasons explain the popularity of rock catchment systems in Kitui:

- Water resources are scarce in Kitui district, but while rainfall is seasonal, erratic and varies greatly from place to place, total amounts are substantial in many areas with mean annual figures for the district ranging from <300mm to >1200mm.
- Only two perennial rivers, the Athi and the Tana, run along the district's borders, 350km apart. Ephemeral sand-rivers flood only during good rains, which might occur for only a few days every second year or so. These floods recharge both natural storage and that in man-made sub-surface dams from where water can be extracted from the sand.
- Groundwater is found at a depth of 20 to 50m but it often contains high concentrations of minerals and can be used for livestock only. Small and large earth dams also provide water but high evaporation rates and seepage consumes most of the water and, due to pollution, the water is used mainly for watering livestock.
- Roof catchment tanks are very popular among the better off, but the cost of a tank and roof is too great for many poorer households.
- The Kitui landscape is dotted with thousands of small and large granite rock outcrops called inselbergs, suitable for rock catchment dams, and these can provide water from a rainfall event of as little as five millimetres.
- Rock catchment dams do not cost the users anything except their own labour. Design, artisans' wages, cement, and G.I. pipes are usually provided by donor agencies.
- Many local Wakamba women have traditionally had to travel long distances to collect water, especially in the dry season. Return day-trips of 20km carrying water on their backs is still common in many areas, while other women may walk up to 50km on a two-day trip to fetch water with a donkey carrying 80-litre containers (Plate 9.14). Given these hardships, the willingness of the women to work on labour-intensive rock catchment dams closer to home is not surprising.

Programmes for constructing rainwater tanks at schools

The first major school water-tank programme began in the semi-arid district of Kitui. In this district 1.5 million people now rely on rainwater harvesting because the region has no permanent rivers and only saline groundwater. In the early 1980s, DANIDA supported the construction of about 300 hemispherical underground ferrocement tanks, described in Chapter 5 and Appendix 5. Initially, these had flat roofs consisting of corrugated-iron sheets supported by treated poles, and storage volumes of 80m^3. These tanks were constructed mainly at schools and used long, V-shaped hanging gutters with

Plate 9.14 *Women with donkeys collecting water from a distant source in Kitui, Kenya.* (Photo: John Gould, 1984)

Plate 9.15 *Women's group constructing a 12m³ ferrocement tank in Nakuru District, Kenya.* (Photo: John Gould, 1991)

splash-guards fitted to the uneven roofs of rural schools to ensure minimal rainwater wastage. During the late 1980s, KWAHO improved the DANIDA design of the hemispherical ground tank by replacing the iron sheet roof with a self-supporting dome of ferrocement, thus increasing the storage capacity to 90m³. KWAHO built several hundred of these tanks, and some with volumes of 120m³, at schools throughout Kenya. Since 1990, UNICEF and DANIDA have embarked on a third school water-tank programme and have built more than 1200 46m³ ferrocement water tanks serviced by V-shaped gutters with splash-guards. These were constructed in association with 1000 double-pit latrines at schools in Kitui District.

The Mutomo Soil and Water Conservation/KIDP Project
The Mutomo Soil and Water Conservation Project has been one of Africa's most successful rural water-supply initiatives in recent years and provides an important demonstration of the potential for a range of rainwater catchment systems. Many of these have been replicated elsewhere, sometimes in a modified form, both in Kenya and in other parts of Africa. From 1983 to 1989, the project was run with direct support and control from DANIDA and assisted hundreds of self-help groups. Many of these were involved in repairing and completing 20 existing rock catchment dams, and in constructing 90 new ones of various designs, the biggest having a reservoir capacity of 6000m³ (see Box 2.2 for further background information). In addition, the project supported the construction of around 200 surface and sub-surface rainwater tanks, 126 shallow wells, 25 sand and sub-surface dams and 12 earth dams, as well as being involved in a few spring-protection and tube-well schemes (Lee and Nissen-Petersen, 1989). From 1989 onwards, the project, while still funded by DANIDA, became known as the Kitui Integrated Development Programme. During this phase of the project, which involved increased local control, the emphasis shifted to focus on the repair, extension and completion of existing rock catchment dam schemes built by other agencies in Kitui District. From the outset of the project, a key component was the high level of self-help community involvement and the use of locally available materials to keep costs down. Today, some 200000 Wakamba people fetch nearly all their domestic water from about 350 rock catchment dams. The construction of new rock catchment dams, as well as the extension of existing ones, is still going on as they have become the most popular water source for rural communities in Kitui (Box 9.1).

Diocese of Nakuru rainwater project
Church-based development initiatives have been very significant in mobilizing communities to address their water problems. In Nakuru and the surrounding districts, both the Anglican and Catholic churches have been actively involved in rainwater-tank construction programmes for many years. The Anglican Diocese of Nakuru (ACK), for example, which covers more than six districts (Nakuru, Nyandarua, Narok, Baringo, Kericho, Samburu and part of Laikipia) has been involved in the construction of over 3000 tanks

(Cumberlege, 1993). Many of these have been built by self-help groups, 90 per cent of which are made up entirely of women who have contributed between US$2 and $10 monthly to a revolving fund to finance the 10–15m³ household ferrocement tanks (Plate 9.15). By 1993, over 400 sub-surface tanks with volumes of 90–120m³ had been constructed in the area, and about half were lined using rough stones and a weak lime–cement mix. Due to high turbidity and bacteriological contamination, however, SIDA sponsored a jar-construction programme to collect roof runoff specifically for drinking and cooking purposes.

The role of donors
A large number of bilateral, multilateral, religious and non-governmental donor organizations have supported rainwater harvesting projects in Kenya over the last few decades. The level of involvement varies, but several agencies have played a major role in supporting the development of rainwater catchment systems in Kenya and their expansion to other parts of the continent. The role of the Catholic Church in Machakos and the Anglican ACK in Nakuru were discussed above, and UNICEF and ActionAid have also actively promoted roof catchment systems. In Kitui District, DANIDA's Mutomo Soil and Water Project provided an important model in the 1980s for demonstrating the potential for several types of rainwater system, especially rock catchments and large surface and ground tanks. SIDA has also been a long-running supporter of household rainwater catchment systems projects in Kenya. In the three years up to June 1998, they provided support for 29 projects with a total budget of around US$1.5 million. SIDA has also worked closely with the Ministry of Health on projects with women's groups constructing 3m³ rainwater jars and 4–10m³ ferrocement tanks, funded mainly through revolving funds and with some external support for advisory services, training, transport and some materials. In order to encourage wider regional replication and adoption of some of the rainwater catchment techniques that have worked well in Kenya, support has also been provided for technology development, training, and dissemination of construction methods and techniques.

Thailand

The Thai rainwater jar programme
Thailand established itself as a leader in household rainwater catchments systems in the 1980s with the impressive development and implementation of several ferrocement tank designs. An 11m³ ferrocement tank design was widely implemented, especially in the north east of the country where they are a common sight in rural areas as many thousands have been built (Trai-tongyoo, 1987). It was, however, the development of the 2m³ Thai jar design which had the greatest impact.

The Thai jar programme is undoubtedly the world's best-known, government-initiated, domestic rainwater-supply project. Through this programme, millions of 2m³ wire-reinforced cement rainwater storage jars have been constructed for household roof catchment supplies since the mid-1980s. Actual jar capacities range from 1 to 2m³, but most are around 1.8–2m³, (see Chapter 5 for technical details). The programme was an unusual combined initiative involving a broad range of stakeholders including house-holders, communities, NGOs, universities, and the private sector, all sup-ported by the government at local, provincial, and national levels. The result of this novel bottom-up meeting top-down approach was a programme of rainwater-jar construction unprecedented in the way it improved the access of rural people to potable water supplies, especially in the north-east of the country. International donor agencies also supported the programme, thus giving it further momentum and global recognition and encouraging its wider replication.

The results of the programme were quite staggering, with around 10 mil-lion rainwater jars constructed in just over five years (Figure 9.6). The programme began officially in November 1985 when a national committee was established to administer it. Originally, the planned implementation strategy aimed to involve villagers in both financial management and con-struction, and provide government support for training, tools, research and administrative costs. The idea was to mobilize huge resources from the millions of project recipients in the form of free labour and contributions to the revolving funds. It was estimated that the cost of constructing the 6 million jars initially planned could be cut from around US$132 million to just $25 million by mobilizing these village-level resources (Wirojanagud

Figure 9.6 Graph showing the rapid growth of the Thai rainwater jar programme (1981–91)

(Source: Gould, 1992)

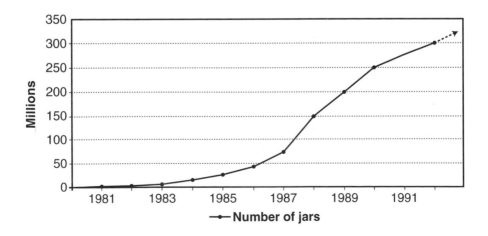

234

and Vanvarothorn, 1990). The government offered start-up loans for village revolving funds ($250 per village), administrative costs, and funds for training courses and research.

Initially, some revolving funds were established where villagers formed groups, and standard contributions of around $4 per month were made. However, as the project took off and gained widespread support, government funds became more readily available and grassroots community-based revolving-fund and implementation initiatives were increasingly replaced by commercial jar-manufacturing enterprises. During 1986 alone, approximately 1.7 million 1–2m³ jars were constructed in north-east Thailand (Wirojanagud and Chindapraisirt, 1987). During this frenzied construction phase, revolving funds were seen by many as a hindrance to rapid implementation. As a result, the programme evolved in a different way to that envisaged. Wirojanagud and Vanvarothorn (1990) explain that, in many cases, districts provided construction materials, tools and training while people contributed labour to construct their own jars under supervision from experienced technicians.

Increasingly, it seemed the private sector took on responsibility for production as it was able to produce good-quality jars at ever lower prices due to economies of scale. Many villagers, trained through government-funded programmes, got jobs with small contractors and some even set up tank-building enterprises themselves. The government at local, regional and national levels remained a major donor to the project, funding construction to the tune of almost 1.6 billion baht (US$64 million) through the Rural Job Creation Programme alone during the 1980s. Finance also came from donors, NGOs and even the private sector, with 2500 tons of cement being donated by one company.

In some cases, groups of villagers were paid through the Rural Job Creation Programme to construct jars at a central location and distribute them to households. With so many people acquiring the skills of tank construction, and with such a high demand for jars, small tank-building business enterprises flourished. These enterprises catered for private demand as well as being subcontracted by many districts. Thailand was undergoing an economic boom at the time and this, combined with the programmes, economies of scale, government subsidies, and fierce private sector competition, helped to push the price of a 2m³ household jar down to around US$20, thereby enabling many householders to purchase jars outright.

The advantage of the mode of implementation that was actually followed, over that originally planned, was that it enabled far more rapid rates of construction and overall implementation than had been originally envisaged. There were, however, a number of drawbacks to this strategy. Since many of the tanks were centrally produced and simply delivered to villagers at a subsidized cost, the benefits of active villager participation were diminished. In the initial phase of the programme, many basic but vital design elements were overlooked in the rush to build tanks as rapidly as possible. For example, many of the tanks built at the start of the programme had neither taps nor covers. Although these were later universally adopted in the standard tank design, a preoccupation with the 'hardware' construction and design aspects of the programme continued, and 'software' aspects, such as system operation and user hygiene education were left as afterthoughts. Only in 1990, towards the end of the main construction phase of the programme, was considerable effort directed towards hygiene education campaigns to encourage users to avoid serious contamination of the water being consumed from the rainwater jars (Tunyavanich and Hewison, 1990).

Although the Thai case study provides a good example of what is possible, it would be unrealistic to expect other countries to implement successful, nationwide rainwater-tank programmes either as quickly or as cheaply. Several factors greatly favoured the rapid development of the rainwater jar programme in Thailand. These included:

- a real felt need for water and a preference for the taste of rainwater
- a period of national economic growth and increasing private affluence
- the availability of cheap cement, and skilled artisans with experience of a similar traditional technology (the Thai Jar)
- a pool of indigenous engineers, technicians and administrators committed to rural development programmes.

Nevertheless, the implementation of the programme was more successful in some parts of the country than in others. In the south of Thailand, the wider availability of alternative sources and a lower preference for the taste of rainwater resulted in far less jar construction.

The Thai rainwater programme – other issues

In many respects the popular assessment of the Thai programme as a 'model development success story' has been based on conventional and simplistic measures of achievement, such as the number of systems constructed. If more substantive measures of development, such as sustainability and improvements relating to health and livelihoods are considered, a more balanced view of the programme's achievements becomes evident. In several respects the programme was a success, particularly, in technical terms, since an affordable, durable and technically appropriate tank design was developed and widely replicated. Another major achievement of the programme was that many artisans were trained in jar and tank construction and much employment was created (albeit mainly short term). By comparison with the above achievements, the broader development aspects related to the programme, including health, hygiene education and community participation in financing and management of the scheme, were less impressive. For example, the degree of community participation in the programme was far less than originally envisaged. This was due in part to the rapid expansion of the project, and the fact that the very active role of the private sector eclipsed that of the community, most of whom failed to establish revolving funds (Wirojanagud and Vanvarothorn, 1990).

Another problem was that, despite the provision of better-quality water supplies close to home, some concerns over water quality persisted, at least

236

among officials if not villagers. A major field survey into rainwater quality revealed that even when the rainwater collected in tanks and jars met drinking-water standards, the continuation of unhygienic water-handling practices was often leading to secondary contamination of rainwater supplies (Wirojanagud et al., 1989). This may explain why even when official data revealed an increase in access to safe water from 25 per cent in 1981 to 77 per cent in 1990, no clear reduction in diarrhoeal diseases or morbidity was noted. In fact, due to better provision of health facilities and better reporting they appear to have increased! (Hewison, 1996). There were also continuing health problems in some areas due to insect-vector-related diseases, such as dengue fever, which may have even been exacerbated to some extent by the widespread construction of water jars. One other significant health issue which continued to persist after the rainwater systems were completed was that, because the tanks often dried up during the rainy season, villagers often returned to traditional contaminated sources at this time, unaware of the health risks incurred (Tunyavanich and Hewison, 1990).

While technically most of the designs developed in Thailand have performed well, there were some problems at the beginning of the programme. The most significant design flaw related to an attempt to develop a low-cost bamboo-reinforced tank. The problem arose due to termite, fungal and bacteriological attack of any exposed bamboo leading to leakage, or even bursting of the tanks (Vadhanavikkit and Pannachet, 1987). Many of the tanks had to be retrofitted with steel belts to reduce the risk of the potentially dangerous impact of a tank failure. The failure of bamboo (and other organic materials) as a substitute for steel reinforcement was discussed in Chapter 1. In the case of Thailand, around 50000 bamboo-reinforced tanks were constructed before the problems of the design were fully realized.

United States

Rain barrels were a common feature of many early homesteads during the colonization of the western states by settlers in the nineteenth century. Nevertheless, although rainwater collection for domestic supply has been steadily replaced in most rural localities on mainland America by borehole and treated, piped, surface supplies, the practice has far from died out. In a nationwide survey of regional health officers conducted by Lye (1992a), it was estimated that around 200000 rainwater systems are in use to meet or supplement the domestic water requirements of small communities and individual households (Grove, 1993). While these are most prevalent on some of the many US island outposts in both the Pacific and the Caribbean, they are also present in the continental interior. While detailed information on types and numbers of systems is sparse, one report by Kincaid (1979) stated that 67000 rainwater cisterns were operational in the state of Ohio alone. Among other mainland states where domestic rainwater use is still common are Arizona, California, Florida, Kentucky, New Mexico, Pennsylvania, Texas, and Virginia.

In recent years, a combination of growing environmental awareness and increasing pressure on conventional water sources has led many water authorities to reconsider the option of rainwater collection, and many municipalities are now starting to actively promote the technology. In Austin, Texas a subsidy of 30 per cent of the cost of any roof catchment tank, up to a ceiling of $500, has recently been introduced.

It was California, however, that was the first mainland state to start actively encouraging the implementation of rainwater tanks, in the late 1970s. The spur for this was the growing pressure on the state's water resources, escalating costs, and the impact of the 1976–7 drought. In response to these pressures, the California Water Conservation Tax Law was passed in 1980 through which all taxpayers could apply for tax credits of up to 55 per cent (to a limit of $3000) to subsidize the cost of implementing rainwater, greywater or combined storage cisterns (Ingham and Kleine, 1982). The granting of this tax credit, which also applied to the installation of water-conserving fixtures such as low-flow showerheads and low-flush toilets, was contingent on compliance with health regulations particularly related to greywater and combined systems. These required such water use to be restricted to non-contact garden irrigation applied through a sub-surface system, e.g. drip irrigation. Although this incentive programme ran for a few years and many people took advantage of it, following a review in 1982, a decision was taken to eliminate the Water Conservation Tax Law. According to Walker (1984), the main reasons for this were abuse of the tax credit, the reduced pressure on water resources due to wetter conditions following the drought, and a need to conserve tax revenues. Apparently, many householders had applied for the credit to install expensive bathroom fittings with little or no water-conservation benefit.

On most of America's many island communities, e.g. Guam, the Caroline Islands, Marshall Islands, Puerto Rico, and the Florida Keys, rainwater collection is widespread, especially on smaller islands lacking alternative freshwater sources. On the US Virgin Islands, with a population of 110 000, every new building is required by law to incorporate a cistern to store roof runoff. The capacity must be equivalent to 400 litres per $1m^2$ of roof area. Cisterns are usually built into the basement of the building and form an integral part of the house design, with tank capacities generally ranging from 5 to $100m^3$. Although the population of the Virgin Islands is relatively small, the three main islands receive around 1.8 million tourists per year, putting considerable pressure on the limited water resources. To increase the overall water availability, rainwater is also harvested from several hillsides covered with impervious materials. In other places, rainwater runoff is used to recharge aquifers artificially, such as at the University of the Virgin Islands, where four wells are recharged from runoff from a 20ha natural catchment (Krishna, 1992).

On the islands of Hawaii, rainwater systems are quite common in rural areas, and at isolated households where the cost of providing piped supplies becomes prohibitive. In the Tantalus mountains above Honolulu, where some of O'ahu Island's wealthier residents reside, over 100 households are dependent almost exclusively on rainwater for all domestic purposes, including drinking. In a survey of the microbiological quality of the rainwater, samples from 18 household tanks were analysed and most failed to meet the high US drinking-water standards (Fujioka and Chinn, 1987). Since there was no evidence of residents suffering any health problems, and most of the indicator bacteria suggested contamination by animals and birds rather than human faecal sources, the findings did not provoke undue alarm.

During the late 1970s, drought conditions resulted in water shortages in several counties on Hawaii. To alleviate the situation, local authorities put a moratorium on the issuing of building permits unless developers could provide their own water sources (Fok, 1982). Such measures represent a short-term 'crisis management' approach to the problem. Recently, efforts to find sustainable permanent solutions to water-shortage problems are being attempted. In Hawaii there are some special local issues relating to rainwater use, especially on the main island, due to the impact of volcanic activity on rainwater acidity. This can potentially be a problem due to the leaching out of lead from roofs, flashing and pipe solders by the acidic rainwater, and special precautions are required. In the past, these special problems have caused concerns over the potential public health threat of promoting rainwater use. Despite this, in 1994 the Hawaii House of Representatives requested the University of Hawaii's Water Resources Research Centre to develop guidelines for county planning and building departments to regulate the construction of private rainwater catchment facilities (Fok, 1997).

10

The future of rainwater catchment systems

THE FOCUS OF this book so far has been on the use of rainwater catchment systems for domestic water supply. The emphasis has been on the development of the technology, design, construction and various aspects of implementation based on experiences from around the world. Most of the examples cited have been from developing countries, and especially from poorer rural communities. This choice has been deliberate since these communities are the ones most urgently in need of improved water supplies, as it is here that most of the world's 'unserved billion' live. In these poorer communities a simple household roof catchment system can have a dramatic impact on improving people's lives. This is especially the case in places such as semi-arid Africa, where traditional sources in rural areas are often distant and unsafe. Despite this emphasis on the communities with greatest water needs, examples of the use of rainwater catchment systems in richer countries have also been touched upon, including case studies from Japan, Germany and the USA. In this final chapter, a broad overview of the possible future development of the technology is presented, and issues such as the role of rainwater catchment systems in sustainable development are discussed.

Building on traditions

The future collection and utilization of rainwater will undoubtedly serve many purposes other than just domestic water supply. These include water for irrigation, aquaculture, air conditioning, flood control, local climatic control, groundwater recharge, landscaping and fire-fighting. Much of the future interest in rainwater collection relates to a broader approach to rainwater utilization. This approach is not new as many of the above uses of rainwater are very ancient indeed. An interesting historical example of non-domestic rainwater use is found in Beijing, the Forbidden City, from where emperors ruled China from 1406 for over 500 years. In this spectacular wooden palace complex, several beautifully decorated, giant brass cauldrons used for storing rainwater runoff collected from paved terraces remain in place today. These were strategically positioned for fire-fighting purposes, and while they did not always stop arsonists and accidents from burning down parts of the palace over the centuries, they do provide clear evidence of the long tradition of rainwater collection from the very heart of China, and its use for purposes other than just domestic consumption. It is partly on the foundations of such ancient traditions that the renewed interest in rainwater utilization in China and calls for its greater use in the twenty-first century are based (Zhu and Liu, 1998). In Japan, too, where rainwater utilization also has a long history, the application

240

history, the application of rainwater utilization in the future, particularly in urban contexts, is now being actively promoted (Murase, 1998; TIRUC, 1994).

Similar calls for re-examining the appropriateness of traditional rainwater harvesting practices in the face of the failure of conventional 'mega-projects' have also recently been made in India. Here, as in other parts of the world, there seems to be a new recognition of the achievements of past generations and the lessons we might learn from them to help us survive and prosper in the future. In their recent book, *Dying Wisdom*, Agarwal and Narain (1997) make a plea for the urgent reconsideration of the future relevance of this ancient but still relevant and highly appropriate technology.

Rainwater utilization and sustainable development

Following the international recognition of the ethos of sustainable development in the late 1980s, there has been a growing realization of the urgent need to implement the policies, practices and lifestyles that this implies. Problems relating to resource depletion, pollution and global climatic change all need to be overcome if more sustainable modes of development are to be achieved. Rainwater catchment systems represent a technology which is fundamentally in tune with efforts to create a more sustainable society. This is because rainwater catchment systems are small scale, involve the use of a renewable resource and, hence, generally have very limited environmental impact.

Rapid population growth, urbanization and rising water demand are putting conventional centralized water-supply systems, and the water resources on which they depend, under increasing pressure. While this is not apparent to ordinary consumers most of the time, during droughts or prolonged dry periods it can become an acute problem leading to water restrictions and, in extreme cases, the cutting off of supplies. Even comparatively humid countries, such as the UK and New Zealand, where abundant water supplies were once taken for granted, have seen the emergence of water restrictions and hosepipe bans in some areas during recent dry summers. During such temporary 'water crises', water utility companies are often enthusiastic about their consumers turning to other sources such as rainwater barrels for gardening to help reduce demand and reduce the pressure on the supply system. This explains why they often promote small rainwater tanks, especially for garden use, in their consumer information leaflets on water-conservation measures, even if they may not be enthusiastic about more general use of rainwater for supplementary supplies.

In some parts of the world, such as Southern Africa, where more chronic water shortages loom in the near future, several approaches are being adopted to try to stem the problem. These include a greater emphasis on integrated water resources management, demand management and water conservation, of which rainwater collection is a part. South Africa has led the way in the region with the launching of an ambitious National Water Conservation Campaign by the government in 1996.

241

Water shortages are also looming in parts of Japan. Current developments in Tokyo and several other large Japanese cities suggest that in the mega-cities of the twenty-first century, rainwater catchment systems are likely to play an increasingly important role. Not only will they reduce the overall water demands of the growing cities but they may also reduce problems of urban flooding. Furthermore, the additional costs of providing rainwater tanks should be offset by savings in the cost of expanding the capacity and extent of the stormwater drainage infrastructure.

Addressing the issue of global warming caused by human activities is another facet of sustainable development in which rainwater catchment systems may have a role to play. Evidence that human-induced climatic changes due to emissions of carbon dioxide and other greenhouse gases (e.g. methane, nitrous oxide, ozone and chlorofluorocarbons) are taking place seem increasingly to be borne out by the facts. Several of the hottest years in terms of mean global temperature were recorded during the 1990s. If these signs are a precursor to the long-predicted global warming, it is suggested that not only will mean global temperatures rise but that climate may become more unstable, with a higher frequency of storms and droughts in many regions. The recent floods and droughts resulting from the strong El Niño effect in the Pacific may be indicative of what will become commonplace in the future. Should these long-term predictions turn out to be true, the role of rainwater catchment systems both for providing supplementary supplies during droughts and emergency supplies following storms, typhoons and hurricanes may be even more important than they are today.

There are several key pointers to suggest that the growing worldwide interest in water conservation in general, and rainwater catchment systems in particular, will continue. Apart from the increasing pressure on conventional water sources, the use of rainwater systems is broadly in line with the policies being set by many governments and international institutions worldwide in their attempt to introduce more sustainable modes of development for the twenty-first century and beyond.

Moving from 19th to 21st century technology

Since the industrial revolution, many ancient, small-scale, decentralized rainwater supplies around the world have been replaced by large-scale centralized 'modern' water-supply systems. These conventional water-supply systems, built from the nineteenth century onwards for their economies of scale and which now often incorporate sophisticated treatment facilities, have indeed contributed to increasingly convenient and safe water supplies in large parts of the world. While these 'modern' systems play an important role and are appropriate in many contexts, they are not appropriate everywhere. One problem is that there is enormous wastage in conventional treated water-supply systems. In richer countries and cities, people flush their toilets with water cleaner than that available for drinking in many poorer rural areas, only to pipe it back for further processing at a sewage-treatment plant before it is discharged or reused. Most people, unaware of where their water comes from, or where their wastewater is going to, seem resigned to continue paying for these services. This apparent willingness to pay for water and wastewater services in wealthier countries in this unquestioning way is probably due to some of the following factors:

- Water and wastewater services remain relatively inexpensive compared to incomes in many places, and charges are often fixed or hidden.
- Householders are either unaware of alternatives, such as rainwater catchment systems, or the additional expense and disruption of retro-fitting existing houses with these systems is not considered worthwhile. (Building them into new houses is usually cheaper.)
- Water utility companies have an overall vested interest in discouraging the substantial use of rainwater for routine purposes such as toilet flushing, clothes and car washing as these may erode their revenues, especially where water use is metered.

In Chapter 9, we have seen that in countries such as Germany, where in many cities both water and rainwater drainage charges are high and the costs to consumers clearly itemized, interest in installing rainwater tanks and seepage wells is growing. While German householders in over a quarter of the country have a genuine vested interest in investing in rainwater collection systems, these have also been strongly promoted and subsidized by many local governments. In Osnabrück, cost-recovery times for rainwater systems have been estimated to be around 16 years (or just 12 years with a local government subsidy) even at current water-supply and rainwater drainage charges (Wessels, 1994). If, as seems likely, the real cost of water supply and wastewater services increases in the future in the face of growing scarcity and stricter environmental controls, there will be a growing incentive for the incorporation of rainwater catchment tanks as standard features in new homes both in Germany and around the world. The German experience, as well as that from Japan, provides an insight into what may become increasingly common during the twenty-first century, as the true and increasing cost of clean water supplies and wastewater treatment recognized.

Rainwater utilization in the 21st century and beyond

While much has been written about the history of rainwater utilization and the current state of the art around the world (see Chapter 1), relatively few commentators have ventured to make predictions or proposals regarding the long-term future development of the technology. Fok (1992) does provide a rare far-sighted analysis of the potential for greatly increasing the use of rooftops as resource collectors for both water and energy in the future. Fok suggests that while rainwater catchment systems and solar-voltaic technologies may not appear economically competitive compared with supplies from major utility companies, the picture may be distorted. Conventional economic comparisons do not normally include the environmental or social costs of major centralized projects, and if these factors are included a different picture emerges. Faced with growing pressure on water and energy resources, the marginal and environmental costs of providing the additional water and energy required by many of the world's rapidly growing cities is often very high. In this context, rainwater catchment systems and renewable energy technologies can often provide both appropriate and economically attractive alternatives. In situations where the capacity of the public water-supply system is subscribed to its limit, part of the responsibility and cost of water supply can be shifted to the private sector by requiring the inclusion of household rainwater systems in plans submitted for the issuing of building permits.

One futuristic view of the way in which rainwater catchment systems may feature in the urban landscapes of tomorrow comes from a proposal for a 'City of Rain' at a 23ha site in Singapore. In this visionary design, a young Singaporean architect explores the multi-functional use of rainwater in a tropical city of the future (Teck, 1989). In this concept the whole site 'city' is raised above all roadways and parking areas to reduce the risk of any pollution of the rainwater which would be collected from all roofs and paved areas. The rainwater is stored in tanks and in a moat surrounding the site. The proposed uses for the rainwater include a wide range of non-potable water functions, such as toilet flushing, water landscape features (fountains and pools), air-conditioning, and cooling of buildings. A central feature of the 'City of Rain' plan is a 'Rain Monument', consisting of a huge funnel shaped like an inverted pyramid, suspended between four tower blocks and beneath viewing galleries bridging diagonally between the towers. A cross-sectional view of the proposed design is shown in Figure 10.1. Water flowing through the 'funnel' would consist of rainwater and also hot water from the air-conditioning system. The rainwater would be circulated by pumps, which could be powered by energy from solar panels housed on the funnel. By pumping the water from the main storage tank to the tops of the towers and through the funnel, a spectacular cascade of rain would produce a fine mist for cooling the surroundings.

Looking even further into the future, it seems likely that while rainwater collection will probably continue to be important in one form or another, its utilization may take place in a context quite unfamiliar to that of the present. One possible scenario is that many areas of today's utilitarian urban sprawl may be cleared in the future and replaced with a relatively small number of very large buildings, each equivalent in size to a modern town. The surrounding land would be reclaimed and converted to parkland and woodland, with some of the original ecosystems restored. In this scenario, one could imagine pyramid-shaped mega-buildings, perhaps 500 to 1000m in height, designed to be self-sufficient as far as possible in both energy and water. All the rainwater runoff would be collected and recycled through the building. Not only would the rainwater provide the main source of water for these self-sufficient buildings, but it would also help to cool the buildings in summer by spraying water from the top and letting it run down the sides, providing evaporative cooling. In winter, the system could be used to melt snow or ice on the sides of the

Figure 10.1 Proposed architectural design for rainwater collection in Singapore

THE CITY OF RAIN

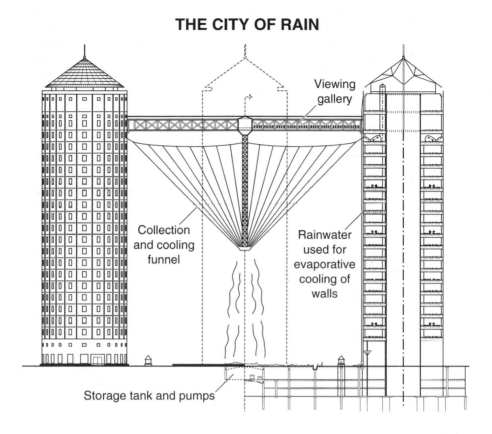

Viewing gallery

Collection and cooling funnel

Rainwater used for evaporative cooling of walls

Storage tank and pumps

The 'Rainwater Monument'

In this futuristic design, rainwater is used for toilet flushing, gardens, water landscape features and cooling the buildings and surrounds.
(Adapted from a drawing by Kevin Lim Chiow Teck, 1989)

building. Internal and external gardens, fountains, ponds and aquariums would also help to regulate the temperature inside the buildings and provide aesthetically pleasing recreational terraces on the outside. Large storage tanks, each containing several thousand cubic metres of rainwater, and possibly constructed in cavities between floors, could be located at many different levels within the structure to assist in moderating the internal temperature. These reservoirs would also provide an emergency water supply for fire-fighting purposes. Since much of the rainwater could be stored at high levels in the building, the supply could mainly be gravity-fed to reduce energy

245

consumption. Where water needs to be pumped to higher levels, pumps would be driven by photovoltaic panels, or in winter by power produced from methane derived from the building's sewage/waste-recycling facility.

While it may seem far-fetched to imagine that in the future a significant proportion of urban dwellers may live in very large buildings, a number of long-term trends suggest that this will be the case. The earth's population is already predicted to reach close to 10 billion before it stabilizes sometime around the end of the twenty-first century and the populations of the world's already crowded mega-cities are set to more than double. Just as cities have been growing in size throughout history so have buildings, particularly in the last century. These trends have created serious problems of growing congestion, overcrowding, crime and environmental degradation. Finding solutions to these problems may require some revolutionary and highly innovative thinking and changes of lifestyle. The construction of these self-sufficient mega-buildings, surrounded by recreational areas and countryside, linked through high-speed transit systems could provide one of several responses to the growing crisis.

The challenges of the new millennium

As we enter the third millennium, many people continue to marvel at humankind's technological 'achievements'. In purely technical terms, many of these accomplishments in fields such as the exploration of the solar system, genetic engineering and computer technology are indeed impressive, while the sophistication of many modern military systems is both awesome and frightening. Yet, in the context of these developments, it is nothing short of outrageous that humanity has failed to successfully apply simple technology to meet some of the most basic human requirements. For many people in poorer regions, the provision of adequate food, water and shelter remains only a distant dream. Because it is the 'cutting-edge' technologies that tend to steal the limelight and fire the imagination, many people have long imagined that the twenty-first century and beyond would be characterized by lifestyles dominated by high technology. For many, personal computers, the Internet, satellite communications and other recent innovations are already having a major impact on their lives; for large numbers of people in poor rural and peri-urban areas, these developments remain irrelevant. However much high technology is developed, it is clear that basic technologies still have a fundamental role to play in improving people's lives, and for many the impact of even the provision of a simple household rainwater system can be dramatic (Plate 1.1).

Over the next few decades the world is faced with two major challenges relating to water-supply provision, which rainwater utilization could help to address. The first relates to rural areas, which are often poor and remote from large-scale water sources such as big dams (which can be custom-built for wealthy cities!). Here the challenge is to try to ensure that convenient, clean water supplies and improved sanitation becomes the norm for every household, as soon as possible. While the most affordable and appropriate technology should be used to do this, rainwater catchment systems clearly have an important role to play, both in areas lacking good alternative water sources and elsewhere as supplementary supplies. The second challenge relates to urban areas where pollution and interference with the natural hydrological cycle has created many problems relating to health, flooding and local climatic changes, such as the 'urban heat island effect'.

For those currently promoting rainwater utilization in cities, the emphasis is on treating runoff, avoiding certain water uses, and mitigating flooding problems. The real challenge in the future, however, will be to remove atmospheric pollution altogether so that pollution-free rainwater can once again be collected in city centres. This, of course, will require a fundamental change in transport modes and policy as well as very strict control of both domestic and industrial emissions into the atmosphere. Restoring the hydrological cycle in cities by again allowing the infiltration of rainwater into the soil and groundwater will also require major physical changes to the urban landscape. With more rainwater retained and stored within the urban area, many of these problems will be greatly reduced. Potentially, most cities could become self-sufficient in terms of water resources. Tokyo is a good case in point; despite the massive water demand of the city, Murase (1998) has estimated that consumption is less than the total rainfall received by the city.

Conclusion

In the preceding chapters, the long tradition and recent revival of rainwater catchment systems for domestic supply around the world has been documented. Several indications, such as the growing pressure on potable water sources world wide, would suggest that the current interest in, and increasing rates of implementation of rainwater systems are likely to continue for some time to come. In the early part of the twenty-first century, rainwater catchment systems will assist significantly in meeting the challenge of ensuring that all have access to clean water in their homes. While rainwater collection is only one of a range of technologies available for this purpose, it is normally always an option and one which, in recent years, has become increasingly popular.

Household rainwater catchment systems have the potential in many parts of the world to provide a substantial part of domestic water needs and, if properly designed and maintained, roof catchments can provide water suitable for drinking purposes. Experience from many countries has shown that privately owned systems at individual households are those that are operated and maintained the most effectively. Communal systems, for example at schools are less likely to be well-maintained as the lines of responsibility for maintenance, including cleaning of the tank and gutters or any repair work, are frequently unclear. Due to less frequent inspection, cleaning and maintenance of communal systems, these are more likely to suffer from contamination and leakage problems, especially from poorly maintained taps.

Apart from domestic supply, the utilization of rainwater in urban areas also seems likely to increase in future due to the broad range of benefits it offers, from reducing pressure on alternative supplies, to protection against floods, fire and as emergency supplies following natural disasters. In earlier chapters we have seen that interest in more sustainable forms of development in general, and rainwater catchment systems in particular, is growing. In many circumstances, rainwater supplies have the potential to meet people's water needs with a minimum of environmental disruption.

In the same way that solar technologies offer the opportunity to become self-sufficient in energy in most parts of the world, rainwater catchment systems and water harvesting for plant production offer the opportunity to become self-sufficient, or at least more self-reliant, in water supplies. Whether one is a villager in the rural 'South' looking for an improved or supplementary water supply, or a city dweller in the urban 'North' looking for ways to save water and adopt a more environmentally sustainable lifestyle, rainwater catchment systems for domestic supply have much to offer.

The renewed interest in rainwater catchment systems for domestic supply in recent decades has led to the development of improved and more cost-effective technologies, particularly for water storage. Potentially, the technology could in the future become a standard feature of almost every home, in every country, supplying some or all of the household's water needs.

APPENDIX 1

Glossary

Abanbar (Persian)

Traditional, communal, excavated rainwater reservoirs housed in distinctive roofed buildings and still used in modern-day Iran.

Aggregate (Ballast)

Crushed stones normally between 8mm and 32mm

Ahars (see *Khadin*)

Large earth bunds used in Northern India (Bihar) to retain floodwater.

Anahaw Palms

Type of palm commonly used for roofing in the Philippines from which rainwater can be easily collected.

Anthill powder

Made from crushed anthills/termite stacks and can sometimes be used as a partial substitute for Portland cement.

Barrios (Spanish)

Marginal informal squatter areas in Central American cities.

Bowser

Water truck- or tractor-towed tanker used for transporting domestic water by road.

Bund

Low earth wall, ridge or dyke used to divert or retain rainwater runoff.

Calcrete

Hard sedimentary deposit consisting of material cemented together by calcium carbonate.

Catchment

Any discrete area draining into a common system; e.g. a river catchment is all drained by one river.

Caxio

Open, hand-dug, sub-surface rainwater cistern dug into micaceous rock in some parts of north-eastern Brazil with typical volume of 50m³ or more.

Chultun

Excavated underground rainwater tank lined with 'stucco' (cement/lime) found in limestone area of Yucatan Peninsular, Mexico.

Cistern

Tank for water storage.

Curing

The process of assisting mortar and concrete to harden by keeping it moist for a period of weeks.

Discount Rate

The future economic value of a resource compared with its present value.

Djabir (Arabic)

A rectangular rainwater tank traditionally made using burnt lime and coral, but more recently with cement, common along the East Coast of Africa and parts of the Arab world.

Favelas

The large, squatter slum areas typical of large South American cities.

Ferrocement

Construction method involving the reinforcement of cement mortar using wire and/or wire mesh.

Flat Batter Dam

A purpose-built surface reservoir and ground catchment system constructed using graders and bulldozers and common in Western Australia for farm and small community water supplies.

Floodwater Harvesting	This term, which is often referred to as floodwater farming, water spreading or spate irrigation, involves the diversion or spreading of turbulent channel flow, often from runoff originating several kilometres away, for supplementary irrigation, flood and erosion control or groundwater recharge.
Foul Flush Device	Any system or device designed to discard the initial roof runoff at the start of any storm (also known as first flush).
Ghala Tank	A cement tank constructed by plastering cement directly on to a basket framework (common in East Africa in the 1970s and 1980s but now largely obsolete due to leakage problems).
Glide	Stone or tile ridge constructed at an angle on the roof to divert rainwater into a tank and to avoid the need for gutters.
Guttersnipe	A special type of self-cleaning foul flush device which can be attached to the downpipe just beneath the gutter.
Hafir (Arabic)	Excavated water reservoir filled by storm runoff for livestock and domestic water supply.
Harambee (Swahili)	Tradition of community spirit, including the provision of free labour on communal projects.
Infiltration Capacity	Limiting rate at which rainfall can be absorbed by the soil surface through the process of infiltration.
Karai (Swahili)	Steel basin used for carrying mortar and other material.
Khadin (Ahar)	Large earth bunds used in Northern India (Rajasthan) to retain floodwater.
Kundis	Large, traditional, saucer-shaped ground catchment systems with central covered cisterns found in Rajastan, India.
Kuskabas (Sailabas)	Inundation farming technique used in Pakistan.
Loess	Fine windblown deposits common in central and NW China.
Lomas	Fog-zone vegetation community found in the coast foothills of the Andes in Chile and Peru.
Mabati (Swahili)	Local term for corrugated-iron sheets commonly used throughout East Africa.
Mega-city	Large city with more than one million inhabitants.
Microcatchment	Small ground catchment system used for concentrating surface runoff around trees or crops.
Murram	Clay containing soft pebbles and sometimes used for rural road construction.
Nil	A cement slurry made from mixing cement and water which can be used as a substitute for waterproof cement.
Pan	Wind-blown depression common in the Kalahari and other deserts, which occasionally fills with rainwater and often contains salt and other evaporite deposits.

Peri-urban	Area on the periphery of city, often including informal settlements.
Permaculture	A term derived from the words 'Permanent Agriculture' and 'Permanent Culture' to describe a design system for sustainable production involving minimum input and maximum output.
Pila (Spanish)	Small, open, cement water tank holding up to about 500 litres common in squatter areas in Honduras.
Pointing	The process of finishing (or repairing) joints in brickwork or masonary with mortar.
Precipitation	A general term for water which falls from the atmosphere as rain, sleet, snow and hail. [Note: Strictly speaking, fog, dew and frost are not forms of precipitation as they condense or are deposited on to surfaces by impaction.]
Rainwater Catchment	Collection and storage of runoff primarily for domestic use and water supply.
Rainwater Harvesting	A general term for most types of rainwater catchment (but excluding floodwater harvesting) for both agriculture and domestic supply.
Roaded Catchment	A type of ground catchment system common in Australia in which the catchment is graded into a series of inward-sloping roads to divert rainwater runoff towards a storage reservoir.
Rojison (Japanese)	A Japanese rainwater cellar, found in urban areas, for communal use.
Runoff Coefficient	The ratio of the volume of water which runs off a surface to the volume of rain which falls on the surface.
Runoff Gardening	A small-scale type of runoff farming which can be applied to the household 'kitchen' garden.
Runoff Farming	The diversion and concentration of rainwater runoff on to crops, trees or pasture.
Sailabas (Kuskabas)	Inundation farming technique used in Pakistan.
Sandriver	Ephemeral river beds which may contain water beneath the sand, but carry visible surface water following heavy rainfall, normally for only a few weeks each year.
Shuijiao (Chinese)	Chinese underground bottle-shaped water cellar, usually up to 15m³ in volume, especially common in the loess plateau region of central China.
Swales	Long, shallow, level excavations made to intercept and hold runoff water to encourage soil-water storage.
Tankas	Local name for rainwater tanks in parts of Northern India.
Thai jar	1–2m³ ferrocement rainwater jar, modelled on traditional clay jars, used to store water with volumes typically less than 250 litres.

251

Teleiats	Mounds of rocks found on hillsides and hilltops in the Negev Desert (once thought to be used for harvesting dew) but probably a result of clearing slopes to enhance rainwater runoff.
Threshing Floor	A specially constructed mud and dung-plastered floor, surrounded by a low wall, used as a surface for threshing grain and, more recently, for collecting rainwater runoff.
Urban Heat Island	An effect causing elevated air temperatures in the centres of large cities due to solar energy being trapped by paved surfaces and buildings.
Water Harvesting	An umbrella term for a whole range of methods of concentrating and storing rainwater runoff, including roofs (rooftop harvesting), the ground (runoff harvesting), and from channel flow (floodwater harvesting). The term is, none the less, most often closely associated with runoff farming and use of microcatchments for agro-forestry and crop production.

Units

1m = 1 metre = 100cm = 1000mm
1m = 3.28 feet
1 cubic metre = 1m³ = 1000 litres
1″ = 1 inch = 2.54 cm
1 hectare = 2.47 acres = 15 mu
1 British imperial gallon = 0.83 US gallons = 4.55 litres
1 US gallon = approx 5.5 litres

Formulas

Where:
r = radius
d = diameter
h = height
π = 3.14 (approximately)
Circumference of a Circle – πd
Area of a Circle – πr^2
Volume of a Cylinder – $\pi r^2 h$
Surface Area of a Cylinder – $2(\pi r^2) + \pi dh$
Volume of a Sphere – $4/3(\pi r^3)$
Surface Area of a Sphere – $4\pi r^2$
Volume of a Hemisphere – $2/3(\pi r^3)$
Surface Area of a Hemisphere – $2\pi r^2$

Useful contact addresses

The Ajit Foundation
396 Vasundhara Colony, Tonk Road,
Jaipur 302 018, India
Fax: +91–141-519938
Email: visquar@jp1.vsnl.net.in

ASAL Consultants Ltd.
P.O. Box 38, Kibwezi, Kenya

BTC (Botswana Technology Centre)
P/Bag 0082, Gaborone, Botswana
Fax: +267–374677
Email: botec@info.bw

CSE (Centre for Science and Environment)
41, Tughlakabad Institutional Area,
New Delhi, 110 062, India
Fax: +91–11-698 5879
Email: cse@sdalt.ernet.in
Website: www.cseindia.org

DALTECH (Centre for Water Resources Studies)
Centre for Water Resources Studies,
Dal Tech, Dalhousie University,
PO Box 1000, Halifax, Nova Scotia,
Canada B3J 2X4.
Email: scottrs@newton.ccs.tuns.ca

DTU (Development Technology Unit)
Engineering Dept, Warwick University,
Coventry CV4 7AL, UK
Fax: +44 1203–418922
Email: dtu@eng.warwick.ac.uk

FAKT (Association for Appropriate Technologies)
Gänsheidstrasse 43, D-70184, Stuttgart,
Germany
Fax: +49–711-210 9555
Email: 100557.3651@compuserve.com

fbr (Fachveeninigung für Betriebs und Regenwassernutzung e.v)
Specialist Association for Rainwater
Utilization
Kasseler Str. 1a, D-60486, Frankfurt am
Main, Germany
Fax: +49–69-9707 4648
Email: fbrev@t-online.de

GWP (Global Water Partnership)
GWP, Sida, S-105 25, Stockholm,
Sweden
Fax: +46–8-698 5627
Email: gwp@sida.se
Website: www.gwp.sida.se

IDRC (International Development Research Centre)
P.O. Box 8500, Ottawa, Canada K1G
3H9
Fax: +1–613-238 7230
Email: info@idrc.ca
Website: www.idrc.ca

IFIC (International Ferrocement Information Centre)
Asian Institute of Technology, P.O.
Box 4, Klong Luang, Pathumthani
12120, Thailand
Fax: +66–2-516–2126
Email: geoferro@.ait.ac.th

IRC (International Water and Sanitation Centre)
P.O. Box 93190, 2509 AD, The Hague,
Netherlands
Fax: +31–70-358 99 64
Email: general@irc.nl
Website: www.oneworld.org/ircwater/

IRCSA (International Rainwater Catchment Systems Association)
P.O. Box 38638, Nairobi, Kenya
Fax: +254–2-556943
Email: bambrah@AfricaOnline.co.ke

IT Publications (Intermediate Technology Publications)
103–105 Southampton Row, London,
WC1B 4HH, UK
Fax: +44–171-436 2013
Email: itpubs@itpubs.org.uk
Website: www.oneworld.org/itdg/

IWRA (International Water Resources Association)
4535 Faner Hall, Southern Illinois
University, Carbondale, IL 62901–4516,
USA
Fax: +1–505-277–9405
Email: iwra@siu.edu
Website: www.iwra.siu.edu

KRA (Kenya Rainwater Association)
P.O. Box 72837,
Fax: +254–2-560438
Email: gscons@arcc.or.ke

Khon Kaen University
Water Resources and Environment
Institute, Faculty of Engineering,
P.O. Box 26, Khon Kaen University,
Khon Kaen 40002, Thailand
Fax: +66–43-237 604

PDA (Population and Community Development Association)
8 Sukhumvit 12, Bangkok 10110,
Thailand
Fax: +66–2-2558804

People for Promoting Rainwater Utilisation
1–8-1, Higashi-Mukojima, Sumida City,
Tokyo, 131 Japan
Fax: +81–3-3611–0574
Email: murase-m@tc4.so-net.ne.jp

Public and Environmental Health Service
Dept. of Human Services, P.O. Box 6,
Rundle Mall SA 5000, Australia
Fax: +61–8226 7102
Email: ehb@health.sa.gov.au

Raindrop **(Published by the Rainwater Harvesting Information Service)**
P.O. Box 38638, Nairobi, Kenya
Fax: +254-2-556943
Email: bambrah@africaonline.co.ke

RELMA (Regional Land Management Unit)
P.O. Box 63403, Nairobi, Kenya
Fax: +254-2-520762
Email: r.winberg@cgnet.com

RHIS (Rainwater Harvesting Information Service)
P.O. Box 38638, Nairobi, Kenya
Fax: +254-2-556943
Email: bambrah@africaonline.co.ke

RWH Forum (Rainwater Harvesting Forum Secretariat)
c/o ITDG, 5 Lionel Edirisinghe
Mawatha, Kirulapone, Colombo 5,
Sri Lanka
Fax: +94–1-856188
Email: tanujaa@itdg.lanka.net

SA WATER (South Australian Water Corporation)
GPO Box 1751, Adelaide, SA 5001
Fax: +61–8-8359 2567
Email: marilla.barnes@sawater.sa.gov.au

SIDA (Swedish International Development Agency)
S-105 25 Stockholm, Sweden
Fax: +46–8-698 5653 / 208864
Email: ingvar.andersson@sida.se
Website: www.sida.se

UNDP-World Bank Water and Sanitation Program
The World Bank, 1818 H Street, NW,
Washington, DC 20433, USA
Fax: +1202–522-3313
Email: info@wsp.org
Website: www.wsp.org

UNICEF
UNICEF House, 3 United Nations
Plaza, New York 10017, USA
Fax: +1212 888–7465
Email: netmaster@unicef.org
Website: www.unicef.org

VITA (Volunteers in Technical Assistance)
1600 Wilson Boulevard, Suite 500,
Arlington, VA 22209, USA
Fax: +1–703–243 5639
Email: vita@vita.org

WaterAid
Prince Consort House, 27–29 Albert
Embankment, London SE1 7UB, UK
Fax: +44–171–793 4545
Email: wateraid@compuserve.com
Website: www.oneworld.org.wateraid

Waterlines
– see IT Publications

Water Resources Research Centre
University of Hawaii at Manoa, 2540
Dole St, Homes Hall 283, Honolulu,
Hawaii 96822, USA
Fax: +1–808-956–5044

WEDC (Water, Engineering and Development Centre)
Loughborough University,
Loughborough, LE11 3TU, UK
Fax: +44–1509–211079
Email: wedc@lboro.ac.uk
Website: www.lboro.ac.uk/departments/
cv/wedc/

WISY (Winkler Systems)
OT Hitzkirchen, Oberdorfstrasse 26,
D-63699, Kefendrod-Hitzkirchen,
Germany
Fax: +60–54-912129
wisyag@t-online.de

Conference contact addresses

**9th International Rainwater Catchment
Systems Conference** (1999)
Johann Gnadlinger,
P.O. Box 21, 48900–000 Juazeiro – BA,
Brazil
Fax: +55–74-811–5385
Email: ircsa@netcap.com.br

**8th International Rainwater Catchment
Systems Conference** (1997)
Jamal Ghoddousi/Bahram Aminipouri,
SCWM Research Centre, P.O. Box
13445–1136, Tehran, Iran
Fax: +98–21-6407214
Email: rain1@neda.net

**7th International Rainwater Catchment
Systems Conference** (1995)
Changming Liu,
CAS, Bldg 917, Datun Rd, Beijing
100101, China
Fax: +86–311-5814362
Email: cmliu@pku.edu.cn

**6th International Rainwater Catchment
Systems Conference** (1993)
G.K. Bambrah
P.O. Box 38638, Nairobi, Kenya
Fax: +254–2–556943
Email: bambrah@africaonline.co.ke

Conference on Fog and Fog Collection
(1998)
P.O. Box 81541, 1057 Steeles Avenue
West, North York, Ontario, M2R 2X1,
Canada
Fax: +1–416-739–4211
Email: fogsite@ibm.net

**National Conference on Rainwater
Harvesting** (1998)
CSE (Centre for Science and
Environment)
41, Tughlakabad Institutional Area,
New Delhi, 110 062, India
Fax: +91–11-698 5879
Email: cse@sdalt.ernet.in
Website: www.cseindia.org

**Tokyo International Rainwater
Utilization Conference** (1994)
Makoto Murase,
Dept. of Environmental Protection, 23–
20 Azumabashi-1-chrome,
Sumida City, Tokyo, Japan
Fax: +81–3-5608–6405
Email: murase-m@tc4.so-net.ne.jp

Contact details for the authors

John Gould
107 Studholme Street,
Christchurch 8002,
New Zealand
Email: john.gould@xtra.co.nz

Erik Nissen-Petersen
P.O. Box 38
Kibwezi
Kenya

APPENDIX 3

Internet resources and computer models

DUE TO THE rapid development of information technology and, in particular, the Internet, it is increasingly possible to access information quickly and cheaply from anywhere in the world. All that is required is a personal computer with a modem, and access to a good, clear telephone link. There is already a huge quantity of information about almost every topic imaginable, including rainwater catchment systems. Much of the material on rainwater systems is targeted at local audiences and, although it can sometimes take time to sift through many sites before the specific information required is located, given time and a bit of practice it is usually possible to find information on even seemingly obscure topics. One major advantage with accessing material from the Internet is that it is usually fairly up-to-date. Feedback and communication with the source authors of the material is also often possible by email. While a number of user-friendly computer models for aiding rainwater system sizing and determining performance in different places have been developed, few are currently freely accessible through the Internet. The Sim Tanka Software produced by the Ajit Foundation (see below for website details) is one rainwater model which can be downloaded free from the Internet. This situation will undoubtedly change soon as more people post models on the Internet. For those interested in developing computer models, the email contacts of a few individuals who have developed rainwater system design models are given below in the section on computer models.

The following list of Internet websites is just a tiny sample of many thousands of sites on various aspects of rainwater catchment systems accessible through the Internet. For anyone unfamiliar with searching for information through 'the Net', it is useful to employ a search engine. These search tools can check millions of sites in a few seconds and pick out any that relate to given key search terms, for example 'rainwater catchment'. If too many sites are located it will be necessary to narrow the search by being more specific or adding extra search terms, e.g. 'rainwater catchment China' or 'gutter sizing'. One user-friendly website which will allow you simply to ask for information in the form of a simple question is *Ask Jeeves* (see second entry below for the website address). This runs several search engines simultaneously and is a fast way to start any search for information on any subject, whether it be looking for rainfall data or finding out what the weather will be like tomorrow! The *InterWater* guide to databases and GARNET are good starting points for conducting any searches on any water-related topic.

Internet websites

(Use following prefix for websites if required: http://)

The Ajit Foundation
Email: visquar@jp1.vsnl.net.in
Website (Sim Tanka Software):
www.geocities.com/rainforest/
canopy/4805

ASK JEEVES
Email: jeeves@askjeeves.com
Website: www.askjeeves.com

CSE (Centre for Science and Environment)
Email: cse@sdalt.ernet.in
Website: www.cseindia.org

GARNET (Global Applied Research Network in Water Supply and Sanitation)
Email: d.l.saywell@lboro.ac.uk
Website: www.lboro.ac.uk/
departments/cv/wedc/garnet/

GWP (Global Water Partnership)
Email: gwp@sida.se
Website: www.gwp.sida.se

IDRC (International Development Research Centre)
Email: info@idrc.ca
Website: www.idrc.ca

Interwater Guide to Databases
Email: general@irc.nl
Website: www.wsscc.org

IRC (International Water and Sanitation Centre)
Email: general@irc.nl
Website: www.oneworld.org/ircwater/

IRCSA (International Rainwater Catchment Systems Association)
Email: bambrah@AfricaOnline.co.ke
Website: www.lboro.ac.uk/
departments/cv/wedc/garnet/
tncrain.html

IT Publications (Intermediate Technology Publications)
Email: journals.edit@itpubs.org.uk
Website: www.oneworld.org/itdg/

IWRA (International Water Resources Association)
Email: iwra@siu.edu
Website: www.iwra.siu.edu

JRCSA (Japan Rainwater Catchment Association)
Email: takeyame@life.shimane-u.ac.jp
Website: takeyam.life.shimane-u.ac.jp/
jircsa/homepage.html

One World (A Network of over 150 NGO Websites)
Website: www.oneworld.org/itdg/

SA WATER (South Australian Water Corporation)
Email: marilla.barnes@sawater.sa.gov.au
Website: www.sacentral.sa.gov.au/
agencies/saw

SIDA (Swedish International Development Agency)
Email: ingvar.andersson@sida.se
Website: www.sida.se

Sourcebook Harvested Rainwater
Email: bowrbird@texas.net
Website: www.greenbuilder.com/
sourcebook/rainwater

Texas Rainwater Harvesting Project
Website: www.ci.austin.tx.us/watercon/
rainwater.html

UNDP-World Bank Water and Sanitation Program
Email: info@wsp.org
Website: www.wsp.org

UNICEF (United Nations Children's Fund)
Email: netmaster@unicef.org
Website: www.wsp.org

WaterAid
Email: wateraid@compuserve.com
Website: www.oneworld.org/wateraid

Waterlines
Email: itpubs@itpubs.org.uk
Website: www.oneworld.org/itdg/
publications.html

Waterlines Technical Briefs
Email: itpubs@itpubs.org.uk
Website: www.lboro.ac.uk/orgs/well/
briefs/contents.html

WEDC (Water, Engineering and Development Centre)
Email: wedc@lboro.ac.uk
Website: www.lboro.ac.uk/
departments/cv/wedc/

Conference websites

9th International Rainwater Catchment Systems Conference Brazil (1999)
Email: ircsa@netcap.com.br
Website: www.ircsa.com.br

National Conference on Rainwater Harvesting India (1998)
Email: cse@sdalt.ernet.in
Website: www.cseindia.org

Conference on Fog and Fog Collection Canada (1998)
Email: fogsite@ibm.net
Website: www.tor.ec.gc.ca/armp/ Events.html

Computer models

The following are examples of some user-friendly computer models which can be run on most personal computers using widely available software packages. These can be applied to local conditions if the appropriate rainfall data and other basic rainwater system variables are provided.

1. Sim Tanka

Sim Tanka is software developed by the Ajit Foundation in Jaipur, India in a spirit of co-operation and in the hope it may help small communities in meeting their water needs in a sustainable and reliable manner. *No guarantees of any kind are, however, implied.* The software will run on Windows 95 and Windows NT operating systems only. The programme requires 15 years of rainfall data and simulates the performance of rainwater harvesting systems, thereby providing a useful predictive tool. The model can assist in determining appropriate tank volume requirements or the fraction of the water demand that can be reliably supplied from existing systems. The model uses a stochastic simulation technique (the Monte Carlo Simulation) to simulate fluctuation in rainfall. A non-technical discussion of the model and underlying assumptions behind Sim Tanka can be found in the December 1996 issue of *Raindrop*, available from the Rainwater Harvesting Information Service in Nairobi (see Appendix 2). The Sim Tanka software can be downloaded free from the following website:

http://www.geocities.com/rainforest/canopy/4805

For further information, email Vikram Vyas at: visquar@jp1.vsnl.net.in (or see Appendix 2 for the Ajit Foundation contact details).

2. Spreadsheet methods

A number of models have been developed for use on standard spreadsheet packages such as Quattro, Lotus or Excel. These are all based on the balance equation method through which the amount of water in the tank at the end of a given period (e.g. each month, week or day) is calculated. This is done by adding the rainwater inflow, less the water demand for the period, to the amount of water that was in the tank at the start of the period. Obviously, the amount of water stored cannot exceed the tank volume and, if the storage at the end of a period is zero, then a failure is recorded. Once rainfall data have been input along with basic system parameters, such as roof area, tank volume, and runoff coefficient, the demand can be manipulated through trial and error to determine the minimum tank size required to meet household demand, or until an acceptable level of household water security is achieved. A simple step-by-step explanation of this approach is shown in Box 3.2. A more detailed example of the use of this approach is given by Burgess (1996) in the June issue of *Raindrop*. For further details contact Stephen Burgess direct at email: sburgess@maf.org or P.O. Box 3404, Eldoret, Kenya.

Some slightly more sophisticated, yet still user-friendly spreadsheet-based rainwater system design programmes applicable for use, using Lotus or Quattro-Pro packages, have been developed by Brian Latham in Canada. These are based on the mass curve method and are designed for general application anywhere. For further details regarding these programmes contact Brian Latham at lathamb@inac.gc.ca or Box 1682, Yellowknife, Canada.

3. Nova Scotia Cistern Sizing Model
This programme, developed at Dalhousie University in Nova Scotia, is a user-friendly package enabling considerable flexibility in the selection of rainwater catchment system design variables. The programme allows for the specification of cistern capacity, collection area, .catch coefficient, daily household water demand and cistern storage at the start of system use. Each set of design criteria chosen is evaluated using the computer model, and rated. The rating is based on the probability that the design specified is able to meet the daily household water requirements. This deterministic computer model was developed to simulate system operation and predict probability of future performance scenarios on the basis of historical daily rainfall data. The model is not available in the public domain as it is set up specifically for use in Nova Scotia with rainfall data files already incorporated. The model could feasibly be adapted for use anywhere that has long-term daily rainfall records available from a network of stations, and it has already been modified for use in Ontario. For more information about this model contact Rick Scott direct at email: scottrs@newton.ccs.tuns.ca or at the Centre for Water Resources Studies, Dal Tech, Dalhousie University, PO Box 1000, Halifax, Nova Scotia, Canada B3J 2X4.

APPENDIX 4

Construction manuals and design information

A VAST AMOUNT of material on water tank construction is available world wide. The following lists are by no means comprehensive, but provide just a small sample of some of the resources that are available which relate to topics covered in this book.

Related books

Appropriate Building Materials, Stulz R. and Mukerji K. (1993) 3rd Edition, SKAT/Gate, IT Publications, London, 404p.

Community Water Development, Kerr C. (1989), IT Publications, London, 300p.

Design and Construction of Small Earth Dams, Nelson K.D. (1985), Australian Land Series, Inkata, Melbourne, Australia.

Dying Wisdom: The Rise, Fall and Potential of India's Traditional Water Harvesting Systems, Agarwal A. and Narain S. (1997), State of India's Environment 4, CSE, New Delhi, 404p.

Ephemeral Rivers in the Tropics, Sandström K. (1997) EPOS, Sweden.

Ferrocement Water Tanks and their Construction, Watt S. (1978) IT Publications, London, 118p.

Fogwater Collection System, International Research and Development Centre, (1993), P.O. Box 8500, Ottawa, Canada, 16p.

Groundwater Dams for Small-Scale Water Supply, Nilsson A. (1984), IT Publications, London, 64p.

Groundwater Dams in Sand-rivers Nissen-Petersen E. (1995), ASAL Consultants Ltd and UNDP/UNCHS & Myanmar (Burma).

Guidance on the Use of Rainwater Tanks, Cunliffe D. (1998), National Environmental Health Forum Monographs, Water Series 3, Public and Environmental Health Service, Dept. of Human Services, P.O. Box 6, Rundle Mall SA 5000, Australia, 28p.

Rain and Stormwater Harvesting in Rural Areas, UNEP (1983) Report by the United Nations Environment Programme, Tycooly International, Dublin, 238p.

Rain Catchment and Water Supply in Rural Africa, Nissen-Petersen E. (1982), Hodder and Stoughton, London, 83p.

Rainwater: An Under-Utilized Resource, (1995) Swedish International Development Authority (SIDA), P.O. Box 30600, Nairobi, Kenya, 30p.

Rainwater Catchment Systems for Household Water Supply, Gould J. (1991) ENSIC Review No. 31, P.O. Box 2754, A.I.T., Bangkok, Thailand, 57p.

Rainwater Harvesting and Water Use in the Barrios of Tegucigalpa, Brand A. and Bradford B. (1991), Agua para el Pueblo/UNICEF Honduras, 52p.

Rainwater Harvesting for Domestic Water Supply in Kisii, Kenya, Omwenga J.M. (1984), Published MSc. Thesis, Tampere University, Finland, 132p.

Rainwater Harvesting: The Collection of Rainfall and Runoff in Rural Areas, Pacey A. and Cullis A. (1986), IT Publications, London, 216p.

Rainwater Reservoirs above Ground Structures for Roof Catchment, Hasse R. (1989), Gate, Vieweg, Braunschweig/Wiesbaden, Germany, 102p.

Rural Water Supplies and Sanitation, Morgan P. (1990), Macmillan Education Ltd., London, 358p.

Soil and Water Conservation in Semi-arid areas, Hudson, N. (1987), FAO Soils Bulletin, No.57, 172p.

The Worth of Water: Technical Briefs on Health, Water and Sanitation, Pickford J. (1991), IT Publications, London, 144p.

Water Conservation for Communities in Arid Areas of South Australia, McLaren N., D. Heath and A. Morias (1987), SA Water (formerly EWSD), South Australian Water Corporation, GPO Box 1751, Adelaide, SA 5001, Australia, 24p.

Water from the Sky, (1989) A Workbook on the Ferrocement Rainwater Tank for Managers of Development Projects, Capiz Development Foundation, P.O. Box 72, Roxas City, Capiz, Philippines, 80p.

Water Harvesting: A Guide for Planners and Project Managers, Lee M. and Visscher J. (1992), Technical Series Paper 30, IRC PO Box 93190, The Hague, Netherlands, 106p.

Water Harvesting in Five African Countries, Lee M. and Visscher J. (1990), Occasional Paper Series 14, IRC PO Box 93190, The Hague, Netherlands, 106p.

Manuals and design information

Collection and Storage of Roof Runoff for Drinking Purposes, Vadhanavikkit C. et al., (1984), Vol. 3 – Construction: Materials, Techniques and Operational Studies, IDRC Canada/Faculty of Engineering, Khon Kaen University, Khon Kaen, Thailand, 113p.

Journal of Ferrocement, IFIC (International Ferrocement Information Centre) Asian Institute of Technology, P.O. Box 4, Klong Luang, Pathumthani 12120, Thailand.

Machakos Diocese: Rainwater Tank Programme, de Vrees L., (1987), Development Office, Catholic Diocese of Machakos, P.O. Box 640, Machakos, Kenya, 17p.

Raindrop (Biannual Newsletter) – Produced by WASH 1988–1993 and by the IRCSA since 1994 (International Rainwater Catchment Systems Association) P.O. Box 38638, Nairobi, Kenya.

Rainwater Roof Catchment Systems, Information and Training for Low-Cost Water Supply and Sanitation, Participants Notes 4.1, Schiller and Latham (1986), World Bank, New York, 44p.

Rainwater Tanks: Their Selection, Use and Maintenance, South Australian Water Corporation, (1998), GPO Box 1751, Adelaide, SA 5001, Australia, 24p.

Thai-Australia Village Water Supply Project: Construction of a 2000 litre Water Jar, P.O. Box 70, Khon Kaen, Thailand 4000, (AusAID–Australian Agency for International Development, GPO Box 887, Canberra City, ACT 2601 Australia, 10p.

Waterlines (Technical Briefs), Quarterly Journal Produced by IT Publications, 103–105 Southampton Row, London, WC1B 4HH, UK.

Other manuals and information sources

Manuals available from ASAL Consultants Ltd
1	10 Water Tanks for Roof and Ground Catchments	70p.
2	8 V.I.P. Latrines	36p.
3	Rock Catchment Dams and Tanks	35p.
4	How to Build Cylindrical Water Tanks with Domes	33p.
5	How to Build an Underground Tank with Dome	33p.
6	How to Repair Various Types of Water Tank	37p.
7	How to Build and Install Gutters and Splash-guards	20p.

Manuals being prepared for 1999
8   Earth Dams Built Manually
9   Sub-surface and Sand Dams in Sandrivers
10   Hand-dug Wells and River intakes in Sandrivers.

The current prices for manuals in 1998 range from US$10 to $18 including packing and postage by registered mail within Kenya. For deliveries to other countries, please add $10 for quick and secure postage by EMS. Ten per cent discount is given on purchases of more than 10 manuals. For further details contact: ASAL Consultants Ltd., P.O. Box 38, Kibwezi, Kenya.

Harvesting Rainwater in Semi-arid Africa, 6 manuals, Nissen-Petersen E. (1990), Danida and ASAL Consultants Ltd., P.O. Box 38, Kibwezi, Kenya.
How to build 6 photo-manuals, Nissen-Petersen E. (1992), Danida and ASAL Consultants Ltd., P.O. Box 38, Kibwezi, Kenya.
Manual on Rehabilitation of Open Wells in Sudan, Nissen-Petersen J. (1995), Danish Red Cross & Kruger Consultants & ASAL Consultants Ltd, Denmark.

Videos

Videos available or in preparation from ASAL Consultants or SIDA
Construction of Water Tanks for Rainwater Harvesting
(42 minutes English/Kiswahili, price US$25)
Being prepared by ASAL Consultants for 1999
– *Rock Catchment Dams and Tanks*
– *Manually Constructed Earth Dams*
– *Sub-surface and Sand Dams in Sandrivers*
– *Deep Hand-dug Wells and River-intakes in Sandrivers*
For further details contact: ASAL Consultants Ltd., P.O. Box 38, Kibwezi, Kenya.
or
SIDA, P.O. Box 30600, Nairobi, Kenya Fax: +254–2-220863.

Video available from FAKT
Mvua ni Maji – Rain is Water: Rainwater Harvesting by Women's Groups in Kenya (English 27 minutes)
For further details contact:
FAKT (Association for Appropriate technologies)
Gänsheidstrase 43, D-70184, Stuttgart, Germany
Fax: +49–711-210 9555 Email: 100557.3651@compuserve.com

Tank construction procedures

Based on the experience of ASAL Consultants Ltd.
P.O. Box 38, Kibwezi, Kenya.
and
Steve Burgess, Eldoret Region Company
P.O. Box 6495, Eldoret, Kenya.
Fax: 254 321 62472. Email: sburgess@maf.org

Contents   **Page**

Design of a formwork for the water tank
Construction procedures
Bill of Quantities for the water tank

Note:
1. All these designs require proper curing on completion (see Chapter 5 and Box 5.1).
2. All measurements are in cm unless otherwise stated.

WATER JAR BUILT OF FERROCEMENT

Storage volume 3m³ (3000 litres).

Construction cost approx. US$150 = US$50 per m³

Introduction

This water jar is larger than most jars and, therefore, is often called the 'Jumbo Jar'. Its design is adapted from the smaller but immensely popular Thai Jar, more than 10 million of which have been built in Thailand.

The Thai Jar is an adapted version of the ancient 200-litre jar made of burned clay of which every household in the Delta of Myanmar (Burma) has a dozen. The Jumbo Jar is especially popular with women's groups who find it easy to build on their own.

Design of a 3m³ jar

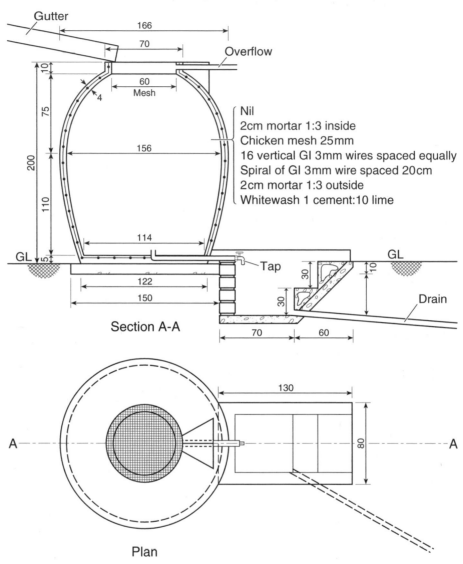

Gutter

166

70

Overflow

10

60
Mesh

4

75

Nil
2cm mortar 1:3 inside
Chicken mesh 25mm
16 vertical GI 3mm wires spaced equally
Spiral of GI 3mm wire spaced 20cm
2cm mortar 1:3 outside
Whitewash 1 cement:10 lime

156

200

110

114

GL

5

Tap

122

150

30

30

70

60

GL

10

Drain

Section A-A

130

A

80

A

Plan

Dimensions are in cm

266

Design of mould for a 3m³ jar

The mould is made of 15 metres of canvas 1.2m wide, consisting of 5 side panels and 1 floor panel sewn together with strong thread and overlaps of 10cm at all joints.

To make a mould, start by drawing a side panel in full size on the canvas and cut it accordingly. Use this side panel to mark the other 4 side panels and cut them. Finally, cut the floor panel, then sew all 6 panels together.

Make space for a string to be pulled and tied for the manhole at the top of the mould.

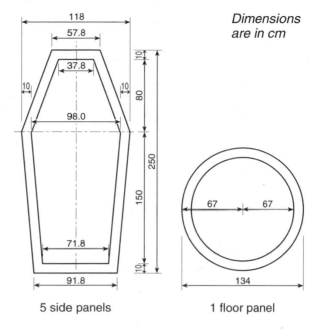

Dimensions are in cm

5 side panels

1 floor panel

Mould

Mould filled with sand
In some areas the only material available for stuffing a mould may be sand.

Since 3m³ of sand weighs about 5 tonnes, a mould made of canvas will burst unless most of the sand is kept in buckets, stacked on layers of timbers separating the rows of buckets.

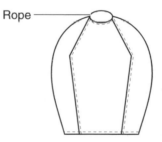

Rope

Mould stitched together

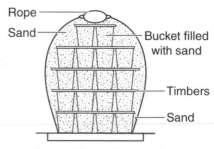

Rope
Sand

Bucket filled with sand

Timbers

Sand

Mould filled with sand

Construction procedures for a 3m³ jar

Foundation

The jar should be situated 90cm from the wall of the house.

The radius of the foundation is 75cm. Draw the circumference of the foundation using a string tied to a peg in the centre of the jar. Dig out soil within the circle until firm soil is reached, or the height to the eave of the roof is 220cm. Level the excavation.

Fill the excavation with 10cm of concrete 1:3:4; make it level and compact it well.

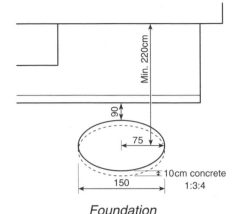

Foundation

Reinforcement of floor

Cut 8 lengths of 7m-long 3mm galvanized wire (GI). Bend the wire ends to avoid injuries.

Mark the middle of each wire on to it using pliers. Tie the 8 wires together at the marks as spokes in a wheel. Make a ring of 3mm GI wire, 116cm in diameter, and place upon spokes and tie together.

Tie two 136cm lengths of chicken mesh with overlaps of 10cm to the ring of the wire. Place the wires and mesh on the foundation.

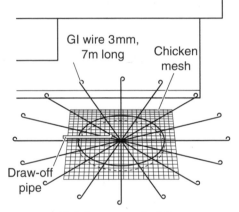

Reinforcement of floor

The draw-off pipe is made of 90cm of 18mm GI pipe on to which an elbow and a nipple are screwed to the inner end, and a socket and a tap to the outer end. Place the pipe upon the foundation.

Mould

The mould is then placed on the foundation and stuffed with light, dry materials, e.g. sawdust, hay or dung. Sand may be used if its weight is taken up by buckets.

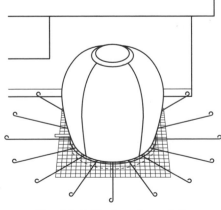

Mould stuffed on foundation

268

Construction procedures for a 3m³ jar (continued)

Reinforcement of wall
Chicken mesh is wrapped tightly around the stuffed mould while the chicken mesh lying under the mould is bent up against the side of the mould.

The 16 wires sticking out from under the mould are now tied on to a ring of GI wire at the top of the mould and spaced equally.

The end of a roll of GI wire is tied on to the foundation and wrapped tightly around the mould as a spiral spaced 20cm to the top of the mould.

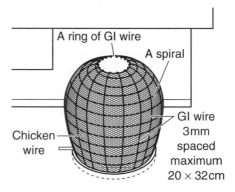

A ring of GI wire

A spiral

GI wire 3mm spaced maximum 20 × 32cm

Chicken wire

Reinforcement of wall

External plaster
Mortar 1:3 is smeared on to the mould in a thin layer. After a couple of hours more mortar is plastered on to the mould until the mortar is 2cm thick.

While the plaster is cured for 3 days, the tap station is built.

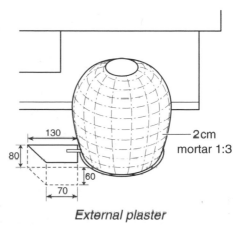

130

80

70

60

2cm mortar 1:3

External plaster

Internal plaster and finish
After 3 days, the mould and its contents are removed. The jar is cleaned before mortar 1:3 is plastered on to the internal side of the jar in 2 layers, each layer being 1cm thick. The floor is made of 5cm-thick plaster of 1:3. On the same day, cement and water are mixed with Nil and, with a steel trowel, pressed into the moist plaster for waterproofing.

Place 2 concentric rings of plain sheet 10cm high and 60cm diameter on top of the jar. Fill the space with 1:3 mortar to form a manhole and a lip. Place a pipe for an overflow through the lip. Cover the manhole with mesh to prevent insects and debris entering the jar.

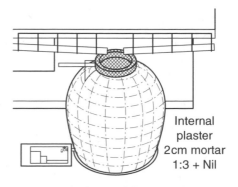

Internal plaster 2cm mortar 1:3 + Nil

Internal plaster and finish

BILL OF QUANTITIES FOR A 3m³ WATER JAR
BUILT OF FERROCEMENT

Item	Specification	Units	Quantity
Materials			
Cement	50kg	Bags	6
Lime	25kg	Bags	1
Sand	Coarse & clean	Tonnes	3
Crushed stones	10 to 20mm	Tonnes	1
Rubble stones	100 to 500mm	Tonnes	1
Bricks/blocks	Variable	Number	50
Water	200 litres	Oil drums	3
PVC pipe	50mm	Metres	3
G.I. pipe	38mm (1½")	Metres	0.5
G.I. pipe	18mm (¾")	Metres	0.9
Tap, elbow, nipple and socket	18mm (¾")	Unit	1
G.I.wire	3mm	Kg	5
Chicken mesh	25mm, 0.9m	Metres	18
Mosquito mesh	Plastic	Metres	0.5
Coffee mesh	Galvanized 5mm	Metres	1
Labour			
	Skilled masons	Working days	1 × 5
	Labourers	Working days	1 × 5
Formwork			
Canvas reusable for 10 jars	1.2m wide sewn into a mould	Metres	15
Cost US$ 150	Ksh 9000 in Kenya (1998)	Labour and materials only	

Exchange rate US$ 1 = Ksh 60

WATER TANK BUILT OF CONCRETE *IN SITU* (FORMWORK)

Storage volume 5m³ (5000 litres)

Construction cost approx. US$300 = $60 per m³

Introduction

The success of this tank, several thousands of which have been built by unskilled people without external assistance in Kenya, can be put down to sheer simplicity: mixing and pouring concrete into a mould or formwork. People learn how to build the tank when they assist neighbours building *their* tank using formwork borrowed from the Diocese of Machakos.

Design of a 5m³ water tank built of concrete *in situ*

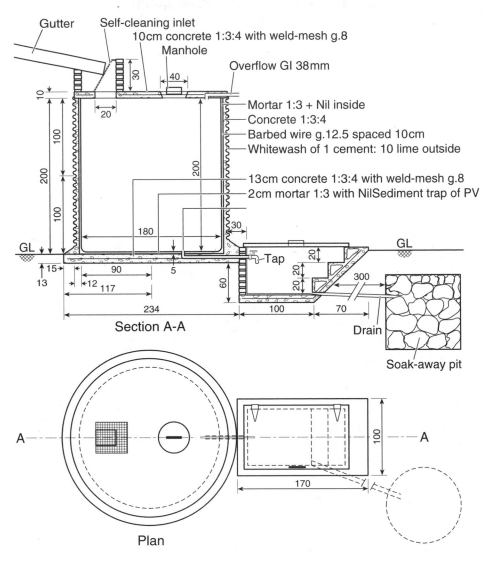

Gutter

Self-cleaning inlet
10cm concrete 1:3:4 with weld-mesh g.8
Manhole

Overflow GI 38mm

Mortar 1:3 + Nil inside
Concrete 1:3:4
Barbed wire g.12.5 spaced 10cm
Whitewash of 1 cement: 10 lime outside

13cm concrete 1:3:4 with weld-mesh g.8
2cm mortar 1:3 with NilSediment trap of PV

Tap

GL

GL

Section A-A

Drain

Soak-away pit

A — A

Plan

Dimensions are in cm

Design of formwork for a 5m³ water tank built of concrete *in situ*

The two circular sets of steel plates for the formwork can be made in two ways:

(a) Corrugated galvanized iron (GI) sheets used for roofing can be rolled into semi-circular shapes in a special machine used by workshops making cylindrical water tanks from GI corrugated-iron sheets

(b) Much cheaper formwork can be made from old oil-drums by an artisan skilled in metal works:

The tops and bottoms are cut out of four oil-drums and the seam of each drum cut open.

Two circles are drawn on the ground; one having a radius of 90cm for the inner form and the other circle having a radius of 100cm for the outer form.

The artisan beats two oil-drums to fit half of each circle. Then each set of oil-drums is bolted together to form a circle.

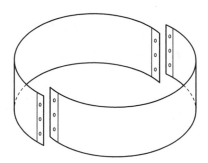

Outer form
radius 100cm
height 100cm

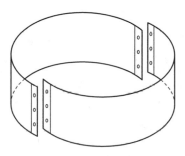

Inner form
radius 90cm
height 100cm

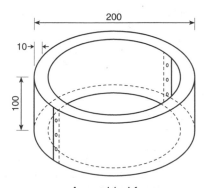

Assembled forms

Internal plaster & finish

273

Construction procedures for a 5m³ water tank built of concrete *in situ*

Excavation

A circle with a radius of 117cm is drawn on the ground, 90cm away from the wall of the building from which rainwater will pour in to the tank.

The excavation should be at least 15cm deep, and 250cm below the eave of the roof and until firm soil is reached. The floor of the excavation is then made level.

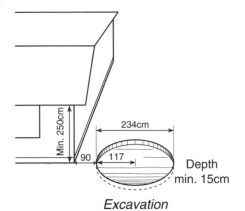

Excavation

Foundation

Two sheets of weld-mesh, tied with overlaps of 20cm, are cut into circles with a radius of 112cm, 5cm shorter than excavation.

A draw-off pipe is made of 90cm of 18mm GI pipe with an elbow and a nipple screwed on to the inner end, and a socket and a tap fixed to the outer end.

Now compact a 7cm layer of concrete 1:3:4 into the excavation. Place the circular sheet of weld-mesh on the concrete. Then place the draw-off pipe on the weld-mesh where the tap stand will be.

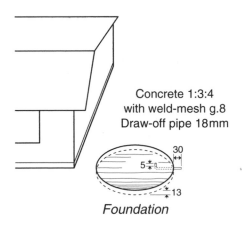

Concrete 1:3:4
with weld-mesh g.8
Draw-off pipe 18mm

Foundation

Compact a 6cm layer of concrete 1:3:4 on to it and level it off with a rough surface. Keep the foundation moist under cover while building the remaining part of the tank.

Mould in first position

Place the two circular moulds on the foundation, 10cm apart.

Fill concrete 1:3:4 into the mould while laying a spiral of barbed wire g.12.5 with a vertical spacing of 10cm in the concrete. Knock the mould to remove any air bubbles from the mould to get air out of the concrete.

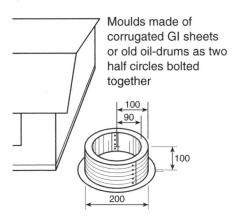

Moulds made of corrugated GI sheets or old oil-drums as two half circles bolted together

Mould in first position

Construction procedures for a 5m³ water tank built of concrete *in situ* (continued)

Mould in second position

Next day, remove the mould and place it on top of the concrete wall.

Now repeat the procedure of filling the mould with concrete and a spiral of barbed wire spaced 10cm.

Remove the mould. Plaster the interior of the tank with 2cm of mortar 1:3 and NIL (cement slurry) on the same day.

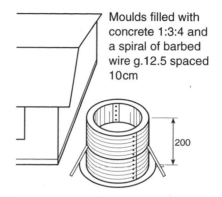

Moulds filled with concrete 1:3:4 and a spiral of barbed wire g.12.5 spaced 10cm

200

Mould in second position

Formwork for roof

Make a framework of timber (6" × 1") supported by props in the tank. The timber should be flush with the top of the tank wall.

Cut two sheets of weld-mesh into a circular sheet 5cm shorter than the outer edge of the tank wall.

Cut a hole for a plastic basin, to act as the mould for the manhole, in the weld-mesh, and place it on the formwork.

Place the overflow pipe under the weld-mesh vertically over the tap in the foundation.

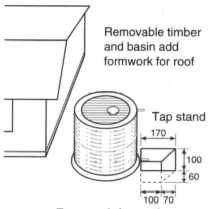

Removable timber and basin add formwork for roof

Tap stand

170

100

60

100 70

Formwork for roof

Roof and finish

Pour 10cm of concrete 1:3:4 into the basin and on to the formwork. Lift the weld-mesh into the middle of the concrete and smoothe it to finish.

Build the tap stand and gutter inlet while curing the tank.

After seven days remove the formwork and whitewash the external surfaces of the tank with 1 cement: 10 lime.

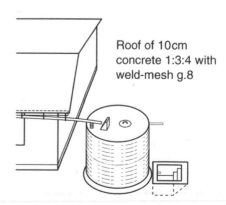

Roof of 10cm concrete 1:3:4 with weld-mesh g.8

Roof, gutter and tap stand

BILL OF QUANTITIES FOR A 5m³ WATER TANK
BUILT OF CONCRETE *IN SITU* (FORMWORK)

Item	Specification	Units	Quantity
Materials			
Cement	50kg	Bags	12
Lime	25kg	Bags	1
Sand	Coarse & clean	Tonnes	3
Crushed stones	10 to 20mm	Tonnes	3
Rubble stones	100 to 500mm	Tonnes	1
Bricks/blocks	Variable	Number	50
Water	200 litres	Oil-drums	8
Weld-mesh	2.4 × 1.2m g8	Sheets	4
Barbed wire	Gauge 12.5	Kg	20 (1 roll)
G.I. pipe	38mm (1½")	Metres	0.5
G.I. pipe	18mm (¾")	Unit	0.9
Tap, elbow, nipple and socket	18mm (¾")	Unit	1
PVC pipe	50m (2")	Metres	3
Mosquito mesh	Plastic	Metres	0.5
Coffee mesh	Galvanized	Metres	1
Lockable door	Steel	0.9 m × 1.5m	1
Labour			
	Skilled masons	Working days	1 × 8
	Labourers	Working days	2 × 8
Formwork			
Reusable for 20 tanks.			
2 circular metal forms	Radius: Inner 90cm Outer 100cm Height 100cm	Unit	1
2 circular	Radius:	Unit	1
Bolts for form	6 mm × 25 mm	Number	6
Timber and nails	6" × 1" timber	Metres	30
for roof	3" nails	Kg	5
Cost US$300	Ksh 18 000 in Kenya (1998)	Labour and materials only	

Exchange rate US$1 = Ksh 60

WATER TANK BUILT OF BRICKS OR BLOCKS

Storage volume 10m³ (10 000 litres).

Construction cost approx. US$500 = US$50 per m³

Introduction

This type of water tank can be built cheaply of locally available materials such as burnt bricks, compressed-soil blocks, quarry, concrete or rubble-stone blocks, the latter being rubble stones concreted into blocks.

The technique for building the tank is similar to that of building a circular house of mud bricks, a skill that most rural artisans can master.

Design of a 10m³ water tank built of bricks or blocks

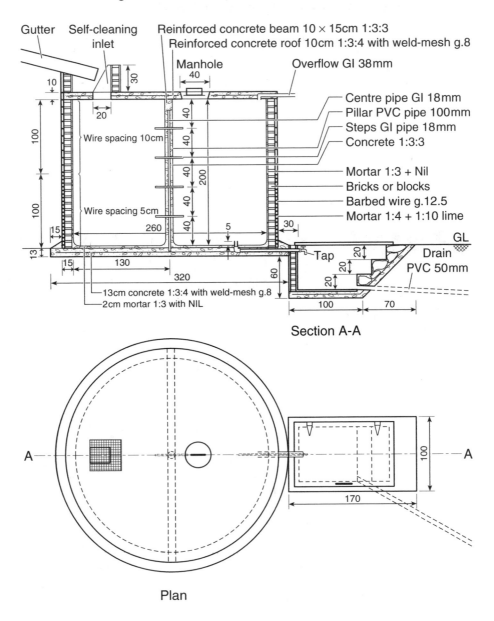

Section A-A

Plan

Dimensions are in cm

Design of formwork for a 10m³ water tank built of bricks or blocks

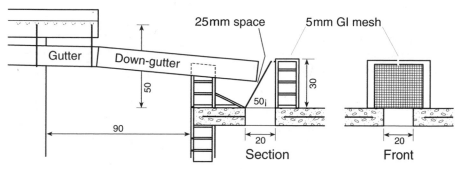

Gutter

Down-gutter

25mm space

5mm GI mesh

50

90

50ʲ

30

20

Section

20

Front

Down-gutter and self-cleaning inlet

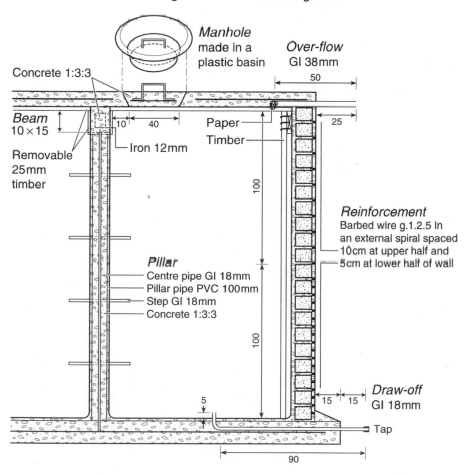

Manhole made in a plastic basin

Over-flow GI 38mm

50

Concrete 1:3:3

Beam 10 × 15

10   40

Paper

Timber

25

Removable 25mm timber

Iron 12mm

100

Reinforcement
Barbed wire g.1.2.5 In
an external spiral spaced
10cm at upper half and
5cm at lower half of wall

Pillar
Centre pipe GI 18mm
Pillar pipe PVC 100mm
Step GI 18mm
Concrete 1:3:3

100

5

Draw-off
GI 18mm

15   15

Tap

90

Dimensions are in cm

Construction procedures for a 10m³ water tank built of bricks or blocks

Excavation

The excavation has a radius of 160cm and is situated 90cm from the gable of a house. The centre of the tank should be equi distant to the two corners of the gable, shown as X on the sketch.

The foundation is dug to a depth of 15cm into firm soil and 250cm under the eave of the roof.

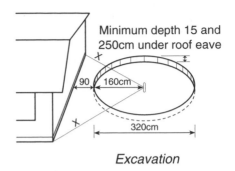

Minimum depth 15 and 250cm under roof eave

Excavation

Foundation, centre and draw-off pipes

Weld-mesh is cut with 20cm overlaps into a circular sheet with a radius of 315cm.

The draw-off pipe is made of a 90cm-long GI pipe of 18mm diameter. An elbow and nipple are fitted to one end and a socket with a tap is attached at the outer end.

The centre pipe is a 210cm-long GI pipe of 18mm diameter.

7cm of concrete 1:3:4 is laid in the excavation. The weld-mesh and draw-off pipe are placed on the concrete. The centre pipe is placed vertically on the weld-mesh, exactly at the centre.

Then 6cm of concrete 1:3:4 is compacted on to the weld-mesh and made level with a rough surface.

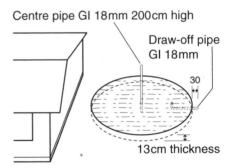

Centre pipe GI 18mm 200cm high

Draw-off pipe GI 18mm

13cm thickness

Foundation, centre pipe and draw-off pipe

Wall built of bricks and blocks

The centre pipe must be exactly vertical because a radius wire is tied to it to give the exact position of the outer corners of the brick or blocks in the circular wall of the tank.

To find the size of the vertical joints without cutting any brick, lay out a circle without mortar. Every vertical joint must overlay the middle of its underlying brick.

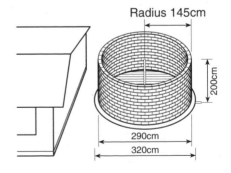

Radius 145cm

290cm

320cm

200cm

Wall built of bricks or blocks

280

Construction procedures for a 10m³ water tank built of bricks or blocks (continued)

Pillar, beam and reinforcement

When the wall is 200cm high, a 185cm-long PVC pipe of 100mm diameter is placed around the centre pipe to make a pillar. Steps of GI pipes 18mm in diameter are inserted into the PVC pipe by heating them over a fire. Then the PVC pipe is filled with concrete 1:3:3 and left to set.

Formwork for a concrete beam 10cm wide and 15cm high is made and placed on top of the pillar and against the wall of the tank, where a seat is cut at each end into the wall.

Barbed wire, g.12.5, is wrapped tightly around the tank and nailed in a spiral spaced 5cm at the lower half of the tank and 10cm at the upper half.

Plaster

The outside of the wall is plastered with 2cm of mortar 1:4.

The interior wall and floor are plastered with 2cm mortar of 1:3 and cement slurry (NIL) pressed into the moist mortar with a steel trowel for waterproofing.

Roof and tap stand

Four lengths of twisted 1/4" iron rods are laid in the formwork and the form filled with concrete 1:3:3.

Weld-mesh, g.8, is cut into a circular sheet 5cm shorter than the outer side of the tank wall and laid on the formwork.

A basin — formwork for the manhole and the draw-off pipe — is also placed on the formwork.

10cm of concrete 1:3:4 is placed on the formwork and the weld-mesh is lifted into the middle. Inlet holes are 20cm × 20cm.

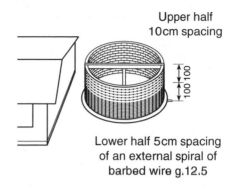

Upper half
10cm spacing

Lower half 5cm spacing
of an external spiral of
barbed wire g.12.5

Pillar, beam and reinforcement

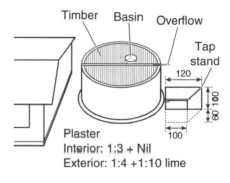

Timber   Basin   Overflow

Tap stand

120

100

Plaster
Interior: 1:3 + Nil
Exterior: 1:4 +1:10 lime

Plaster, formwork and roof

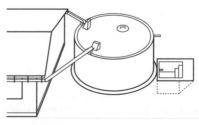

Roof, gutter and tap stand

281

BILL OF QUANTITIES FOR A 10m³ WATER TANK BUILT OF BURNT BRICKS, COMPRESSED SOIL BLOCKS, CONCRETE BLOCKS OR RUBBLE-STONE BLOCKS

Item	Specification	Units	Quantity
Materials			
Cement	50kg	Bags	21
Lime	25kg	Bags	4
Sand	Coarse & clean	Tonnes	4
Crushed stones	10 to 20mm	Tonnes	4
Stone blocks	100 to 500mm	Tonnes	1
Burnt bricks	10 × 12 × 20cm	Number	700
OR compressed soil blocks	12 × 14 × 29cm	Number	455
OR concrete and stone	14 × 20 × 40cm	Number	230
Water	200 litres	Oil-drums	10
Weld mesh	2.4 × 1.2m g8	Sheets	9
Barbed wire	Gauge 12.5	Kg	30
Twisted bar	Y 12	Metres	13
G.I. pipe	38mm (1½")	Metres	0.5
G.I. pipe	18mm (¾")	Metres	4
Tap, elbow, nipple and socket	18mm (¾")	Unit	1
PVC pipe	100mm (4")	Metres	2
PVC pipe	50mm	Metres	3
Coffee mesh	Galvanized	Metres	1
Mosquito mesh	Plastic	Metres	0.5
Lockable door	Steel	0.9 × 1.5m	1
Labour			
	Skilled masons	Working days	1 × 10
	Labourers	Working days	2 × 10
Formwork			
Reusable for 20 tanks			
Timber and nails for roof	6" × 1" timber	Metres	70
	3" nails	Kg	8
Cost US$500	Ksh 30 000 in Kenya (1998)	Labour and materials only	

Exchange rate US$1 = Ksh 60

WATER TANK BUILT OF FERROCEMENT

Storage volume 11m³ (11 000 litres).

Construction cost approx. US$550 = US$50 per m³

Introduction

Water tanks built of ferrocement are held in high esteem and are being promoted by development agencies and organizations. However, it is sometimes forgotten that the use of ferrocement requires special skills, equipment and materials that are not easy to obtain in remote regions.

The next three ferrocement water tanks presented in this manual are similar in design and construction procedures but vary in storage volume. Thousands of these tank designs have been made in a dozen countries over the last decade. This experience has resulted in the ferrocement tanks presented here.

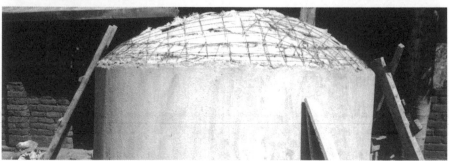

Design of an 11m³ water tank built of ferrocement

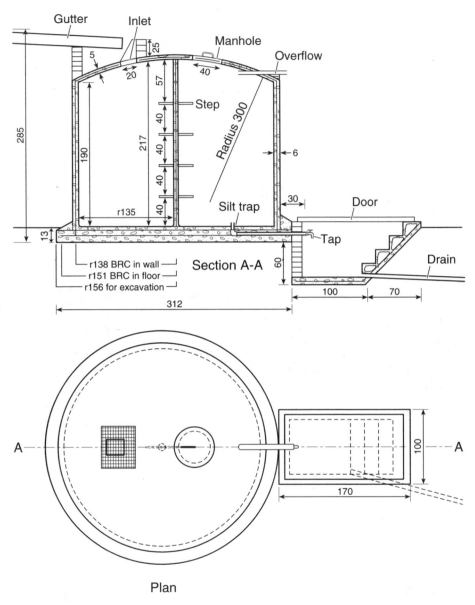

Section A-A

r138 BRC in wall
r151 BRC in floor
r156 for excavation

Plan

Dimensions are in cm

Design of dome for an 11m³ water tank built of ferrocement

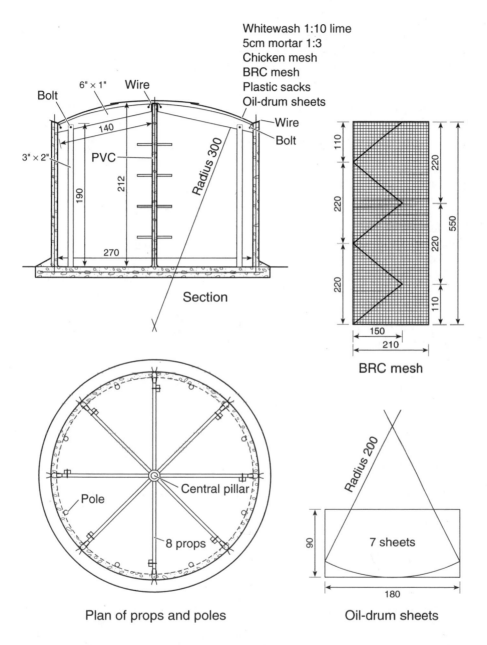

Whitewash 1:10 lime
5cm mortar 1:3
Chicken mesh
BRC mesh
Plastic sacks
Oil-drum sheets

Bolt
6" × 1" Wire
Wire
Bolt
140
3" × 2"
PVC
Radius 300
190
212
270

Section

110
220
220
220
220
550
110
150
210

BRC mesh

Pole
Central pillar
8 props

Plan of props and poles

Radius 200
90
7 sheets
180

Oil-drum sheets

Dimensions are in cm

285

Construction procedures for a 11m³ water tank built of ferrocement

Excavation

At the middle of the gable of the house, a circle is drawn 90cm from the wall, with a radius of 156cm.

The excavation should be at least 285cm below the eave of the roof and at least 15cm deep, or until firm soil is reached. The floor of the excavation must be made level.

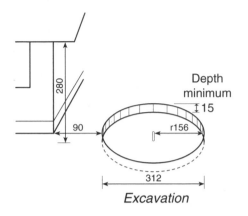

Depth minimum
15

r156

280

90

312

Excavation

BRC mesh for floor and wall

Two lengths of 302cm are cut from a roll of BRC mesh and tied together to form a square sheet of 302cm × 302cm. The sheet is then cut into a circle with a radius of 151cm.

A length of 907cm is cut from a roll of BRC mesh; the ends are tied to form a cylinder with a radius of 138cm.

The vertical wires at the bottom are bent to each side alternately.

The cylinder is then placed evenly on the circular sheet and tied to it with binding wire.

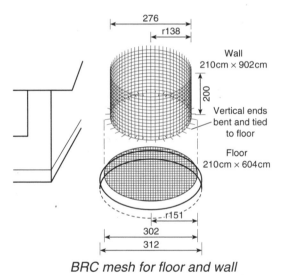

276

r138

Wall
210cm × 902cm

200

Vertical ends
bent and tied
to floor

Floor
210cm × 604cm

r151

302

312

BRC mesh for floor and wall

Foundation

Concrete 1:3:4 is mixed and placed in a 7cm-thick layer in the excavation without moistening the soil.

The BRC mesh and draw-off pipe are placed on the concrete.

A 6cm-thick layer of concrete 1:3:4 is compacted on to the first layer of concrete and left with a rough surface.

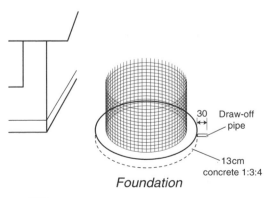

30   Draw-off
pipe

13cm
concrete 1:3:4

Foundation

286

Construction procedures for a 11m³ water tank built of ferrocement
(continued)

Wall

Chicken mesh is wrapped tightly around the BRC mesh and tied on to it by twisting the chicken mesh.

A 3mm GI wire is wrapped tightly four times around the chicken mesh at floor level from where it continues as a spiral to the top of the BRC mesh where it is wrapped around four times. The spacing of the spiral is 5cm at the lower half of the wall and 10cm at the upper half. Plastic sacks are hung against the outer side of the wall and kept tight with a spiral of sisal string starting from the top.

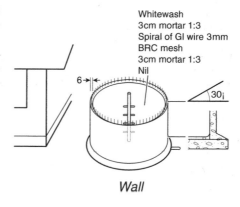

Whitewash
3cm mortar 1:3
Spiral of GI wire 3mm
BRC mesh
3cm mortar 1:3
Nil

Wall

Mortar 1:3 is smeared on to the inside of the tank against the plastic sacks. Next day, a 2.5cm layer of mortar is plastered on top of the first layer and floor and finished with Nil. Then the sacks are removed and the outer wall is plastered with 2.5cm of mortar 1:3.

Formwork for dome

Erect the formwork and oover its plastic sacks with BRC mesh, and bend the vertical BRC ends in the wall over the dome.

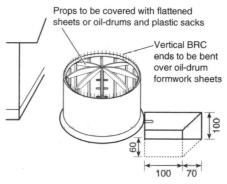

Props to be covered with flattened sheets or oil-drums and plastic sacks

Vertical BRC ends to be bent over oil-drum formwork sheets

Formwork for dome

Compact lightly a 5cm mortar 1:3 on to the dome while lifting the BRC mesh into the middle of the mortar. Use a plastic wash-basin as formwork for the manhole and make 20cm × 20cm inlet holes.

Cover the finished dome with plastic sacks weighed down by sand or soil. Do not walk on the dome for seven days, until the formwork can be removed.

Inlets, overflow and tap

Build the imlets and install the overflow pipe over the tap stand, which can be closed with a door. Seal the joint between dome and wall.

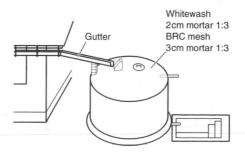

Whitewash
2cm mortar 1:3
BRC mesh
3cm mortar 1:3

Gutter

Dome, inlet, manhole and overflow

287

BILL OF QUANTITIES FOR A 11m³ WATER TANK BUILT OF FERROCEMENT

Item	Specification	Units	Quantity
Materials			
Cement	50kg	Bags	22
Lime	25kg	Bags	1
Sand	Coarse & clean	Tonnes	5
Crushed stones	10 to 20mm	Tonnes	2
Rubble stones	100 to 500mm	Tonnes	1
Bricks/blocks	Variable	Number	50
Water	200 litres	Oil-drums	15
BRC mesh	No. 65	Metres	24
Chicken mesh	25mm, 0.9m	Metres	38
Twisted iron	12mm (¹/₂")	Metres	3
G.I. wire	3mm	Kg	10
G.I. pipe	38mm (1¹/₂")	Metres	0.9
G.I. pipe	18mm (³/₄")	Metres	0.9
Tap, elbow, nipple and socket	18mm (³/₄")	Unit	1
PVC pipe	100mm (4")	Metres	2.2
PVC pipe	50mm (2")	Metres	3
Coffee mesh	Galvanized	Metres	1
Mosquito mesh	Plastic	Metres	0.5
Lockable door	Steel	0.9 × 1.5m	1
Labour			
	Skilled masons	Working days	1 × 10
	Labourers	Working days	2 × 10
Formwork			
Reusable for 30 tanks			
Timber, bolts, sheets, etc. for dome	6" × 1" timber	Metres	12
	2" × 3" timber	Metres	16
	Poles 2 metres	Number	8
	Plastic bags	Number	20
	Sisal twine	Kg	2
	Bolts 6 × 100 mm	Number	8
	Oil-drum sheets	Number	7
Manhole	Plastic basin	Number	1
Cost US$550	Ksh 33 000 in Kenya (1998)	Labour and materials only	

Exchange rate US$1 = Ksh 60

WATER TANK BUILT OF FERROCEMENT

Storage volume 23m³ (23 000 litres).

Construction cost approx. US$750 = $33 per m³

Introduction

This ferrocement tank is similar to the 11m³ model, but by doubling its capacity to store 23 000 litres, it becomes the ideal size for most households in climatic conditions of three to five months without any rainfall.

Design of a 23m³ water tank built of ferrocement

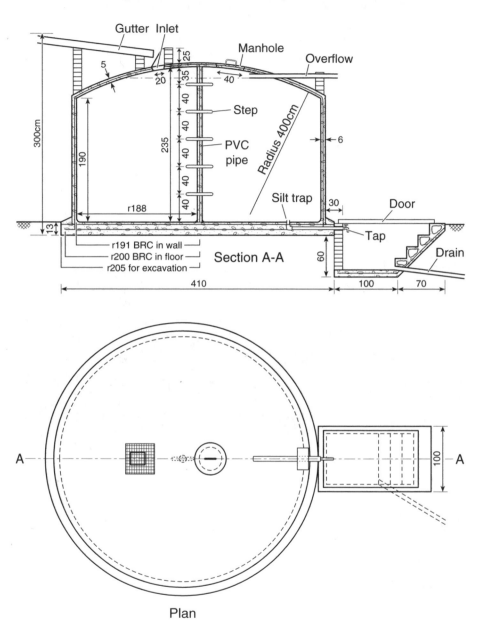

Gutter Inlet

Manhole

Overflow

5

25

35

20

40

300cm

235

190

40

40

Step

40

PVC
pipe

Radius 400cm

6

40

r188

40

Silt trap

30

Door

13

Tap

r191 BRC in wall
r200 BRC in floor
r205 for excavation

Section A-A

60

Drain

410

100

70

A

100

A

Plan

Dimensions are in cm

Design of a dome for a 23m³ water tank built of ferrocement

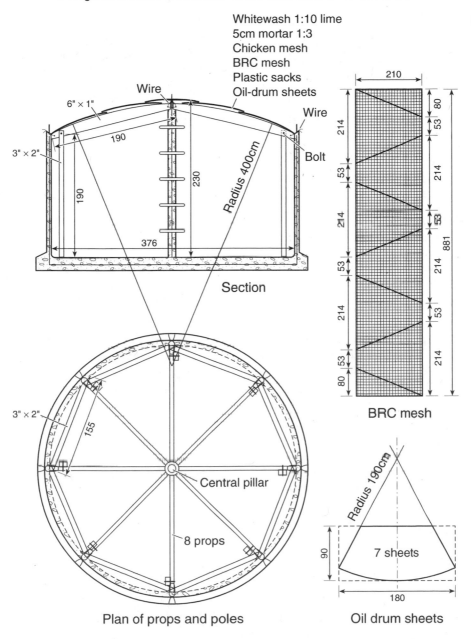

Whitewash 1:10 lime
5cm mortar 1:3
Chicken mesh
BRC mesh
Plastic sacks
Oil-drum sheets

Wire

Wire

6" × 1"

190

3" × 2"

190

230

Radius 400cm

Bolt

376

Section

210

80

53

214

214

53

53

214

881

53

214

53

214

53

214

80

BRC mesh

3" × 2"

155

Central pillar

8 props

Plan of props and poles

Radius 190cm

90

7 sheets

180

Oil drum sheets

Dimensions are in cm

Construction procedures for a 23m³ water tank built of ferrocement

Excavation

At the middle of the gable of the house, a circle is drawn 90cm from the wall, with a radius of 205cm.

The excavation should be at least 300cm below the eave of the roof and at least 15cm deep, or until firm soil is reached. The floor of the excavation must be made level.

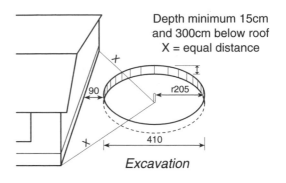

Depth minimum 15cm
and 300cm below roof
X = equal distance

90 r205

410

Excavation

BRC mesh for floor and wall

Two lengths of 400cm are cut from a roll of BRC mesh and tied together to form a square sheet of 400cm × 400cm. The sheet is then cut into a circle with a radius of 200cm.

A length of 1240cm is cut from a roll of BRC mesh; the ends are tied to form a cylinder with a radius of 191cm.

The vertical wires at the bottom are bent to each side alternately.

The cylinder is then placed evenly on the circular sheet and tied to it with binding wire.

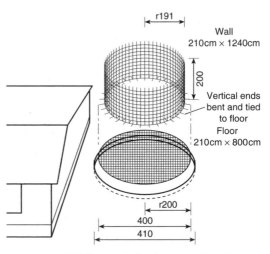

r191

Wall
210cm × 1240cm

200

Vertical ends
bent and tied
to floor
Floor
210cm × 800cm

r200

400

410

BRC mesh for floor and wall

Foundation

Concrete 1:3:4 is mixed and placed in a 7cm-thick layer in the excavation without moistening the soil.

The BRC mesh and draw-off pipe are placed on the concrete.

A 6cm-thick layer of concrete 1:3:4 is compacted on to the first layer of concrete and left with a rough surface.

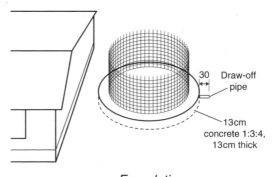

30   Draw-off
pipe

13cm
concrete 1:3:4,
13cm thick

Foundation

Construction procedures for a 23m³ water tank built of ferrocement
(continued)

Wall

Chicken mesh is wrapped tightly around the BRC mesh and tied on to it by twisting the chicken mesh.

A 3mm GI wire is wrapped tightly four times around the chicken mesh at floor level from where it continues as a spiral to the top of BRC mesh where it is wrapped around four times. The spacing of the spiral is 5cm at the lower half of the wall and 10cm at the top half.

Plastic sacks are hung against the outer side of the wall and kept tight with a spiral of sisal string starting from the top. Mortar 1:3 is smeared against the plastic sacks on their inner side. Next day, a 2.5cm layer of mortar Is plastered on top of the smear and floor and finished with Nil.

The sacks are removed and the outer wall is plastered with 2.5cm of mortar 1:3.

Formwork for dome

Erect the formwork and cover its plastic sacks with BRC mesh, and bend the vertical BRC ends in the wall over the dome. Compact lightly a 5cm mortar 1:3 on to the dome while lifting the BRC mesh into the middle of the mortar. Use a plastic wash-basin as formwork for the manhole and make 20cm × 20cm inlet holes.

Cover the finished dome with plastic sacks weighed down by sand or soil. Do not walk on the dome for seven days, until the formwork can be removed.

Inlets, overflow and tap

Build the inlets and install the overflow pipe over the tap-stand which can be closed with a door. Seal the joint between dome and wall.

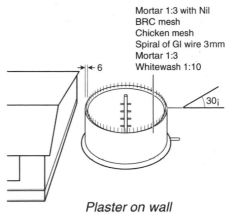

Mortar 1:3 with Nil
BRC mesh
Chicken mesh
Spiral of GI wire 3mm
Mortar 1:3
Whitewash 1:10

Plaster on wall

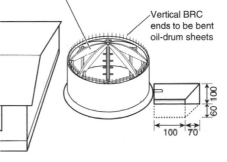

Props to be covered with oil-drum sheets and plastic sacks.

Vertical BRC ends to be bent
oil-drum sheets

Formwork for dome

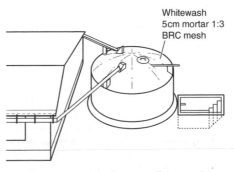

Whitewash
5cm mortar 1:3
BRC mesh

Dome, manhole, overflow and tap

293

BILL OF QUANTITIES FOR A 23m³ WATER TANK BUILT OF FERROCEMENT

Item	Specification	Units	Quantity
Materials			
Cement	50kg	Bags	30
Lime	25kg	Bags	1
Sand	Coarse & clean	Tonnes	7
Crushed stones	10 to 20mm	Tonnes	3
Rubble stones	100 to 500mm	Tonnes	1
Bricks/blocks	Variable	Number	50
Water	200 litres	Oil-drums	25
BRC mesh	No. 65	Metres	33
Chicken mesh	25mm, 0.9m	Metres	50
Twisted iron	12mm (½")	Metres	3
G.I. wire	3mm	Kg	20
G.I. pipe	38mm (1½")	Metres	1.3
G.I. pipe	18mm (¾")	Metres	0.9
Tap, elbow, nipple and socket	18mm (¾")	Unit	1
PVC pipe	100mm (4")	Metres	2.4
PVC pipe	50mm (2")	Metres	3
Coffee mesh	Galvanized	Metres	1
Mosquito mesh	Plastic	Metres	0.5
Lockable door	Steel	0.9 × 1.5m	1
Labour			
	Skilled masons	Working days	2 × 10
	Labourers	Working days	3 × 10
Formwork			
Reusable for 30 tanks			
Timber, bolts, sheets, etc. for dome	6" × 1" timber	Metres	16
	2" × 3" timber	Metres	30
	Plastic bags	Number	30
	Sisal twine	Kg	3
	Bolts 6 × 120mm	Number	8
	Oil-drum sheets	Number	10
Manhole	Plastic basin	Number	1
Cost US$550	Ksh 45 000 in Kenya (1998)	Labour and materials only	

Exchange rate US$1 = Ksh 60

Introduction

This 46m³ water tank is capable of storing sufficient water to meet household requirements for five to eight months without any rain.

Most of the approximately 4000 tanks which have been built in Kenya to date are situated at rural schools to provide clean drinking-water for the pupils.

Design of a 46m³ water tank built of ferrocement

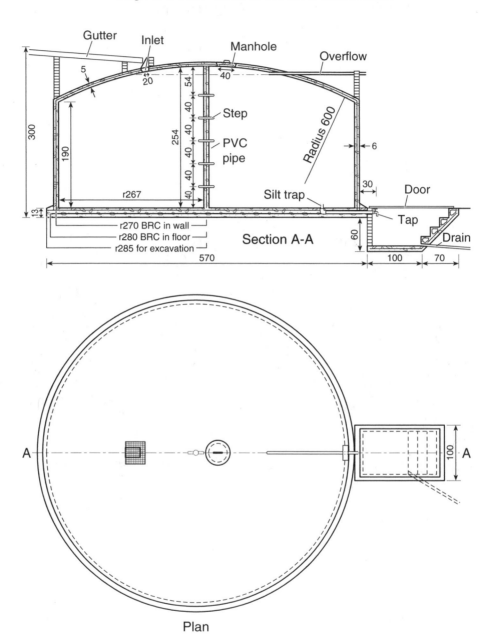

Section A-A

Plan

Dimensions are in cm

Design of a dome for a 46m³ water tank built of ferrocement

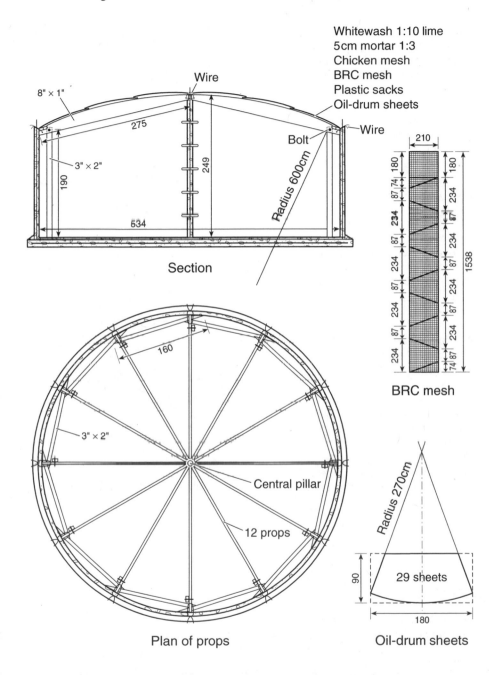

Whitewash 1:10 lime
5cm mortar 1:3
Chicken mesh
BRC mesh
Plastic sacks
Oil-drum sheets

Section

BRC mesh

Plan of props

Oil-drum sheets

Construction procedures for a 46m³ water tank built of ferrocement

Excavation

At the middle of the gable of the house, a circle is drawn 90cm from the wall, with a radius of 285cm.

The excavation should be at least 300cm below the eave of the roof and at least 15cm deep, or until firm soil is reached. The floor of the excavation made level.

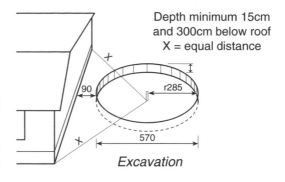

Depth minimum 15cm and 300cm below roof
X = equal distance

Excavation

BRC mesh for floor and wall

Two lengths of 560cm are cut from a roll of BRC mesh and tied together to form a square sheet of 560cm × 560cm. The sheet is then cut into a circle with a radius of 280cm.

A length of 1740cm is cut from a roll of BRC mesh and tied into a cylinder with a radius of 270cm.

The vertical wires at the bottom are bent to each side alternately.

The cylinder is then placed evenly on the circular sheet and tied to it with binding wire.

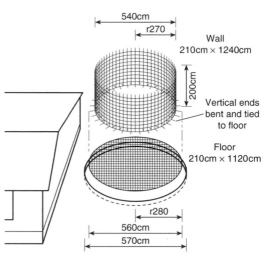

Wall
210cm × 1240cm

Vertical ends bent and tied to floor

Floor
210cm × 1120cm

BRC mesh for floor and wall

Foundation

Concrete 1:3:4 is mixed and placed in a 7cm-thick layer in the excavation without moistening the soil.

The BRC mesh and draw-off pipe are placed on the concrete.

A 6cm-thick layer of concrete 1:3:4 is compacted on to the first layer of concrete and left with a rough surface.

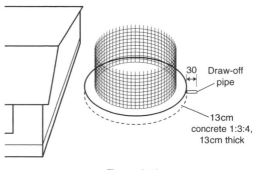

Draw-off pipe

13cm concrete 1:3:4, 13cm thick

Foundation

Construction procedures for a 46m³ water tank built of ferrocement (continued)

Wall

Chicken mesh is wrapped tightly around the BRC mesh, twisted and tied on.

A 3mm GI wire is wrapped tightly four times around the chicken mesh at floor level from where it continues as a spiral to the top of BRC mesh where it is again wrapped around 4 times. The spacing of the spiral is 5cm at the lower half of the wall and 10cm at the top half.

Plastic sacks are hung against the outer side of the wall and kept tight with a spiral of sisal string starting from the top. Mortar 1:3 is smeared against the plastic sacks on their inner side. Next day, a 2.5cm layer of mortar is plastered on to the smear and floor and finished with Nil.

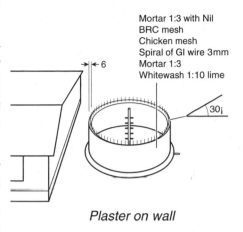

Mortar 1:3 with Nil
BRC mesh
Chicken mesh
Spiral of GI wire 3mm
Mortar 1:3
Whitewash 1:10 lime

Plaster on wall

The sacks are removed and the outer wall is plastered with 2.5cm of mortar 1:3.

Formwork for dome

Erect the formwork and cover the plastic sacks with BRC mesh. Bend the vertical BRC ends in the wall over the BRC mesh in the dome. Compact lightly a 5cm mortar 1:3 on to the dome while lifting the BRC mesh into the middle of the mortar. Use a plastic wash-basin as formwork for the manhole. Make 20cm × 20cm inlet holes.

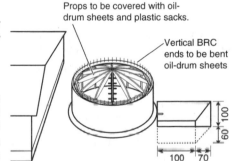

Props to be covered with oil-drum sheets and plastic sacks.

Vertical BRC ends to be bent oil-drum sheets

Formwork for dome

Cover the finished dome with plastic sacks weighed down by sand or soil. Do not walk on the dome for seven days, until the formwork can be removed.

Inlets, overflow and tap

Build the inlets and install the overflow pipe over the tap-stand which can be closed with a door. Seal the joint between dome and wall.

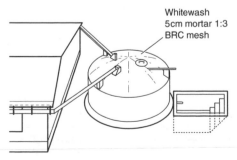

Whitewash
5cm mortar 1:3
BRC mesh

Dome, manhole, overflow and tap

BILL OF QUANTITIES FOR A 46m³ WATER TANK BUILT OF FERROCEMENT

Item	Specification	Units	Quantity
Materials			
Cement	50kg	Bags	50
Lime	25kg	Bags	2
Sand	Coarse & clean	Tonnes	10
Crushed stones	10 to 20mm	Tonnes	4
Rubble stones	100 to 500mm	Tonnes	1
Bricks/blocks	Variable	Number	50
Water	200 litres	Oil-drums	35
BRC mesh	No. 65	Metres	33
Chicken mesh	25mm, 0.9m	Metres	80
Twisted iron	12mm (¹/₂")	Metres	3
G.I. wire	3mm	Kg	25
G.I. pipe	37mm (1¹/₂")	Metres	1.8
G.I. pipe	18mm (³/₄")	Metres	3.4
Tap, elbow, nipple and socket	18mm (³/₄")	Unit	1
PVC pipe	100mm (4")	Metres	3
PVC pipe	50mm (2")	Metres	3
Coffee mesh	Galvanized	Metres	1
Mosquito mesh	Plastic	Metres	0.5
Lockable door	Steel	0.9 × 1.5m	1
Labour			
	Skilled masons	Working days	2 × 14
	Labourers	Working days	3 × 14
Formwork			
Reusable for 30 tanks			
Timber, bolts, sheets, etc. for dome	6" × 1" timber	Metres	36
	2" × 3" timber	Metres	46
	Plastic bags	Number	50
	Sisal twine	Kg	5
	Bolts 6 × 120mm	Number	12
	Oil-drum sheets	Number	29
Manhole	Plastic basin	Number	1
Cost US$1200	Ksh 72 000 in Kenya (1998)	Materials and labour only	

Exchange rate US$1 = Ksh 60

This large water tank requires a large roof catchment if it is to fill up with rainwater. The tank is, therefore, most commonly built at rural schools, with large roofs, in arid and semi-arid regions.

A word of warning: water tanks of this size can be built successfully only by well-trained artisans, and in stable soil conditions.

Design of a 90m³ water tank built of ferrocement

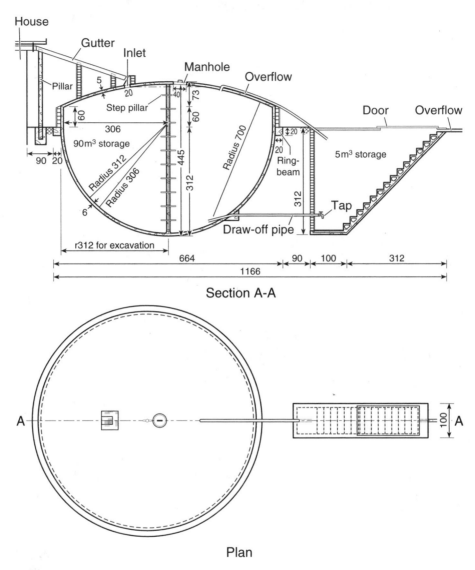

Section A-A

Plan

Dimensions are in cm

Design of a dome for a 90m³ water tank built of ferrocement

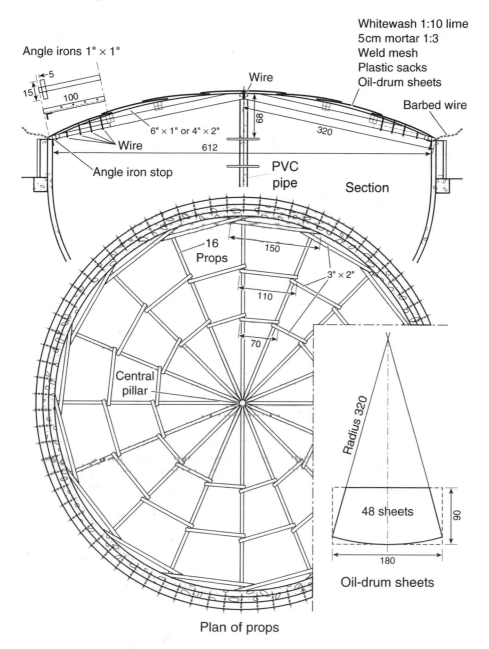

Angle irons 1" × 1"

5

15

100

Whitewash 1:10 lime
5cm mortar 1:3
Weld mesh
Plastic sacks
Oil-drum sheets

Wire

Barbed wire

68

320

6" × 1" or 4" × 2"

Wire

612

Angle iron stop

PVC
pipe

Section

16
Props

150

3" × 2"

110

70

Central
pillar

Radius 320

48 sheets

90

180

Oil-drum sheets

Plan of props

Dimensions are in cm

303

Construction procedures for a 90m³ water tank built of ferrocement

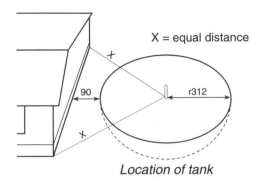

X = equal distance

Location of tank

Excavation

At the middle of the gable of the house, a circle with a radius of 312cm is drawn 90cm from the wall.

The excavation is made hemispherical using a radius wire of 312cm tied to the peg at one end, with the other end showing the side of the wall. The peg and its soil pillar are the last to be removed.

Circular wall

A 20cm × 20cm seat for a ring beam is excavated at the rim of the hemispherical excavation and filled with concrete 1:3:3 reinforced with a spiral of 8 rounds of barbed wire gauge 12.5.

A 60cm-high circular wall of bricks or blocks is built on to the ring beam.

Eight rounds of barbed wire are wrapped tightly around the wall and spaced 10cm apart. The wire is covered with 2cm of 1:4 mortar.

Hemispherical wall

A 3cm-thick coat of mortar 1:3 is thrown on to the excavation.

Chicken mesh is nailed on to both walls with minimum overlaps of 10cm. Barbed wire, g. 12.5, is nailed on to the chicken mesh in a spiral spaced 20cm.

Lines of barbed wire are nailed on to the walls 30cm apart and protruding 30cm from one side of the rim across the centre to the opposite side of the rim.

Ring beam of concrete 1:3:3
with 8 rounds of barbed wire

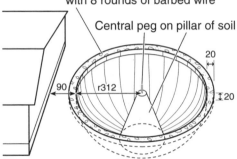

Central peg on pillar of soil

Excavation and ring beam

Internal reinforcement

Mesh of barbed wire g. 12.5, and chicken mesh nailed on to 3cm of mortar 1:3 and covered with 3cm of mortar 1:3 + Nil

External reinforcement

8 rounds of barbed wire g. 12.5

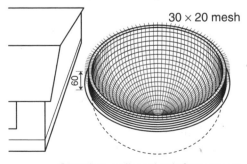

30 × 20 mesh

Circular wall and reinforcement

Construction procedures for a 90m³ water tank built of ferrocement
(continued)

A 3cm-thick layer of mortar 1:3 is plastered on to the reinforcement and covered with Nil.

Formwork for dome
Erect the formwork (see previous page) and cover the plastic sacks with weld mesh g.8 overlapping by a minimum of 20cm. Bend the protruding ends of barbed wire over the weld mesh.

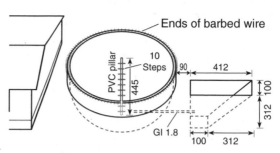

Central pillar and draw-off pipe

Compact lightly a 5cm mortar 1:3 on to the dome while lifting the weld mesh into the middle of the mortar.

Use a plastic wash-basin as formwork for the manhole. Make 20cm × 20cm inlet holes.

Cover the finished dome with plastic sacks weighed down by sand.

Do not walk on the dome for seven days, until the formwork is removed.

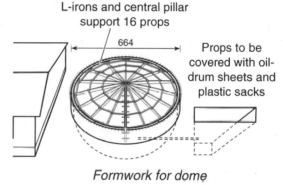

Formwork for dome

Inlets, overflow and tap
Build the inlets and install the overflow pipe over the tap stand, which can be closed with a door.

The tap stand is waterproof so that any overflow can be stored. A concrete roof and a lockable door are fixed over the tap stand.

Seal the interior joint between dome and wall.

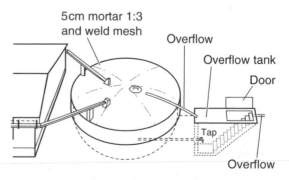

Dome, overflow, tap and gutter

BILL OF QUANTITIES FOR A 90m³ WATER TANK BUILT OF FERROCEMENT

Item	Specification	Units	Quantity
Materials			
Cement	50kg	Bags	73
Lime	25kg	Bags	2
Sand	Coarse & clean	Tonnes	17
Crushed stones	10 to 20mm	Tonnes	1
Bricks/blocks	Variable	Number	500
Water	200 litres	Oil-drums	45
Weld mesh	2.4 × 1.2m g8	Sheets	25
Chicken mesh	25mm, 0.9m	Metres	100
Twisted iron	12mm (½")	Metres	5
Barbed wire	Gauge 12.5	Kg	100
G.I. pipe	38mm (1½")	Metres	4
G.I. elbow	38mm (1½")	Number	1
G.I. pipe	18mm (¾")	Metres	9
Tap, elbow, nipple and socket	18mm (¾")	Unit	1
PVC pipe	100mm (4")	Metres	5
Coffee mesh	Galvanized	Metres	1
Mosquito mesh	Plastic	Metres	0.5
Lockable door	Steel	0.9 × 2.0m	1
Labour			
	Skilled masons	Working days	3 × 14
	Labourers	Working days	4 × 20
Formwork			
Reusable for 30 tanks			
Timber, bolts, sheets, L-iron for dome	6" × 1" timber	Metres	60
	2" × 3" timber	Metres	60
	Plastic bags	Number	50
	L-iron 25 × 25mm	Number	16
	Sisal twine	Kg	3
	Oil-drum sheets	Number	48
Manhole	Plastic basin	Number	1
Cost US$1900	Ksh 114 000 in Kenya (1998)	Materials and labour only	

Exchange rate US$1 = Ksh 60

Making and installing gutters with splash-guard

V-shaped gutters are made on the construction site by the builders. Galvanized-iron sheets, gauge 26 and 190 × 200cm are cut into strips 33.3cm wide.

A lip 1.6cm wide is bent along one side of a strip using two home-made mallets against the sharp edge of a U-iron 5cm × 10cm × 200cm long, on to which a 5cm-wide timber has been bolted.

The sheet is bent by hand along the edge of the timber while the lip is held tightly against the U-iron.

The sheet is now turned round so the hand-bend edge can be made tight against the U-iron using the mallets.

While in this position, the other lip is bent over the timber by hand. The sheet is then turned round again to make a sharp corner on the lip by using the mallets against the edge of the iron.

A strong gutter has now been made with its two sides being 15cm wide, each supported by a lip 1.6cm wide.

A splash-guard is made in a similar way, but requires only a slight bend along the middle.

Gutter hangers are made by bending 3mm GI wire around nails in the profile of the gutter.

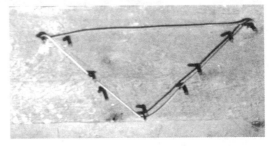

V-shaped gutters are installed by first nailing a line of splash-guard on to the eave of the roof. The splash-guard should protrude about 2cm over the eave to prevent dirt on the roof from blocking the splash-guard.

A transparent hosepipe is tied to each end of the splash-guard and filled with water until its level reaches the bottom of the splash-guard at the end opposite the tank.

The length of the roof is now measured in metres. The required gradient of 1cm per 1m sloping towards the tank is found by converting the length in metres to centimetres and measuring downward from the water level in the pipe near the tank.

If, for example, a roof is 20m long, then the drop is 20cm.

A gutter hanger is attached to each end of the splash-guard at the found gradient. A builder's line is drawn between the bottom of these two hangers.

Starting from the tank, gutters are laid in hangers suspended from the splash-guard by 1mm GI wires which are adjusted along the builder's line.

Upon reaching the far end of the gutter, its sides are bent over each other.

At the other end, the gutter is extended straight to the tank by supporting it with two timbers nailed in a V.

Tools and equipment for building water tanks

A builder and his assistant need the following tools for building a water tank. Should more than two builders be involved, or should more than a few tanks be built, the quantity is increased accordingly.

Item	Specifications	Quantity
Tape measure	15 to 30m	1
Tape measures	2 to 3m	2
Mason hammer	Any handy size	1
Mason trowels	Medium size	2
Mason chisel	Any handy size	1
Square steel trowel	Any handy size	1
Pliers	Medium size	2
Hacksaw with blades	Medium size	1
Carpenter's saw	Medium size	1
Carpenter's hammer	Steel handle	1
Crowbar	Approx. 60cm long	1
Wooden float	Approx. 10cm × 50cm	2
Straight edge	200cm long	1
Spirit level	Approx. 100cm long	1
Builder's line	Thin nylon, 50m	1
Sisal twine	2kg roll	1
Sisal brush	Preferably flat 10cm	1
Shovels	Medium size	2
Mattock/pick-axe	Medium size	1
Karias/metal basins	Medium size	5
Buckets for water	Heavy plastic	2
Oil-drums for water	Or any large container	2
Wheelbarrow	Medium size	1
Sieve for sand	90cm × 180cm with GI mesh	1
Double collapsible ladder	Approx. 240cm long	1
Plastic sacks	Larger sizes for curing	50
Gauge box	For mortar & concrete	1
Formwork for dome or roof	Depends on type and size	1

Tools and equipment for gutters and splash-guards

Tin snips	Handy size	2
Mallets	2 × 10 × 30cm timber	2
Pliers	Handy size	2
Carpenter's hammer	Steel handle	1
Carpenter's chisel	Handy size	1
Carpenter's saw	Handy size	1
Crowbar	90cm long	1
Builder's line	Thin nylon, 50m long	1
Transparent hosepipe	Any size but 15m long	1
Double collapsible ladder	Approx. 300cm long	2
Gutter bender bench	5 × 10cm U-iron 200cm long	1

Tank repair

FOR A DETAILED, illustrated account of how to repair a variety of water tanks, interested readers may also wish to consult the manual *How to Repair Various Types of Water Tank* by Nissen-Petersen (1992d), updated in 1998 and available from ASAL Consultants (see Appendix 4 for details). The manual describes how to carry out major repairs on different types of tank with volumes ranging from 2m³ to 80m³. The tank repair methods discussed include the relining of unreinforced-cement jars, and surface tanks made of corrugated iron, ferrocement and concrete blocks. Repairs of hemispherical sub-surface ferrocement tanks are also described.

Repair of ferrocement tanks

The repair of small leaks in ferrocement and certain other tanks using rapid-setting cement or sodium silicate was described in Chapter 5, as were some techniques for dealing with leaks in plastic and metal tanks, which can be hard to repair. The technique of applying different sealants, bonding agents and waterproof coatings has also been described by Enyatseng (1998), and various products are available on the market. The following description is for a method outlined by Hasse (1989, p66–69) for the repair of ferrocement water tanks.

The repair of ferrocement tanks is reasonably straightforward provided some basic rules are followed. Key among these is that the quality and mixture of the materials used should be the same as that used for the initial construction work. Both the cement:sand ratio and the sand used should ideally have the same properties as that originally used. If a different mixture or sand type is used, differential expansion stresses may result in a new leak developing. This can also occur if more water is used than in the original construction, due to shrinkage on drying, so care should be taken to ensure the mortar is not too wet.

If the reinforcement has not been damaged, relatively small leaks can be repaired by chipping away the mortar around the leak from the inside of the tank, using a hammer and chisel, until the chicken wire is just exposed. This should be done carefully to make sure that no cracks are caused on the external wall. An area with a diameter of 15cm should be chipped away. If the leak is not visible from the inside of the tank, a long thin nail can be hammered through from the outside to reveal the location of the area needing repair. If the area requiring patching is dry, it is necessary to wet it both on the inside and outside of the tank several times until an area of at least 0.5m² is really moist. New mortar can then be applied from the inside and the surface smoothed using a trowel. If a nail was used to locate the leak from the outside, this must be removed and any small hole also filled from the outside. The repaired area must be protected from the sun by being covered with plastic and kept moist. A layer of nil should be applied to the area. If the tank cannot be filled, the new mortar must be regularly splashed with water twice a day for a few weeks to ensure it is properly cured.

Larger repairs involve a similar approach but these are rarely required unless a tank has been damaged by a vehicle or fails when first filled, due to poor workmanship. If the reinforcement has been damaged, all the mortar should be chipped away and any damaged chicken wire removed. Any fencing wire or chicken mesh can be rebent into position. Welded reinforcement mesh should not be rebent as this may cause further damage. If it is first cut, it can be rebent into position and tied tightly using binding wire. If chicken wire has to be replaced, a patch consisting of a double layer should be tied to the reinforcement mesh using binding wire. Again, the area should be thoroughly moistened with water before any new mortar is applied, as described above. A coat of nil can then be applied and thorough curing of the repaired area undertaken.

References

ABS 1994, *Environmental Issues, People's Views and Practices*, Australian Bureau of Statistics, Canberra.

ADB 1993, 'Appendix D: Health Aspects of Water Supply', Asian Development Bank, 'Thailand Small Towns Water Supply Project – Feasibility Study TA No. 1685-THA', Team/Gibb/Adescon/Coffey, Bangkok & Manila.

Agarwal A. and Narain S. 1997, *Dying Wisdom: The Rise, Fall and Potential of India's Traditional Water Harvesting Systems*. State of India's Environment 4, A Citizen's Report, CSE, New Delhi, 404p.

Agnew C. and Anderson E. 1992. *Water Resources in the Arid Realm*, Routledge. 329p.

Ahmed S. and Fok Y. 1982, Stochastic Dynamic Models for Rainfall Processes, *Proceedings of the International Conference on Rain Water Cistern Systems*, Honolulu, p46–53.

Alaerts G., Hartvelt F. and Warner J. 1997, Capacity Building – Beyond the 'Project' Approach, *Waterlines*, Vol. 15, No. 4, pp2–5.

Aminipouri B. and Ghoddousi J. (Editors) 1997, *Proceedings of the 8th International Rainwater Catchment Systems Conference*, Ministry of Jihad, Tehran, Iran, 1579p.

Andersson, I. 1989, Rural Water Supply Development in the Context of Structural Adjustment (part 1) *Waterlines*, Vol.8, No.2, pp28–30

Andersson I. 1990, Rural Water Supply Development in the Context of Structural Adjustment (part 2) *Waterlines*, Vol. 8 No. 3, pp 20–23.

Appan A., Villareal, C. and Wing, L. 1989, The Planning, Development, Implementation of a Typical RWCS: A case study from Capiz. *Proceedings of the 4th International Rainwater Cistern Systems Conference*, Manila, Philippines, pp1–12.

Aristanti C. 1986, Dian Desa's Rainwater Catchment Programme, *Proceedings of Regional Seminar and Workshop on Rainwater Catchment*, Khon Kaen, Thailand, pp132–4.

Ariyabandu R. 1991, Rainwater Cisterns – A New Approach to Supplement Rural Water Supply Systems in Sri Lanka, *Proceedings of the 5th International Rainwater Cistern Systems Conference*, Keelung, Taiwan, pp607–19.

Austin J., Otterstetter H. and Rosensweig F. 1987, Institutional and Human Resource Development, *Waterlines*, Vol. 5, No. 4, pp2–5.

Bailey N. 1959, *Cisterns for Rural Water Supply in Ohio*, Dept. of Natural Resources, Columbus, 21p.

Bambrah G., Otino F. and Thomas D. (Editors) 1993, Participation in Rainwater Collection for Low Income Communities and Sustainable Development, *Proceedings of the 6th International Rainwater Catchment Systems Conference*, Nairobi, Kenya, 502p.

Bang Y., Bown D. and Onwubiko A. 1981, Prevalence of larvae of potential yellow fever in domestic water containers in south-east Nigeria, *Bulletin of the World Health Organization*, Vol. 59, No. 1, pp107–14.

Barlow R., Crick F., Fraenkel P., Derrick A. and Bokalders V. 1993, *Windpumps: A Guide for Development Workers*, IT Publications, London, 144p.

Bastermeyer T. and Lee M. 1992, Drinking-Water Source Deterioration: An Urgent Problem, *Waterlines*, Vol. 11, No. 1, pp9–12.

Biamah E., Choge J. and Cherogony R. 1993, Djabia Rainwater Harvesting Systems for Domestic Water Supply in Lamu, Kenya, *Proceedings of the 6th International Rainwater Catchment Systems Conference*, Nairobi, Kenya, pp281–93.

Bo L. 1993, Rainwater for Domestic Use in China, *Proceedings of the 6th International Rainwater Catchment Systems Conference*, Nairobi, Kenya, pp71–6.

Body P. 1986, *The Contamination of Rainwater Tanks in Port Pirie*, Report No. 8, Dept of Environment and Planning, South Australia, Adelaide, 29p.

Brand A. and Bradford B. 1991, *Rainwater Harvesting and Water Use in the Barrios of Tegucigalpa*, Agua para el Pueblo/UNICEF, Honduras, 52p.

Burgess S. 1996, Rainwater Catchment Systems – Roof Tank Sizing, *Raindrop*, Series 2, Vol. 5, pp4(i-iv).

Calvert K. and Binning R. 1977, Low-Cost Water Tanks on Pacific Islands, *Appropriate Technology*, Vol. 4, No. 3, pp21–23.

Campbell D. 1993, Practical Weapons in the War Against Malaria and Dengue Fever, *Raindrop*, Vol. 8, pp3–8.

Chareonsook O. et al. 1985, Prevalence of Aedes Mosquito in Big Cement Jars and Rainwater Tanks, *Communicable Disease Journal*, Thailand (Written in Thai with English Summary), Vol. 11, No.3, pp247–63.

Chareonsook O. et al. 1986, The Entero-pathogenic Bacteria and PH of Rainwater from Three Types of Container, *Communicable Disease Journal*, Thailand (Written in Thai with English Summary), Vol.12, No.1, pp50–8.

Chindaprasirt P. 1995, Self-help training Program for Small Water Resources Development in Rural Areas, *Experiences in the Development of Small-scale Water Resources in Rural Areas*, (Edited by Tharun G. et al. 1995), CDG, SEAPO, Thailand, pp145–52.

Churchill A. et al. 1987, *Rural Water Supply and Sanitation*, World Bank Discussion Paper, World Bank, Washington, 113p.

Corbet P. 1986, Using Dragonflies to Suppress Mosquitoes in Domestic Water-Storage Containers, *Waterlines*, Vol. 4, No. 3, pp10–11.

Crabtree, K., Ruskin R., Shaw S. and Rose J. 1996, The Detection of Cryptosporidium Oocysts and Giardia Cysts in Cistern Water in the U.S. Virgin Islands, *Water Research*, Vol. 30, No. 1, pp208–16.

Crasta F., Fasso C., Patta F., Putzu G. 1982, Carthaginian – Roman Cisterns in Sardinia. *Proceedings of the International Conference on Rain Water Cistern Systems*, University of Hawaii, Honolulu, pp37–45.

Critchley W. and Siegert K. 1991, *Water Harvesting, A Manual for the Design and Construction of Water Harvesting Schemes for Plant Production*, FAO, Rome, 133p.

Cullis A. and Pacey A. 1991, *A Development Dialogue – Rainwater Harvesting in Turkana*, IT Publications, London, p191.

Cumberlege O. 1993, Making Every Drop Count, *Waterlines*, Vol. 11. No. 3, pp23–26.

Cunliffe D. 1998, *Guidance on the Use of Rainwater Tanks*, National Environmental Health Forum Monographs, Water Series 3, Public and Environmental Health Service, Dept. of Human Services, P.O. Box 6, Rundle Mall SA 5000, Australia, 28p.

de Vrees L. 1987, *Machakos Diocese: Rainwater Tank Programme*, Development Office, Catholic Diocese of Machakos, P.O. Box 640, Machakos, Kenya, 17p.

Dixit A. and Upadyaya S. 1991, Rainwater Cistern Use in Nepal: Problems, Prospects and Promotion, *Proceedings of the 5th International Rainwater Cistern Systems Conference*, Keelung, Taiwan, pp639–50.

Dodge C. and Zelenika M. 1987, Rehabilitation of Hafirs in Sudan, *Waterlines*, Vol.6 No.1, pp24–7.

Doody M. 1980, Gibraltar's Water Supply. *Inst. Water Engineers – Transactions*, pp151–4.

Dorfman J. and Valentijn J. 1993, *The Use of Natural Fibres, Water Soluble Resin and Inflatable Moulds*, Unpub. Report, Life Source International Ltd, Newport, USA, 5p.

Dugan G., Tomomitsu M. and Lau L. 1984, Chemical Constituents of Rainfall in Hawaii, Effect of Ocean Influence and Volcanic Eruptions, *Proceedings of the 2nd International Conference on Rain Water Cistern Systems*, U.S. Virgin Islands, E2, pp1–13.

Enyatseng G. 1988, *The Evaluation of Ferrocement Water Tank Repair Methods*, Ind. Report No. 11, Botswana Technology Centre, P/Bag 0082, Gaborone, Botswana, 28p.

Erskine J. 1995, The Role of Women in Water and Sanitation Development, Nakuru, Kenya, *Proceedings of the 7th International Conference on Rain Water Cistern Systems*, Beijing, China, Vol.2 Part 8, pp11–20.

Eslam Z. and Nejad Z. 1997, The Value of Rainwater and Importance and Storage in Iran, *Proceedings of the 8th International Rainwater Catchment Systems Conference*, Ministry of Jihad-E-Sazandegi, Tehran, Iran, Vol. 1, pp400–3.

Esrey S., Potash J., Roberts L. and Shiff C. 1990, *Health Benefits from Improvements in Water Supply and Sanitation: Surveys and Analysis of the Literature on Selected Diseases*. W.A.S.H. Technical Report No. 66, USAID, Washington, D.C.

Evenari M., Shanan L. and Tadmor 1971, *The Negev: The Challenge of the Desert*, Harvard University Press, Cambridge, USA.

Evenari M. et al. 1961, Ancient Agriculture in the Negev., *Science* Vol.133, pp976–86.

Falciai M. and Bresci E. 1997, Fog Capture and Utilization in the Coastal Peruvian Desert. *Proceedings of the 8th International Conference on Rain Water Catchment Systems*, Tehran, Iran, Vol. 2, pp801–8.

Falkenmark M. (ed.) 1982, *Rural Water Supply and Health*, Scandinavian Institute of African Studies, Uppsala, Sweden, 118p.

Falkenmark M. 1989, The Massive Water Scarcity Now Threatening Africa – Why Isn't it being Addressed?, *Ambio*, Vol. 18, No. 2, pp112–118.

Feachem R. and Cairncross A. 1978, *Small Water Supplies*, London School of Hygiene, London, 78p.

Feachem R. 1988, Interventions for Diarrhoea Control: Effectiveness and Costs, Background paper No. 1, *Community Epidemiology/Health Management Network Meeting Report*, Khon Kaen, Thailand.

Fewkes A. and Frampton D. 1993, Optimizing the Capacity of Rainwater Storage Cisterns, *Proceedings of the 6th International Conference on Rain Water Catchment Systems*, Nairobi, Kenya, pp225–36.

Fewkes A. 1995, Field Testing of a Rainwater Collector, *Proceedings of the 7th International Conference on Rain Water Catchment Systems*, Beijing, China, Section 10, pp1–10.

Finch, H. 1994, Development of the Guttersnipe, *Proceedings of the Tokyo International Rainwater Utilization Conference*, Sumida City, Tokyo, Japan, pp360–6.

Fok Y. 1982, Integrating Rain Water Cisterns with Public Water Supply Systems, *Proceedings of the Rainwater Cistern Systems Conference*, Honolulu, Hawaii, pp317–22.

Fok, Y. 1992, Rooftops: The Under-utilized Resource, *Proceedings of the Regional Conference of the International Rainwater Catchment Systems Association*, Kyoto, Japan, Vol. 1, pp164–74.

Fok Y. 1994, Can Rainwater Utilization Save Cities?, *Proceedings of the Tokyo International Rainwater Utilization Conference*, Sumida City, Tokyo, Japan, pp3–13.

Fok Y. 1997, Rainwater Catchment Systems: Development of Guidelines, *Proceedings of the 8th International Rainwater Catchment Systems Conference*, Tehran, Iran, pp260–267.

Fok, Y., Fong R., Murabayashi E., Lo A. 1982, Deterministic and Probabilistic Processes of Weekly Rainfall, *Proceedings of the International Conference on Rain Water Cistern Systems*, Hawaii, Honolulu, pp83–91.

Freeman H. et al. 1979, *Evaluating Social Projects in Developing Countries*, Development Centre, OECD, Paris, 247p.

Fujioka R. 1993, Guidelines and Microbial Standards for Cistern Waters, *Proceedings of the 6th International Conference on Rain Water Cistern Systems*, Nairobi, Kenya, pp393–8.

Fujioka R. and Chinn 1987, The Microbiological Quality of Cistern Waters in the Tantalus Area of Honolulu, Hawaii, *Proceedings of the 3rd International Conference on Rain Water Cistern Systems*, Khon Kaen Univ., Thailand, F3, pp1–13.

Fujioka R. Inserra S. and Chinn R. 1991, The Bacterial Content of Cistern Waters in Hawaii, *Proceedings of the 5th International Conference on Rain Water Cistern Systems*, Keelung, Taiwan pp33–45.

Fujioka R., Rijal G. and Ling B. 1995, A Solar Powered UV System to Disinfect Cistern Waters, *Proceedings of the 7th International Conference on Rain Water Cistern Systems*, Beijing, China, Section 9, pp48–57.

Gaddal A. 1991, Hafirs in Sudan, *Proceedings of the 5th International Conference on Rain Water Cistern Systems*, Keelung, Taiwan, pp651–60.

Geiger W. and Dreiseitl H. 1995, *Neue Wege Für Regenwasser*, Oldenbourg, Munich, Germany, 293p.

Ghoddousi J. 1995, An Outlook to the Development and Use of Rainwater Harvesting in Iran, *Proceedings of the 7th International Rainwater Catchment Systems Conference*, Beijing, China, Vol 1. (4), pp26–36.

Gieske, A., Gould J.E. and Sefe F. 1995, Performance of an Instrumented Roof Catchment System in Botswana, *Proceeding of 7th International Rainwater Catchment Systems Conference*, Beijing, China, Vol. 2, Section 10, pp60–9.

Gnadlinger J. 1993, Rainwater Cisterns for Rural Communities in the Brazilian Semi-Arid Tropics, *Proceedings of the 6th International Conference on Rain Water Cistern Systems*, Nairobi, Kenya, pp295–304.

Gnadlinger J. 1995a, Cisterns for Rural Low-Income Communities in N.E. Brazil, *Proceedings of 7th International Rainwater Cistern Systems Conference*, Beijing, China, Vol.2, (Section 6) pp1–10.

Gnadlinger J. 1995b, Lime – the Great Sealer: Constructing Low-cost, Subsurface rainwater Tanks in Brazil, *Waterlines*, Vol.14, No.2, pp11–14.

Gonzalez, F. 1972, *The Water Supply in Gibraltar*, Unpublished paper presented at Barcelona Water Conference, Gibraltar Public Works Department, ITDG, Rugby, UK.

Gordillo T., Gonzalez E. and Gaona S. 1982, History of Yucatan Cisterns, *Proceedings of the International Rainwater Cistern Systems Conference*, Honolulu, Hawaii, pp16–22.

Gould J. 1985, *An Assessment of Rainwater Catchment Systems in Botswana*, Unpublished MSc Thesis, University of Alberta, Edmonton, Canada, p222.

Gould J. 1987, An Assessment of Roof and Ground Catchment Systems in Botswana, *Proceedings of the 3rd International Conference on Rain Water Cistern Systems*, Khon Kaen University, Thailand, C2 pp1–17.

Gould J. 1989, Strategies for Overcoming the Obstacles Associated with 'Software' Aspects of Rainwater Catchment System Implementation, *Proceedings of the 4th International Rainwater Cistern Systems Conference*, Manila, Philippines, pp1–16.

Gould J. 1991, *Rainwater Catchment Systems For Household Water Supply*. ENSIC Review No.31, P.O. Box 2754, A.I.T., Bangkok, Thailand, 57p.

Gould J. 1992, Developments of Roof Catchment Systems in Rural S.E. Asia, *Proceedings of the International Rainwater Catchment Systems Association Regional Conference*, Kyoto, Vol.1, pp275–86.

Gould J. 1995a, Developments in Rainwater Catchment Systems Technology and Implementation Strategies in the 1980s and Lessons for the 1990s. *Experiences in the Development of Small-scale Water Resources in Rural Areas* (edited by Tharun et al. 1995), CDG, SEAPO, Thailand, pp95–106.

Gould J. 1995b, *An investigation of the potential role for rainwater catchment systems in rural water supply in Botswana*, Research Report, Dept. of Environmental Science, University of Botswana, 62p.

Gould J. 1995c, Developments in Rainwater Catchment Systems in Eastern and Southern Africa, *Proceedings of 7th International Rainwater Cistern Systems Conference*, Beijing, China, Vol 1. (4) pp44–55.

Gould J. 1996, Rainwater Utilization in Botswana: Problems and Possibilities, *Science, Technology and Development*, Vol.14, No.3, pp72–87.

Gould J. 1997, Problems and Possibilities Relating to Rainwater Utilization in Botswana, *Proceedings of the 8th International Conference on Rain Water Catchment Systems*, Tehran, Iran, Vol. 2, pp696–706.

Gould J. 1998, Review of Recent Developments in Rainwater Catchment Systems Technology in Eastern and Southern Africa, *Science, Technology and Development*, Vol. 16, No. 1, pp247–256.

317

Gould, J. and McPherson, H. 1987, Bacteriological Quality of Rainwater in Roof and Ground Catchment Systems in Botswana, *Water International*, Vol. 12, No. 3. pp135–8.

Grove S. 1993, Rainwater Harvesting in the United States – Learning Lessons the World Can Use, *Raindrop*, Vol. 8, pp1–10.

Guangen H. and Jianming Z. 1997, A Study of Roof Rainwater Catchment Project Application and Dissemination, *Proceedings of the 8th International Rainwater Catchment Systems Conference*, Tehran, Iran, Vol. 1, pp1198–9.

Haebler R. and Waller D. 1987, Water of Rainwater Collection Systems in the Eastern Caribbean, *Proceedings of the 3rd International Conference on Rain Water Cistern Systems*, Khon Kaen University, Thailand, pp1–16.

Hare A. 1900, *Venice* (5th Edition), G. Allen, London.

Hassanizadeh S. 1984, Rain Water Cisterns in Iran, *Proceedings of the 2nd International Conference on Rain Water Cistern Systems*, U.S. Virgin Islands, B2, pp1–20.

Hasse R. 1989, *Rainwater Reservoirs above Ground Structures for Roof Catchment*, Gate, Vieweg, Braunschweig/Wiesbaden, Germany, 102p.

Hayama S. 1994, Sofia University, Yotsuya Campus: Solar System and Rainwater Utilization, *Proceedings of the Tokyo International Rainwater Utilization Conference*, Sumida City, Tokyo, Japan (English and Japanese), pp159–60.

Health Department of Western Australia. 1996, *Is the Water in your Rainwater Tank Safe to Drink?*, Environmental Health Service, P.O. Box 8172, Stirling St., Perth WA 6849, Australia.

Heggen R. 1982, Optimal Catchment Design by Marginal Analysis, *Proceedings of the International Conference on Rain Water Cistern Systems*, Hawaii, Honolulu, pp135–43.

Heggen R. 1989, Hydraulics of Rainwater Catchment Gutters, *Proceedings of the 4th International Conference on Rain Water Cistern Systems*, Manila, pp1–9.

Heggen R. 1993, Value of Daily Data for Rainwater Catchment, *Proceedings of the 6th International Conference on Rain Water Cistern Systems*, Nairobi, Kenya, pp413–18.

Heggen R. 1997, Theohydrology/Hydrotheology, Rainwater Catchment in its Broadest Perspective, *Proceedings of the 8th International Conference on Rain Water Catchment Systems*, Tehran, Iran, Vol. 2, pp406–15.

Hewison K. 1996, Public Health Aspects of Rural Water Supply and Environmental Sanitation in Northeast Thailand and the Lao PDR, in Mekong Basin Natural Resource Management Project. Report for AusAID, Murdoch University and University of Sydney.

Hewison K. and Tunyavanich N. 1990, Rainwater Storage in Cement Jars in N.E.Thailand, *Water Resources Development*, Vol 6., No. 2, pp129–36.

Heyworth J., Maynard E. Cunliffe D. 1998, Who Drinks What?: Potable Water Use in South Australia, *Water*, Jan/Feb Issue, pp9–13.

Higuchi T. 1994, My Snow-Water-Recycling-House and my Vision in Heavy Snowfall Districts, *Proceedings of the Tokyo International Rainwater Utilization Conference*, Sumida City, 20–23 Azumabashi-1-Chrome, Tokyo 130, Japan, pp581–9.

Hoey P. and West S. 1982, Recent Initiatives in Raintank Supply Systems for South Australia, *Proceedings of the International Conference on Rain Water Cistern Systems*, Honolulu, Hawaii, pp284–93.

Hofkes E. (Ed.) 1982, *Small Community Water Supplies*, International Reference Centre for Community Water Supplies and Sanitation, John Wiley, Chichester, UK, 442p.

Hollick M. 1982, Water Harvesting in Arid Lands. *Scientific Reviews on Arid Zone Research*, Scientific Publishers, Jodhpur, India, Vol. 1, pp173–247.

Hood D. 1994, Rainwater and Public Health, *Tephra*, Vol. 13, No.4, pp24–6.

Hoque R. 1991, The Necessity and Scope for Rainwater Harvesting in Bangladesh, *Proceedings of the 5th International Rainwater Cistern Systems Conference*, Keelung, Taiwan, pp586–97.

Howsam P. 1998, Water Law and the Right to a Basic Water Supply, *Waterlines*, Vol. 16. No. 3, pp4–7.

Hubbard A.J. and Hubbard G. 1905, *Neolithic Dew Ponds and Cattleways*, Longmans, Green & Co., London.

Hudson, N. 1987, Soil and Water Conservation in Semi-arid areas, *FAO Soils Bulletin*, No. 57, 172p.

Iddings S. 1984, Village Technology for Spherical Tanks, *World Water*, (August Issue), pp38–40.

IDRC 1993, *Fogwater Collection System*, International Research and Development Centre, Canada. 16p.

Ingham A. and Kleine C. 1982, Cistern Systems: The California Perspective, *Proceedings of the Rainwater Cistern Systems Conference*, Honolulu, Hawaii, pp323–31.

ITDG 1969, *The Introduction of Rainwater Catchment Tanks and Micro-Irrigation to Botswana*, ITDG.

Jarman J. and Johnson C. 1996, Collaboration or Collision Course? NGO/government Partnership in Tanzania, *Waterlines*, Vol. 15, No. 2, pp7–10.

Joklik O. 1995, Potabilization of Rainwater, *Proceedings of the 7th International Conference on Rain Water Cistern Systems*, Beijing, China, Section 9, pp33–47.

Kaneko M., Arikawa Y. and Tamura S. 1992, Use of Rainwater Supply on Isolated Islands, *Proceedings of the Regional International Rainwater Catchment Systems Association Conference*, Kyoto, Japan, Vol.1, pp127–38.

Kenna J. and B. Gillet 1985, *Solar Water Pumping: A handbook*, IT Publications, London, 132p.

Kenyon, A. 1929, The Ironclad or Artificial Catchment, *Journal of Agriculture*, Department of Agriculture, Victoria, No. 27, pp86–91.

Kerr C. 1989, *Community Water Development*, IT Publications, London, 300p.

Khan M. and Faroda A. 1997, Water Harvesting for Sustainability in the Indian Arid Zone of Rajastan, *Proceedings of the 8th International Rainwater Catchment Systems Conference*, Ministry of Jihad-E-Sazandegi, Tehran, Iran, Vol. 1. pp357–65.

Kincaid T. 1979, Alternative Individual Water Sources. *Quality Water for Home and Farm*, Proceedings: Third Domestic Water Quality Symposium, American Society of Agricultural Engineering, pp73–8.

Kingori T. 1995, The Role of Women in Roof Catchment Water Tank Projects in the Catholic Diocese of Nakuru, Kenya, *Proceedings of the 7th International Conference on Rain Water Cistern Systems*, Beijing, China, Vol.2 Part 8, pp21–5.

Kolarkar, A.S., Murthy K. and Singh N. 1980, Water Harvesting and Runoff Farming in Arid Rajastan, *Indian Journal of Soil Conservation*, Vol.8, No.2, pp113–19.

Kolsky, P. 1997, Engineers and Urban Malaria: Part of the Solution or Part of the Problem? *Waterlines*, Vol. 16, No. 2, pp10–12.

Kone S. 1991, Malian Experience in Rain Water Cistern Systems, *Proceedings of the 5th International Rainwater Cistern Systems Conference*, Keelung, Taiwan, pp598–606.

König K. 1996, *Regenwasser in der Architekt*, Ökologische Konzepte (German), Staufen, Germany.

König K. 1998, *Rainwater in Cities, Ecological Concepts*, Available from fbr, Kassler Str. 1a, D-60486, Frankfurt am Main, Germany, p11.

Koplan, J., Deen R., Swanston W. and Tota B. 1978, Contaminated Roof-Collected Rainwater as a Possible Cause of an Outbreak of Salmonellosis, *Journal of Hygiene*, Cambridge, Vol. 8, pp303–9.

Kovacs, G. 1979, Traditions of Rainwater Harvesting in Europe. *Report to UNEP Rain and Stormwater Harvesting Project*, Nairobi, 30p.

Krishna J. 1989, Cistern Water Systems in the U.S. Virgin Islands, *Proceedings of the 4th International Conference on Rain Water Cistern Systems*, Manila, Philippines, E2, pp1–11.

Krishna J. 1992, Rainwater Catchment Systems in the U.S. Virgin Islands, *Proceedings of the Regional International Rainwater Catchment Systems Association Conference*, Kyoto, Japan, Vol.1, pp244–9.

Krishna J. 1993, Water Quality Standards for Rainwater Cistern Systems, *Proceedings of the 6th International Conference on Rain Water Cistern Systems*, Nairobi, Kenya, pp389–92.

La Hire, P. de 1742, *The Philosophical History and Memoirs of the Royal Academy of Sciences*, London.

Laing I. 1981, Rainfall Collection in Australia. Proceedings of Workshop: *Rainfall Collection for Agriculture in Arid and Semi-Arid Regions*, (edited by Dutt et al.), University of Arizona, Commonwealth Agricultural Bureau, Farnham, UK.

Laing I. 1991, Rainwater Tanks, *Farmnote*, No. 84/90, Western Australia Department of Agriculture, 4p.

Latham B. 1983, *Rainwater Collection Systems: The Design of Single Purpose Reservoirs*. MSc thesis, Dept. of Civil Engineering, University of Ottawa, Canada, 232p.

Latham B. 1984a, *Rainwater Collection Activities in Indonesia and Thailand*, Report to Canadian International Development Agency, Box 2423, Station D, Ottawa, 145p.

Latham B. 1984b, Building a Thai Jumbo Water Jar Using a Brick Mould, *Waterlines*, Vol. 3. No. 2, pp26–8.

Latham B. and Gould J. 1986, Lessons and Field Experience with Rainwater Collection Systems in Africa and Asia, *Aqua* Vol.4, pp183–9.

Layton S. 1987, Business – A Way of Transferring Technology, *Proceedings of the 3rd International Conference on Rain Water Cistern Systems*, Khon Kaen University, Thailand, E1, pp1–12.

Lee M. and E. Nissen-Petersen, 1989, The Use of Low-Cost, Self-Help Rain Water Harvesting Systems for Community Water Supply in Southern Kenya, *Proceedings of the 4th International Rainwater Cistern Systems Conference*, Manila, Philippines, B4, pp1–12.

Lee M. and Visscher J.T. 1990, *Water Harvesting in Five African Countries*, Occasional Paper Series 14, IRC, PO Box 93190, The Hague, Netherlands, 106p.

Lee M.D. and Visscher J.T. 1992, *Water Harvesting: A Guide for Planners and Project Managers*, Technical Paper 30, IRC, PO Box 93190, The Hague, Netherlands, 106p.

Lijuan L. and Guoyou Z. 1997, Different Purposes of Rainwater Catchment in China and their Environmental Effects, *Proceedings of the 8th International Rainwater Catchment Systems Conference*, Tehran, Iran, Vol. 1, pp378–82.

Liu C. and Mou H., 1993, Rainwater Catchment Systems in Agricultural Regions of North China, *Agricultural Systems and Ecology*, pp1–7. (Chinese).

Lloyd B. 1982, Water Quality Surveillance, *Waterlines*, Vol.1, No. 2, pp19–22.

Longland F. (Ed. P. Stern) 1936/1983, *Field Engineering*, IT Publications.

Lugonzo-Campbell J. 1989, Replacing Community Participation with NGO Participation – A New Approach, *Proceedings of the 4th International Rainwater Clstern Systems Conference*, Manila, Philippines, B2, pp1–12.

Lye D. 1992a, Microbiology of Rainwater Cistern Systems: A Review, *Journal of Environmental Science and Health*, A27 (8), pp2123–66.

Lye, D. 1992b, Legionella and amoeba found in cistern systems, *Proceedings of the Regional Conference of the International Rainwater Catchment Systems Association*, Kyoto, Japan, pp534–7.

Maddocks D. 1973, *Report on Rainwater Catchment Project in Jamaica*, ODA London, unpublished report, available from ITDG.

Maddocks D. 1975, *Methods of Creating Low-cost Waterproof Membranes for use in Construction of Rainwater Catchment and Storage Systems*, Unpublished report, ITDG.

Maikano G. and Nyberg A. 1981, Rainwater Catchment in Botswana, *Rural Water Supply in Developing Countries*, Proceedings of a Training Workshop, Zomba, Malawi, Pub. 167e, IDRC, Ottawa, pp123–5.

Marjoram T. 1987, Rural Water Supply in the South Pacific, *Proceedings of the 3rd International Conference on Rain Water Cistern Systems*, Khon Kaen, Thailand, E3, pp1–11.

Mather D. 1996, Lasting Solutions – Governments and Communities Re-Examine their Roles, *Waterlines*, Vol. 15, No. 2, pp2–3.

McCallan E. 1948, *Life on Old St. David's*, Bermuda Hamilton: Bermuda Monument Trust.

McKenzie J.E. 1981, *A Study of the Social Environment Surrounding the Provision of Water Supply in Selected Areas of Papua New Guinea*, Master's Thesis, Univ. of Adelaide, 125p.

McLaren N., Heath, D. and Morias A. 1987, *Water Conservation for Communities in Arid Areas of South Australia*, EWSD, South Australian Water Corporation, GPO Box 1751, Adelaide, SA 5001, Australia, 24p.

McPherson, H., McGarry, M., Gould, J. and Latham, B. 1984, *Low Cost Appropriate Water and Sanitation Technologies for Kenya*, GTZ report to the Min. of Water Development, Maji House, Nairobi, 257p.

Meemken W. 1994, Possibilities for the Sensible Utilization of Rainwater, *Proceedings of the Tokyo International Rainwater Utilization Conference*, Sumida City, Tokyo, Japan, pp79–90.

Michaelides G. 1986, *Investigations into the Quality of Roof-Harvested Rainwater for Domestic Use in Developing Countries*, PhD Research Thesis, University of Dundee, Scotland, UK.

Michaelides G. 1989, Investigation into the Quality of Roof-Harvested Rainwater for Domestic Use in Developing Countries: A PhD Research Study, *Proceedings of the 4th International Rainwater Cistern Systems Conference*, Manila, Philippines, E2, pp1–12.

Michaelides G. and Young R.J. 1984, Diverting the Foul Flush from Roof Catchments Used for Potable Water Supply, *African and Asian Water and Sewage*, Vol. 3, No. 4, pp18–21.

Minami I. 1995, Technical Development of Rainwater Catchment Systems, *Proceedings of the 7th Rainwater Catchment Systems Conference*, Beijing, China, Section 1, pp58–62.

Minami I., Amuza A. and Yangyuoru M. 1992, New Rainwater Catchment System for Concrete Buildings, *Proceedings of the Regional Conference of the International Rainwater Catchment Systems Association*, Kyoto, Japan, Section 1, pp406–16.

Mollison B. 1992, *Introduction to Permaculture*, Tagari Publications, Tyalgum, Australia, 198p.

Morgan P. 1990, *Rural Water Supplies and Sanitation*, Macmillan Education Ltd., London, 358p.

Mou H. and Wang H. 1993, Rainwater Use and Recent Development in China, *Proceedings of the 6th International Rainwater Catchment Systems Conference*, Nairobi, pp63–70.

Mou H. 1995, Rainwater Utilization for Sustainable Development in North China, *Waterlines*, Vol. 14. No. 2, pp19–21.

Mou H. et al. (Editors) 1995, Rainwater Utilization for the World's People, *Proceedings of the 7th International Rainwater Catchment Systems Conference*, Chinese Academy of Sciences, Beijing, China, Volumes 1 and 2, 1185p.

Mou H. and Wang H. 1997, Approaches of Rainwater Harvesting and Retention in Urban Areas, *Proceedings of the 8th International Rainwater Catchment Systems Conference*, Tehran, Iran, Vol. 2, pp678–86.

Moysey E. and Mueller E.F. 1962, *Concrete Farm Cisterns*, Dept. of Agricultural Engineering, Univ. of Saskatchewan, Saskatoon, Canada, 8p.

Murase M. 1987, *Have you Seen Miyake Island? A Rainwater Utilization Proposal*, Dept. of Environmental Protection, 23–20 Azumabashi-1-chrome, Sumida City, Tokyo, Japan, 5p. (Japanese).

Murase M. 1994, Can Rainwater Utilization Save Cities, *Proceedings of the Tokyo International Rainwater Utilization Conference*, Sumida City, Tokyo, Japan pp33–40. (English and Japanese).

Murase M. 1998, Rainwater Utilization and Sustainable Development in Cities, *Stockholm Rainwater Harvesting Workshop*, Global Water Partnership, Stockholm, 6p.

Murase M. 1998, Rainwater Utilization and Sustainable Development in Cities, *Wasser-Wirtschaft – Zeitschift für Wasser und Umwelt*, Vol. 88, No. 7–8, pp401–3.

NAS (National Academy of Sciences) 1974, *More Water for Arid Lands: Promising Technologies and Research Opportunities*, Washington D.C., 153p.

Nelson K.D. 1985, *Design and Construction of Small Earth Dams*, Australian Land Series, Inkata, Melbourne, Australia.

Neri L, Li C. and Schiller E. 1984, Use of Rainwater For Drinking Purposes: Its Health Implications, *Proceedings of the 2nd International Conference on Rain Water Cistern Systems*, US Virgin Islands, E6, pp1–24.

Nilsson A. 1984, *Groundwater Dams for Small-Scale Water Supply*, IT Publications, London, 64p.

Nissen-Petersen E. 1982, *Rain Catchment and Water Supply in Rural Africa*, Hodder and Stoughton, London, 83p.

Nissen-Petersen E. 1985, Water from Rocks, *Waterlines*, Vol. 3, No. 3, pp7–12.

Nissen-Petersen E. 1986, Water from Sand, *Waterlines*, Vol. 4, No.3, pp7–9.

Nissen-Petersen E. 1990a, *Rock Catchment Dam with Self Closing Tap*, Manual No. 3, Harvesting Rainwater in Semi-arid Africa Series, ASAL Consultants, P.O. Box 38, Kibwezi, Kenya, 33p.

Nissen-Petersen E. 1990b, *How to Build a Cylindrical Water Tank with Dome. (46m³)*. A photo manual, ASAL Consultants, P.O. Box 38, Kibwezi, Kenya ASAL/DANIDA, 33p.

Nissen-Petersen E. 1992a, *How to Build a Cylindrical Water Tank with Dome. (46m³)*. A photo manual, ASAL Consultants Ltd/DANIDA, P.O. Box 38, Kibwezi, Kenya, 33p.

Nissen-Petersen E. 1992b, *How to Build an Underground Tank with Dome. (46m³)*. A photo manual, ASAL Consultants Ltd/DANIDA, P.O. Box 38, Kibwezi, Kenya, 29p.

Nissen-Petersen E. 1992c, *How to Build and Install Gutters with Splash-Guards*. A photo manual, ASAL Consultants Ltd/DANIDA, P.O. Box 38, Kibwezi, Kenya, 14p.

Nissen-Petersen E. 1992d, *How to Repair Various Types of Water Tank*. A photo manual, ASAL Consultants Ltd/DANIDA, P.O. Box 38, Kibwezi, Kenya, 37p.

Nissen-Petersen E. 1996, *Ground Water Dams in Sand Rivers, A Manual on Survey, Design, Construction and Maintenance*, UNDP/UNCHS Myanmar and ASAL Consultants, P.O. Box 38, Kibwezi, Kenya, 68p.

Nissen-Petersen E. 1998a, *10 Water Tanks for Roof and Ground Catchments*, SIDA Training Course Manual, ASAL Consultants, P.O. Box 38, Kibwezi, Kenya, 70p.

Nissen-Petersen E. 1998b, *Rock Catchment Dams and Tanks*, SIDA Training Course Manual, ASAL Consultants, P.O. Box 38, Kibwezi, Kenya, 35p.

Nissen-Petersen E. 1999 (in press), *Sub-surface and Sand in Sand Rivers*, Manual, ASAL Consultants, P.O. Box 38, Kibwezi, Kenya.

Nissen-Petersen E. and Lee M. 1990, Rain Water Harvesting in Semi-Arid Africa. Manual 1. *Affordable Water Supply Water Tanks with Guttering and Hand-Pump Series.* ASAL Consultants, P.O. Box 38, Kibwezi, Kenya, 52p.

O'Brien L. 1990, Report on Rainwater Harvesting Project in Togo, *Raindrop*, Vol. 3, pp1,5–6.

O'Meara C. 1982, Rain Water Cistern Utilization in Selected Hamlets of the Republic of Belau, Western Caroline Islands, *Proceedings of the International Conference on Rain Water Cistern Systems*, Honolulu, Hawaii, pp266–75.

Ockwell R. 1986, *Assisting in Emergencies: A Resource Handbook for UNICEF Field Staff*, UNICEF, New York.

Omwenga J. 1984, *Rainwater Harvesting for Domestic Water Supply in Kisii, Kenya*, Published MSc Thesis (pub. No. 17), Dept. of Civil Engineering, Tampere University of Technology, Finland, 132p.

Opiro K. 1993, Finding the Catchment Coefficient for Rainwater Harvesting from Trees, *Proceedings of the 6th International Conference on Rain Water Cistern Systems*, Nairobi, Kenya, pp275–80.

Owen M. and Gerba C. 1987, A Case History of Disinfection of Water in Rural Mexico, *Proceedings of the 3rd International Conference on Rain Water Cistern Systems*, Khon Kaen Univ., Thailand, F4, pp1–17.

Ozis, U. 1982, Outlook on the Ancient Cisterns in Anatolia, Turkey, *Proceedings of the International Conference on Rain Water Cistern Systems*, University of Hawaii, Honolulu, pp9–15.

Pacey A. et al. 1977, Technology is Not Enough, The Provision and Maintenance of Appropriate Water Supplies, *Aqua*, Vol. 1, No. 1, pp1–58.

Pacey A. and Cullis A. 1986, *Rainwater Harvesting: The Collection of Rainfall and Runoff in Rural Areas*, IT Publications, London, 216p.

Pakianathan E., 1989, A Study of Diversion and Delivery Systems in Rain Water Cisterns in India, *Proceedings of the 4th International Rainwater Cistern Systems Conference*, Manila, Philippines, H1, pp1–11.

Parker R. 1973, *The Introduction of Catchment Systems for Rural Water Supplies – A Benefit/Cost Study in a S.E. Ghana Village*, Dept. of Agricultural Economics and Management, University of Reading, UK, 45p.

Patterson R. 1985, Rural Domestic Water Consumption Rates and Associated Catchment Storage Combinations, *Hydrology and Water Resources Symposium*, 14–16 May, Sydney, Institution of Engineers, pp39–42.

Penman H. 1970, *The Water Cycle*, Scientific American, Inc.

Perrens S. 1975, Collection and Storage Strategies for Domestic Rainwater Systems in Australia, *Hydrology Papers*, Institution of Engineers, Canberra, Australia, pp168–72.

Perrens S.J. 1982a, Design Strategy for Domestic Rainwater Systems in Australia, *Proceedings of the International Conference on Rain Water Cistern Systems*, Hawaii, Honolulu, pp108–17.

Perrens S.J. 1982b, Effect of Rationing on Reliability of Domestic Rainwater Systems, *Proceedings of the International Conference on Rain Water Cistern Systems*, Hawaii, Honolulu, pp308–16.

Petersen, S. 1993, Rainwater Catchment from Salt Pans for Domestic Use in Botswana, *Proceedings of the 6th International Conference on Rain Water Catchment Systems*, Nairobi, Kenya, pp169–76.

Pickering K. and Owen L. 1994, *An Introduction to Global Environmental Issues*, Routledge, London and New York, 390p.

Pickford J. 1991, *The Worth of Water: Technical Briefs on Health, Water and Sanitation*, IT Publications, London, 144p.

Pinfold J., Horan, N., Wirojanagud W. and Mara D. 1990, The Bacteriological Quality of Water Collected in Rainjars in Rural N.E.Thailand, *Water Research*, Vol. 27, No.2, pp297–302.

Pinfold, J., Horan, N., Wirojanagud W. and Mara D. 1993, The Bacteriological Quality of Rainjar Water in Rural N.E.Thailand, *Water Research*, Vol. 27, No. 2, pp297–302.

Postel S. 1992, *The Last Oasis: Facing Water Scarcity*, Worldwatch Environmental Alert Series, Earthscan, London, 240p.

Prempridi T. and Chatuthasry C. 1982, Past and Present Use of Ponds as Rain-Water Storage in Thailand. *Proceedings of the 2nd International Conference on Rain Water Cistern Systems*, St. Thomas, U.S. Virgin Islands, C2, pp1–21.

Ray D. 1983, *Rainwater Harvesting Project: Socio-economic Case Studies*, Vol. 1 and Vol. 2, Report for ITDG, (Cited in Pacey and Cullis 1986), ITDG.

Ree W., Wimberley, F., Guinn W. and Lauritzen C. 1971, Rainwater Harvesting System Design, Paper ARS 41–184, *Agricultural Research Service*, U.S. Department of Agriculture, 12p.

Ree W. 1976, Rooftop Runoff for Water Supply, U.S. Dept. of Agriculture Report, ARS-S-133, *Agricultural Research Service*, U.S. Dept. of Agriculture, 10p.

Reed B. 1998, Sunshine and Fresh Air: A Practical Approach to Combatting Water-borne Disease, *Waterlines*, Vol. 15, No. 4, pp27–9.

Reij, C., Mulder, P. and Bergmann L. 1988, *Water Harvesting for Plant Production*, World Bank Technical Paper, No. 91, 123p.

Richards R., Kranmer J., Baker D. and Krieger K. 1987, Pesticides in Rainwater in the northeastern United States, *Nature*, Vol. 327, No. 6118, pp129–31.

Riddle J. and Speedy R. 1984, Rainwater Cistern Systems: The Park Experience, *Proceedings of 2nd International Conference on Rain Water Cistern Systems*, U.S. Virgin Islands, E4, pp1–7.

Rijal G. and Fujioka R. 1995, A Home-Owner's Test for Bacteria in Cistern Waters, *Proceedings of the 7th International Conference on Rain Water Cistern Systems*, Beijing, China, Section 9, pp58–64.

Rippl, W. 1983, *The Capacity of Storage Reservoirs for Water Supply*, USDA Report, ARS-S-133, 10p.

Robertson A. 1950, *The Hafir – What, Why, Where and How?*, Ministry of Agriculture Bulletin No.1, Khartoum, Sudan.

Romeo C. 1982, Water Quality Arguments for Rain Catchment Development in Belau, *Proceedings of the International Conference on Rain Water Cistern Systems*, Honolulu, Hawaii, pp257–66.

SA Water 1998, *Rainwater Tanks: Their Selection, Use and Maintenance*, South Australian Water Corporation, GPO Box 1751, Adelaide, SA 5001, Australia, 24p.

Salas J., 1989, Community Participation Around the Ferrocement Rainwater Catchment System: The Capiz Experience. *Proceedings of the 4th International Rainwater Cistern Systems Conference*, Manila, Philippines, B8, pp1–19.

Salas J., 1995, Women's Issues in Rainwater Collection Projects, *Proceedings of the 7th International Rain Water Catchment Systems Conference*, Beijing, China, Volume 2, Part 8, pp1–6.

Schemenauer R. and Cereceda P. 1991, Fog-water Collection in Arid Coastal Locations, *Ambio*, Vol. 20, No.7, pp303–8.

Schemenauer R. and Cereceda P. 1992, Water from Fog-covered Mountains, *Waterlines*, Vol. 10, No. 4, pp10–13.

Schemenauer R. and Cereceda P. 1993, High Elevation Fog as a Water Resource for Developing Countries, *Proceedings of the 6th International Conference on Rain Water Catchment Systems*, Nairobi, Kenya, pp255–60.

Schemenauer R. and Cereceda P. 1994, The Role of Wind in Rainwater and Fog Collection, *Water International*, Vol. 19, pp70–6.

Schiller E. and Latham B. 1982a, Rainwater Roof Catchment Systems, *Information and Training for Low-Cost Water Supply and Sanitation*, Ch4.1, Trattles D., World Bank, 198p.

Schiller E. and Latham B. 1982b, Computerized Methods in Optimizing Rainwater Catchment Systems, *Proceedings of the International Conference on Rain Water Cistern Systems*, Hawaii, Honolulu, pp108–17.

Schiller E. 1982, Rooftop Rainwater Catchment Systems for Drinking-Water Supply, *Water Supply and Sanitation in Developing Countries*, Ann Arbor Science, pp85–100.

Scott R., Mooers J. and Waller D. 1995, Rain Water Cistern Systems – A Regional Approach to Cistern Sizing in Nova Scotia, *Proceeding of 7th International Rainwater Catchment Systems Conference*, Beijing, China, Vol. 2, section 10, pp38–48.

Scott R. and Waller D. 1987, Water Quality Aspects of a Rainwater Cistern System in Nova Scotia, Canada, *Proceedings of the 3rd International Conference on Rain Water Cistern Systems*, Khon Kaen Univ., Thailand, F1, pp1–16.

Sharpe W. and Young E. 1982, Occurrence of Heavy Metals in Rural Roof-Catchment Cistern Systems, *Proceedings of the International Conference on Rain Water Cistern Systems*, Hawaii, Honolulu, pp249–56.

Shata A. 1982, Past, Present and Future Development of Catchment Areas in the Mediterranean Coastal Desert of Egypt, *Proceedings of the International Rainwater Cistern Systems Conference*, Honolulu, Hawaii, pp23–32.

SIDA 1995, (Nissen-Petersen E. and J. Mbugua) *Rainwater: An Under-Utilized Resource*, Swedish International Development Authority (SIDA), P.O. Box 30600, Nairobi, Kenya, 30p.

Simmonds A. 1993, The Ability of Rural Women in Tanzania to pay for Rainwater Harvesting, *Proceedings of the 6th International Conference on Rain Water Catchment Systems*, Nairobi, Kenya, pp369–76.

Simmons G. and Smith J. 1997, Roof Water: A Probable Source of Salmonella Infections, *New Zealand Public Health Report*, Vol. 4, No. 1, 5p.

Skinner B. 1990, *Community Rainwater Catchment*, Unpublished Report, Water Engineering and Development Centre (WEDC), Loughborough University, UK, 109p.

South Australian Health Commission 1995, *Guidelines on the Collection, Care and Control of Rainwater in Tanks*, South Australian Health Commission, P.O. Box 6, Rundle Mall 5000, Adelaide, Australia, 16p.

Stone L. 1994, Solar Cooking in Developing Countries, *Solar Today*, Vol.8, No.6, p27.

Takeyama K. and Minami I. 1995, Rainwater Utilization in Izumo Dome and Some Reformations for Automatic Rainwater Cachment Systems , *Proceedings of the 7th Rainwater Catchment Systems Conference*, Beijing, China, Section 10, pp113–20.

Teck K. 1989, The City of Rain: The Architecture of Rainwater Collection in Singapore, *Proceedings of the 4th International Rainwater Cistern Systems Conference*, Manila, Philippines, Section K1, pp1–17.

Tharun G. 1995, Project Casework Training Approach for Self-help Training Program for Small Water Resources Development, *Experiences in the Development of Small-Scale Water Resources in Rural Areas*, (Edited by Tharun G. et al. 1995), CDG, SEAPO, Thailand, May 1990, pp153–72.

Tharun G. et al. (Editors) 1995, Experiences in the Development of Small-scale Water Resources in Rural Areas, *Proc. of the International Symposium on Development of Small-scale Water Resources in Rural Areas*, Carl Duisberg Gesellschaft, SEAPO, Thailand, 21–25 May 1990, 238p.

Thomas P. and Greene G. 1993, Rainwater Quality from Different Roof Catchments, *Water, Science and Technology*, Vol. 28, No. 3/5, pp291–9.

Thomas T. 1998, Domestic Water Supply Using Rainwater Harvesting, *Building Research and Information*, Vol. 2, No. 2, pp94–101.

Thoya J. 1995, The Role of Rural Women in the Development and Sustainability of Rainwater Catchment Systems, *Proceedings of the 6th International Conference on Rain Water Catchment Systems*, Nairobi, Kenya, pp363–8.

Thurman R. 1993, Comparison of Drinking-Water Collected in Concrete and Galvanized Rainwater Cisterns with Untreated Tap Water, *Australian Microbiologist*, Vol.14, No.4., 113p.

TIRUC 1994, *Proceedings of the Tokyo International Rainwater Utilization Conference*, Dept. of Environmental Protection, 23–20 Azumabashi-1-chrome, Sumida City, Tokyo, Japan, 633p. (English and Japanese).

Traitongyoo T. 1987, Promoting Village Participation in Water Tank Construction, *Waterlines*, Vol.5, No.4, pp12–13.

Tun-Lin W., Kay B. and Barnes A. 1996, Understanding Productivity, A Key to *Aedes aegypti* Surveillance, *American Journal of Tropical Medicine and Hygiene*, Vol. 3, No.6, pp595–601.

Tunyavanich N. and Hewison K. 1989, Water Supply and Water Use Behaviour: The Use of Cement Rainwater Jars in N.E.Thailand, *Proceedings of the 4th International Rainwater Cistern Systems Conference*, Manila, C2, pp1–23.

Tunyavanich N. and Hewison K. 1990, Rural Water Supply, Sanitation and Health Education in Thailand: Can Success Follow Success? *Waterlines*, Vol. 8, No. 3, pp6–9.

UNEP 1983, *Rain and Stormwater Harvesting in Rural Areas*, Report by the United Nations Environment Programme, Tycooly International, Dublin, 238p.

Vadhanavikkit C., Thiensiripipat and Viwathanathepa S. 1984, *Collection and Storage of Roof Runoff for Drinking Purposes*, Vol. 3 – Construction Materials, Techniques and Operational Studies, IDRC Canada/Faculty of Engineering, Khon Kaen University, Khon Kaen, Thailand, 113p.

Vadhanavikkit C. and Pannachet Y. 1987, Investigations of Bamboo Reinforced Concrete Water Tanks, *Proceedings of the 3rd International Conference on Rainwater Cistern Systems*, Khon Kaen, Thailand, Section C13, pp1–6.

Villareal C. et al. 1989, *Proceedings of the 4th International Rainwater Cistern Systems Conference*, Manila, Philippines, 470p.

Vyas V. 1996, The Ajit Foundation's Project on Modelling Water Resources for Rural Communities in Arid and Semi-Arid Regions, *Raindrop*, Series 2, Vol. 6, p4(i-iv).

Walker W. 1984, Rainwater Cistern Systems: Legal, Institutional and Policy Considerations, *Proceedings of the 2nd Rainwater Cistern Systems Conference*, St. Thomas, U.S. Virgin Islands, Section G2, pp1–10.

Wall B. and McCown R. 1989, Designing Roof Catchment Water Supply Systems Using Water Budgeting Methods, *Water Resources Development*, Vol. 5, No. 1, pp11–18.

Waller D.H. 1982, Rain water as a water supply source in Bermuda, *Proceedings of the International Conference on Rain Water Cistern Systems*, Hawaii, Honolulu, pp184–93.

Waller D. and Inman D. 1982, Rain Water as an Alternative Source in Nova Scotia, *Proceedings of the International Conference on Rain Water Cistern Systems*, Honolulu, Hawaii, pp202–10.

Wamani W. and Mbugua J. 1993, Rainwater Harvesting in Kenya: A State of the Art and Related Socio-Economic Issues, *Proceedings of the 6th International Rainwater Catchment Systems Conference*, Nairobi, Kenya, pp327–38.

Watt, S. 1978, *Ferrocement Water Tanks and their Construction*, IT Publications, London, 118p.

Wegelin M. and Sommer B. 1998, Solar Water Disinfection (SODIS) – Destined for Worldwide Use? *Waterlines*, Vol. 16, No. 3, pp30–2.

Wessels R. 1994, Establishment of Rainwater Utilization Plants in Osnabruck, *Proceedings of Tokyo International Rainwater Utilization Conference*, Sumida City, Tokyo, pp249–75.

White G., Bradley D. and White A. (1972), *Drawers of Water: Domestic Water Use in East Africa*, University of Chicago Press, 306p.

Whiteside M. 1982, *How To Build a Water Catchment Tank*, Mahalapye Development Trust, Botswana Government Printers, 32p.

World Bank 1992, *World Development Report*, Washington D.C. 240p.

WHO 1993, *Guidelines for Drinking-Water Quality*, (2nd Edition), Vol. 1, World Health Organization, Geneva, 188p.

Wirojanagud W. et al. 1989, *Evaluation of Rainwater Quality: Heavy Metals and Pathogens*, IDRC, Ottawa, 103p.

Wirojanagud P. and Vanvarothorn V. 1990, Jars and Tanks for Rainwater Storage in Rural Thailand, *Waterlines*, Vol. 8, No. 3, pp29–32.

Wirojanagud P. and Chindapraisirt P. 1987, Strategies to Provide Drinking-Water in the Rural Areas of Thailand, *Proceedings of the 3rd International Conference on Rain Water Cistern Systems*, Khon Kaen, Thailand, B5, pp1–11.

WISY 1998, *System for Filtering and Collecting Rainwater*, (Product leaflets), WISY, Oberdorfstr. 26, D-63699, Kefendrod-Hitzkirchen, Germany.

WRI (World Resources Institute) 1996, *World Resources 1996–97*, Oxford University Press, New York.

Yaziz M., Gunting H., Sapiari N. and Ghazali A. 1989, Variations in Rainwater Quality from Roof Catchments, *Water Research*, Vol. 23, pp761–5.

Yuan T. and Benjing W. 1997, Utilization of Rainwater Resources in the Gansu Province, *Proceedings of the 8th International Rainwater Catchment Systems Conference*, Tehran, Iran, Vol. 2, pp1218–20.

Zhu Q. and Wu F. 1995a, Rainwater Catchment and Utilization in Gansu, China, *Proceedings of the 7th International Conference on Rain Water Cistern Systems*, Beijing, China, Vol.1 Part 1, pp18–27.

Zhu Q. and Wu F. 1995b, A Lifeblood Transfusion: Gansu's New Rainwater Catchment Systems, *Waterlines*, Vol. 14. No. 2, pp5–7.

Zhu Q. and Liu C. 1998, *Rainwater Utilization for Sustainable Development of Water Resources in China*, Paper presented at the Stockholm Water International Symposium, Stockholm, Sweden, 8p.

Index

USA 11, 15, 39, 143, 144, 204, 237–9
uses of water 3, 7, 17, 48–9, 219, 240, 244–5, 247

Victoria State Rivers and Water Supply Commission 202
volcanic activity 143, 144, 205, 223, 224, 239

Wakamba people 232
walls of tank 117, 119, 120
Wanganui, New Zealand 205
WASH (Water, Sanitation and Health) project 199
washout pipe 83–5
Wasini island, Africa 10
wastage 242
waste water 49, 242–3
water 3–7, 147–8, 150, 163
    for construction 109, 110, 111
    see also acidic; collection/carrying; safety of; saline; shortages; treatment of; uses of; waste
water quality 15, 19–20, 70, 141–55, 202, 205, 239
    stored water 144–6, 150, 155–7
    unsafe/unsuitable to drink 17, 100, 143, 145, 147, 207, 219, 244

see also contamination; non-potable water; health; treatment of; WHO
water supply 45, 55–6, 188, 204, 241, 242, 243, 244
    no alternative 12, 205, 207, 211, 223, 238
    see also backup supply; collection/carrying; emergency supply; trucking in water
WaterAid 184
water-holes 99
water-jar wells 218
waterproofing 95, 112, 120, 125
web-sites and internet 63, 64, 155, 199, 205, 246, 256, 257, 258
wells 99, 100, 188
West Indies 11, 147
whitewash 110
WHO 17, 141, 142, 144, 145, 146
WISY 222
women 164–5, 168, 173, 191, 195, 233
wooden tanks 93

Yerebatan Sarayi (Istanbul), Turkey 8

Zhejiang Province, China 217
Zimbabwe 142
zinc 144
Zutshwa, Botswana 29, 32